Journey from the Bush

The Ken Lewis Story

Edited by
Brian Lynch

Prestige Press

A catalogue record of this book is available from the British Library

First Edition: December 2012

ISBN: 978-1-84375-615-6

To order additional copies of this book please visit:
http://www.prestige-press.com/kenlewis

Published by Prestige Press
Email: info@prestige-press.com Web: http://www.prestige-press.com

Andrew

March 2013

Whenever Brandon has needed your help and advice, you have been there for him. Andrew for that I sincerely thank you. Brandon is very lucky to have you on his side!.

Ken

To Lynn,

my wife, my best friend, my world

....also to my family and friends, because they mean so much to me!

Acknowledgements

I must take this opportunity to offer my heartfelt thanks to the following people who have worked so hard in helping me to write and produce this book.

Brian Lynch, whose editorship and narrative style has transformed my diary entries and memories in to this biography.

The irreplaceable Chris Howes for the many arduous hours spent proof reading.... from Brian's initial drafts right through to the final proof! Thanks to Chris too for spotting the odd error in some of my recollections and for purging the occasional repetition.

Peter Ives who kindly took the cover photograph and the picture of Lynn used in the dedication. In fact, as a great friend and our long-time family photographer, many of the photographs in the book itself are those snapped by Peter over the course of many years.

Thanks also to my publisher, David Pearman of Prestige Press, who has designed, produced and published the book.

My thanks also goes to those of you who have made contributions to the last chapter.

Finally, thank you to Chel for encouraging (or should I say nagging) me to write the book in the first place and, of course, to Lynn for all her help and wise counsel as well as putting up with all the disruption to our normal schedule during this whole process, which seemed to have lasted a lifetime!

Contents

Author's Note

When people retire, or leave their jobs after long service, it's often convenient to fall back on the old Sinatra hit about doing things their way; but since I have no intention of either retiring or giving up work, I will resist the temptation.

However, Frank does mention having few regrets and, having now completed this book, I struggle to find any to complain about either. Of my 'few' I would say that perhaps the most significant was not meeting Lynn earlier in our lives.

Had we done so we could have had so many more wonderful years together, perhaps closing in on our 50 years by this time. Yes, I regret missing those years, but am grateful for the ones we have spent with each other and look forward to many more to come.

Together we built a fine family and we're hugely proud of all the children. As we go to press Brandon has just been promoted and is now the Junior Minister for Local Government. Prior to this he spent some 12 years helping to build Woodlands Schools in to the extremely succesful schools they are today. Bradley is an extremely successful businessman in the City of London and provided considerable import into the nurseries and schools as well. Cheralyn, after completing a BA with Honours in Psychology has taught A level students at Brentwood School and has recently obtained a Masters in Forensic Psychology. She has also followed Brandon into politics and is a local councillor.

However, if I do have another 'regret', in a way it relates to them. On my 60th birthday our children bought me something I have coveted for much of my life – a drum kit. Not just any old drum kit, but one of the types used by no less than Ringo Starr – a kind of Rolls Royce in percussion. What a wonderfully thoughtful gift it was, and one which I use as often as I can. My regret however is that when I had the chance, I was always too busy to learn to play the drums properly and should have done that much earlier in life. But I'm still working on it!

Ken Lewis

Introduction

The Forties and the Fifties

War, peace and austerity

We are all the product of our environment and experience. The humbler our origins the more impressive our achievements in life are, and that applies to Ken Lewis as much as it does to anyone. It would be easy to start simply by saying he was born into wartime austerity but to know the man we need to know the facts of life for everyone at that time, because that is part of the environment that shaped him.

The forties really was a decade of war, peace, austerity and social change, and its first five years have been well documented in every form. We have re-fought the great battles a thousand times over on cinema and TV screens since, but what was it like for the people?....etc.

Well, the decade started badly of course with the war and blitz, and went steadily downhill for the next five years. On January 8th 1940, rationing was introduced for the first time since 1918. People were allowed four ounces of butter, 12ozs of sugar, and 4ozs of bacon or ham; in February meat would go on ration as well. The ration books would be with us until long after the war (July 1954 in fact), but there is validity to the argument that, as a nation, we had the most healthy and sensibly balanced diet in our history. Through necessity we became a nation of 'Dig for Victory' smallholders, as parks, gardens and any small spaces were used to grow vegetables and fruit to eat to eke out the rations.

Dig for Victory was a slogan that, like others, was a constant reminder of the war, as if one was needed. There was, for example, the campaign urging people not to gossip about the war, with three million posters carrying slogans like 'Careless Talk Costs Lives' and 'Be like Dad and Keep mum', homing in on the fact that real information about the location of ships, troops and munitions could easily reach German ears if their spies picked up loose talk, even in food queues.

Despite going badly in the early years, the war never stopped people enjoying themselves, whether it was community singing in the shelters and tube stations, listening to ITMA (It's That Man Again with Tommy Handley) or going to the pictures and theatres. In fact advance tickets for the wartime London premier of the Hollywood classic 'Gone with the Wind' reached £10,000 by April 1940. The West End may have been dimmed for the blackout, but clearly it was still doing great theatre and cinema business.

The war news got worse as the evacuation from Dunkirk sent a clear signal that, what would be hailed by Churchill as our 'Finest hour' was not far away. As the people braced themselves for invasion, nobody could be really sure what was going to happen British towns had been bombed before, by the Zeppelins in the First World War, but they were nothing in comparison with the blitzkrieg unleashed by the Luftwaffe in 1940.

The ack-ack gunners could fight back by blazing away at the invader coming across the Channel or North Sea and the Spitfires and Hurricanes would fly into history, but ordinary people could only crouch in their shelters and go about their work as normally as they could. Some children were evacuated to 'safer' parts of the country – but many parents determined to live, or die, as a family.

And they did – or at least those who survived the bombing did. After the raids kids played on the bombsites and scrabbled through gardens for shrapnel or shell cases. Their mothers, many of them with their men away on active service, struggled with the restrictions of the ration book. The men that did remain were either too young, old, unfit for service, in jobs keeping the communications and transport services operating, or working in the factories, mines and shipyards. Even when their normal working day was done, many did fire watching duties or joined the Home Guard. It's jokingly called Dad's Army, but those men were very serious about their intentions if the Nazis had come and they would have died fighting in the streets.

They were years of queues and grey bread, where blacked out homes, streets and buses, along with bombsites, doodlebugs and V2 rockets were a fact of life. Yet despite everything, morale stayed high – partly thanks to the example set by the King and Queen, but mainly due to the leadership and inspirational speeches of Winston Churchill. Britain suffered, but in adversity its communities thrived.

So for many at home and abroad it was a shock when, in 1945 and with the European war won, Churchill was so spectacularly removed from office by the biggest (until then) Labour landslide in history. He was replaced with the unassuming Clement Attlee, who led the most radical government in terms of social change this country had ever seen, and arguably would see until Margaret Thatcher arrived on the scene many years later.

Attlee brought the 'brave new world' people had dreamed of, but felt they had been cheated of, in 1918. With a slogan of 'Let us face the future', he put together a team, which produced a programme of nationalisation and social reform, whose jewel was the Welfare State. It was a concept, which envisioned a 'cradle to the grave' Utopia, which had actually been outlined by Liberal Sir William Beveridge in 1942 at Churchill's behest. Ironically it would be guided through Parliament into reality by one of Churchill's bitterest critics, Aneurin Bevan; yet, seven years later, the people would bring the old warrior back to Downing Street, with his pledge to 'Set the people free'.

But neither pledge would be easily achievable, and those who burnt their ration books and identity cards on VE-night would find they had been premature, because post-war peace brought even greater degrees of austerity. The war had bankrupted the nation and while there was talk of rebuilding, the reality was grim. It would be decades before the bombsites were all cleared and, while employment was at a high level for the first time in the century, the black market was as strong during the late forties as it had been during the war.

The Welfare State though, had brought some plusses. Children had free milk, (and dinners at school if they wanted them); mothers were supplied with dried milk, orange juice, malt and other vitamins necessary to bring up their babies. The 'bombed out' families lucky enough to have been allocated one of the 'prefab' homes Churchill had ordered near the end of the war as a 'quick-fix' temporary solution, found they were comfortable, weatherproof and even had a luxury most working class homes never had – a fridge. Some even stand and are lived in to this day.

But the post-war forties were tough. By May 1946 even bread was rationed – something which had not happened even during the war. Strikes by dockers, road haulage workers and left wing unions who had viewed a

Labour government as their personal fiefdom, began to sap the people's will – particularly those who had voted Labour for the first time.

February 1947 brought even greater privations when one of the worst winters on record coincided with major fuel shortages. Heavy snowstorms and sub-zero temperatures combined with serious fuel shortages to bring Britain almost to its economic knees. Over four million workers were laid off because of power cuts – with coal trains unable to battle their way through 20-ft high snowdrifts to the power stations. Thousands of homes went without heat or light for long periods of the day, adding to the misery and the RAF was even called in to drop food to stranded villagers and their animals. One tiny isolated Devon hamlet sent the authorities a telegram on February 12th saying it had had no bread since January 27th.

Not everything had changed though. The BBC issued scriptwriters with guidelines regulating the conduct of radio hero Dick Barton who, with his pals Jock Anderson and Snowy White, captivated millions of impressionable small boys at 6.45pm each evening, (with an 'Omnibus edition' on Saturday mornings). The rules were designed to protect Dick's character and they included the demand that 'Sex plays no part in his adventures, he never lies and never swears'. Rule 5 concerns the violence involved with such an adventure, pledging that such violence would be 'restricted to clean socks on the jaw'.

Those guidelines probably say more about the moral, social and ethical standards of the forties than anything else.

The Fifties

Rebellion, racism and rock n roll

The fifties was a decade when the Cold War became even more firmly entrenched in people's minds. Russia, which had 'taken over' many of the old Eastern European states (as Churchill had warned in 1946 with his 'Iron Curtain' speech), gained a new ally in the shape of Communist China. The success of Mao Tse Tung in seizing control of that massive country, unsettled the whole region.

One of the consequences that arose from that had its roots on February 7th 1950 when Vietnam (formerly French Indo-China) was divided into two parts with the northern half coming under Soviet communist influence, the south being 'free' but supported by America. The Vietnam War that resulted would cost the lives of countless thousands, including hundreds of American troops – but even before that a similar situation arose in Korea.

On September 9th 1948 the northern (Soviet controlled) part of Korea had declared itself, as the Democratic People's Republic of Korea, while the southern half, which was still occupied by U.S. troops, became simply the Republic of Korea. The political divide was a guarantee of confrontation that finally spilt over on June 25th 1950 when North Korea sent troops across the 38th parallel into the south.

It precipitated a war that involved the United Nations fighting for the south on one hand, and communists from China and elsewhere, on the other. It would be three years before peace but not victory on either side, was finally achieved in that, still divided, country.

Back in Britain however, there were some very positive signs that the country was finally emerging from the war that had ended in 1945. In May 1950, for instance, petrol ceased to be rationed after ten years, and gradually most rationing also came to an end. The end of petrol rationing in particular, opened the door to more travel.

In May 1951 the King opened the Festival of Britain. Staged in London, and in other parts of the country, a hundred years after the Victorian's Great Exhibition the festival was a showcase for British industry and technology as well as being a post-war morale booster for the nation as a whole. It included the South Bank Festival Hall, which is still used extensively, and a 'Dome of Discovery' (which was later dismantled).

It would be the last big event George VI, who during the war with his Queen had endeared themselves to the people, just as Churchill through his leadership had, would open. Within a year he was dead and a 'new Elizabethan age' had begun but Britain was, often reluctantly, dismantling the empire that had its roots in the first one. We were still fighting – rebellions in Malaya, Burma, India and in parts of Africa such as Kenya and many conscripted soldiers, sailors and airmen would die or be injured defending the empire.

There was good news too – on the very day Elizabeth was crowned, news came that a British team had climbed Everest. Later that year, soccer idol Stanley Matthews would win his FA Cup medal and legendary jockey Gordon Richards would win his elusive Derby. Everything seemed to be pointing to the new Elizabethan Age being as exciting as the first. There were other significant improvements too.

Austerity had begun to ease and the return to Downing Street in October 1951, of the old warrior Winston Churchill leading his first peacetime Tory government, led to the lifting of many socialist restrictions, especially on business. Mass unemployment appeared to be a thing of the past and there was a growing confidence that things could only get better. Certainly by the end of the fifties Britain was significantly better off than it had been at the end of the forties.

In 1951 Churchill promised to make Britain 'strong and free' and, slowly but surely, things did improve. So much so, that the Tories were re-elected under his successors (Eden and Macmillan) for the next 13 years – even surviving the military disaster on the Suez Canal which brought Eden down. He was replaced by 'Supermac' Harold Macmillan, a very shrewd operator who once, probably truthfully told the people 'You've never had it so good.

On a lighter side, one of the most significant moments of the decade took place in April 1954 when a little known American band called Bill Haley and the Comets, burst on the scene with Rock Around the Clock. 'Rock n Roll' unleashed a mass of young talent, both in America and the UK, appealing to a young audience which was wealthier and more rebellious than previous generations, inhibited by poverty and unemployment, had been.

Rock n Roll proved to be the key that generated huge new markets in terms of fashion and style, but it was really an indicator that the old order had finally started to change. It was a phenomenon that created new 'stars', who shoved many of the old style entertainers to the shadows. It also shaped the way post-war Britain developed generally through the second half of the twentieth century.

The fifties became the decade of the young, and even though conscription was still in force, there was a growing sense of greater freedom for the young generation. With it came the milk and 'frothy coffee' bars, the juke boxes and the Teddy Boys, whose 'uniform' and hairstyles reflected the end of utility clothes, boring suits and the unimaginative ' short back and sides' haircuts.

The fifties paved the way for the even more relaxed and 'swinging' sixties, but sadly it also saw racism, with a level of viciousness not seen since the dark days of Mosley's Fascists. Immigrants from the old empire began to arrive seeking their fortunes, and there were race riots involving young people in places like Notting Hill and Brixton, where many West Indian immigrants were living.

To sum up the fifties would be to see the decade as one where Britain was at peace – apart, of course, from being involved in military actions and rebellions all around its Empire. It was a period when, with memories of wartime privations fading, there was optimism that the good times and national prosperity were in sight. There was full employment, people had money in their pockets and were better educated and more ambitious.

There was rebellion and racism – but there was also Rock n Roll, and that made a real social difference for it was a great leveller, especially as far as racism went. The fifties encouraged ambition, because the young ones no longer 'knew their place'. Whether the next decade, the sixties, justified such confidence is a judgement to be considered by others.

Chapter 1

Roots and the early years

Lewis – out of frustration

We are, each of us and whoever we are, the product of our history and our achievements, be they individual or collective. Whether the rewards of success are financial or in terms of experience, status or influence the real beneficiaries are our children and they need to know the story so that they can learn and build on it for themselves, our grandchildren and theirs. It is their legacy.

That is why I am writing this account of my own very personal journey and the foundations it was built on. Like plants anything of any consequence, be it a building, a company – even a football team like my beloved Queens Park Rangers – needs to have roots. Ours grew out of the appalling poverty of the Victorian East End of London to the governing benches of the House of Commons and I think we can be proud of that.

My (our) story really began in a distant land a long time before I was born when, sometime around 1880 a young Polish Jew called 'Lucjusz' Mayhover decided to join thousands of Jews fleeing from persecution in Poland and Russia. Actually his name may not have been Lucjusz. The truth is that I really have no idea what his first name actually was, but my reason for choosing it will become clear shortly.

Jews have been arriving in England since the time of William the Conqueror but were not always welcomed, being driven out many times for one reason or another. Hitler was not the first ruler to conjure up reasons for anti-Semitism for populist reasons and will probably not be the last.

It was Oliver Cromwell who, recognising the benefits in terms of financial, organisational and manufacturing expertise the Jews brought with them, opened the doors to them fully. It can be said that a great deal of the Great Britain success story since then has been down to the integration of Jews into our society – bankers, traders, industrialists, entrepreneurs, politicians and philanthropists. One Jewish born (though not practising) politician, Benjamin Disraeli who virtually founded the modern Conservative Party, became one of our most successful prime ministers and a favourite of the Queen.

But the Victorian England that young Lucjusz arrived in was a long way from the plush surroundings of the Palace of Westminster. His new country may well have been an improvement on the Poland he and so many more Jews had fled from, but it was still one where the 'underclasses' suffered incredible hardship whatever their race and nationality. As well as the Jewish immigrants and the indigenous English poor, they included many thousands of Irish families people starved out of their homeland by the potato famine. In both cases, usually because they couldn't afford to go any further, they tended to make their homes in the squalid and already crowded slums of the East End.

Apart from many photographs taken of conditions in those days, over the years we've all seen many films about Jack the Ripper going about his murderous business in the East End at that time. His crimes apart, it means that on film and in books we've also seen the very grim backdrops, characterisations and other graphic illustrations of his world – the one young Lucjusz Mayhover arrived in. A Dickensian London of dingy gas-lit alleys, cobbled streets and overcrowded hovels full of desperately poor men and women reeking of beer or gin.

He would have probably arrived, perhaps by steamer from Hamburg, at the Irongate Wharf, near Tower Bridge. At that time thousands of Jews, fleeing the Russian and Eastern European 'pogroms', and penniless Irish immigrants were arriving there every week. The immigration officers would have been rushed off their feet, understandably making them very impatient especially with the foreign speakers.

Here they would have been confronted by yet another young man who spoke no English and who would have had difficulties understanding them. The officials needed to put the names of all the immigrants onto their entry papers and records but many of them, Lucjusz included, had problems understanding let alone answering questions about their names. In most cases they only spoke Polish, and possibly Yiddish, in Eastern European accents and that would have been frustrating the officials with lines of people queuing up in front of them.

He kept repeating his name but of course in Polish until, family legend has it, they finally gave up out of sheer exasperation. Ignoring his real surname Mayhover, they impatiently stamped his entry papers as Lewis, the closest they could get to Lucjusz (if that was indeed his name). He was in, and that was how Lewis became the family name.

Mum and Dad

Because so many immigrants around that time were in fact refugees, be they from anti-Semitism in Eastern Europe or starvation in Ireland, they were usually virtually penniless when they arrived. They could not afford to go any further so they tended to settle close to the port they'd arrived at, be it Liverpool, Glasgow or London. It's the reason most of those ports in the late 19th and early 20th century had large concentrations of Jewish and Irish settlers prepared to put up with social conditions that were at least an improvement on the ones they fled.

So it's not surprising that the newly arrived Polish refugee, now called Mr. Lewis did the same. He would have found that the one redeeming feature was that within that melting pot of social deprivation race or religion did not matter – they all suffered equally. In fact because of those conditions religion played a huge role – whether it was the large numbers of Christian (Catholic especially) churches, the synagogues or the rallying calls of other Christian-based groups like the Salvation Army doing their best by providing soup kitchens and shelter for the really worse off.

Poverty was the common denominator and there is well authenticated evidence of hungry and ragged children going to school barefoot, of men without work hanging around on street corners or in the pubs trying to forget their troubles through cheap alcohol. It was one where desperate mothers took their treasured possessions to the pawnshops to get the money to feed their families.

London's East End wasn't alone in such deprivation of course – up and down the land in those days the big cities had their 'underclass'. The shameful downside to rich Victorian Britain was a desperately poor one, struggling to survive in dirt and disease. Perhaps their only real strength would have been in that sense of the 'in it together' community. It was in such a world that Mr. Lewis found himself, but he did have one strong card in his favour – self-reliance and the propensity of his race for hard work.

I don't know how he did it but clearly he proved successful enough to find himself a wife – a small chubby and very friendly Jewish lady who always had a smile on her face. I vaguely remember her as always being pleased to see me and giving me a cuddle whenever I entered the room. Grandad was also successful enough to raise, despite the times they lived in, a large family – in fact my dad was one of eleven children.

Henry Lewis, my Dad, was born in the East End on February 16th 1902 and went to school in Hackney. Hard working parents meant the kids were expected to pull their weight too, so by the age of 12 he was balancing school with work while helping with the younger children at the same time. That of course was around the time the world was going mad with the first of the twentieth century's two world wars. (Ironically his own son would be born during the second one).

When he did start work proper it was on the very lowest rung of a ladder that led up to the very top of his career tree in catering. He started as a commis waiter – the one who sets the table and brings the condiments to the diners rather than the meals themselves. He must have impressed even then, because he soon moved up the scale to waiter and wine waiter before eventually becoming the Banqueting Manager at the prestigious Clarendon Restaurant in Baker Street.

It was also a career that led him by chance, despite being determined never to marry, to meet my mother. Her name was Margaret Alice Spicer, also born in the East End (Poplar) but on 16th May 1912, ten years after dad was born. She had a brother, Jim, and two sisters and by all accounts all the girls were described as 'stunners' – one of them, some time between the wars, becoming a London beauty queen.

Mum was always praised for her dress sense too but she'd had her problems in her younger days. Apparently, thanks to a father who was an abusive alcoholic who had all his kids taken away for their own safety, she and her young sister were put into care in Hutton for a while. That was in Hutton Poplars where a lot of undernourished and/or orphaned kids from Poplar and the East End lived and went to school. She was living then, ironically perhaps just a mile or so down the road from Hutton Mount, where we have lived for many years. Perhaps I should try to explain a little about Hutton Poplars as a way of showing what Mum experienced in her youth.

It was opened in 1905, just seven years before she was born, as a 'Training School or Residential Home' for destitute children living in Poplar – hence the name. It followed a terrible fire at a home in Poplar in which a lot of children had died and was built after public donations out in the Essex countryside, largely at the instigation of famous old socialist MP George Lansbury. It housed from 400 to 700 children at a time in its early days when East End Victorian orphanages and workhouses were overcrowded.

It would have been an amazing place for such children with its own shop, dormitories, a school and even an indoor swimming pool, along with staff quarters and training facilities. Some MPs complained that with parquet floors and central heating it had all the comforts of a public school like Eton than an orphan's training school. In fact, like mum not all the children were orphans, but over the sixty years it was open many thousands of poor East End boys and girls passed through its doors.

They were not always welcomed by locals but many of the children who lived there still live in Brentwood to this day. I don't know much, if anything, about Mum's life in those days but it seems that one awful morning she woke up to find her five year old sister dead in the bed next to hers. What a dreadful moment that must have been.

Then, at the age of 18 she went blind but, thanks to the wonderful work done at Moorfields Hospital, she regained her sight two years later. She got a job as a waitress in the West End where dad was also working, though not in the same establishment he was in.

For obvious reasons staff in restaurants cannot have their lunches at the usual times because they are too busy so, when the weather was good, they would often spend a late lunch eating their sandwiches outside somewhere. Mum and dad were both eating theirs in the Savoy Gardens on the Thames Embankment, when they got talking. Those conversations led to dates but Mum always told me that his first serious words to her were: 'Don't fall in love with me, because I am not the marrying type.' Some chat-up line, eh?

Now while 20th century social conditions may have improved in the thirties compared to earlier years, many conventions hadn't. One clear one was that marriage between a good Jewish boy and a good Catholic girl was out of the question. That wasn't anti-Semitism though because 'mixed marriages' between Catholics and Protestants was frowned upon by the former too. Love, however is always stronger than convention and in September 1935 the young couple were quietly married in the famous Caxton Hall registry office.

I emphasise quietly because the 33-year old Henry never actually told his mum about it. Indeed he kept the fact that she had a Catholic daughter-in-law from her for two years. Believe it or not for those two years he regularly went home to his mum for Sunday lunch, but as a single man. Finally they decided to tell the old lady the truth and went to see her together. I have no idea how that particular meeting went, but grandmother clearly got over the shock because Mum became her favourite daughter-in-law.

Schooldays are not always the happiest....

Mum and dad desperately wanted a family but for a long time nothing happened – well apart from the war, the Battle of Britain and the Blitz of course. Then on June 20th 1943, as the tide of war began to turn in the Allies favour, I arrived in the Ducane Hospital in Wormwood Scrubs – yes, right next to the prison.

Me, aged around 2. Something makes me think Mum wanted a daughter.

The Blitz was over but London was still getting the occasional visits from the Luftwaffe and within a year or so the 'doodlebugs' (Hitlers V1 weapons) began dropping fairly indiscriminately on London. They were followed by his V2 rockets but within a few months of my being born, Mum and I were evacuated to St Ives in Huntingdonshire where we saw out the rest of the war.

When it finally ended in 1945

she brought me home to join dad who by that time was living in Shepherds Bush. That's where I spent my formative years and is where my lifelong love for our local team, Queens Park Rangers, began. The war was over but it had all but bankrupted the country and for many years austerity, including food rationing, was a way of life. For many years to come London bore the scars of the war, with bombsites – particularly in the devastated East End of my grandfather – everywhere.

Pictured here at a very young age

The country elected a Labour government but, in truth, any government whatever its politics would have struggled at that time but for us kids of course the worst thing was that sweets were still on ration. Well, that and starting school of course, where from start to finish I was never an outstanding scholar.

That began when I was five and, bearing in mind that I had a Jewish father and Catholic mother, I was enrolled in the St Vincent's Catholic School to be taught by nuns. I suppose that says a lot about dad's commitment to his, or to be honest, lack of commitment to religion. I was only there for a couple of years anyway but I can still remember my mother commenting that I hadn't learned much there but they had taught me good manners.

They hadn't curbed my natural curiosity or my adventurous spirit, because I was about seven when I got 'arrested'. I was staying with friends in Hackney and we went over to Victoria Park where we saw a sign telling us not to cross a bridge to an island where it was forbidden to go. Well, I ask you. What does that sort of challenge do to any kid? Yes, we climbed over the fence and walked across the bridge onto the island.

We found huge beds of daffodils and thought it would be a good idea to pick some to take home to mum. So when we walked back over the bridge carrying our 'swag' it was to find a load of park-keepers there

Mum, Dad and me at Butlins Holiday Camp.

In my new uniform on my first day at Latymer Foundation School.

The class of Latymer School, 1953.
I'm still friends with most of my old schoolmates today.

waiting for us. They took our names and a few months later we had to appear in Juvenile Court, where we were ticked off and our parents fined.

I was switched then to the Latymer Foundation School in Hammersmith where I suddenly found myself exposed to real lessons and real teachers. It was all so different and I do remember how scared I was at first and how strange it felt to be sitting at a real desk. I was also learning things and doing tasks that I did not always understand but somehow I managed to get through the next four years. Some of that was due to the help I was getting from one of my teachers in particular – Mr. Childs, a man who eventually became my Godfather.

My love for all things 'cowboy' started at a young age. Here's me in my outfit at Butlins when I was seven.

He was neither Jewish nor Catholic but Church of England, so you can see that at that stage I was living in a quite confused religious period of my life. I do owe that man a lot though because, largely thanks to his private tuition, I managed to pass my 11+ exams and in those days that meant a lot, delighting parents, because it opened the doors to grammar schools and that was my next move.

In 1954, largely thanks to my father and against all the academic odds, I was offered a place in one of the oldest and most prestigious schools in London. I know the name St Marylebone Grammar School (SMGS) doesn't stand out much from the usual lists of grammar schools for most people but this one did.

Founded in 1742 by King James it had a history of scholastic achievement, producing many men who became very successful in their fields. One of its patrons, in 1827, was the Duke of Wellington who twelve years earlier had achieved historic fame by beating Napoleon at Waterloo. The Iron Duke, who would also become Prime Minister, became one of many patrons who also included royalty.

Among its famous old boys we can claim the great orchestra conductor Sir Thomas Beecham, footballer John Barnes and author Len Deighton, musician/writer Benny Green – even pop singer 'Adam Ant' was one. There were many others, lesser known perhaps but highly distinguished in their fields – in business and industry, the church and the armed forces. Though it no longer exists as a school the 'old boys' society – the Old Philologians – still meets every year in London for its annual lunch.

So how did a poor Jewish/Catholic kid from Shepherd's Bush get to enter such illustrious portals? The short answer is that his father happened to be a pretty good waiter, well by that time he was a little more than that. Henry Lewis had followed his career path since starting as a commis waiter very successfully. When the school's legendary headmaster, Philip Wayne, started eating his lunch in the nearby Clarendon Restaurant he often fell into conversation with its Banqueting Manager, Henry Lewis, my dad.

They became friends and as a result, having passed my 11+ to at least qualify for that kind of school, Mr. Wayne offered me an interview. The memory of that day stays with me to this day because as mum and I walked through its old-fashioned and imposing gates I remember feeling totally inadequate and nervous. We sat in a big hall waiting for a man to open the big oak door that led into the headmaster's office.

He gestured us to sit down in a chair that seemed miles away from the big desk he was sitting behind. The interview never really got off to an encouraging start. 'As I know your father so well I thought it only fair to interview you,' he said. It was an opening line that didn't say a lot about my academic abilities but I just remember thinking to myself that...'good old Dad at least got me through the door'.

It's been a long time since then of course and I don't remember too much about the interview apart from one question he asked and that stays in my memory. He wanted to know what I did in my spare time, like at weekends for example.

'I like to go to the local park,' I told him quite truthfully.

'What do you do while you are there? Do you collect anything?' he asked.

I told him yes, that I collected girls' phone numbers so I could ask

Aged eleven with Mum and Dad at the Georgian Hotel in Haslemere

them out, and a broad grin spread across his face. It never occurred to me that he'd meant something a little more serious, but he'd realised that I'd answered his question honestly and in the only way I knew how. Let's not forget I was only eleven at the time and didn't realise how funny this would look to a grown up person, but I suppose it ended the whole interview on a good note.

We were thanked for coming and told we could expect a letter about the decision. When it did come, and it is still in my possession, Dad read it and passed it over to me without comment. It reads: 'Dear Mr. Lewis. Your son did not exactly shine at his interview today as I am sure Mrs. Lewis would have explained. However, due to our relationship I have agreed to find your son a place at St Marylebone Grammar School.' I was in but as you will see in many ways as things turned out Dad and Mr. Wayne did me no favours.

It was lucky in more senses than one because Mr. Wayne was on the point of retirement and was very soon replaced by Mr. Harold Llewellyn-Smith who was head at the school for the rest of my time there. Other teachers included the deputy head Mr. W R C 'snapper' Snape, Mr. C

Bosley, a Welshman and E McNeil. I remember the last two particularly because on the afternoon of September 13th 1954, the day before I actually started at the school, along with 91 other boys, I was called into the school library for what these days we would call our induction.

There we were confronted by these two young teachers who had been deputised to tell us about the school and what was expected of us in 'the Beehive'. I have no idea why but the motif on the school badge was a beehive. That led to my father, who had a wicked 'Cockney' sense of humour, grinning that 'boys in the beehive must behive'.

Bosley and McNeil told us a lot about our new school that afternoon, about its history, traditions and what would be expected of us, but one thing in particular. They told us that relationships among the 92 of us would not only be quickly formed but lasting. They predicted that if we stuck together, became friends and were honourable with each other we would still be communicating with each other in fifty years' time.

Now, to a bunch of 11-year olds that was a lifetime away and seemed impossible but their words were meant to be taken seriously and as things turned out, remarkably accurate. As you will see later in this book it became a fact of life for so many of us in that room back in 1954. The school may no longer exist but its history and traditions live on.

Having already mentioned the more distinguished students that SMGS turned out I have to confess that I was not one of them. I generally found school pretty boring and didn't attend many lessons. In fairness, though Dad had got me into it, the school was way above my capabilities and I struggled, coming bottom in most subjects – well in every sense except one, sport.

I enjoyed the rugby field and was captain of the second team for several years so Wednesday afternoons in particular, were very special. We walked round the corner to Marylebone Station where we could catch a train to our home ground in Sudbury. Even from a young age and despite our love of sport, a lot of smoking went on in the carriages not marshalled by the teachers on those trips. Wednesday afternoons it would be either rugby or cross country running, so was the only day I attended school regularly.

There was one regular habit though. Chilton Court which had its own restaurant where my father was Banqueting Manager was a short distance away. That meant I did not have to endure too many school dinners – not epicurean delights in any schools, even mine, in those days. I'd often walk down Baker Street to have lunch with Dad but because the headmaster still lunched there many times, I had to eat in the staff quarters.

The short walk back to school took me past a sweetshop and I still have some amazing memories of the different sweets I used to buy with money Dad gave me after lunch without Mum ever finding out. Nor was it the only time he came to my aid financially.

Going to the dogs...

Like many kids then I was doing a paper round to get extra pocket money and in Shepherds Bush our local paper shop was called Strudwicks. They paid me ten shillings (50pence yes, but it went a lot further then) a week to get up at 6am seven days a week to deliver newspapers. Sunday papers were not as big and bulky as they are now but they were still bigger than the dailies and I would hate to have to deliver them today.

I did have a bike which helped of course but my biggest problem was actually getting up in the mornings so it was usually Dad who did that. I would drag myself out of bed, put some clothes on over of my pyjamas and cycle off. Very often after delivering the papers I'd get back home in time to go back to bed for an hour before having to get up for school. Then, on a Saturday morning as I set out on my round I was handed my 'wages' in the shape of a ten-shilling (ten bob) note, because the coins only came in with decimalisation.

One Saturday morning that sticks in my mind was the one when I got home without the ten bob. I had lost it somewhere as I was delivering the papers and it caused a big row at home when Mum stopped Dad from making up my lost cash. 'He has to learn. You just can't give him the money back,' I remember her telling him and eventually he caved in and agreed with her.

I'd worked hard and got up early for a week and had nothing to show for it. It looked like the end of the world but later on, Dad quietly took me aside and, making me swear not to tell mum, handed me a ten shilling note. Of course I never did tell her but as I will explain there were in fact many things about Dad that I never told her.

In fact we developed a pretty strong father/son bond when I was around seven years old and he and Mum separated for a while. These were the days of course when the finality of divorce was usually confined to famous (and rich) film stars but marriages still went through rocky patches. I don't know the circumstances behind the split but for a while Mum and I moved into my Aunt Irene's house a few streets away from the family home in Shepherd's Bush where Dad stayed.

He was allowed to see me on Sundays when he took me either to London Zoo or to Speakers Corner in Hyde Park. I think I got to know and appreciate him that much better during those days than at any other time but before I leave the subject of newspapers a few years later I managed to get a newspaper stand concession in Lime Grove, the BBC TV studios. I often sold newspapers to the stars, especially like the singing group the King Brothers who made many hit records and were regulars on shows like the '6-5 special'. They were regularly voted as the nation's top singing group and were great guys, very friendly and more importantly they always bought three papers from me.

Going back to dad, one of the things I never told mum about him was that he often took me to 'the dogs' at Stamford Bridge. Chelsea FC still play there of course but, around the football pitch in those days there was also a greyhound race track (and speedway track too if memory serves me right), which was very popular until racing there ended in 1968. I would stand watching what was happening between races while Dad, telling me not to follow him, went to the tote windows to place a bet. Telling an inquisitive kid not to follow him is a waste of time of course and that's exactly what I used to do.

He would say he was going to place a bet at the two-shilling window but whenever I watched him he always went to the ten-shilling one. One day I confessed that, on my way back from the toilet, I'd seen him going to the ten shilling window. He looked at me, smiled and said: 'Son, you did not see that at all because I promised your mum I only bet two shillings at a time.'

I got the message of course but, in his day, Dad was an inveterate gambler and one of my uncles once told me a story on how to judge Dad and his ability to be calm, placid and never moody. It seems that his family, well his brothers at least, were gamblers and had even been bookies – on the track of course because off-course bookmaking was illegal. I know I learned to tic-tac myself at a very young age.

One day Dad and one of the uncles got a very hot tip on a particular dog in a race that he could not possibly lose. Dad raised every penny he could – £125, an enormous amount of money for working people in the forties – to put on the dog. The uncle had done the same but there was a photo-finish and their 'dead cert' dog was placed second. Dad had put his entire bet on the nose i.e. to win. According to my uncle, Dad just looked round, shrugged his shoulders and said 'Oh dear – well, we came close'.

Not another word was said at the time but Dad went home to Mum who exploded and was miserable for months. Mum was more of a firebrand and the incident demonstrated that Dad had a calm

In my late teens and without the whiskers!

temperament in adversity. It is such stories, family legends really, that have stayed with me all through the years.

Of course I was still at school at the time, miserably inadequate in the classroom, revelling on the sports and rugby field, but there was always one other bright spot – the annual camp. Once a year it was compulsory to attend the Forest Green School Camp – which belonged to SMGS and was down in deepest Surrey.

One day in the summer, on a Wednesday morning, we would be picked up by coach outside the school and driven away to spend the next seven days at Forest Green. There, living in tents and getting loads of fresh air, we would dig ditches supposedly learning to be surveyors. Apart, that is, when we weren't sneaking out to the local pub, The Parrot, and finding girls to date – our teachers would have been blissfully unaware of this of course, mainly because they were in a different pub or bar.

One history of the school commenting on the camp, which was acquired for the school thanks to a £10,000 cash gift in 1929 from newspaper baron Lord Rothermere, confirms my recollections:

'The Forest Green camp attracted quite considerable coverage in the

national press, no doubt prompted by Wayne himself, as it provided the opportunity for city boys to experience life under canvas, cooking over open fires, self-help opportunities like digging their own swimming pool and the laying of a concrete cricket strip.

All of the school forms visited the camp for one week stays and during the time spent there followed projects on geography, biology and surveying. In the forties and fifties there was one evening devoted to 'the scheme' which involved one half of the boys defending the tower on Leith Hill and the others being the attack force.

Good relations were built up with the local population and there was for the senior boys a cricket match most weeks against the village side. For some youngsters it provided their first introduction to cider and other strong beverages at The Parrot, where occasionally the staff were in one bar and the boys in the other!'

Philip Wayne of course had retired by the time I started school but I think Forest Green is another reason I'm grateful to his memory. When he died at the age of 74 in 1963 he was buried at Cranleigh not far from his beloved Forest Green.

On Sundays parents were allowed to visit and take us out for a decent meal, but those five years of summer camp remain as some of the happiest in my memory. It was where some very special friendships, many of them lasting to this day, were forged. Wonderful days but there came one when, for the first and only time, I distinguished myself at school.

That was in 1959 when I left school, two years early, having been the only boy in the school's history to have failed every exam. I never even managed to get a GCE (General Certificate of Education). My schooldays, apart from the sports side and the camp, were not particularly happy but in one other area I am grateful. St Marylebone Grammar School really did help boys become young men and, as those two teachers had predicted when they welcomed us to it, friendships made there really have stood the test of time.

But they were over and in 1959, at the age of 15, I was out looking for a job.

Chapter 1A

The Sixties

Wind of change

In February 1960 British Prime Minister Harold Macmillan made a speech, prophetic at the time, which included a phrase that also summed up the sixties as an era. 'The wind of change is blowing through this continent' he told the then white and apartheid ruling South African Parliament.

Macmillan was talking about the rise of African nationalism, which was heralding the end of imperialism there, but he could equally have been predicting so many other changes under way in the world by then.

In America it would be the era of the 'Camelot' of the Kennedy's which itself led to its own wind of change in the form of the civil rights movement, and of political assassination which would include two of the Kennedys, along with Civil Rights activist Martin Luther King. It would be the era of space exploration with men walking on the moon, of the Anglo-French Concorde aeroplane, East-West confrontation over Cuban missiles and of De Gaulle denying Britain a seat at the growing European table.

By the time 1960 dawned, World War 2 had been over for fifteen years but the world had still not fully recovered from its effects. The Cold War between Russia and the West had intensified with a new wall in Berlin dividing the two Germanys, though an economic miracle was happening in West Germany (and Japan).

The Cold War – or at least its ramifications given that both sides possessed weapons of mass destruction – also led to the rise of pacifism. Throughout the decade, the 'Ban the Bomb' movement went from strength to strength. It marched regularly into central London to demonstrate, with some very powerful speakers like philosopher Bertrand Russell and playwright John

Osborne, not to mention most of the Labour Party leaders, among their ranks.

On the business front the Tory government, with one eye on the 1964 election, made huge ten percent cuts in the car and domestic appliance purchase tax that existed before VAT. Chancellor Selwyn Lloyd was warned that a business boom based on hire purchase credit and import growth would not be good news; but he went ahead anyway.

A few months later he would be one of the victims of the purge that became known as the night of the long knives, when Macmillan sacked seven members of his cabinet. It was an event of which Liberal MP Jeremy Thorpe famously said: "Greater love hath no man than this – that he lay down his friends for his life". Then in October 1964 the ruling Conservatives lost power, for the first time since Churchill had led them back to Downing Street in October 1951. Labour, now under Harold Wilson, took over.

A year earlier Wilson had said, at party conference, that a new kind of Labour Party would be running the country. 'We are redefining our socialism in terms of the scientific revolution. The Britain that is going to be forged in the white heat of this scientific revolution will be no place for restrictive practices or outdated methods on either side of industry', he had predicted.

The will may have been there, but it would actually take another Tory prime minister – and a female one at that twenty years later – to really make a successful attack on the restrictive practices and outdated method Wilson had condemned.

Wilson had no better luck in persuading De Gaulle to let the UK join the Common Market (as it was then) than the Tories had had. The French president who had been sheltered in Britain during the war, wanted an end to the UK/USA special relationship, the dismantling of the Sterling area and proof that the British had begun to think like 'good Europeans'.

Worse was to come for Wilson. In November, seven months after the French rebuff, he had to devalue the pound. Despite his bland political and largely nonsensical assurance that it did not affect 'the pound in your pocket', the fact was that even during the war the pound was worth $4.03 – whereas it was now worth $2.40.

Another name to make it big in the sixties (apart from Carnaby Street and the Beatles of course) was the Chairman of British Rail, Dr Richard Beeching. In the cause of rationalisation he closed down a quarter of the rail network – 2128 stations and axed almost 70,000 jobs. Today, with all the efforts to *persuade people to use the railway, rather than roads, to transport goods and people, in hindsight his actions look to have been very short sighted.*

To summarise the sixties would be to suggest that, as Macmillan had said at the start, they did prove to be a period of great change. Despite the devaluation, people generally felt more prosperous, and new mortgage schemes such as the Greater London Council's 100 percent mortgage, had given more people the opportunity to move out of the cities to new environments. Wilson's plans to revolutionise Labour thinking never really took off, but there was relatively full employment throughout the decade. We even won football's World Cup.

The sixties did produce a society able to shake off many of the old social (and sexual) inhibitions of the past, as the popularity (with both sexes) of the mini-skirt exemplified. Certainly it resulted in a much more liberal and open minded attitude than the one held by a High Court advocate at the start of the decade, in November 1960.

That was when Mr. Mervyn Griffith-Jones was prosecuting Penguin Books because it had published a paperback version of the notorious Lady Chatterley's Lover. It was a case seen now as having been a turning point in attitudes, but his plea to the jury is very revealing. "Is it a book you would wish your wife, or your servant, to read?" he asked.

The jury felt they could.

Chapter 2

The sweet smell of Dagenham

Fair fa' your honest, sonsie face,
Great chieftain o the puddin'-race!
Aboon them a' ye tak your place,
Painch, tripe, or thairm:
Weel are ye wordy of a grace
As lang's my arm.

Carnaby Street and coffee bars

It might seem odd to start this chapter with part of a poem by a Scottish poet about a traditional Scottish dish, but be patient with me. There would come a time when Robert Burns and his praise of the haggis would have a great effect on my career, but in 1959 all I was concerned with was getting my first job after leaving school.

At that time with Britain, and London especially, on the brink of the 'swinging sixties' there was plenty of work about and many more career opportunities than there seems to be today. For a West London kid who'd left school with nothing in the way of certificates and qualifications the place to be then was the West End and especially Soho.

That was where all the excitement was – in the coffee bars where 'frothy coffee' had replaced the old milk bars and shakes, a new young and vibrant music revolution with the likes of Tommy Steel and Cliff Richard dragging the kids in with their guitars and home-grown rock n roll. In roads like Carnaby Street new fashion boutiques, not just for the girls but for the boys too, were springing up as young people, flushed with cash, were enjoying their youth.

Carnaby Street was a very different sort of place than Saville Row,

London's more traditional tailoring environment in Mayfair, of course but it was a company there – J Heathcote & Co. – who offered me my first job. At the helm of this textile manufacturing company was Mr. J Heathcote Amery who at that time was Chancellor of the Exchequer though of course it wasn't him who interviewed me.

I was offered the job of an office junior (a 'gofer' – i.e. 'go for this, go for that') at the staggering wage of £5 a week – £4.10 (£4.50p) after tax. For some reason we were paid in ten shilling notes, so I got nine of them every Friday afternoon so I gave up my paper round.

I started my career by working in the office as an order clerk. That was simply processing orders and often delivering rolls of nylon and other materials to the many West End dressmakers that were operating in London then. In fact most of the major dressmakers and fashion houses used our company to buy the materials for their garments and we were often given complimentary tickets for fashion shows at Courtaulds, just round the corner from Saville Row.

Once established in the firm we were expected to have some knowledge of the industry so they sent me down to Tiverton in Devon. This was not only the Heathcote Estate (and his constituency) but was where the mills that made the textiles were. I spent a few weeks there learning all I could about textiles etc., staying in a very nice local hotel which was very exciting for a sixteen year old boy – and even more so for one who had left home by then.

Well it wasn't so much a case of just voluntarily leaving home as a naughty teenager with a mother who stood no nonsense and insisted on her son not staying out late. One particular night she told me that if I wasn't home by 10pm she would pack my suitcases and they would be on the doorstep in the morning. Mum was true to her word – I walked a young lady home from church club, got home late and next morning my cases were on the doorstep.

I remember just picking them up, going to work and telling my boss who gave me the day off to find somewhere to live. I had just reached my sixteenth birthday. There were a couple of family friends, Flo and Ed Barret, in Alperton (Wembley) who I knew would help me out and, after making a call I caught a train and spent a couple of nights with them. Then I managed to get my own lodgings, – a room in a B&B which also housed some great Irish labourers.

Back to Tiverton where staying in that hotel, with all expenses paid, meant a lot and I even got to play rugby at a local club for the Heathcote team. Everything ends sooner or later however and after a few wonderful months in Devon I had to come back to London where I had to face the realities of life. I realised I was not earning enough to cover my lodgings, fares and my social life. I needed to find a better paid job or extra work.

Around this time I thought it might help me find girlfriends if I was in uniform but, national service having finished, I had no intention of joining up as a full time serviceman. I went along to the Territorials at the White City. The

Barry Thompson and me standing in Arminger Road, Shepherds Bush

colour on the berets (red) looked better than others so I joined the Royal Marine Forces Volunteer Commando Corps (RMFVRCC).

These were airborne 'troops' and my first training session was enough. I had to climb up a rope ladder and, holding onto a couple of pieces of rope, jump out of an improvised barrage balloon at 100ft. The whole thing terrified me, but then I found out that our next jump would have been with a proper parachute out of a real balloon hundreds of feet above Wormwood Scrubs, the very place I'd been born. That did it for me.

I switched berets for a green one in the Commando Corps Reserves where we just seemed to go canoeing in places like Gibraltar or crawling through dirty ditches staying out all night learning to shoot.

At the end of the day I decided the khaki wasn't doing a lot for me and anyway while I was out on night manoeuvres, my mates were out pinching all the girls. At the end of my two-year stint, trying to get out of most things, I called it a day.

Life of a salesman

I've never been afraid of hard work (those Jewish roots perhaps) and since I was only working five days a week, the weekend was 'available' so to speak. There was still plenty of work around in those days, and that included casual or part time jobs. It didn't take me long to find a Saturday job with a firm called Rowse of Ealing. This was a large department store with a lot of different areas, so where did I find myself? Textiles – where I had to cut up yards of materials while also serving the public direct.

Apart from that, I suppose it was an extension of my full time job and it certainly helped with the personal finances, but I still wanted more. On Sundays I managed to get a job selling Walls Ice Cream in Harrow from a barrow we picked up in its Stonebridge Park depot on the North Circular. They hadn't got around to bikes so, from 8am until 5pm and whatever the weather I would be pushing this barrow (yes through streets broad and narrow if you like) around Harrow and Kenton.

We weren't paid a salary, just a commission on each ice cream sold and believe me the competition was intense. Despite that there was just one day when I never sold a single ice cream but the depot manager took pity on me and gave me sixpence for a Mars bar on the way home. Believe me, it was the best Mars bar I ever tasted.

So there I was – working seven days a week but my evenings were free and it was ice cream, this time Lyons Polar Maid Ice Cream. This particular job offered the opportunity of working in different venues and one was the Bertram Mills Circus which was held at Olympia for a few months a year and I sold ice cream there. I also sold it during evening racing at Sandown Park but my busiest time was selling Lyons Ice Cream at the Ideal Home Exhibition.

All told I was working seven days and six nights (I never worked Sunday nights), but I did make a lot of friends and learned a lot about people during those working hours. Sunday nights were kept free to be spent in a pub in Acton with a family called the Thomsons. Their eldest son Tony played drums for a jazz group there and I would stand mesmerised watching him. I always thought that is what I would like to do one day and my interest in the drums has remained with me to this day.

So now I was earning good money but it was a pretty frenetic life-style and apart from not having seen my parents for a while, I wasn't eating properly either and the inevitable happened. I collapsed in Earls Court one evening. Somehow someone found my father's telephone number and he rushed to my side to take me out for a decent meal. He took me to the Golden Arrow in Hammersmith and he took me there many times after that, but always without mum knowing. As I said before we had a pretty special 'bonding' and he was keeping an eye on me. After a couple of years he persuaded me to go home to see Mum and somewhere down the line bridges were mended and I would often call in for a while.

I really did love my seven days a week working routine and Sunday nights were always there to look forward, to but by the time I was eighteen I had the urge to change direction and look for new challenges. With all my experience selling ice creams for example behind me, I started to look at what opportunities there were for salesmen. It wasn't long before a particular advert caught my eye.

Taking the biscuit

Huntley & Palmers, once known as the most famous biscuit company in the world, was founded in 1822 in Reading and when they advertised a sales job I applied and was interviewed. They told me I would have to attend a salesman's course in Reading and that sounded good to me but what was even more attractive was that the job carried a company car with it.

The interview went well and I was offered the job but there was a little hitch and that was that one requirement for joining the company as a salesman was that you had to be twenty-one and I wasn't. I was eighteen but I did look older than my years and thought I could pass for 21 so I took the risk when I filled in the application form and lied about my age. I kept my birthday and month the same – just put the rest back by three years.

It worked too because I passed the interview and was sent to a Reading hotel where they had set up a room to look like a normal grocery store. It was in there that we did our induction training before being sent out with regular salesmen in and around the Home Counties to learn how to sell biscuits to grocers (when we had more local grocers than superstores of course).

After a month working with, and learning from other salesmen I started being sent to different areas where the regular man was on holiday as a 'relief salesman'. I did that for a long time spending a lot of my time in London's East End – from Mile End and Bethnal Green to Aldgate. In fact most of London north of the river, even in my beloved West End and Soho where there was always a lot of small grocery stores.

I found I was really enjoying my new career, doing well and opening new accounts. Then, when I was getting close to my twentieth birthday the firm sent me a letter congratulating me, saying I had done well enough to be put on the permanent staff with my own area. Such a promotion opened up the opportunity of joining the Huntley and Palmers pension scheme, a form for that was attached to the letter and therein laid a problem.

Among the paperwork they sent was a request for me to send in my birth certificate. I, of course had lied about my age when I'd joined and I still wasn't twenty-one so I did what any red-blooded young Englishman would do – I ignored it and carried on as usual.

A month or so went by and another request for the paperwork came, and then another a few months later. I ignored them all. Eventually I was summoned to the Sales Manager's office in Fenchurch Street where I was pretty sure I knew what would happen. He told me I'd been doing a good job and that I was a natural salesman. Sadly he said my administration skills were atrocious and that they had written to me many times but I had still not completed the form to go permanent or sent in the documentation, including my birth certificate.

I'd realised then that I had to come clean, telling them I was only twenty. I knew it would cause an upset but hadn't realised just how much of one. He was clearly appalled, called in other members of the staff and it quickly became the crime of the century.

You see the requirements for having to be 21 on joining was more to do with the company's motor insurance than anything else. Their motor insurance stated that all their employees using a company car on the road must be 21 or over. I had, therefore been driving while uninsured for almost two years.

I had to go there and then leave the car behind, grab my possessions and head back to my one bedroom home in Shepherds Bush, with my 21st birthday approaching out of work and looking for a new job.

Butterkist

The driving licence issue apart one thing my life selling biscuits had shown me was that I not only had a flair for selling but it was work I enjoyed, so when it came to looking for a new job that was where I began looking. Being part of that scenario with Huntley & Palmer meant I also saw trade magazines like '*The Grocer*', and other similar publications. In one of them I spotted an ad for a van driver to sell popcorn in the London area, so I applied.

The advertisement had been placed by a company called Clarks Cereal Products, who had been manufacturing Butterkist, sweet sugary-butter coated popcorn, since before the war. Little did I know, when I applied, just how important that very simple product would become and where it would take me in the future. I was offered an interview in its factory in Dagenham where some of my mother's family lived.

The factory itself was at the end of a long road called Blackborne Road which was not easy to find (we had no Satnav in those days of course). In fact I started to panic a bit about being late for my interview when my sense of smell, as I arrived in front of some big gates with that strong sweet odour filling my nostrils, told me I had arrived at what would one day become the world's biggest popcorn plant.

The company actually had its origins in another part of Essex, in Southend when Cecil Hugh, fresh back from working in New York in the thirties, decided that a version of the popular American product could compete with the whelks and cockles in that favourite venue of East Enders. It was often called the 'Cockney's Mecca' and they would arrive in droves by train, coach or

Cecil Hugh, General Manager of Clarks and my mentor.

47

Tower Bridge steamer for their days out, so it's not surprising that Hugh felt it was the place.

But he was wrong and it proved to be a difficult birth so eventually he decided he had to look for help and he managed to link up with a London company called George Clark and Co who passed him on to their agents Clarks Cereal Products who agreed to supply Hugh with the puffed cereals he needed. That link developed into a merger with Butterkist now being produced in Clark's Tower Warehouse in Wapping before moving to more premises in Bow Road – perhaps not the best place to be when war was declared and the London blitz began and the inevitable happened.

As the war ended the company, which apart from the bombing etc. had boomed during the war, was looking for new premises. Dagenham, already the home of Fords and May & Baker also had a vast potential workforce and the council was looking to attract more firms to it. So Butterkist came to Blackborne Road where in 1964 I arrived to seek work selling popcorn from a van.

I was interviewed by a very tall man called Mike Adler who explained that I would be getting a basic salary of around £10 a week but a commission of one shilling (5p in today's money) for every box of Butterkist I sold from the van. We had to come to the factory every morning, load up with boxes of Butterkist and drive off to our areas, which for me was the East End and then the West End too.

I found that, having so recently been selling biscuits, I adapted quite well to selling popcorn and within six months I was earning pretty good money. I had been asked to move closer to Dagenham and since I had only ever rented furnished accommodation and my total possessions could be packed into a suitcase, that was no problem. In fact the company even put me up in a motel in Stratford for a year so I was even saving money as well as making it, until I moved into a flat in Earls Court.

One day I was summoned to head office and – with my previous experience of that in mind – was not something I approached with confidence. But to my delight I was asked if I would be interested in becoming a 'Relief Representative' – the firm's name for salesmen. The company had 22 men on the road who could be taken ill or go on holiday so someone was needed to fill the gap when they did.

It not only sounded good but meant I switched from a company van to a brand new Ford Anglia and got to stay in hotels with an allowance for

Our Ref: MMA/RVT   23rd July, 1964.

Mr. J. K. Lewis,
4, Adrian Lodge,
100/102, Sunningfields Road,
Hendon,
London, N.W.4.

Dear Mr. Lewis,

      I wish to confirm our conversation of last
evening when I offered you the position of North London
Representative.

      Your basic salary will be £750 per annum with
£1 per week lunch allowance. You will also be given a bonus
on your over-all ability, attitude towards your work and
actual turnover obtained on the area. This bonus is paid
monthly at the Company's discretion and you can expect a bonus
after you have completed your second time round a journey. We
will pay expenses that are incurred on behalf of the Company
for example staying out expenses etc.

      Your appointment will be subject to satisfactory
references and your being covered by the Guarantee Society.

      Will you please confirm your acceptance of the
position by telephone and in writing.

      I hope your stay with the Company will be a long
and happy one and look forward to your joining us on Monday
August 17th.

               Yours faithfully,
       for CLARKS CEREAL PRODUCTS LIMITED

              M.M. ADLER
          DEPUTY SALES MANAGER

P.S. Will you please return the Guarantee Society Form plus
    the two references, I omitted to take from you last evening,
    to this office personally.

*The letter of appointment confirming the start of my journey at House of
Clarks. I could never have imagined what a journey it would prove to be!*

dinner. At that time I was also, having been engaged for a while to a girl
called Jean, about to be married so a promotion would be very welcome.
It was an easy decision for me, though perhaps not for Jean because it
would take me away from home for periods.

    I took the job and had a great time travelling to different parts of the
country – getting lost just about everywhere – and having lots of fun. Jean
and I got married in April 1964 and we moved into a flat in Hendon.

Then I was called to the office again and this time was offered my own territory, but not just any territory because as South of England Rep for Clarks Cereal Products, Dagenham was in my patch. It also included Essex, Suffolk, all of London north of the Thames, Hertfordshire, Middlesex, Buckinghamshire, Cambridgeshire and Bedfordshire, but of course the Dagenham part meant I was directly under the eye of the management.

Unlike the other Reps, who only came into HQ once a year and made most of their contacts to it by phone or letter, because I had to call on my customers on a five week basis I had to go into the office once every five weeks too. As a result I became pretty well known to the staff and to the Sales Manager in particular.

I did pretty well for the next nine months and gradually moved up the sales target ladder. That meant bigger bonuses of course but it also meant I had to work harder and harder. My marriage suffered accordingly and since Jean and I had obviously married too young it wasn't stable enough to survive and within a couple of years we were divorced.

The last time I actually saw Jean was in a West End dancehall on July 30th 1966 when I was celebrating with friends. I know the date exactly because what we were celebrating was the first, and so far only, time England won the World Cup and we'd been there to see it. I'd been to see the 3rd/4th place playoff when Portugal beat the USSR and managed to persuade a tout to sell me at 25 shillings (£1.25p) ticket for £4 for the final.

For a couple of years before then I had been going into betting shops to back England to win the cup and of course as it got close to the tournament the odds dropped but I'd seen every game England played so finally managing to get one for the final where we were due to play Germany was wonderful.

In fact I was sitting right behind one of the goals – the one Germany equalised in almost at the end of the game. We had to suffer/enjoy extra time but finally we saw the great Bobby Moore lift the trophy and was carried on the shoulders of the team as little Nobby Stiles did his impish dance in front of them. It was a wonderful experience and the memory of that day will live with me forever, especially as a lifelong supporter of a little club, third division when I started supporting them, though as I write QPR are now playing in the Premiership.

Football has always played a very important part in my life, going back to when I was five or six and my grandfather would walk me to the next street, Loftus Road where QPR played. When old enough I would go on my own and even become a club steward, so I was one of those lucky schoolboys who got paid half a crown (twelve and a half pence), wore a steward's badge and watch the game. In the fifties there was never any trouble at the games.

QPR had never (until now) come to the forefront of football. They usually only had small crowds but they were as passionate about their team as any others and they produced some football legends of their own with players like Rodney Marsh, goalkeeper Phil Parkes who went to West Ham for over ten years and former England captain Gerry Francis.

One of our biggest moments, until promotion in 2011, happened the year after the World Cup final in 1967 and again at Wembley, when third division QPR not only won promotion but beat a number of higher division clubs to reach the League Cup final against another team better known by its initials West Bromwich Albion (WBA) who were in the first division. We actually beat them 3-2, coming back from a two-goal deficit.

So there are a couple of years in my life that include two little pieces of history for me. I was there for both and still have the tickets, programmes and some pretty important pictures of both these events in my office today. I am proud to have been part of both days but otherwise life moved on and I stayed on in the Hendon flat for a long time.

Not long afterwards we received notification from Cecil Hugh, our General Manager who I'd seen but never actually met, that the Sales Manager who'd taken me on and who I had got to know quite well, was leaving to take over at Schwarz

My World Cup Final ticket when England won the Cup. I was there! Little could I have imagined that my career would see me on first-name-terms with many of my heros of that very special day!

51

Pickles. This was quite a shock because in those days people with good jobs tended to stay there, so I guess he was moving on to bigger and better things.

Burns Night

Now I can satisfy your curiosity about the relevance of Robert Burns' tribute to the haggis that I started this chapter with, because it had what proved to be a dramatic effect on my life and career. In a way I guess it could even be called its fulcrum.

As well as the World Cup, 1966 was the year I became a member of the Manufacturing Confectioners Commercial Travellers Association (MCCTA) and was elected to be Minutes Secretary, Assistant Social Secretary and Press Officer. All these jobs were quite new to me of course and quite challenging, but they did give me another aspect of the industry I was working in. They also helped me meet many colleagues who on the streets were 'competitors' and that helped me appreciate that competitors do not have to be 'enemies'.

Now, January 25th each year is Burns Night and not just in Scotland either. I guess by that time we are over the Christmas and New Year celebrations and ready for new ones so a lot of English companies and people join the Scots in the celebration of their great poet with whisky and haggis. The MCCTA used to celebrate this occasion in the Russell Hotel in London and this particular one in 1966 was to change my life.

When I arrived it was to find myself on a table of eight, with the others being Sales Managers with other companies. I was still only a lowly, well not lowly perhaps, Rep of course. There being no drink/drive laws as they stand now then we did spend a lot of the evening 'toasting' the haggis in the usual style and getting on famously. In fact one of them, the Sales Manager of Barker & Dobson even tried head hunting me, suggesting I give up selling popcorn and join them.

It was around this time that we had lost our own Sales Manager, but there was something about Clarks Cereal Products Ltd that felt right to me. So I resisted the temptation to leave our small company to go to the biggest one in our industry for a bigger salary. Of course by that stage in the evening I was pretty drunk. He asked me why and I told him it was because I was able to do what I wanted, go on the road and come back whenever I wanted so it was quite a relaxing life.

He said; 'Alright, I will contact your Sales Manager and tell him that whenever I go past your flat your car is always there and that you are never at work. Then, when you have got the sack you can come and work for me.'

'We don't have a Sales Manager. He left a few months ago and no one has been appointed yet so that one won't work,' I replied, drunkenly of course.

The evening was getting later and I, along with the others, was getting more and more drunk without realising the others on the table were winding me up. I was getting a bit annoyed as well but they started saying that if the company had no Sales Manager why hadn't I been offered it? They pointed out that as the local rep in Dagenham I was the obvious choice so clearly they did not think much of me not to have offered it to me.

They pushed me harder asking if I'd applied for the job and by 2am when I drove home to Hendon I was pretty well worked up. Before even thinking of going to bed I sat down and wrote a letter to my General Manager saying I wanted the job, telling him I was covering the Dagenham area and that should have been reason enough. I was too drunk to recognise that I never had any actual experience in managing staff but I went out there and then and posted it at 3am before going home and finally getting to bed.

Next morning, sober by then of course, I realised with horror what I'd done and dashed down to the post office to retrieve it. No chance! I was nervous of what Mr. Hugh would think of me and my cheek in writing the letter but once a letter is in the post it belongs to the Queen until it's delivered.

I now worried for the next few days because, apart from the content of the letter, I didn't know if my spelling and grammar had been ok. All I could remember was that I said I wanted a better job and for the next few weeks I sweated. Then I got a very polite letter from Mr. Hugh saying thanks, but no thanks because, as I feared, of my lack of experience. He said the job would continue to be advertised but for me to carry on as I was, which was a great relief.

Three months later another letter arrived from Mr. Hugh asking me to attend head office for a meeting with him. It didn't mention an interview

DIRECTORS
SIR PHILIP A WARTER
G S PITT

WIRE
CREAMBARLI DAGENHAM

TELEPHONE
DOMinion 0221/4

CLARKS CEREAL PRODUCTS LTD

DAGENHAM

ESSEX

GENERAL MANAGER'S OFFICE

Our Ref: ACH/PK   14th February, 1967.

Mr. J. K. Lewis,
4 Adrian Lodge,
100/2 Sunningfields Road,
Hendon,
LONDON. N.W.4.

Dear Mr. Lewis,

  The details which I was able to reveal in our conversation yesterday regarding the plans for the future will be of considerable encouragement to you.

  I am impressed with the initiative that you have shown in the past in securing business, and this will stand to your credit for the future.

     Yours sincerely,

     A. C. Hugh.
     GENERAL MANAGER.

This is a letter I received from Cecil Hugh following my appointment as Assistant Sales Manager

and I feared that someone had spotted me going off to watch football or to a dog track for an afternoon meeting. Well you always think the worst.

When the day came I was met by a very friendly Mr. Hugh who indicated I should sit down in a massive chair in front of his desk. He explained that he'd not been satisfied with the quality of the applicants he'd already seen for the Sales Manager's job and had decided to offer me the job of Assistant Sales Manager.

He said he would continue to look for a Sales Manager to whom I would be responsible and from whom I would be learning the business.

I would be driving a Rover 2000 instead of my old Anglia, get a fifty percent pay rise and was shown into my own office.

In one hour my life had changed dramatically, all thanks to Burns Night earlier that year, a wind-up by competitors and of course the booze that had loosened my writing arm. I was now 'Management' and that ladder, along with my energy, would take me to the very top of my own 'world cup' and it didn't take long for that journey to begin.

Chapter 3

Onwards and upwards

Head-hunted

So, thanks to a Burns Night wind-up and an excess of spirit – Scotch spirit mainly – I was now Assistant Sales Manager, without a Sales Manager but my own office, a boost in salary and an executive's car. It was a whole new world but I only found out later that not only had they not had any suitable applicants for the top job, they hadn't had any for the one they offered me either.

This was probably because the salary they were offering in both positions was too low for the industry, but hey, who cares? It was a step up and, although I didn't know it then, there would be more to come. I spent a few days moving my desk and chair about and reading books I didn't always fully understand while trying to look busy. Finally I decided it was time I went out on the road and that seemed to please my General Manager Mr. Cecil Hugh, the man who'd started the company all those years earlier.

He'd not actually had any contact himself with any of the twenty-two salesmen (reps) we had throughout the UK so for the next six months that is what I did. I met up with each of them, discussed various ideas and organised a Sales Conference. That had never happened before so, with the help of an excellent sales team, my new job was starting to take off. Some were getting on a bit and I could see changes were necessary and that kept me busy for the next year.

Then I was suddenly called to a meeting with two very important people – Company Chairman George Pitt and Managing Director Sir Philip Warter. Mr. Pitt had been instrumental in helping the firm move after being bombed out during the blitz. A director then of British & Foreign Wharfs (and of the famous Yardley perfume company in Stratford) he'd made a factory in Stratford available for Butterkist to move into. Before being knighted Sir Philip had also been a saviour in helping the company move into better premises before the war. He owned the ABC cinema group and in the early sixties was recruited by the government to help Lord Beeching reorganise the railway network.

Two very important people obviously, so why they would want a meeting with the firm's Assistant Sales Manager was beyond me. They sat me down in Hugh's office and told me how impressed they had all been with my first year as Assistant Sales Manager and had agreed they need look no further for a Sales Manager, the very job I'd drunkenly asked for a year earlier. Now they offered it to me and gratefully I accepted it.

I was now, at the age of 24, the General Sales Manager of a company that was starting to move with twenty-two salesmen and with a year's experience I hadn't had before. Once again I mentally thanked Robert Burns and the 'wind up' merchants who egged me on that night.

One other immediate result was that I started to get 'head hunted' by other companies. The ink had hardly dried on my new contract when a competitor, Pims Popcorn which was owned by Watney's, approached me. I wasn't really interested but decided to go and talk to them anyway as a means of touring their plant and learning all I could about them.

It was a much smaller outfit than Clarks but it did teach me one thing – i.e. that there will always be a competitor. I always had it in mind that one day we might just swallow them up and we did. Five years after the tour I went to Victoria where Watney Mann had its head office and did the deal to buy Pims Popcorn, leaving us the only producers of popcorn in the land.

It wasn't only them either, because I can see from my diaries that I was also contacted by Wilkinson Sword Edge who made, among other things, razor blades about the same time. In fact within a month of my promotion I was approached by three different companies with job offers. My intention by then however was to stay in the popcorn business and, thankfully as things turned out, I did.

Popcorn giant acquires 'only serious rival'

CLARKS Cereal Products, the Dagenham-based "Butterkist" people, have taken over "their only serious rival" — Pims Popcorn, of Wembley, a subsidiary company of Watney Mann, the brewers.

Negotiations for the deal had been in progress since last April.

The equipment and machinery at the Wembley factory will be transferred to Dagenham, and the Pims product will be made there from now on — "in the largest popcorn plant in the world."

The take-over was initiated by Mr J. K. Lewis, general sales

Mr J. K. Lewis

manager of Clarks since 1968, who has just been appointed to the board.

He started with the company in 1963 as a merchandiser with a "Butterkist" van.

Mr Lewis told CTN: "We expect to improve the product of Pims Popcorn and give it wider distribution than it has previously experienced, while our main objective will continue to be the uxpansion of our own product.

"All Pims customers can be assured of the service offered by our company, which is second to none."

From March 1, Clarks will become sole agents in the United Kingdom for the confectionery market for the El Van range of soft drinks

Press coverage of Clarks' purchase of Pims Popcorn

Big day at Wembley

No, I don't mean the day we won the world cup but one just as important – Saturday March 4th 1967 when one set of club initials met another set. It was Wembley which was hosting the first ever League Cup Final and my club, little third division QPR, was there to play first division West Bromwich Albion (WBA). Wow!

It will have been noted that, apart from business and work, I was rather keen on football and of course, apart from England, that meant Queens Park Rangers. I had managed to buy nine tickets for a game nobody, even ourselves, expected a QPR victory but we did anticipate a great day out. Well, even today, it's not often a low division club gets to the dizzy heights of Wembley and we were going to make the most of it.

I dressed up the car in a glory of blue and white – ribbons and bows, balloons out of the window and QPR stickers on the bumpers – squeezed as many pals into it as I could and off we went to this very special day. Win, lose or draw we would be enjoying the experience and show manager Alex Stock and 'our lads' that we were behind them all the way.

By one of those ironic coincidences earlier that year the club had sold one of our best players, Clive Clark, to West Bromwich Albion where he'd done well and helped them to Wembley. Even worse, for us, in the first half of the game he scored two goals against us and we went in at half time 2-0 down.

Not surprisingly we were a little bit disheartened by then but then the team came out for the second half and upset the odds by scoring three goals to become the first lower division club to win the League Cup. Mark Lazarus, Rodney Marsh and club captain Mike Keen forgot they were only third division players and WBA were a top first division club, by scoring a goal apiece to run out winners with Keen picking up the trophy. We could hardly believe it and we revelled in the sheer joy of the moment.

The fact that we were not supposed to win the game was illustrated by the fact that the winners were entered into the following year's European Competition... well provided they were the first division club. So, despite being beaten out of sight at Wembley it was WBA who went on into Europe, but our disappointment was at least salvaged up to a point, because we became Third Division champions that year.

The Tuesday after the final we were playing Bournemouth at home. We beat them 1-0 but what a night that proved to be, because the team paraded with the cup in front of more delirious QPR supporters than we'd ever seen turn up for a mid-week game before. To add to my week of joy I even won the pools that week – well I got twenty-two and a half points a third dividend which netted me fifteen shillings (75 pence), not a lot but better than losing fifteen bob.

I had an even better result that same week when Mr. Hugh called me in for a chat, promised me a new car and held out a future with good prospects and the opportunity to travel abroad. All before I actually reached my 24th birthday but there was still more icing on the cake because almost on the very last game of the season QPR beat Oldham to clinch the Third Division title. We would be playing the slightly bigger boys the following year, and my cheque for next season's season ticket was already in the post.

Diving in

Cecil Hugh called me into his office one morning to tell me he'd decided I needed to learn 'marketing'. I'd been pretty good as a salesman of course but marketing was something else and it seemed that one needed a certificate in marketing to help you push your company forward.

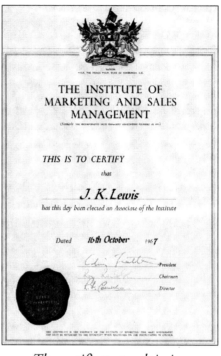

THE INSTITUTE OF
MARKETING AND SALES
MANAGEMENT

THIS IS TO CERTIFY
that

J. K. Lewis

has this day been elected an Associate of the Institute

Dated *16th October* 1967

President
Chairman
Director

He was right of course because the right kind of marketing makes it easier for your sales force to succeed, so on June 1st that year I was enrolled in the Harrow Technical College, where I spent a year getting a Marketing Certificate. I now had my first official title – Member of the Institute of Marketing (M. Inst. M) – and it felt good to be able to put these letters after my name.

The certificate proclaiming me a Member of the Institute of Marketing which hung on my office wall

To be honest no one was ever quite sure what they meant but they were put on all the letters sent out by the company in my name. I'm not sure they changed my life much but, being 'certified' (or should that be certificated?) they did get me another pay rise which was just as well because I had a new hobby.

I guess all work and no play really does make Jack, or whoever, a dull boy and it was my pal Gareth Thompson who decided I should take up deep sea diving – the swimming kind, not clumping around on the seabed in lead shoes wearing a helmet. I did my early lessons, learning about the equipment under six feet of water in the Wood Green Swimming Baths.

Once you had qualified on completing the course you were then allowed officially to go swimming with a partner and from thereon Gareth and I would spend many happy weekends diving in Lulworth Cove in Dorset. We'd set up camp at Corfe Castle but the diving took place in Lulworth Cove where, apart from there being a hut where we could fill our air tanks, there was a nice little cafe. It wasn't far from London, an easy journey in those days, and fortunately Gareth was a highly experienced diver so I was always in good and safe hands.

Diving became quite an obsession with me and opened up a whole new world of course. We began looking for other areas to dive and soon found Dunwich on the East Coast where there was an underground city that had formed over many centuries. The corrosion there was so bad that at times you could see coffins sticking out of the rocks because there was a church and graveyard at the bottom. I understand that it has all gone now but in those days, if you had an experienced partner and some heavy duty lights it was possible to see parts of the old ruins that, centuries before, had fallen into the sea about a quarter of a mile from the shore.

We spent many weekends diving between the South and East coasts but sadly never had the opportunity to dive foreign waters.

Essex man

Still talking about 1967 it was in that active year when I really began to get to grips with my new job that I finally left West London (but not QPR of course) to discover Essex. In September the lease on my Hendon flat expired and since my new position demanded I spend more time in our Dagenham office it was no longer really a sensible option.

Mr. Hugh, as generous and helpful as ever, agreed that I should live at the company expense in the Harleen Motel, just off Stratford Broadway – a lot closer to Dagenham than Hendon. It was very nice and to make it even better the motel had a late night drinking licence so a variety of people, not necessarily residents, would come in off the street for a pint or three. I got talking to one of them, he was called Peter Kalisher, who revealed he had a big house in Gidea Park, even closer to Dagenham and in which he let rooms.

So I moved into a room costing me £3.50 a week, sharing a bathroom with several other like-minded drinking and friendly people. Gidea Park was a nice area and only around fifteen minutes from my office. I also paid a shilling for each bath and I see from my notes that December was an expensive month because I had six baths, whereas I usually had five.

I'd given up the sales area I'd been covering for Clarks, taking on a new rep, so I had more time for the company and other things, such as my social life. Peter and I were around the same age and had become close friends, touring local pubs, clubs and drinking holes etc. and also places like the old Ilford Palais where we became regulars.

By this time of course I was really getting to grips with my new job. I was going out with reps to meet customers while trying to open new accounts in order to push the business forward. I also had to face up to one of the less attractive responsibilities of my new position – having to fire some people and interview new ones, because the sales force I'd inherited had not been terribly effective. I was now in a position and felt strong enough to build my own team.

I was managing to split my time between the business and football quite successfully and in 1968 was lucky enough to meet a man called Reg Powell, who owned a West End advertising agency called CFP. Mr. Hugh, who'd known Reg previously, and I discussed the idea and we decided to appoint CFP to help promote the business with advertising, conferences and all kind of promotional activities. It worked out very well with Reg and I gelling from the start, helping me progress the business.

There was a good example that year of business and football coming together very nicely, but its origins lay four years earlier. Back in 1964, on my 21st birthday as it happens, I happened to be in Ipswich calling on a customer called Mr. Zagni who ran ice-cream vans and supplied a lot of local caterers. He commented on the very nice mohair suit I was wearing and I explained that it was my birthday and was going out to celebrate later. I will always treasure his reply.

'Well we don't need an order today, but we can't not give you one on this special day'. Thereupon he gave me an order to send in a couple of weeks later. Business then was quite personal and a lot friendlier and less cutthroat than it seems to be today. Mr. Zagni and I became good friends and that paid off in 1968 on the day QPR played Ipswich Town.

Gareth (Thompson) and I had been unable to get any tickets for love or money for that game and we were desperate to see it. I phoned Zagni and he told us to get to his warehouse by 11am that morning. We duly arrived and he gave us white coats, put us on one of his vans that sold hot dogs and burgers etc. Then he drove us straight to the stadium in Portman Road and into the ground. We helped him unload his stock into the various catering bars there before taking off our coats and watching the game. This, of course, was in the days before seated stadiums and tickets.

After the game, which we drew 2-2 as it happens, we helped him get the van started and finished up at his house for tea and cheese rolls. A perfect example of my business and my sport coming together, thanks to a customer who became a friend.

In fact that year was an even more memorable QPR one because on May 11th I travelled up to the Midlands to watch my team not just beat Aston Villa 2-1 but to clinch promotion to the First Division. This of course was something that the supporters of a small club from Shepherd's Bush could never have dreamed of, even after our League Cup triumph and previous year's promotion to Division 2.

We could now look forward to playing the likes of Manchester United, Arsenal, Spurs and Liverpool – the very cream of English football that we had never seen our team play. The bottle of champagne used to celebrate that win over Aston Villa is still in my possession..... er, empty of course.

Mrs. Carpenter... and new horizons

Business-wise it was an active year too because, among other things, I attended my first ever conference, a Cinema Conference in Edinburgh. Why cinemas? Well, apart from the fact that our MD Sir Philip Warter was Chairman of ABC Cinemas our popcorn of course was a popular seller in them.

It meant a round of dinner dances, exhibitions and a different film premier every night of course, but someone had to do it. Seriously though, it gave me the chance to mix and meet with a lot of the company's major customers in the cinema industry, though it didn't help with our new product.

We'd produced a new, mint flavoured, version called Mintkist which for some reason or another we thought could do well in Scandinavia. It didn't. I spent a lot of time travelling in that area but it seemed that mint popcorn did not catch their imagination any more than it did at home.

I spent a lot of time going round the UK collecting just about everything we'd sold but they were useful trips in other ways. After all I couldn't go round the country with our salesmen without spending a little time visiting football grounds and stadiums. On one day alone I got to see Newcastle's St James' Park and in Sunderland went to Roker Park where they used to play at the time. It was nice seeing some of the places our little Loftus Road team would not normally play in.

There was a sadness that year too because Mr. Childs, who had been my teacher from the age of 5 to 7 and had subsequently become my Godfather, died. A strict disciplinarian in his day he became very close to the family but sadly I was unaware of his death when I popped in to see him on a Wednesday only to find he'd died a couple of days before. A real gentleman, who had such a positive effect on my life and for which I will always be grateful.

Still learning I was starting to understand the American side of our business for of course our corn was imported from that country's great Corn Belt. That is composed of seven states close together and who have the right amount of rain and climate. We dealt with a particular company called Blevins and in 1968 Jim Blevins flew in from the States to visit us in Dagenham and we got on very well indeed. I treasure his words to my boss. 'Send young Ken over to us and we'll take good care of him', words that sent my mind buzzing with anticipation. In the years to come I would cross the Atlantic many times but I still remember the thrill of those words.

But more of that later because possibly one of the most significant events of that year, though it wasn't apparent at the time, followed the resignation of Beryl, my secretary who I seem to remember had found a better job. Within a day or so I had interviewed a Mrs. Skelton and offered her the job. Later she became Mr. Hugh's secretary until she left to take a job at the town hall – popcorn to politics, something my family knows a little bit about too.

In September, the 6th to be precise and the reason I know it will become clear later, Mr. Hugh asked me to interview a secretary for him as well. One of the candidates, a Mrs. Carpenter, seemed to be right for the job so I asked her to come back for a second interview with the boss a week later.

He agreed with my judgement and Mrs. Carpenter started working for him as his secretary the following week. For some reason or other a few weeks later Mr. Hugh asked me to swap secretaries. He said he felt he would be better served by Mrs. Skelton who was an older lady and that the younger, shorter and mini-skirted Mrs. Carpenter would serve the company better working for me. That suited me too, the switch took place and my whole life started to change again – oh yes, Mrs. Carpenter's first name was Lynn.

Not that I spent a lot of time in the office with her in those early days because my passport was starting to get used more and more. One day in the spring of 1969 I was suddenly told I was off to the Netherlands which, in those days conjured up visions of tulips, windmills and canals rather than smoky cafe's and bars. For a young man it was an exciting prospect, particularly since Clarks was paying all the costs. It turned out that an old pal of Mr. Hugh's, who had opened up a confectionery wholesalers business in Holland, had made contact with him saying he would be interested in buying some Butterkist, which had never been on sale in that country.

So there I was, in Amsterdam with a briefcase full of popcorn, but all I had was an address and some money – not even a hotel booked. That wasn't the way it worked in those days, so I simply asked a taxi-driver at the airport to take me to one and he took me to the American Hotel. To be honest there was very little 'American' about it but it was comfortable and in a good position for me to go about and do my business in. It was also next to the American Cinema next door where they showed a lot of American films.

It also had a good tour desk and I thought that, since I was in the country, it would be nice to see some of it, so I booked myself onto a tour. Apart from Amsterdam itself I managed to see Rotterdam, the Hague and Delft where I saw some of its famous pottery being made. So much of it in fact that I began to get impatient to get back to Amsterdam to sell some popcorn, which I did.

At the time I was not sure if the relatively small number of boxes of popcorn I'd agreed to send to Holland to keep Mr. Hugh's friend happy was worth the effort. However, it proved to be a very worthwhile order because that kindly old chap gave me a number of names and addresses of other wholesalers in Amsterdam who could supply the whole country. That meant I could stay a little longer in Holland and really did get some new orders – certainly enough to make me feel the trip had been successful and my boss felt the same too, though I don't recall if we had many repeat orders from that country.

He was delighted and out of that trip to sell a few boxes of popcorn on the other side of the North Sea, I not only got another rise but a new title as well. I was now the company's Export Manager and that really did open up a lot of new horizons. I guessed it gave me the right and opportunity to travel the world, all expenses paid with a briefcase full of packets of popcorn.

In fact the very next week I was sent off on another trip across the sea – well to the Channel Islands at least, to Guernsey where Mr. Hugh had some more connections. It proved to be quite easy to sell Butterkist there because although it had been advertised and sold in the cinemas it had never been on sale generally. Then I flew on to Jersey where I got a lot of information, a few orders and many promises.

To be honest I was starting to like this 'jet-set' idea of flying around the world on a kind of 'have briefcase, will travel' basis. However, apart from a quick overnight trip to Germany for an exhibition and visit to a chocolate manufacturer, I was stuck back in Dagenham for a long while.

Not that life was suddenly boring there. As a member of the MCCTA (Manufacturing Confectioners Commercial Travellers Association) by then I was also its Social Secretary and organising trips like the one to the Sun newspaper called 'Put the paper to bed'. For those not in the know, this is the final process involved in printing the paper before it goes out onto the streets and while times and technology have changed I suspect it's still called that.

As far as my dizzy aspirations for global travel were concerned however the firm's new Export Manager only managed a repeat trip to the Channel Islands that year. In fairness it was a successful trip resulting in a number of orders for the products we were selling at the time. Things there were working out pretty well for us and there was even talk or my doing a TV commercial.

On the other hand I did get to know my own country a little better that year and not just football stadiums either, though I did successfully find Molineaux in Wolverhampton to see the 'Wolves' play on one trip. I spent a lot of time with my reps and learning to appreciate the beauty and history of places like York and touring the North East in Middlesbrough and Newcastle. I was actually in Newcastle visiting an old family friend when I had to rush back for my birthday celebration when I was being treated to a night seeing Des O'Connor at the Palladium.

The following week I saw Val Doonican, but that was in Blackpool where I went to on business. Blackpool was a good place to stay anyway because it was only a short flight to the Isle of Man where I'd never been. That was, well in a way it was, export potential and I hadn't been abroad as Export Manager for months, though I was still mixing business with pleasure in those days. I spent some time in Devon and Cornwall but rushed back so I could see the premier of a new film – Hair – the film version of a stage show featuring naked people and which had shocked audiences, though it probably wouldn't these days.

I enjoyed Manchester and Liverpool (business with football pleasure of course). They were full of really friendly and pleasant people who always made me welcome and of course I always loved the 'scouse' humour of the Liverpudlians. In fact over those years I made some pretty good friends, possibly because I became known as the 'Popcorn man from QPR' and in those days the Rangers offered them no threat footballwise.

Some of those relationships made in those days have stood the test of time and in fact one of them, Roy Hall who owned a warehouse in Manchester even asked me to be Best Man at his wedding. For an 'Export Manager' I was doing a pretty good job visiting places all over the UK – Cardiff, Bristol, Porthcawl, Keynsham, Port Talbot, Swansea especially. I made a lot of friends in the Welsh Valleys in those years.

I also remember being invited, as a guest of the Portsmouth Chamber of Commerce, to make a speech on how popcorn was made. To be honest I didn't really know and had to make a lot of it up as I went along. After all I was on the outside of the business when it came to production rather than on the inside where you didn't get expenses. Then, suddenly near the end of the year, I was asked to go on a Government Board of Commerce tour to Scandinavia, so once again my horizons went beyond our shores.

The idea was that a group of around twenty people were approved by the Government to help the export drive by going abroad and it was a really mixed bunch of us that travelled that day. One guy was selling chinchillas while another, Jack Plautus, had a case full of cosmetics. Two other guys together – and I do mean they were together – were selling new IT equipment. For the bigger boys on the trip Fords had a representative and some other really big businesses were there helping to boost exports. Me? I was selling popcorn.

I hadn't met any of this group before of course and it was a rather strangely lonely experience even though we were welcomed at all the UK embassies. I suppose that sense of loneliness was emphasised because at the time I was also starting to get on friendly terms with my secretary Lynn Carpenter, and I seem to remember writing and phoning Dagenham a lot during that trip.

To Russia with popcorn

We actually kicked off in Denmark where I found how different life in that part of the world was. Compared with the people I had been dealing with in the UK, life seemed to be much more free and easy and the Danes were far more relaxed. After four days we moved to Sweden – very similar experience – and another embassy party before going on to Finland.

The Finns are a very hardy race and their saunas were very different from those we'd had in the other countries. I was never, and still remain unconvinced, too sure about all those sticks and birches and it was pretty cold standing around on those rooftops in September wearing just a towel. I was never quite sure which of the group talked me into this, it could have been Plautus, but we did it.

I mention Jack because we became particularly friendly on that trip. He, you will remember was selling cosmetics and he came up with the idea that his goods might be welcomed in Russia. I thought, what the hell, they might well like our popcorn as well, not that we were planning to go to the USSR of course, just their embassy in Helsinki.

Well the two countries are neighbours but what we didn't know was the history between Russia and Finland. Stalin, still swallowing up other neighbouring states like Latvia and Lithuania between the wars, attacked Finland just before the start of the Second World War when he also invaded Poland. He got the shock of his life when the Finns not only had the temerity to fight back but initially beat the Red Army. The war ended in 1940 when the Finns signed a peace treaty in Moscow, ceding some territory but never surrendered.

Jack and I were oblivious to all that at the time so we called a cab and asked the driver to drop us outside the Russian Embassy. Instead he stopped at the end of the street and politely told us we would have to walk the rest of the way. Apparently no self-respecting Finn would go anywhere anything Russian, especially an embassy.

So we walked about a mile to the embassy, Jack with his cosmetics and me with my popcorn. We arrived and went into the embassy where of course we had no appointment and had great difficulty trying to explain why we'd turned up with cosmetics and popcorn. We actually got inside the door, probably because we confused them, and were put into a waiting room with the door being locked behind us.

There we were, locked in a room in a Russian embassy in Finland and getting more worried by the minute. It took a good half hour before the door was unlocked and a guy who could speak reasonable English walked in to ask us what we were doing. In fact he went further by asking why we were spying on Russia.

It seemed a bit unlikely that two Englishmen would be spying on Russia in its Helsinki embassy carrying nothing but lipstick and popcorn but it was a worrying development. Visions of being flown by night to Moscow and the Lubianka prison started to flood our minds. Desperately we tried to explain that we'd thought our products might find a market in the USSR but he was not amused.

Politely we were told that the only way we could sell products was if we bought telegraph poles, steel or metals from them. We were, of course, totally out of our depth and very confused. In fairness they could see that and we were politely shown the door and told which way to go to get a taxi. 'You will never get a taxi to come near our embassy', they said. They never even wanted our samples, but we were glad to just get out of there.

The next day we went to Norway, a few ferry rides and another embassy party before going back to London. As far as I was concerned the whole trip (the Russian adventure apart of course) was a great success. Even more important was the letter Mr. Hugh received from the leader of the group on behalf of the government. It said 'Ken Lewis's contribution and involvement had helped the group's success immensely and how much we'd enjoyed having him on the trip'.

It offered Clarks the chance to travel whenever those export groups were put together, with all expenses paid by the government, so no wonder he was pleased even though the trip had not actually resulted in a lot of orders apart for some for Minkist. What Mr. Hugh saw was that his protégé – he had no children and that is what I was to him – was gaining some considerable experience which would stand me in good stead for the future.

Cecil Hugh was a clever man in many ways and was probably my first step on the ladder to any success. I owe him so much... especially of course for my secretary.

D. H. Dumas.

Dear Mr. Hugh,

I hope you will not mind my writing to you like this, but as Managing Director of a group of companies with some considerable experience of employing staff I feel you will not be affended.

Your General Sales Manager Mr. J.K.Lewis conducted himself in such a way during the recent trade mission to Scandinavia that quite apart from the obvious success he had in the possibility of creating new business for your compay, he radiated an extremely satisfactory image in the eyes of the British Counsolat staff in all the countries we visited, and much impressed the other members of the mission. Having organised something like 25 trade missions to all parts of the world, I would regard him as the perfect mission type in as much that he fully understood and complied with the various requirements that must be met by mission members which to some extent must present the group image, yet he took every advantage of opportunities for his own company's business development.

I would like to congratulate you on acquiring his services in the first place and to compliment you on the guidance he has obviously received from you as his employer. I sincerely hope that it will be my pleasure to have your company represented on further trade missions, and where you see fit by Mr. Lewis.

This is a copy of a letter sent to Cecil Hugh after I returned from a British Board of Trade mission to Denmark, Sweden, Norway and Finland. There's little doubt it helped to further my career at Clarks!

Lynn, my new secretary, working in my office

Chapter 4

Lynn

Gassed and robbed in Tel Aviv

One windfall advantage of my new position was that even my holidays could be part funded by the firm if I mixed business with pleasure (again) and sold some popcorn at the same time. So when Mr. Hugh suggested I could use a holiday I took him up on it and decided to go somewhere I'd never been to before.

Given my roots I guess there had always been a subconscious desire to visit Israel and since he had some names to contact as far as selling Butterkist was concerned, I jumped at the chance. I suppose that for many in my situation it would have been like 'going home' but I was simply keen to go there on holiday and also to take a girl friend with me.

Only eighteen months or so before then Israel had been locked into what history called the 'Six Day War' when in June 1967 it had attacked Egyptian, Syrian, Iraqi and Jordanian positions that had been threatening its own borders. The Egyptian leader Nasser in particular had been doing a lot of sabre-rattling and making all kinds of threats about destroying Israel once and for all.

The Israelis, deciding to take the initiative, had had astonishing success and, against all the odds, decisively defeated their enemies on all fronts and in the air. They even gained control of new territories bordering their own land, like the West Bank and the Gaza Strip that they control to this day.

When we arrived and drove out of the Tel Aviv airport the litter of war, in the shape of wrecked and abandoned tanks and armoured vehicles was clear to see, while among the people there seemed to be a very understandable sense of triumphalism similar I imagined to the way we'd felt after winning the Battle of Britain. For us though it was new places, full of adventure and unusual smells. I mention the smells because of what happened next.

We checked into our hotel and that night went to bed fully relaxed. The next morning however I woke to find my trousers, with my wallet in them, gone as had also some of my friend's jewellery. Agatha Christie would have loved this one for one of her characters because there we were, five storeys up with our door locked and the balcony door, which overlooked the beach still closed.

Yes, Poirot would have loved this one, but I phoned down to reception and from the response it was pretty clear that something odd had been going on because, before I could explain, the lady on the phone asked if we'd been burgled. I said we had and she said other guests on that floor had also been robbed and asked that we remain in the room until detectives could talk to us.

A couple of hours later they knocked at our door and when they walked in sniffed and said; 'You've been gassed. Can't you smell it?' We said no because everything smelt different to us so we would not have been able to tell anyway.

It transpired that the burglar, or burglars, had used some sort of gas, just enough to make us more drowsy and into a deeper sleep while rummaging through the rooms. The detectives of course blamed local Arabs although we never saw any evidence of that and within a couple of hours my trousers – minus my wallet of course – were recovered from the beach later that morning, though my girlfriend's jewellery was never seen again.

We had to go to the local Police Station to make a statement of course and also to get a letter for my boss confirming what had happened. We phoned Mr. Hugh from there, telling him of our loss and it appeared he actually had a friend at one of the confectionary wholesaler's addresses I was due to visit. The police very kindly drove us to that address where we were given some money to see us over until Mr. Hugh could wire us some more to repay his friend and continue with our trip.

Quite an experience and a great learning curve for a young man on his first visit to the Middle East (and his roots of course). Oh yes, we also managed to sell a little popcorn too.

Master Maize

Family, even extended family, has always been important to me and I had a Grandad who was not my Grandad and a Nan who was not my Nan either. In my early days when we lived in Shepherds Bush an elderly couple, Mr. and Mrs. Salmon, virtually became my extra grandparents. In fact I grew up believing them to be and they always were in a way, certainly always loving me as their own.

Well, early in 1970 he was taken into hospital in Dover, where he was living by then, with a heart attack, and I spent a lot of time commuting between Essex and Dover as a result. I mention it because I spent the early part of that year covering all parts of the South coast where I had no rep, and getting set up for exhibitions.

Now trade exhibitions had never played a big part in the company's development but it seemed a good idea to me so we prepared for our first

What a great sport Lynn was to don the outfit. She's pictured here with Moira Lister on our stand at a trade fair.

one in London. It also sounded like a lot of fun though there was an awful lot of detail and paperwork involved and that was not my strong point.

However remember I did have a very efficient secretary then known as Lynn Carpenter and she began to attend meetings with stand designers and the like in London. She also helped me to fit her out with the, would you believe, 'Master Maize' costume that she was to wear on the stand giving her, I am sure, a lot of amusement. It wasn't a very flattering outfit and I still have the photo somewhere.

The exhibition, called Contob70, was held in the Horticultural Hall in Victoria and I was booked into the Grosvenor House hotel a short walk from the venue. It was March, bitterly cold and snowing a lot of the time making it difficult for my secretary, who was travelling to London and back every day to man the stand. In fact it got so bad that one evening it was clear that she wasn't going to get home.

Well, being a company man to my fingertips I had no wish to put Clarks to added expense by booking another hotel room we decided we would share mine. Well that's my story and I'm sticking to it, but it started a whole new chapter of my life and I will leave that to your imagination. Certainly I will never forget Master Maize.

Apart from all that it was a busy few months that year with social activities like the Kent Candy Ball, a Sales Manager's Conference at the Cumberland Hotel in London, the Retail Confectioner's Dinner at the Royal Lancaster and, of course I never missed a QPR game either. There was also a visit to the Ideal Home Exhibition's first popcorn stand, but it wasn't ours, and MCCTA meetings taking place all the time too.

I almost became a film star that year too – well perhaps not quite a film star as an advertising one. Cecil Hugh started taking me to London film studios to see how commercials were made because we were looking at the idea of making our own ones for the cinema screens – lot of popcorn etc. eaten in the cinemas. It was quite exciting sitting in cinemas watching private screenings of film adverts and not just in London either.

I was sent to the Cinematographic Exhibitors Exhibition (CEA) conference in Edinburgh and remember finding my way round that beautiful Scottish city. It lasted a week – conferences all day and parties all night because people involved in that industry know how to entertain. In between times we even managed a visit to the Zoo.

I had also become part of the Cinematic and Television Benevolent

Fund (CTBF) and I went to work at their retirement home's summer fete. Called Glebelands it is in Wokingham (Berks) and offers a home for those in the industry who had fallen on hard times. I was amazed at the different residents there – some had been famous stars and producers but there were also former projectionists, cinema managers and even ice-cream ladies, all happily living together under the same roof.

I was still travelling extensively through the UK that year – Yorkshire and its beautiful coastline, ending up in a conference in Harrogate, a lovely town with great charm and old fashioned courtesies. I had a cousin living in Newcastle who introduced me to some of its nightclubs and of course the exciting atmosphere of St James' Park when their club was at home and this was also World Cup year

A young Lynn and I attending a function at the Royal Lancaster Hotel. Note the sideburns, but still no beard and Lynn's somewhat short dress!

with England defending its title and their personal idols, the Charlton brothers (Bobby and Jack) were still very much part of that team. It was also the first year it was broadcast in colour.

I made a lot of good friends during that period, especially in the confectionery industry. People like George Hagon of Palmer & Harvey (who eventually became my best man), Ian Yates the most eccentric wholesaler in the North of England and Roy Hall. They all became, and remain, good friends.

All this travelling apart however, I was also finding lots of excuses to come back to Essex where I was starting to 'date' my secretary more often. As it happened that year the CEA had scheduled its conference for Brighton – yes Brighton where the very name conjured up all kinds

Here's me with my friends, Roy Hall and Ian Yates when we met up in Alderly Edge, Cheshire. We've been great friends for over forty years!

of ideas. I just went with the flow, phoned her and told her I needed her down there for a few days.

What secretary would argue with her boss if he told her she was needed in Brighton? So yes she arrived, wearing a pure white suit, and it was so nice a day that we went down to the beach – to take notes of course. Sadly (perhaps) many of the beaches along the South coast that year were heavily polluted with a lot of thick black tar. Such tar does not go well with a white suit and we had to go back to the hotel to get it cleaned up. It took all night but at least we had the World Cup in colour on TV to, ahum, pass the time away.

That year I spent my 27th birthday with Lynn, but also remember it because it was the day the World Cup Final was screened in colour for the first time. Sadly it didn't include England, who'd been knocked out in the semi's by Germany, but the final between Brazil and Italy was a great one to watch.

The other big step that year was deciding to buy a house. I'd spent years living in hotels, bedsits and rented accommodation, including the Gidea Park house belonging to Peter Kalisher where I'd lived in the next room to a young married couple, Mick and Pat Bray. I looked around and found a small development of four houses in Hornchurch, so I did a deal on one of them – my first step on the property ladder. All very exciting!

Moving on and moving in

Talking of show business this was also the year I met Alan Breeze. A publican by then but older people will remember him with a lot of affection as the singer in Billy Cotton's band. Pre-war racing driver and World War 1 hero Cotton formed his band during the twenties but it was after the second war that he really became famous with his BBC radio Billy Cotton Band Show 'Wakey Wakey' which successfully transferred to television.

As Cotton's regular male vocalist Alan Breeze was probably one of the best known singers on the air with a bright and breezy style that lived up to his name. It helped him fit in very well with a band and a boss whose trademark was that kind of lively music. When I met him he had a pub in a village in Flixton (Norfolk) called 'The Buck'.

It was actually called the Flixton Buck and had a big sign outside, and still does, saying 'Don't pass the Buck'. Lynn and I didn't because we spent our first night together there in July. The following morning we drove to Lowestoft for the day before going off to Great Yarmouth to see Herman's Hermits, after which we went back to the Buck for the customary boozy night.

More of Alan Breeze and the Buck later, but by that time Lynn was staying with me most but not all nights. She was having a few problems back home when I flew first to Jersey and then on to Guernsey to do some business in July. The airlines were having some industrial problems with strikes and that week there was a lot of fog (summer fog in the English Channel is not unusual) so getting home from Guernsey seemed to be impossible.

However I managed to find a guy with a boat who took me back to Jersey where I got a plane back to Southend Airport. When I got there I found Lynn waiting for me and that night we formally moved in together and have been so ever since.

That did present a problem though because, while my new house was still being built, I was still living in the Gidea Park house where I had just one small bedroom containing a single bed and had to share a bathroom with others in the house. Hardly the greatest of starts, but in the next room were a couple called Mick and Pat Bray and they had been looking for bigger accommodation too. They found a flat in Brentwood, a newish development called Cameron Close right next to the station and they offered us the chance to share with them.

There was also the need of course to buy furniture for two people, rather than for the 'bachelor pad' I'd originally envisaged. Lynn and I went to Harrison & Gibson's in Ilford and had a couple of shocks when we found that it was not only more expensive than we'd thought, but that there would be a six month delay in delivery. We decided to leave things for a while and make the best of what we had.

By this time Lynn was starting to meet members of my family, uncles and aunts and even more of my friends. Most of my friends in the trade she knew from having been my secretary for a few years of course but, even apart from my football following friends, I had many others. Over the weeks that followed I helped Lynn move her personal belongings from her previous address to our shared flat in Brentwood.

After moving to end a previous relationship I went to see Mr. Hugh to tell him of my new situation and how I needed a rise and to my surprise he agreed. Not only did I get more money but a new company car, a Ford Cortina, arrived. Things really were changing in my life, though like anything else there were some rough patches.

I remember taking Lynn out to the Meads Ballroom in Brentwood (no longer there) where you could enjoy a good evening dancing and eating a good meal. We were with friends but I remember getting annoyed when Lynn was asked to dance and stayed on the floor for another few dances. I told our friends I was off and left. I got over it and went home the following morning and we went out for lunch. Sorted!

Meanwhile the new house was coming on, the phone was going in and the curtains going up. Just as well because Mick and Pat, as close friends as you could wish, were clearly getting a little fed up with us because we all had little privacy. We were living it up a bit too, going to the West End on Saturday nights to see a show or late film before going on to an all-night pancake house and getting home in time for breakfast on Sunday. My grandad had recovered from his heart attack so we often went down to Dover on a Sunday to see him and Nan.

Lynn began to visit her Mum, who I met at the garden gate, though her dad would never come out to meet me, but still time was on our side and back at the house things were taking shape. The carpets were going down, I'd found a guy to do our garden and we'd signed up with DER rentals so at least we had TV. One firm was fitting our lights, another putting up mirrors while Mick and Pat were getting as excited about our going as we were. Then the big day arrived.

In August that year we finally moved into our new home in Wingletye Lane Hornchurch. Mind you we had nothing to sit on, no kitchen facilities and no cooking utensils – just a house, curtains, carpets, mirrors, a TV set and a bed. We borrowed a couple of deck chairs from an uncle and aunt, who also delivered a couple of their own chairs so we could now sit down, watch the telly and as for cooking well Lynn would boil eggs in an electric kettle. Mostly we enjoyed a lot of French bread and cheese, Lyons individual fruit pies and wine, oh yes lots and lots of wine. Tough times sure but if a new relationship can survive that, it can survive anything.

Poisoned....by a banana

We were in our new, but empty home and our friends were happy again so Lynn and I felt we deserved a holiday and the Algarve beckoned. We stayed at my cousin's home near Gatwick, left our car there and the next day flew out for our planned two weeks in Portugal.

Now one thing this particular Export Manager had a problem with was foreign food, still preferring the 'safety' of bread, cheese, pies and fruit. While some of the visitors there were getting stung and poisoned by jelly-fish in the sea, I got poisoned by a banana.

For me the Portuguese food all looked, sounded and smelt too foreign to me so I played safe with bananas, for breakfast, lunch and dinner and somewhere down the line I copped an unfortunate one. It was cheap to feed me but I came out in a horrendous rash that Lynn, who was enjoying the local cuisine, said made me look like a map of the world. We tried lots of different remedies but nothing worked and when my cousin picked us up at Gatwick he fell about laughing.

I do remember we got back in time to see QPR beat Bristol City 2-1 but we went to a party that night and I was the centre of attention (and amusement), with my explanation of how I'd got my strange looking face and arms thanks to banana poisoning.

Not to worry, we were moving on steadily, even getting our first colour TV which our friendly DER man came to sort out just in time for the football season. Coincidence, of course, but Lynn got her own back when she discovered a department store in nearby Upminster called Roomes and I seem to have been paying their bills ever since. We (she) even decided to get a decent kitchen so Hygena were on their way very soon.

It was just as well that things at work were going well too though there were one or two, shall we say worrying, moments. For instance in late 1970 I was invited to another Candy Ball – yes, fine except that this was in Belfast where things were getting worse in terms of the troubles there. I'd never actually been to Ireland or met any of our customers or selling agent there, so I said I would go. Lynn was not exactly happy about this but to have refused would not have endeared us to our Irish customers so I flew off to meet our agent, Bill Cleland.

Thankfully it went well. For three days we visited customers, attended the Candy Ball and got home just in time to watch QPR thrash the Orient 5-1. See, the Irish must be lucky for me, so who needs the Blarney Stone? That night Lynn and I met our Channel Islands agent James de Lisle at the MCCTA London Dinner Dance and a week later I was in Manchester for the Dinner Dance there too. For an Export Manager I was certainly getting to know my own country pretty well.

We were making arrangements to spend our first Christmas together, down at Alan Breeze's pub the Flixton Buck in Norfolk. Everything was going so well when, on Friday 23rd October 1970 Lynn (still my secretary as well of course), walked into the office and said: I've had a pregnancy test and its positive'.

Santa Lewis

My diary entry for that day reads: 'Lynn's pregnancy test is positive, absolutely delighted'. The following day, after ordering a new dressing table, we were off to see QPR beat Portsmouth 2-0 so you can imagine it was quite a weekend but now I was an expectant daddy too. We went to meet gynaecologist Mr. Forster, who we were to meet many times in the years ahead. I seem to remember he had three sets of twins of his own so clearly he knew the score.

Our kitchen was nearing completion, with the addition of a new washing machine, so proper meals at home were now possible. I remember taking George Hagon, a family friend now of course, with his six-year old son Paul to see QPR but something clearly went wrong that day. Like me George was an avid QPR fan but eventually young Paul became, and I hesitate to say this, a Chelsea fan. He even had his 40th birthday party at Stamford Bridge, so as you can see there is just no pleasing some people.

Being an excited expectant dad and it being near Christmas I decided I should at least own the proper gear so off I went to Gamages to buy a proper Father Christmas outfit. (Actually I still have it, along with some newer ones too). Lynn was now on monthly hospital check-ups and was doing well enough to come to the MCCTA Christmas party at the Royal Lancaster hotel in London. She knew they gave the ladies gifts there but the evening clearly did her little good because the next day, while I was in the West Country, she was taken into hospital with a scare.

It turned out to be just one of those scares that occur in many pregnancies and she was ok. I came home to be told that such scares were sent to test us but she was certainly well enough to come to QPR that week to see us play Carlisle and for our Christmas trip to Dover to see Nan and Grandad.

I was now driving a new Rover 2000, because Mr. Hugh had decided I'd worked hard enough to warrant a higher status car and it was certainly a step up from the Cortina. It was a hectic Christmas week with all our reps coming down for our Christmas Conference – a busy time with conferences by day, shows and dinners at night and we managed to find all the 'Bier Kellers' in the West End. Then, after the firm's Christmas lunch Lynn and I were off to Norfolk and 'the Buck'.

Look, it was Christmas Eve, I had a new Rover 2000 and a Father Christmas outfit – what would be more natural then for me to drive to Norfolk wearing the appropriate outfit? The traffic police on the route must have been phoning ahead after being stopped the first time because we were pulled over several times on that journey, but not with any malice. It seemed that even coppers having to work late on Christmas Eve had a great sense of humour.

We got to the pub and walked in, me in my Santa outfit, to rapturous applause and I was suddenly inundated with requests to visit local homes where there were children the next day. After a good meal, lots of drink of course, and not much sleep it was Christmas Day, our first together, with Lynn being three months pregnant.

That morning, along with friends and what seemed pretty much the entire population of the village we visited every home, whether they had children there or not. It's not a big village and everyone seemed to enjoy the spectacle of this idiot dressed up as Father Christmas walking the streets, looking for kids but with an empty sack and a friendly wave. 1970 is not a Christmas Lynn and I are ever likely to forget.

It took all morning and then it was back to the Buck for lunch and more drinks. Since we were residents we could legally drink all day and all night, and we did... well except for the one of us who was pregnant of course. The next day we were invited to Alan Breeze's own house, which was opposite the pub, for more drinks. In fact he owned all the farmland around that house. That day was the one that we discovered that Guinness and Champagne go down well together – I think it's called 'Black Velvet'. Even Lynn had a go at that one, though of course in moderation.

Christmas over we headed back to Hornchurch, for our first New Year together. We visited family and friends – Lynn went to see her parents and, as usual, I collected her from the garden gate before we went shopping for our first New Year's Eve party. We held it at home and it was a great success with a couple of dozen friends and neighbours dropping in and staying until around 3am. We spent New Year's Day 1971 going to the movies – we are both still fans of the cinema – and I think we saw Sherlock Holmes and The Jockey Club Stakes.

There was a down side though because QPR went down 2-1 to Swindon; but, hey, out first Christmas and New Year together and looking forward to becoming a family, I could stand losing a football match.

One minor problem that 1971 brought for a sales manager was decimalisation because in a way he has to start thinking in a different currency both normally and at work. It seems easy now (in fact even today I often still think in old money) but it seemed complicated at the time and I was sent on decimalisation courses. Another was finding a new secretary.

Lynn and I were now officially together at work, going in and home together, but she was also starting to get bigger of course. I started to contact employment agencies, but I also met my Chairman, George Pitt's son – let's call him Pitt Junior for now – who wanted to get more involved in the business. Younger than me and, like his dad a chartered accountant, he also seemed very posh to me.

Exhibitions always took place early in the year and in 1971 it was the Interchoc Exhibition in London. Lynn of course was still having regular checkups but I had another problem to work out – how to beat a postal strike and that involved a new way to spend weekends.

We couldn't let it beat us because we needed the cheques of course. So all the reps around the country would be collecting the money during the week, bring it down to Dagenham at the weekend, collect their post etc. and drive back to their areas again. It was a really difficult challenge, quite new to us and very satisfying to solve.

Actually there was another challenge too. Lynn of course was already married so every now and again we had to go to a solicitor's office in London to get that sorted as well. So, sorting out postal strike problems, along with Lynn's and looking for a new secretary and now I had the Chairman's son popping in and out at the same time.

That latter aspect got more worrying as he now seemed to be taking up a lot of time, sometimes all day, and I did not have the time to always be polite. We didn't get off to a great start and it was pretty obvious he was planning to take over from his father, a man I admired greatly and got on well with, eventually. Here we go, I thought and a decade or so later I was proved right.

It was all go at the time. Sales meetings – a new idea of mine – were taking place regularly and our team was taking shape. We also had a mixture of ideas, new and old, coming together in the hope of enlightening the world to the benefits of popcorn. Thanks to the postal strike I was also going round the country meeting the men and sometimes swapping posts. I was also at the stage of interviewing for a new secretary. Whew!

It was a bit of a relief when Easter came and on Good Friday my Uncle Alf and Auntie Doll picked us up and we went off to spend the holiday at the Flixton Buck. On Easter Saturday we went into Norwich, a beautiful city with some really good shopping but, by sheer coincidence of course, Norwich happened to be at home to QPR that day. As it happens we lost

3-0 but that evening we went to the dogs and, without quite knowing what we were doing, we won the Quinella.

This is a gamble where you name the winner and second placed dog in each race with any winnings accumulating up from one race to another. That night there were just three winning tickers in the entire stadium and we had two of them. Needless to say we had a great time in the Buck that night. On Sunday we all went to Great Yarmouth before coming home on Easter Monday where Uncle Alf was quite insistent I took him to see Leyton Orient. Oh yes, I almost forgot – they were playing QPR that day and we won 1-0.

By St Georges Day (23rd April) it was time, with the baby due in mid-June, for Lynn to retire from work. Her job as my secretary meant she had a lot of involvement with the company reps and that day some of them arrived to present her with an inscribed candlestick as a farewell thank-you gift. That night we headed off to the Confectionery Benevolent Dinner at the Dorchester.

As I said before Pitt Junior was getting more involved in the business and he heard that I was off to Brussels to take a stand at the Interchoc Conference in Knock de la Zouch. He said he'd like to go as well, so we arranged to meet at the airport. He turned up with his wife having, without telling me, bought two tickets. Lynn of course was attending pre-natal classes by then so couldn't go. Well his dad was the boss I guess, but it was my first conference abroad and it seemed to go well.

It was also about this time that I met Jim Blevins – the guy from the American Corn Belt and who lived in Elvis country – Memphis, Tennessee. We met many times after that and had some great times with him in the USA, but more of that later.

At that time however I was busy looking for prams and for obvious reasons by then Lynn was quite big. It was a month before she was due to give birth, so she couldn't fly and I had to go to an MCCTA conference in Newcastle on my own and it seemed strange being there without her.

Still at least George Hagon had got me a ticket for the cup final so I was at Wembley to see a London club beat Liverpool 2-1. Sadly it was Arsenal, not QPR.

Chapter 4A

The Seventies

Turmoil, turmoil, everywhere

On January 23rd 1970 the new decade was ushered in when the first 'jumbo jet' (the Boeing 747) landed at Heathrow. It really marked the start of mass air travel on a big scale because it carried twice as many passengers as its predecessor, the 707. Suddenly and particularly since the previous year Concorde had roared into the air from the same airport, the world really began to shrink. People had the money, opportunity and means, to stretch their horizons, and so it was also a good time to be in the hotel business.

Politically the decade got off to another, at the time astonishing, start when against all the odds Edward Heath led the Tories back into government after all the pollsters had predicted an easy Labour victory for Wilson. It was a return to government however, that would result in immense dissatisfaction throughout the country, as a struggle took place between militant unions and the government.

Irish, and Arab (Palestinian), terrorism was gaining in strength while one of the Middle East figures, the Egyptian leader Nasser, died, leaving the whole area in something of a confused state. He was closely followed to the grave by Charles de Gaulle the former French president who had opposed British entry to Europe, (though he had relied on it back in 1944 of course).

America started the decade still deeply embroiled in Vietnam and to a lesser extent in Cambodia, but President Richard Nixon, who would later leave office in disgrace following the notorious Watergate scandal, actually set a peace process in motion and even built bridges between his country and China as well as Russia. In 1973 another Middle East war started after Egypt launched an attack on Israel across the Suez Canal – one they would live to regret after being comprehensively defeated again by the Israeli forces.

By 1974 Heath had to put Britain onto a 'three day' week after an overtime ban imposed by the miners left coal stocks at the power stations at an all-time low. His Christmas was spent grappling with industrial unrest so strong that his government had to bring in an emergency budget cutting millions from public spending, including on schools and hospitals. Forced into a general election in March (based on 'who rules Britain?'), he lost. He tried unsuccessfully to do a deal with the Liberals in an attempt to stay in power, but Harold Wilson was back in charge again, but of a hung parliament so with no real political power and still hamstrung with militant unions.

It did not help things and as a further indication that all was not well in the UK, in January 1976 bankruptcies hit an all-time high, with even some millionaires going to the wall. Even so, it came as a shock when, in March that year, Wilson suddenly announced he was quitting as Prime Minister. There was speculation about his real reasons for going in the way he did, but he proved to be suffering, and subsequently died from Alzheimer's Disease. His successor was James Callaghan, who inherited the whole sorry mess for things got no better.

In September Britain had to go cap in hand to the International Monetary Fund for a £2.3billion loan. The struggle in the Labour movement, particularly between left-wing unions and government realists, became more intense. An increasingly bitter situation in Northern Ireland with the emergence again of the IRA, did nothing to help ease Callaghan's problems.

Strikes were now part of the scene, with Britain often being seen and described, as 'the sick man of Europe' and as a result some disputes got quite violent on the picket line. A so-called 'social contract' drawn up by the government and trade unions, but which depended on wage restraint, had to be abandoned. Although there were sad distractions like the deaths of personalities like Elvis Presley, Charlie Chaplin and Bing Crosby, it was the national economic situation that dominated Britain.

By 1979 that was critical and out of control. Thanks to overwhelming union discontent there was even talk of the declaration of a state of emergency – in fact the winter of 78/79 became known as the 'Winter of Discontent'.

Largely as a result of that the Conservatives, now led by Margaret Thatcher, were twenty percent ahead in the polls when, in March 1979, Callaghan's government was defeated on a vote in the House of Commons. That could mean only one thing – a general election and on May 4th 1979 Great Britain woke up to find, not only that it had a new leader, but she was a woman.

Standing on the steps of 10 Downing Street, Margaret Thatcher promised to transform Britain's economic and industrial climate. "Where there is discord, may we bring harmony. Where there is despair, may we bring hope," she told the country. And she did, but it wasn't easy.

Chapter 5

Brandon

Decisions, decisions!

I do remember that in the lead-up to Brandon's arrival there were a lot of decisions, critical decisions, to be made. For instance Lynn wanted to go to the Furniture Show on a Saturday and I said that was a good idea because we could kill two birds with one stone. Good decision because it meant we could go and watch QPR beating Sunderland 2-0 in the afternoon and then go on to the Olympia round the corner afterwards.

I was still doing a lot of travelling, Lynn was having her medicals and Pitt Junior was still making a nuisance of himself as far as I was concerned, so it made a nice break to take up Mr. Hugh's invitation for us to visit his home in Chigwell. Called Brook Barn, it was a big old place but in it he had his own fully fitted out cinema and lots of films. I guess that was all with the help of our Managing Director, Sir Philip Warter who was Chairman of ABC cinemas at the time, but Lynn and I both loved (still do) the movies so it was a welcome invitation gratefully accepted.

Another of the big decisions I (we) had to make about that time came as a result of my getting tickets for the League Cup Final – that year being between Spurs and Aston Villa. The problem was that it was also a day when QPR were playing Millwall at home. Well come on, what would you do?

I had to put Lynn first of course so we went to Loftus Road for the first half before dashing off to Wembley where Lynn went shopping (her hobby) in Wembley High Street while I saw Spurs beating the Villa 2-0. That was in February 71 of course and a month later, also at

Wembley, another great sporting event launched my interest in a new sport – boxing.

It was the night that Henry Cooper the much loved British heavyweight champion, who'd once floored Muhammed Ali, was beaten on points by the former Hungarian but now British Joe Bugner. It was a very controversial decision taken by referee Harry Gibbs against all the odds and a disbelieving and angry crowd.

He gave it to Bugner by just a quarter of a point, quite a courageous decision given Cooper's popularity. In his book he wrote *'Certainly there were boos and one or two people abused me but you expect that when a title fight as important as this one has turned on a knife edge. A few in the crowd shouted 'fix' but I have never bent a fight in my life and have heard all that kind of thing before.'* Years later I was told that, at the time we lived in Cameron Close with the Brays, Gibbs was actually living just a few yards away in Great Eastern Road.

Sport in many forms has always played a part in my life and you will recall saying how my father used to take me dog racing as a kid. Well by this time Lynn had started to take an interest in the dogs too – well, at least that's my story – and since my parents were living in Westcliff by then we used to go to the track in Southend.

I had in fact been brought up in a dog-racing environment as well as in my dad's interest. I had uncles who owned and raced greyhounds as well as being track bookmakers. With Dad working with them too I was bound to get involved in the game one way or another and I did.

Dad and I would often go to the Southend track and then onto a late night flapping track a few miles down the road in Rayleigh where racing started around 10pm. A 'flapping track' is an unlicensed one where all kinds of dodgy practices can take place, and usually do. Dogs can be raced under different names for example and anything goes, but Dad and I had a system, not complicated but one that involved tic-tacking. That's the long-distance sign system used by bookies to communicate odds with each other.

It was a system that kept us happy and made us feel we were beating the system, even if it was a dodgy one and we had a lot of fun dog racing together in those days.

One other vital decision during that time comes to mind. It was the one to employ Chris Standing (as she was then) as my new secretary and seems to have been another good one for she managed to stick around for the odd forty years or so.

Father's day

Lynn's baby was due to put in an appearance on June 17th but, though I stayed home that day – well at least to midday – there was no sign of anything happening so I went to the office. Pitt Junior was also in that day and wasn't the slightest bit interested that I might have to dash off at any moment but in the event I worked until late that evening. In the meantime our kitchen table and chairs were delivered and we were getting constant phone calls from family and friends asking if there was any news,

There wasn't and the next day (Friday) I had to attend an evening MCCTA meeting. I remember phoning Lynn from the meeting (in a West End pub) to see if she was ok. All she wanted was fish and chips so I picked them up on the way home and we had a late (11pm) supper before going to bed knowing the baby was two days late.

A couple of hours later Lynn woke me. It was 2am in the morning of Saturday 19th June and she told me we had to get to the hospital, like now. 'What, at this time of the morning, wonderful' I thought, to myself of course. Well at least it gave me an excuse to cross red traffic lights on the way to Harold Wood but we got there ok and got Lynn settled in.

I hung around until 5.30am but nothing happened so I went home for some sleep and came back at 1pm – still nothing. In fact that's what I was hoping for and that Lynn could hang on until the following day which, apart from being Father's Day was also my birthday. What a birthday present that would be.

I spent most of that day giving Lynn gas and air until it ran out and she demanded I go out and get some more. It was Hospital Fete day and most of the staff was outside listening to the band so I had to tour the wards looking for more of the stuff. Fortunately, because I was bringing large stocks of Butterkist and sweets in to bribe them with, I was popular with the nurses. Eventually it was midnight and we were back on track.

I'd even been issued with my own set of foot covers, gloves, mask and white coat and the Matron, who had kids who loved Butterkist, was my best friend. It was past midnight and we were all celebrating my birthday so I had time to slip out for a drink. Our friends Mick and Pat were running a late-night drinking club less than a mile from the hospital so off I went to tell them what was happening, and get a beer and sandwich. Then it was off back to Harold Wood where gynaecologist Mr. Forster had been called for and someone else had arrived too.

I got myself enrobed again and was walking back to the delivery room where I'd been so many times before popping out for a drink, but this time I was stopped in my tracks by a big lady. She was the matron who had taken over the shift and who I'd never seen (or Butterkist bribed) before.

'Where are you going?' She boomed. I explained that I was on my way to help deliver our baby but she was unimpressed.

'Fathers are not allowed in here. You go back to the waiting room and wait there until we give you the news,' she said, gesturing for me to retreat. I protested but she was not only adamant but bigger than me so I went back to the waiting room and sat there with the door open wondering how to gatecrash the birth. Then Mr. Forster, in full evening dress having been called out from dinner, walked past the room and saw me.

'What are you doing here? I thought you wanted to be at the birth,' he said. I told him about being refused permission despite the amount of popcorn I had given away. As he walked on I followed him and heard the row he was having with the matron, who lost the battle.

'Come on in, you need to get dressed properly,' she growled. She began to tell me what I needed to wear when I interrupted her to tell her I already had the stuff that had been given to me earlier. I got geared up and started to walk confidently towards the delivery room, when I suddenly got cold feet. I began to feel I would be better off staying outside and watching proceedings through the window when I saw Big Matron staring hard at me. I realised how silly it would be to do that having argued so fiercely to get in, and anyway I really did want to be there for the delivery.

So I went in and stood by the door, as far from Lynn as I could – well that was the intention but I found myself getting closer and closer to her until I was actually holding her hand and watching the proceedings. Suddenly, and I will remember Mr. Forster's words as long as I live, he said 'Look if you are getting this close, you might as well help your baby out'.

Wow! All I could see was this beautiful sight as I helped our son come into the world. Whatever they say about all the blood and that, I never saw any of it. All I was conscious of was seeing my son being born that morning. My diary tells me it was 3am on the 20th June 1971 and our baby weighed 6lbs 15ozs. What a combined birthday and Father's Day present that was.

One thing is sure – Brandon and I will never forget each other's birthdays and I will never ever forget his birth day.

'Brandon cries most of the night'

The excitement of the moment over, Lynn (and our new family) obviously needed to rest and of course I had things to do as well so, after telephoning the world to give them the news, I went back to Mick and Pat's for er... lunch. Then I went back to the hospital where Lynn's Mum and Dad, Bill and Ivy, turned up as well. This was actually the first time I had ever met Lynn's father so clearly I was finally being accepted, but it's odd that I should meet my son before meeting his grandfather.

While Lynn was recovering business went on as normal of course and as it happened the Dagenham Town Show was coming and the day after Brandon's arrival I was in the Civic Centre meeting with the organising committee. Butterkist had always been a great supporter of the annual event that takes place in Central Park during the summer holidays.

It consists of a huge funfair, lots of marquees with fruit and veg stalls, flower displays, dog and cat shows, Fords would be showing off their latest cars and there would be sky-divers dropping in out of the sky. Police dog handlers and bike riders would be giving displays and of course the famous Butterkist stall, manned by staff and family would be adding to the general enjoyment. This was always a big big show, where we gave the good people of Dagenham a great deal, practically giving the stuff away. It was always great PR and we supported it every year and it was something I loved doing.

Anyway that week I split my time between head office and the hospital where I would sometimes meet my own Mum and Dad who were nearby.

I also had some important shopping to do of course, so it was off to Roomes to buy a crib for Brandon. One other important meeting that took place that week while Lynn was still in hospital was the one that took place when my mum and Dad met Lynn's parents for the first time.

It was a great period for firsts all round, especially when her brother Tony and his then girlfriend (later wife) Vivian also turned up – so in a way and though he didn't know it of course – Brandon, the future MP, was bringing all the strands of our families together. Lynn was back on form as she prepared to come home, telling me to get a haircut (nothing new there) and organising my shopping expeditions to places like the butchers, though I had no idea what to buy. The pram was being delivered and all looked well, but then Pitt Junior turned up for a meeting.

This time however he had his father with him and initially I did not feel that was a good omen, but Mr. Pitt had always been good to me. He was perfectly charming that day and had a good influence on the meeting so all was calm and it went well which was a relief because I was looking forward to Lynn and Brandon's homecoming the next day.

What a wonderful day – I remember that that evening we watched TV until around 2am before going to bed looking forward to a nice long sleep. Silly us! Yes Brandon woke up two hours later demanding attention and so it all began. Only those new parents who have been through it will know the massive changes it makes – lots of visitors during the day, and little sleep at night. My diary for that period often reads: *Brandon cries most of the night*.

A week later we had the official wetting of the baby's head – a booze up for all the family so now they were all getting to know each other, thanks to our new son. I remember buying Brandon his first £1 premium bond and of course going to the registrar to get him registered and to collect his Birth Certificate. Then we took off to Dover to show our son, all of three weeks old by then, Dover Castle and also of course to meet Nan and Grandad Salmon.

Life soon began to settle down to what was now normality, Lynn at home looking after Brandon and me on the road (or in the air) looking after Butterkist and our future. After the Town Show it was off to Malta before coming back to a conference in Stockport before flying off again to Gibraltar for another week's business. During this period my new secretary

Chris Standing came round on the Sunday and worked all day – giving her a glimpse of how we would be working in the years to come.

While I was in Gibraltar I got a cable from one of the company's directors Dick Whitehead calling me back home. Purchase tax had been increased while I was away and I had to deal with the new price strategy. When I did get back it was to find Pitt Junior waiting to see if, as an accountant, he could help but to be truthful his business knowledge was of no use at all.

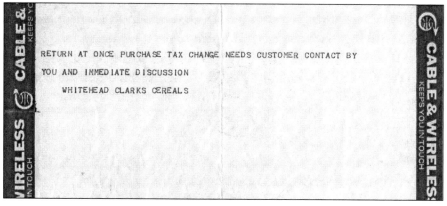

RETURN AT ONCE PURCHASE TAX CHANGE NEEDS CUSTOMER CONTACT BY
YOU AND IMMEDIATE DISCUSSION
WHITEHEAD CLARKS CEREALS

The telegram I received while in Gibraltar requiring me to return home

One Clark's development that did happen however was the announcement that shares were being issued and I was offered some of them; but they came at a price so it meant a visit to the bank and a chat with the manager, this time to sell myself and the company. Then it was away again, this time to Dublin as part of this hectic period. Sadly while I was away a border collie, yes she was called Lassie, I'd given my parents years before, had had to be put down. A sad moment of gloom, in a period of bright optimism.

I was still mixing business with pleasure, virtually burning the candle at both ends, when we celebrated Lynn's parent's 25th wedding anniversary at the Royal Purfleet. We knew the manager and he gave us a room for Brandon with a cot in it so he could sleep while we attended the party. Then, without telling Lynn too much I took Brandon off to be circumcised before dashing off to Edinburgh, on business of course but I came back to take her, Brandon and my parents off to Guernsey for a holiday.

It was also about this time that Lynn's dad Bill was starting to warm to me a bit. He even came to Loftus Road with me to see QPR instead of (well, perhaps as well as) his beloved West Ham United. Actually Brandon was in the QPR programme when he was only six months old. Start as you mean to go on, I say.

In fact Bill and his wife Ivy proved to be a godsend because they were happy to take care of Brandon so that Lynn could join me on some of the social occasions, like the Candy Balls in Purley, Bristol, London and even Jersey, that I had to go to so often.

I also suddenly realised that having a new child in the family could mean me paying less income tax so I went to see the taxman though, with all the questions he asked, I began to wish I hadn't bothered. The thing was that I was still claiming for a previous wife (Jean) and I thought this might be a problem. Later I was proved right – I had made an error of judgement and only time will tell how much of one.

There was one other 'loose end' I began tying up about this time – Lynn's divorce. She had enough on her hands to cope with, me being away so much and Brandon still not helping much by being so restless at night, that on her behalf I began seeing a solicitor and a QC to try to get things moving.

To Blackpool with love

I had a lot of friends and business acquaintances in Manchester and in the autumn that year I was asked to be their guest of honour at a dinner there. A nice thought of course but that meant a speech too but the thing I remember most is that with Brandon being looked after at home by her parents Lynn was able to come with me.

It was a successful speech and the next day (Saturday) I suggested we took a trip to the coast. Lynn had never been to Blackpool or seen its 'Golden Mile' so I said I would take her to lunch there so off we went by train. We had an excellent lunch in a nice restaurant overlooking the sea above Woolworths, after which I suggested we went for a walk along the front.

Suddenly she remarked on how many people were walking in the same direction on such a cold day and I agreed. Then in the distance she saw a football stadium with the floodlights on and the penny dropped – we were walking down Bloomfield Road with everyone else. Surprise surprise – Blackpool were at home to QPR that day and, thanks to an equaliser from Rodney Marsh we drew 1-1.

It was the first time we left Brandon with Bill and Ivy for a long weekend but in early November they took him for another long one when we flew, with customers and staff, to Tunisia. That time of year of course is full of dinners and other social occasions and I remember, as Chairman of the Home Counties branch of the MCCTA having to make one at the Royal Lancaster Hotel in London. I recall it mostly because Pitt Junior, as guest of honour, was also making one but in fairness he made a good job of it. He'd even agreed that the company would pay for the ladies gifts, a very well designed compact with the company motif on it.

Our first family (of three) Christmas was at home when Uncle Alf and Auntie Doll joined us for lunch, while Bill and Ivy, Tony and Vivien joined us in the , evening. It was a busy but happy Christmas and we even got a couple of football matches in and, because Lynn and I had spent our first Christmas together at The Buck in Flixton, we'd pop down there again – minus the Santa Claus suit but with our new son.

By New Year we were back home, having survived our first months as a family, a holiday and Christmas/New Year festivities but Brandon? He was still only sleeping two hours at a time – four if we were lucky – but he was putting on weight and we were going to the matches as a family.

All seemed well but then we suddenly got a call from Ron Murfitt, the guy who had built our house. Lynn had known him since the days she'd worked in an estate agents office and he was good builder as well as a friend. This time he told us he'd bought some land in Upminster and wondered if we'd be interested. It was a nice quiet road and the houses were bigger than ours so we told him we were.

Well, why not? We were doing great business at Clarks and in fact the company's official biographer in his '50 Golden Years', describing the seventies as: '**The decade of acquisition**', wrote:

'The seventies saw other changes. New management developed as earlier management stood down. Cecil Hugh retired in 1971 and Dick Whitehead, who had been with us since the earliest days of the Hugh company, took sole charge of all production. He was assisted in the running of the company by Ken Lewis covering Sales and Arthur Smith as Company Secretary.'

It really was a busy time because among other things I was trying to do a deal with a company in Stratford. Streimers, who made nut brittle and coconut bars as well as other specialist confectionery, had good products but no sales force. We, on the other hand had a limited product range but a good sales force and I wanted to sell their products with ours on a 'buy in and sell out' basis. At the same time I was negotiating to change our carriers to get a reduced cost on delivery, thus increasing our already growing profits, so you can see why we were happy to look at the new house idea.

I think at this stage I ought to explain about my annual UK tour – it will save boring you by repeating it all later. At the start of every calendar year I went off to visit all my twenty reps and two sales managers, beginning in Scotland – always a good place to start in a New Year of course. This 'tour' would take me twenty weeks as I always spent a week with each rep, and after that I would start visiting customer's head offices, most of which were in the South of England. After 'the tour' I would do a few export trips to Europe and/or the Middle East.

So from January to May my usual routine would be to leave home after lunch on Sunday to catch an early evening train or plane. On arrival book into a hotel and have a pre-arranged dinner with the local rep and customers and be ready for an early start on the Monday morning. I usually got home on a Friday evening, or Saturday morning and that was pretty much my routine until the early summer when the holiday camps would be open and it was time to visit their head offices to do business.

I was in Glasgow that year when I got a phone call from Lynn to say a family member had died. He was Jewish so the funeral would be the next day and I would not be able to get back in time, but I'd had some very good advice from our Glasgow rep Jock (of course) Carmalt. He said that when deciding to go to a funeral and trying to make up your mind, decide on the basis that if by not attending you would not be missed, do not go. That was good advice that I've followed ever since.

Sadly the following year I had news that Jock was ill and been taken to Glasgow Infirmary so I caught a flight and got there in time to see him. He was always called 'the gentleman' and as usual he had a smile on his face and a friendly word when he saw me.

The next day his son Graham called me to say his father had passed away during the night. I remember thinking how pleased I was, to have had the opportunity to see him before he died. The funeral was in three days time and, following his advice, I had to decide whether I would be missed if I wasn't there and in this case it was a definite yes. He had been a long time company servant (even longer than me) and I decided that apart from me others in the sales team should attend so Jock's sales manager and the other Scottish rep attended as well. I will always remember Jock Carmalt with affection.

On the brighter side that year Lynn had celebrated her first Mother's Day and also the fact that her brother Tony was marrying Vivien. Actually that caused a bit of a problem because they picked on a date that also happened to be Cup Final Day. Anyway I managed to stay at Bill and Ivy's house to see the first half before dashing off to the wedding just in time, and then rush back to a friend's house to see the end of the game in which Leeds beat Arsenal 1-0. Have I mentioned my love for football before by the way?

We had Brandon's christening that year and my mum had her 60th birthday. I always remember thinking how old that was, but somehow it doesn't seem like that today. Anyway we all went to the White Hart in Brentwood for lunch and then off to St Andrews Church in Hornchurch where, at 4.30pm Brandon was christened and baptised. (Two for the price of one).

We got home around midnight obviously exhausted but our son was still having problems sleeping at night so I had to take him out for a ride in the Rover. We would drive to somewhere like Ilford and he'd sleep the whole way. There were not too many cars about at that time of night, especially with babies in the back and at first we were often pulled over by the police but they gradually got as used to the routine as Brandon did and ignored us.

Unfortunately, a week after the christening, Grandad Salmon died and we all went off to Dover to see Nan. He was a nice old man and seemed to have been around all my life because, as I explained before, I grew up in the same Shepherd's Bush house he and Nan lived in. Bill and Ivy were on holiday in a camp in Dymchurch not far from Dover, and they looked after Brandon while Lynn and I went to Grandad's funeral.

I was of course still dealing with Lynn's divorce and that year was the first time my son and I celebrated our mutual birthdays. It must have been my 29th but of course all the attention was on Brandon and one of the things I remember most was his birthday cake. It was in the shape of a telephone and it was all he played with – in fact nothing has changed much since he still spends a lot of his time on it.

On the business front by 1973 I was also negotiating the acquisition, our first as a company. If you recall years earlier, when I'd been made sales manager, I'd been approached (headhunted), by Pims Popcorn a company owned by Watney Mann. In fact I'd gone to see them, more as a way of looking at the way they worked than any serious idea of

Brandon on the phone on his 1st birthday... nothing changes then!

switching jobs. Well now, five years later, there I was again, in Watney's head office in Victoria negotiating to take Best Foods (who produced Pims Popcorn) over for Clarks. Yes it was a busy time alright and as our biographer reported – 'it was an inspired move'.

'Already the largest popcorn plant in the world, CCP acquired Pims its only serious rival, manufacturers of Pims Toffee Popcorn from Watney. It was an inspired move. Destined to become our other main product Pims expanded at a rate that made it Dagenham's fastest growing brand with sales eventually reaching half of those of Butterkist. Within two years the two products between them reached a staggering 60 million packs a year.'

It wasn't our last acquisition in that decade either. Taking over the Boy Blue label put us into loose and pre-packaged sweets, then the Crusader Confectionery Company. Perhaps I'm leaping ahead a bit too far and too fast here because I haven't even mentioned Brandon's rash yet.

We'd been to the annual party at Glebelands when on the way home Lynn suddenly noticed he'd broken out in a rash and being relatively new parents we took him straight to hospital. It was St Elizabeth's Hospital in the East End and they said for us to take him home because he'd clearly eaten something which had caused the rash. Early the next morning however our own doctor came to the house and confirmed that in actual fact he had the measles.

Chapter 6

Top dogs... and Toostie

When you've got friends and Nestlé

Right from my schooldays in the SMGS I have found it easy to make friends, of the kind that last. In my business and social life that's been the same and so many of them have helped me along life's path.

I remember people like Jock Carmalt, George Hagon (and his son Paul) and Cecil Hugh of course, but also John Golfer, Stanley Kitts and Ralph Peters who were so helpful to me and so influential in my career and helped Clarks to become top dogs in our field. Even today I have a close circle of people like Mike Large, Ron Warmington and so many others I am proud to call friends and who Lynn and I enjoy spending time with.

I have already described how, when I was appointed Sales Manager at Clarks I was suddenly offered several different jobs, such as taking over a similar job at Pims Popcorn (who we later took over). As I recall, being so excited about my promotion, I took none of them really seriously but suddenly one came along that would have sent Charlie Bucket's (in Roald Dahl's story about Charlie and the Chocolate factory) taste buds crazy.

Sometime around 1972 I had lunch in his club with a chap called John Golfer – a really nice man who ran a business in Wood Green called Caxton Chocolate. Over lunch we talked about the possibility of my joining his company to take over the sales side. Both Lynn and I had met John socially on a number of social occasions and we both liked him so I wondered if it would be possible to work with him. At that stage his organisation was much larger than Clarks, but I was doing well in my job there so had to think hard about it.

There was nothing 'back door' about this idea – that wasn't John's way and he actually contacted my chairman, Pitt Junior by then, to tell him he was seriously thinking about offering me a position. In a sense that put me into no-man's land but it's all out in the open and sometimes that works for you. The company gave me permission to spend a day at Caxton's to talk to their sales force and sales manager, which I did.

It soon became obvious however that John's team was not as 'with it' as my own one was. Their Sales Manager kept on talking to me about buyers of major companies who I knew had retired or been moved on and replaced. I felt like being in a bit of a time warp and being young, and I am afraid a bit forthright, I said a few things that ruffled some feathers. However I was still offered the job and invited to think about it.

Back in Dagenham everything had changed and I was told my future there was not only assured but I was even being considered for a seat on the Board. The added inducement of a new and improved contract and another new car helped me make up my mind to stay with Clarks and Butterkist.

I was always appreciative to John Golfer for helping, indirectly perhaps, to make life so much better for me and my young family. We stayed good friends until sadly he passed away many years later.

Then there was Stanley Kitts who owned a company called Daintee Confectionery in Blackpool and who I'd become friendly with during one of my trips north. I came up with the notion that if we expanded our range into sweets he could manufacture them in Blackpool where he had the capacity and equipment to do so. Arthur Smith, our company secretary, and I went up to discuss the idea with him and he agreed.

Stanley also owned the trading name of Boy Blue which he gave us as a gift and we came to an agreement. He would manufacture a vast range of products, deliver them to us and we would add them to our range so that our sales reps were getting an improved range of products to sell to their customers.

Then there was Ralph Peters who had a company called Somportex, but also one called Slush Puppie – a kind of fruity slushed ice drink he was selling all over Europe. But it was with Somportex that we struck a deal – another one involving chocolate, but this time a white chocolate bar he would import from a Dutch company called Boon.

Now this was pretty similar to a Nestlé product already on the market called the Milky Bar (remember the Milky Bar Kid?), but ours would be bigger, packaged differently and would be called the Big Milky. My company had the sole rights to the label and we would be the only people in the UK selling the Big Milky.

I am not sure to this day why, since we were competing directly with Nestlé, how on earth we thought we'd get away with it. Anyway we launched the product, advertised and marketed it, selling and promoting it across the UK – until the letter from Nestlé's solicitor arrived with a writ telling us to stop trading.

To be fair our label was quite similar to theirs and they were claiming encroachment of copyright. In their opinion their customers may have been misled into buying our product instead of theirs. Well, they did have a Milky Bar in a big size so they had a point. In fact there were all sorts of reasons on the writ and it shocked us rigid as our investment in packaging with the Dutch company had been quite substantial.

Not unnaturally our chairman, Pitt Junior, was a touch concerned, thinking we were about to be taken to the cleaners by Nestlé and their lawyers. 'Throwing a wobbly' could be a polite way of describing the meeting we had and as an accountant he clearly had huge numbers running through his head if they took us to the High Court.

But he was not me and he didn't know Ralph Peters and the relationship we had with each other. Ralph said: 'Look, I brought you into this and it's my problem not yours. I will handle it and I will deal with the costs.'

He took me to meet his solicitors and we went on to Nestlé to meet theirs, when he made it very clear he was dealing with it and any bills would be down to him. He had, and still has, a very nice way of dealing with people and you automatically felt you can trust him and that his word is his bond.

So we all went along to Nestlé and I have to say they were absolutely marvellous. They clearly had no intention of hurting small companies such as ours. After all they were, and still are, the world's largest food company. They even agreed that we could continue to sell our product to use up all existing materials, packaging and product but then we had to stop. The agreement was made, signed and the cost borne by Ralph.

However, would you believe it but we'd just put in our biggest ever order for product and materials so it took the best part of a year or two to exhaust all our stock. Still we made a few bob, learned a few lessons and moved on. What did I say to Ralph? 'Another fine mess you got me into' – but my tongue was planted firmly in my cheek and we remain friends to this day.

Mister Toostie

As ever I always tried to mix business with pleasure and while of course QPR was, and remains to this day, my biggest sporting passion there were others. In fact over the years I have developed interests in other sports, like boxing for example, but even while I was growing up greyhound racing was competing with the football.

Dad and my uncles got me into the dogs at a very early age as I have already said and it was an interest that we all, Lynn included, shared. Some years earlier I'd bought a rather elderly dog called Knave of Castletown. Named after a town in Ireland, where it had started its career, it ran for a few years at Hackney and gave us all a lot of fun.

Now I had decided to buy a second one, young with many years ahead of it to race at Romford Stadium. We decided to call him Mister Toostie after the sound Brandon used to make with his mouth and teeth in those days. He was homed in kennels in South Ockendon so on Sundays we could easily visit and take him for walks.

Greyhounds have to have three successful trials before they can race properly (to prove they run rather than fight) and Mister Toostie won his first one at the Romford track with no problems. I, on the other hand, did have a few problems, the principle one being taken away from my office to do Jury Service at Woodford Crown Court.

That came at the same time I was in London with a QC finalising the Big Milky case because, even if you come to a mutual and amicable agreement there are still papers to be dealt with. So the Jury Service call, which you cannot ignore, was a bit of a nuisance. Every morning for a couple of weeks I had to turn up at the Crown Court, only to get released a few hours later. I did manage to get a few days off but was called back to court again almost immediately.

Eventually I was put on a jury, only to be thrown off it again after three days. It appeared that some jurors (not me incidentally) had been

Brandon and Bradley with our dog Mr. Toostie

threatened so all of us had to go and I was released back into the business world.

Mister Toostie, having passed his trials, was also released but into the racing world having his first race at Romford, which he lost – as we all did that day, but soon it was to be our big day. Once a year we sponsored a big race, the Butterkist Cup, at the stadium to which all our staff were invited... to work. At the start of the evening they would be positioned at every entrance handing out packets of Butterkist as people came in. In fairness they also all got dinner that evening as well as being able to watch the races of course.

More about Mister Toostie later, but at this time I was also starting to take groups of customers, with a number of staff as well, on short breaks

CTN, November 16, 1972

Winner all the way

HIS name is Centaur, he started at 7-2, and he led all the way over 650 yards at Romford Greyhound Stadium to beat the favourite and win the "Butterkist Cup" for his owner, Mrs A. Boor.

She is pictured after receiving the trophy from Mr J. Kenneth Lewis, general sales manager of Clarks Cereal Products, the Dagenham-based popcorn people, who sponsored the race.

abroad and a quick tour of Germany, Austria and Italy. They were all prize-winners with sales of Butterkist so it was a good trip but I remember on my return being called to British Home Stores head office in Marylebone. We were supplying them with fudge and jellies at the time.

I was still a bit jet-lagged when I got back and remember leaving my car at the Blackhorse Lane station and getting a train to the BHS head office. Now I remember we discussed business but their buyer, Barry Brown, was a far more experienced and more accomplished drinker than me and when I left I was a bit drunk. I knew I wouldn't be able to drive but managed to find my way to Baker Street and on to Blackhorse Lane where I had the sense to phone my secretary.

Somehow she worked out from my phone call where I was and arranged for a member of staff to fetch me. My car stayed in the car park overnight and thank goodness it was still there the next day.

As I said we were supplying BHS with fudge and jellies thanks to our involvement with a company called Crusader Confectionery. Owned by a man called Jack Carter it was producing them at his factory in South Norwood. We had the Daintee Confectionery range of course but that did not include fudge and jellies, so we arranged for Crusader to supply them and add to our range. Years later I bought Crusader for Clarks but 1972 was also memorable for our 'Turkish delight'.

Not the jelly kind but a range of canned drinks called Elvan produced by a company called IMSA, who also had a franchise in Istanbul to produce Coco-Cola. They were a big business backed by a major Turkish banking organisation called Istanbul Bankasa and were looking for a UK sales force to distribute their range of canned drinks, at the same time I was looking to expand our range of products. Later that year we tied up a deal, both with them and with Daintee. In the same week I attended my first board meeting, so it was a good time to be able to report good business.

I had another good family reason to remember the latter end of 1972 because, with Christmas around the corner, lots of dinner dances were taking place and I was busily visiting customers at home with gifts etc. It seemed like a good time to have a break so Lynn and I decided to take

Opposite: Presenting the Butterkist Cup to Centaur the winner of the race sponsored by Clarks at Romford Dog Track. The PR machine kept turning!

Brandon and my mum and dad for a quick break abroad. We flew to Majorca for a few days and all went well until we came home.

Now my dad was a great character, one of those lovely guys who never missed a trick and he thought it wonderful that there was such a thing as Duty Free. This was something he'd never experienced before and the thought that abroad you could buy cheap alcohol and tobacco, and I do mean cheap, set him thinking.

So on the return flight, unbeknown to me of course, he took full advantage with more packets than he was legally allowed stuffed into his pockets, socks, underwear and any other place he could think of. Of course hiding alcohol is a lot different and much harder.

We reached Customs and guess who was stopped and whose luggage was searched. What alerted the Customs man to Dad was finding a bottle of Schweppes tonic water on him. Why on earth would anyone be bringing tonic water back with them? They took the cap off the bottle and guess what, they found it was pure gin.

He did like his drop of gin and he also had his full allowance but he couldn't resist taking the chance. I think that, after they also found the fags in odd places and looked at this lovely old man they realised he wasn't a big time smuggler. They just smiled, gave him a ticking off and sent us on our way but he loved thinking he'd got away with something.

'You see son, if you don't try you will never know,' he said with a twinkle in his eye. The fact that we could all have finished up with criminal records didn't seem to matter.

A Pims in a poke

The day we returned from holiday we had two bits of important news. For Lynn it was the fact that our new washing machine was arriving but for me it was the arrival of our Company Secretary Arthur Smith and the news he brought.

It seems that he and I were about to become Directors of the company – and me only 29. That Sunday I took Lynn and Brandon, my mum and dad, uncle Alf and auntie Doll for a celebratory lunch at the White Hart in Brentwood. Ok it hadn't yet been confirmed but hey, I was almost there.

The following day Arthur and I, along with Pitt Junior, went to London to sign all the papers relating to our buying Pims Popcorn from Watney Mann. I think the way that turned out became the most valuable business experience I ever had.

I was quite confident that having Pitt Junior, a fully qualified accountant with a background in finance, and Arthur who was equally well trained in finance, that it would be a simple purchase. My own role there was as the negotiator on the business side and everything seemed to go well.

We looked through all the relevant paperwork, including lists of machinery, current stocks, information on staff, numbers and salaries and all the financial statements. The money in the bank at the time amounted to around £30,000 if memory serves me right. It all looked good and we signed the deal – it was our company and we walked out very confident. The euphoria soon vanished.

Within a couple of days we found we'd actually bought a company with no money in the bank, apart from around £100. How? Because none of us had thought to ask about cheque books and what cheques were currently going through the system, that's how. In fact we'd paid around £30k too much for the company. I guess we were not as sharp as we thought we were.

We'd never actually bought a company before and had we asked the right questions we would have probably got honest answers, but we didn't. So we had to make the best of it and get on with the job, which we did pretty successfully as things turned out. A lesson learned and never forgotten.

The following week I went out to Wembley to see our new company, Pims Popcorn. I needed to see the factory, talk to the staff, look at stocks, get customer lists along with all the necessary information as well as sorting out who we needed and would keep. It was a small business so it wasn't a terribly difficult job.

Our intentions had always been to amalgamate the Wembley operation with the Dagenham one, but I made it clear to the staff that while that was our intention it would not be immediately. That way all the staff knew exactly where they stood and of course, albeit it would be a long journey for some, they would all be offered a job. It was, in my view, a good Christmas all around.

A busy time? I should say so. I was having meetings with builder Ron Murfitt, going to cheer QPR on at Loftus Road, going to the dogs in Romford, visiting Best Foods (re Pims Popcorn), in serious negotiations with Crusader Confectionery, who produced some of our product, to buy them out, buying ten new cars at a time for the sales force and.... Toostie won his first race.

You can see from this that, sport apart, the company was growing and it was felt that I should attend a banking course in the City. What did I learn? Well that the banks had some great facilities for food and booze. They certainly lived well in those days – probably still do – but I did meet some nice people and some good banking contacts. One, John Dickson, was to play a really important part in my future but, as always, family always comes first.

I often stayed at the Esso Hotel near Wembley stadium because it was the closest to the Pims Popcorn factory when I got a call from Lynn saying Brandon had a 'heart murmur'. I was still a relatively new dad so had no idea what that meant so I phoned my old doctor in Shepherds Bush, a man I had been with all my life and in fact the doctor who brought me into the world in the first place. He calmed me down, telling me it wasn't as serious as it sounded and that Brandon would grow out of it.

Nevertheless I went home and we took our son to see our family doctor Dr Moses and he confirmed that but arranged for an X-ray to be sure. So it was back to Harold Wood where the result showed up a slightly sticky heart valve that would, as said previously, clear up as he got older. It's amazing that, no matter how many people reassure you that your child is ok you still take precautions. We went off to see heart specialist Dr Nixon in Wimpole Street and, like the others, he said the boy would grow out of it, which he did.

We had another celebration around that time as well because, without telling Lynn why, I went off to Ilford County Court to handle her divorce proceedings in her absence. It was granted that day and I went home with a bottle of champagne to explain why we were celebrating – well that and the fact I paid Ron Murfitt £25 deposit for the new house he was building for us and that we planned to move into.

I was attending seminars in London for Chartered Accountants – another idea by Pitt Junior though God knows why because I rarely understood a word; but at Easter Mr. Toostie won again and that was the kind of finance I did understand. I began to realise that I had quite a good dog here.

When I became president of the MCCTA (Manufacturing Confectioners Commercial Travellers Association) I had to do a lot of travelling up and down the UK of course, making speeches. Butterkist of course was still my main interest and I remember taking a group of our Southern sales force to help me 'blitz' Jersey. Our aim was to get Butterkist into every possible outlet and I remember the night we had a challenge between ourselves to sell one box of Butterkist after midnight.

Yes it was a joke but it was a seaside resort, open all hours so not impossible. In fact it was our Southern Sales Manager, Ron Gwinnell who did it. He simply stepped out of his car, box of Butterkist in his hand, walked up to an ice cream kiosk that was closing up for the night and sold them a box for cash. That was the kind of team spirit we enjoyed and paid off so handsomely for the company.

It was similar to the time when, mixing work with leisure, Lynn, Brandon and I went with Uncle Alf and Aunt Doll on our first cruise as a family. It was on the Oriana and we went to the Mediterranean where one of the stops was Istanbul where I had already arranged to meet some executives of the Elvan Drinks Company, to tour their factory and the adjacent Coca-Cola factory. Very impressive on both counts.

Our new house in Upminster was almost finished and paying a stage payment on a Friday 13th did not feel unlucky, but around that time Clarks was about to have its first AGM in Dagenham. Up to then they'd always been held at the Institute of Chartered Accountants Offices in London, followed by lunch at the Savoy. The Fairlanes Hotel in Hornchurch might not be the Savoy, but that way our shareholders not only had their AGM on site but would then be able to tour the factory which, after all, was theirs.

Kenbrand

Business doesn't always have to be doom, gloom or even boom however because there's always a lighter side if the right people are involved. Take the affair of the vanishing Rolls Royce, for example – a trick even Tommy

Cooper would have been proud of, especially since it happened in Wales where he was born.

Our friend and customer Ian Yates was planning to open his new Cash

Pictured here at the Royal Matlock Spa Hotel
having just been inaugurated as the President of the MCCTA

and Carry in Pontypool, so Lynn and I were invited to join the dinner celebration at the Priory Hotel in Carleon where we stayed. What Ian hadn't told me was that he intended to ask me to make a speech – in fact he didn't actually even ask me never mind warn me. He simply stood up after dessert and announced that I was going to. Thanks pal, but after dinner his sons Jeff and Jimmy helped me get my own back.

Ian had arrived in his beautiful yellow, yes yellow, Rolls Royce which of course he'd parked outside the hotel, so we moved it. Well Jeff found his keys and we actually hid the Roller outside and well away from the hotel. It was an old hotel with lots of mature gardens and we found a very nice three-wheel garden barrow which, in the dead of night, we moved into the parking space Ian's car had been parked.

Lynn and I checked out and left to catch an early train the next morning but I hear it was quite an interesting moment when Ian came out with his Rolls Royce keys in his hand to find it had become an old wheelbarrow overnight. As the great Tommy would have said...'just like that'. Well it couldn't have had anything to do with me, because I was on the train back to London.

Then there was the time Ralph Peters (of Somportex) bought himself a dinghy – well a little rubber one with an outboard motor. His son had taken up sailing and was competing in the National Cadet Championships at Burnham-on-Crouch so Ralph suggested we jointly sponsored this rubber dinghy. It had Somportex on one side and Butterkist on the other and it seemed like a good idea.

I had no idea that I was actually going to be in this boat on the water, because otherwise I would have dressed for the occasion. As it was, when Ralph came to pick me up I was fully dressed in suit and tie and Ralph being Ralph, he said nothing other than commenting on how smart I looked. Privately I was thinking that he actually looked a bit scruffy.

When we got to Burnham I discovered pretty quickly that I was in the dinghy and dressed for the office. I was the laughing stock of everyone there, who were incidentally all more appropriately dressed. He had no yellow Rolls Royce to nick so I made him pick up the tab for dinner that night. However we remain friends to this day.

That does not go for either Ralph, Ian or several more of my business friends and contacts as the Kenbrand episode will show. Having said that, just as before when I was headhunted, there are times when you can turn a negative situation to your own advantage by holding your nerve. I was, and always was, loyal to Clarks, the company which had given me such a great career, but there are times for all of us when we wonder if it's time to move on.

It happened when I was thinking about starting up my own business. After all I had all the contacts, was well known in the trade and had plenty of friends who were prepared to help. I registered a company with the name of Kenbrand for the purpose of buying and distributing confectionery, a business that by now I was well acquainted with and well qualified for of course.

I had a number of colleagues and friends in the trade who were prepared to put money into the company to buy shares and all would benefit in one way or another. I would be Chairman and I had a loyal secretary who was prepared to join me, while Stanley Kitts of Daintee was prepared to manufacture my confectionery products.

There was always Ralph Peters, of course, who would get me some unusual imports with the exclusive UK rights to sell and George Hagon, of Palmer & Harvey, Britain's largest wholesaler who would buy and distribute my products. In fact throughout the UK I had a lot of friends like Ian Yates (he of the yellow Rolls Royce), Roy Hall and Ray Hancock who all had big Cash & Carry groups. Everything was looking good but I made one major mistake – I kept my Kenbrand paperwork in my office on the premises.

Someone, and I knew who it was, must have gone through my files when I was away and discovered that I had not only registered my new company but was all ready to go. I was intending to do this while running Clarks Cereal Products, the company producing Butterkist, Pims Popcorn and Boy Blue at the same time. It was intended to be, as they say, my little earner on the side.

The person who 'found' my paperwork obviously took steps to inform the other directors on what they'd found and, as a result, one day I was called into the 'big office'. Pitt Junior (by then our Chairman) was sitting in the big chair with Dick Whitehead and Arthur Smith the other two directors flanking him. He invited me to sit down and, producing my paperwork, asked me what was going on.

They could see from the files that I had the support not only of all our suppliers but within the industry as a whole, and not surprisingly they were not best pleased. I was quite indignant on the issue of how they came to have my paperwork by rifling my private files but that did not appear to matter. Fact is they had me bang to rights as they say.

I am however pretty good at thinking on my feet. I explained that I had no long-term contract, just a year at a time, and I was looking to improve my finances by starting a business called Kenbrand and running it alongside my normal job. Then, attack being the best means of defence, I told them I was getting pretty fed up with always having to argue with the Board to achieve a better standard of living for my staff, both sales team and secretary, and this was intended to be my little extra bit of security.

A quick switch to logic enabled me to point out that I could have used the company's sales force to move new Kenbrand products around the country so there could have been benefits to Clarks in the shape of extra income. It was pretty clear all round that this was nothing more than an excuse, but it was an answer and I could see that my 'explanations' had had an effect. They asked me to leave the room while they discussed the matter and I did so fairly confidently and with the parting shot of defiance that 'If you want me to resign I will do it now'. I left them with that thought and, at least, an option.

Half an hour later they called me back to tell me that they had well understood my frustrations. They offered me a new five-year contract with an increase in salary, a new and better car and more input on the salaries etc. of the staff under my control. Victory or vindication? Perhaps a bit of both, but the quid pro quo was that I had to give up the idea of Kenbrand and work exclusively for the company with no 'little earner' on the side.

Well at that stage it all sounded good to me. I was concerned about my friends who had agreed to support me and had already put money into Kenbrand, but I decided on the spot to agree the deal. It gave me some pretty good security, with that five year contract, but what of my partners who'd already paid for their shares and had been quite excited about the project? I knew I was going to have to spend a lot of that evening on the phone.

It is in times like these that you find out who your real friends are, and to a man they all said: 'No problems. We fully understand but always remember the company and we are all set up and ready to go if ever you need us.' In fact it was some years yet before I officially de-registered Kenbrand, mainly because it was clearly unnecessary and also to save the annual expenses involved even with inactive businesses.

No money ever went back for the shares that disappeared when the company did and the reason for that is that all my friends refused point blank to accept any reimbursement for the money they paid for their shares. Nor was there any animosity or bad feeling but in fact delight that they had played a part in helping to improve the future of myself and my family.

Both Stanley Kitts and George Hagon remained close friends until, sadly, they passed away while Ralph Peters went off for a life in the USA and Majorca. He always stayed in touch and we met up whenever he came back to the UK on visits. He's now back in the UK permanently and nothing has changed because he is still a great character. Yes he is still scruffy –a big man and always seen with a cigar in his mouth, he always objected to wearing a tie but restaurants like the Savoy that used to refuse him entry because of that now no longer object but even welcome him. Perhaps he really was ahead of his time – at least that is how I like to think of him.

Chapter 7

Upminster... Chicago... Cologne

Go West, young man

Of course when Horace Greeley made his inspirational call to young Americans he was urging them to create new frontiers in the 'wild west' of their own country, but if we look at national boundaries then for us in Clarks it meant crossing the Atlantic to his. So it was that in 1973 I made my first business trip to the U.S.A.

When Dick Whitehead, our Chief Engineer John Lavery and I flew to Chicago it was with several things in mind. In a sense we, or at least our main product, was 'going home', for it was when our founder Cecil Hugh was managing a Woolworths in New York that he spotted the potential of popcorn in the UK. There it was, as our historian wrote, *available on every street corner where, covered in melted butter and sprinkled with salt it was as American as Moms apple pie'*.

Now, almost half a century later, the boys from Butterkist – the sweeter British version, were over there to see how they did it. John Lavery headed up our team of eight full time engineers in our factory and we were keen to see the various types of packaging equipment.

In fact around that time I was starting a new venture for Clarks producing product for other companies, such as Trebor where we agreed to produce new jellies for them. They were already producing their own but, because we'd bought some new wrapping technology in Italy that gave us the ability to wrap jellies many times faster than any other machines available at the time, we could produce more for them.

I should admit at this time that this came about because of a piece of luck and an instant decision and some smart business. We'd been in

Bologna visiting the factory when they let it slip that Trebor were already interested and had gone back to discuss buying it with their Board of Directors. I asked, innocently of course, how many of the machines they could manufacture in a year and they said eight so, there and then, I agreed to buy the lot.

We already knew it was the right machinery for us and buying the lot would give us a year's lead against any other company. In other words we had a full year with no competition on fast wrapping jellies – a good head start in the industry, which is why we were able to offer other companies – including Trebor – a deal using machines we had literally bought from under their noses. In addition to Trebor we began to supply other well-known companies with jellies produced, wrapped and sold to them cheaper than anyone else could – certainly cheaper than they could do themselves.

However it was very different machinery we had in mind when we flew to America, where we visited a number of factories who were packaging popcorn. One of them was the Clover Club Company, which was part of Inter-Pepsi in Colorado Springs just south of Denver. This company had found a way of producing popcorn and nuts where the nuts would actually stick to the popcorn instead of falling to the bottom of the bag.

To be honest this wasn't of great interest to me, but John Lavery was a brilliant engineer – a lecturer at the Engineering College in London – so we did see a lot of machinery, mostly for packaging popcorn, in food companies. We were hosted throughout by our American friends, notably Jim Blevins (who I have mentioned before) of the Blevins Popcorn Company in Memphis.

At the end of the week we had a few days to ourselves and we went to Canada where John Lavery took the opportunity to spend a few days with his sister, while Whitehead and I stayed in Toronto. We also went to see a large confectionery wholesaler who imported UK confectionery, in Hamilton just outside Niagara. They became a good jellies customer for us and Dick and I took the chance to visit the Falls – quite an experience – before meeting up to go home again.

In fact, apart from what we'd seen and the people we'd met, what really stood out for me on that trip was the journey – both out and back. The flight out to Chicago was booked Economy, because in those days there was no Business or Club class. The choice was simply one of Economy or First Class and remember that our Chairman, Pitt Junior, was an accountant.

The three of us sat in the middle of a row. None of us was small but the seats were. All I had to do was just enjoy the flight but the other two had work to do, either actually working or reading up about the sort of equipment we were about to see. With screaming kids and lots of noise around us, Whitehead decided to go and look at the first class section. Apart from one couple it was completely empty.

I was holding the expenses for the trip so he asked me to go with him to see the chief cabin steward. Not known for his tact and diplomacy I almost shrivelled up when he said

Dick Whitehead, Works Director, and myself standing in a field of corn towering over our heads.

he would give the man 'a bung' (I think £100 was mentioned) if he could move the three of us into first class. To my surprise the man said: 'Just a minute sir, I will make sure there are no objections from the couple already there.'

As it happened the couple not only objected, quite vehemently in fact, but asked for the steward's name and warned him that if anyone without a first class ticket entered the cabin he would be reported. There was no choice but to go back to our seats and suffer the noise and distractions for the rest of the flight, whereupon Whitehead instructed me to change our seats on the return flight to first class. I phoned our UK agent and we flew back from Toronto in style.

There is one last recollection I have from that flight, as does Lynn. As we waited in Toronto Airport I realised I still had some of the expenses cash in my pocket. We had taken a lot of cash for food and hotel bills etc. not realising that our hosts would be picking up a lot of the bills for us, so I had some over. In Toronto Airport as we waited for our flight I was looking for a present to take back to Lynn and I spotted a very nice watch. It was in the shape of a horseshoe, representing the Horseshoe Falls at Niagara and Whitehead urged me to use the rest of the expense money buying it for her.

I was shocked but I remember his words very clearly. 'We don't want to take it back, you have put this whole trip together and you deserve a bonus.' Lynn still treasures that watch to this day.

The money's on Toostie, and in Brandon

There are all sorts of little, apparently insignificant compared with whatever else is happening, moments that somehow stick in your mind throughout your life, especially when they backfire and I suppose that's what makes life more interesting. One of these occasions is October 6th 1973 when his father George and I took young Paul Hagon to his first football match. Naturally, since both his dad and I were lifelong supporters it was to Loftus Road to watch QPR.

If memory serves me right Paul was about six years old and we watched the Rangers draw 1-1 with Chelsea and the lad was so impressed he became a lifelong supporter.... of Chelsea. Still having cultivated and encouraged his own son Michael to follow in his footsteps and become a Chelsea supporter Michael turned to Arsenal. See Paul, what goes around comes around.

Meanwhile on the greyhound front Mister Toostie had become such a favourite at Romford, the odds on his whenever he raced were pretty poor. We took him to Hackney Wick instead for his trials and he raced there for a while too but, out of the blue, we had an entirely different emergency to deal with.

I just got back from Jersey where I had been filming a new commercial for Channel TV when I got a frantic phone call from Lynn saying that Brandon had swallowed a coin. Somehow he'd managed to take a Portuguese 50 centavo coin out of a jar where we collected foreign coins, put it into his mouth and swallowed it.

I was sitting at my office desk when Lynn phoned and clearly I didn't take it too seriously because I just advised her to take him to the doctor. Our Sales Manager Ron Gwinnell, who was sitting on the other side of the desk, heard me say it and enquired what it was all about.

I said: 'Oh, it's just my son. He's swallowed a coin and Lynn said he is choking a bit too I said take him to the doctors.'

Ron, bless him, who with four sons had far more experience than me, jumped up and said, 'For God's sake, tell her to be at the door and we will be there in ten minutes.' Whereupon we dashed home as fast as he could drive, picked Lynn and Brandon up and rushed them straight off to Harold Wood hospital. It appears that the size of the 50 centavo was exactly the same circumference as his throat and must have gone down at the perfect slanted angle not to have stayed in his throat and choked him.

We got to the hospital and he went straight in for X-rays but they didn't seem to want to tell us much. In fact they were not exactly terribly pro-active in keeping us informed and taking whatever steps were necessary. I telephoned the Nuffield, a local private hospital, who said 'Bring Brandon here straight away,' so although it was evening time by then we moved him.

They told us to leave him there and that he would probably stay for a few days. They also X-rayed him and told us straight away that the coin had moved down into his stomach. They said it could pass naturally but also warned us that it could cause peritonitis. There was nothing we could do except wait so we left him at the Nuffield for a few days but we also had an appointment with a specialist called Michael Prinn, who these days lives around the corner from us. He suggested that an operation may be needed but advised us to give it a little longer.

The next day I had an appointment to make an important after dinner speech in Bristol and it was a difficult decision but after being assured nothing else was likely to happen I went, while Lynn stayed with Brandon in the hospital. When I got back it was agreed that an operation was now necessary. He had another X-ray and was instantly booked in so at 12.45pm on October 29th he had the operation and of course we both stayed with him.

They successfully removed the coin, which remains in my collection, and a couple of days later our son was released. Apart from going back for a checkup all seemed to be well, apart from the fact he has a slight scar, but we will always be grateful – especially to Ron who was the first to appreciate the possible gravity of the situation.

There was one other nice touch to the story because afterwards I took

Lynn to Torremolinos on the annual staff and customers trip and on the day we arrived back home it was when the biggest bunch of flowers you ever saw arrived. It was from Stanley Kitts (of Daintee) who had known of the problems regarding Brandon's operation and Lynn staying in hospital with him. He felt Lynn deserved 'something special' (his words) for having had and come through such a difficult time.

Meanwhile while we were having money taken out of Brandon, we were doing very well putting money on Mister Toostie who was running well for us at Hackney Wick.

Days of wine and Roses (lime juice)

As I said earlier there are dates that stick in the mind for odd reasons and December 31st (New Year's Eve) 1973 does in mine. Why? Queens Park Rangers 3 Manchester United 0, that's why. It's not a result that happens every day of course so it's one that I still savour and remember with deep satisfaction.

In the Spring of that year we moved into our new home in The Grove Upminster. We had been having regular site meetings with plumbers and electricians as well as seeing new fitted furniture going in and carpets going down. We actually moved in on Wednesday 20th March.

There were some interesting developments at work too because for some reason it was decided that I should learn how to actually manufacture confectionery. God knows why, because I was never likely to do so but I guess that since we had a couple of confectionery companies by then I ought to know something about it. So I spent a week on a course in Leatherhead, which was not far from where our chairman Pitt Junior lived.

It had been his idea and he was curious about how it was going and invited me to dinner at his house one evening. We never did get on very well so it was a bit tense but in the event the evening passed reasonably well. In fact later that year he even came with me on a trip to Eire, visiting a confectionery company in Cork, before travelling by train to Dublin where I had to give a speech at an MCCTA dinner.

Then, seen as a pretty good sales and marketing man by Pitt Junior, I was asked to get involved in one of the family's other businesses. Among them was the British & Foreign Wharf Company which in fact had been a very big part of the Butterkist story because it actually owned Clarks Cereal products into which the original company formed by Cecil Hugh was merged.

Just before the war the British & Foreign Wharf company which until then had simply concentrated on bottling bonded spirits and wine, went into bottling wine generally. They leased a massive building in Wapping and, since it was too big for their own use, rented some of the space out to other companies including, apart from Clarks, space for bottling the famous Roses Lime Juice. This scheme was the brainchild of its managing director Mr. (later Sir) Philip Warter who would later play a big part in the Butterkist story himself.

Another important name that came into the story then was a British & Foreign Wharf company director Mr. George Pitt (Pitt Senior), who became Clark's chairman. It was however his son Pitt Junior of course who wanted me to take a look at the family wine business near the Surrey Docks. Its MD Arthur Taylor said they needed some help with sales and marketing, so I was introduced to a company that imported and bottled wine. Wonderful!

Samples flowed easily of course and it was a great boon to me not to have to buy my wine any more because I was given it by the case. In return all I had to do was look at their options relating to selling even more of their product and one idea I gave them was to consider their own label for supermarket groups and that seemed to work out pretty well. By that time the big superstores were really growing into major supermarkets and their wine, spirits and beer sections were a considerable financial boost to that growth so the timing was good.

I worked with the company for a day a week for most weeks and it was something completely different from confectionery. They were really nice people to work with and gave me something completely different to interest me at the same time.

Around this time my great friend Gareth Thomson told me that he and his wife Betty had decided to ditch the UK to start a new life in Australia. Gareth had been a friend since my early days in the confectionery industry. We often used to meet up in the East End when I was selling popcorn and he was the Area Agent for Pez Confectionery and he often came to watch QPR with me.

Lynn and I decided to give them a farewell party in our new house and a couple of days later I drove them to Heathrow. I remember the journey being quick, but quiet and I sensed apprehension in Betty who wasn't keen to go, while I was about to lose one of my best friends. Gareth, on the other hand, was excited and ready to start a new life. They had no children then but he'd sold the house, resigned from his job and was quite adventurous. As I drove home after leaving them at Heathrow that day the radio was playing 'Leaving on a jet plane'.

I remember him turning up at our house with one of the biggest blue and white teddy bears you could ever get. The colours of course represented the QPR colours and he wanted to leave Brandon something for his approaching 3rd birthday. Then they went off to their new life in Adelaide where they still are to this day. Lynn and I have made a few visits there since, and they never fail to return to the UK for any of our important functions, special birthdays, weddings etc.

I do remember that they left a few days before the start of the 1974 world cup in West Germany won, yes by West Germany. Ironically it was the series England failed to qualify for but one country that did was... Australia. Still the final was a great game between the Germans and the Netherlands who had already won a lot of friends with their 'total football' style.

The teddy bear wasn't the only present Brandon got for his third birthday of course because it was time for his first bike so we went shopping in the bicycle shops. We celebrated it with a family party in the garden of our new house when the family came over for dinner. We also started getting the family portraits that currently adorn various places in our home taken.

Then, for one reason and another we were already looking at other properties and the area of Emerson Park, not far from Upminster, came to mind. Lynn was pregnant again and we realised we'd need a bigger place and more garden so we decided to look around to see what building was going on there.

Morecambe and Wise

I doubt if I will ever forget the look on the copper's face when we opened my garage to find it stuffed full of boxes and packets of popcorn and sweets. In fact he'd arrived as a potential buyer, because we'd decided to move from Upminster, and as he viewed the house itself he seemed pretty happy with it.

Then I opened up the garage door and, well a policeman is always a policeman, so I had a lot of explaining to do, telling him the Dagenham Town Show was due that weekend and about our part in it. However he and his family seemed like pretty nice people and eventually they did buy the place.

Our final decision to move to a bigger house in Emerson Park was largely down to the fact that Lynn was pregnant again. She was also expecting something else too and in preparation for that began taking her first driving lessons. In fact she had quite a few because she wanted to get a first time pass before she got too big, but with the House of Clark's AGM and the Butterkist Cup at Romford coming up it was quite a hectic time all round.

A bit too much really because Lynn, back under the care of Dr Forster, was not feeling too well and having to spend some days in bed. Sadly, on August 6th she lost the baby – a really sad moment for us all. Losing a child, at any age, is a terrible thing but having a miscarriage is just as traumatic and emotional experience, especially for the mother of course but also for the father who can only offer her comfort and reassurance. I felt a break was needed so I quickly booked a week for us all, including my parents, at Butlins in Bognor Regis.

I decided to give Lynn a birthday treat too so I took her for a night out at the Circus Tavern which is a big night spot catering for around 2,000 people. We went with Ron and Sue Wenn (Ron was the buyer for Keymarkets) to see Freddie 'the parrot' Davis. Sadly he did not seem to be a major attraction because there were only about a dozen people, including ourselves, in the place that night. Not one of Lynn's most memorable nights out and I am not sure it did me a lot of good with Keymarkets either.

I had better luck a few weeks later when I went with a group from the

British & Foreign Wharf company to the Granada Theatre in East Ham to see Morecambe and Wise who were putting on a show for TV. It was a great evening and proved to be the start of their long-running and very successful television shows. We were celebrating ourselves at the time because the BBC had heard that we had made it into the Guinness Book of Records, because we had the world's largest popcorn plant, and wanted an interview. We were back at the Circus Tavern at Christmas though, but this time to see Joe Brown and the Bruvvers in what proved to be a much better evening than our previous visit.

On the home front the policeman (Mr. McQuater) and his family who, having bought our Upminster house, wanted to move in. Our own new house in Emerson Park was not ready so we had to start looking for temporary accommodation in the shape of a small flat.

Brandon, who had started school by then, was starting to wonder how Father Christmas was able to move so easily from department store to department store and sometimes even to garden centres. Oh yes, there was one other thing that happened that Christmas that sticks in the mind – Lynn passed her driving test on December 4th at the first attempt. She has never let me forget it.

Pools winners

I have only ever been to one Rotarian Lunch and that was in Scotland. One of our customers, Tom Hannah, was Provost in a little town called Johnstone and it was he who invited me to lunch. What I didn't know when I sat down to enjoy a nice lunch with some good wine was that as a first time guest you are expected to say a few words.

It's a good job that by that time I was well used to making speeches but there I was in a room full of Scots all of whom, apart from my host and his son, were strangers to me. Somehow I got through it by talking, what I usually talked about, football and the difference between the English and Scottish leagues, but I mention this because of another incident involving a Hannah.

At the time back at home Lynn got her first car, a bright red DAF so she was happy, settled, had some independence for the first time... and was pregnant again. Me? I was off to Cologne with another great friend, Sandy Hannah – nephew of my Rotarian host.

Now Sandy was a bit of a late night bird and when most people are heading for bed he was ready to go out drinking champagne. We were staying at a little place just outside Cologne called Leverkusen which had its own late night drinking club – well in truth it was a little more than that because it had lady hosts who saw you to the bar and then helped you drink.

I realised this the moment we went in and pointed out to Sandy that this was no ordinary pub but he was always flash with his money and insisted we were staying to drink champagne. The hours went by and the money was flowing as fast as the champagne. I was getting desperate to get out because I was a bit worried about the bill because I only had a few German marks left.

As it happened when the final bill did come we had nothing like the amount needed between us whereupon a couple of 'heavies' appeared and accompanied us back to our bedrooms. I had no more marks but fortunately Sandy didn't have a problem there and had money in his room so the 'gentlemen' collected it from him, along with a generous tip for our 'hostesses'.

To be honest I was never completely sure we were even drinking genuine champers, but there was no point arguing about that with those gorillas. We went to bed, overslept and missed our plane from Cologne to London. We had to take a long and very expensive taxi ride to Dusseldorf, where we were able to get a plane home. Sandy remains a great friend.

In April that year we were due to move out of our Upminster home but our new one in Emerson Park was still not finished so we moved into a small flat in Hornchurch. It was on the main road and there was no telephone (mobile phones were still the stuff of science fiction then) so we felt a bit cut off. We were a bit concerned of course because Lynn was months away from giving birth and bearing in mind the problems of the previous year we obviously needed to keep in touch. I resolved not to be away and we moved Brandon into a new local playschool so Lynn didn't have to travel so far.

I did have to do some travelling though and I remember giving a speech in Welsh at an MCCTA dinner in Cardiff. Well not completely – I did spend a year learning the language, or at least trying to. I could only manage a paragraph before reverting to English but I believe my audience appreciated my trying. We also had another Butlins holiday in Barry Island with my parents but before we did, I met Alan Britain.

Lynn and I had been looking at the idea of installing a swimming pool in the garden of our new Emerson Park house when it was ready. One of the companies we looked at was Britannia Swimming Pools owned by Alan Britain, who I had never met before. He was extremely helpful and came to look at the site to see the best place to put a pool. Then he came to the flat for a cup of tea when he explained that the pool would take a few weeks to build and would cost £2,000. He also pointed out that installing it while the builders were still on site made sense because the mess involved would not affect us.

To be honest Lynn had never been really keen on the idea with young children about but also because of the cost, knowing we could not afford it. I told Alan we would have to think about it because while it was a wonderful idea we did not really have that sort of money to spare, especially with a new baby on the way. I told him we would think about it while we were away and call him with our decision when we got back.

Anyway we got back on the Saturday and on the Sunday morning I popped round to see the site to see how the building was going. I was somewhat shocked, maybe pleasantly surprised, definitely bewildered and concerned financially to see that a pool had already been installed in the garden. It wasn't finished but the hole was dug, the pool tiled and the pipes were in place. My immediate reaction was to phone Alan before going home to tell Lynn news I knew she would not be pleased about.

As it turned out I had no means of contacting Alan because in those days he had no business card – and still doesn't. All we knew was that he had a small site next to Upminster Station so would have to wait until Monday morning. I decided to go home, collect Lynn and, without mentioning the little back garden surprise she had in store, take her to see how building was going.

We arrived and went round the back and I have never been able to make up my mind about what she was thinking when she saw it but I will always remember the words. 'It's in the wrong place', she said.

Now I had no preconceived ideas about where the pool was to go but Lynn would have had it in an area more convenient to the back door. The fact is however that what had been nothing more than an idle thought

– part of a wish list really – had become a reality. We both just stood and stared at it, mostly wondering how we were going to pay for it, but there was nothing we could do until the next day anyway.

We still didn't have a telephone in the flat so we couldn't be contacted either but bright and early on Monday Alan Britain turned up there and asked if we had had the opportunity yet of seeing our new property. We just stared back at him and said we had. 'You put a pool in. We didn't order it, were only thinking about it, and we didn't know where we would get the money to pay for it.'

He just laughed and asked for a cup of tea. Alan, as we came to know, was always one to ask for a cuppa, use the phone (not this time mate) or the loo but he was new to us and we weren't sure how to take him. He explained that he had employees with nothing to do and he had to pay them for a week's work anyway. He said he knew we wanted the pool but also that we never had the money so, rather than lay the men off, he thought he'd go ahead and build the pool on the basis that one day we would pay him something.

I was amazed that anyone would have such trust but Lynn, of course, told him it was in the wrong place. He explained to her that his knowledge of pools was that you always put them in the area that had the most sun but wasn't too close to the house which creates shadows. I don't think that she was ever convinced but to me it made sense.

As for me I couldn't get over the fact that this man had told someone he'd only just met briefly, and living in a small flat with virtually no furniture that he trusted him. It seemed odd to me but he said he'd had to make a judgement, that he was going to finish the job, get it working and whenever we had some money he assumed we would pay him.

That level of trust created a bond that remains to this day. Alan and his wife Sue have been close friends of ours ever since. The debt however, drove me crazy – debt always does – and I took him straight to the bank that morning and, taking out what little money we had I gave it to him. He expected me to pay him back over two or three years but in fact I paid it off in full in just eleven months which surprised him as much as it surprised Lynn and me.

He was also a very a patient man too because, knowing nothing about swimming pools I was constantly calling him out, day, night or at weekends, because when something went wrong I didn't know what to do. Often that would involve him arriving, turning on a switch that I'd forgotten to do and after having his cup of tea everything went back to normal.

It just shows that there are still people in this world who are prepared to take a gamble on people they trust. We became very good friends and even though these days they live in Spain we keep in regular contact and, whenever he visits the UK he still drops in for his cuppa.

Chapter 8

New house, new baby

The Rolls moved in before us

Ruby weddings (40 years) are always a bit special in families and a heavily pregnant Lynn and I spent a lot of time organising the celebration for my mum and dad's one. We booked a hall in Hornchurch, arranged for all the catering and when my parents arrived it was to be greeted by an array of friends and relatives from both sides of the family – some of whom they'd not seen for many years.

Colour TVs were becoming the norm and we had a nice set waiting for them as our present. Obviously such events are always a bit tearful and I still have a letter from them thanking us and telling us how emotional the whole experience was. It's nice to be able to look back and think about something nice you've done for parents in years gone by and especially when they are no longer with us. It was a fun affair with plenty to eat and drink, so everyone had a good time and they stayed with us overnight as we only lived a few miles away from the hall.

That was followed by the Dagenham Town Show and the Clarks AGM but we were also about to complete on our new Emerson Park home and that led to a bit of a battle of wits between Lynn and myself. On July 17th when we signed the final contract and collected the keys I was heading off to the AGM and we were just a couple of months from the arrival of the new baby.

I was negotiating with a removals company – South Park Removals who, having used them previously I was planning to use again. The house was almost ready but not quite but Lynn, being heavily pregnant, was keen to move in and settle down. We were still living in that small flat

133

with no telephone but I was trying to make everything about the house perfect so I was putting off the removal date with all sorts of excuses – which Lynn of course saw through every time I offered them.

She would ring South Park herself to tell them she wanted a date and very soon, whereupon they would phone me at the office to warn me of her call. I would give them all sorts of reasons why they couldn't do it so they would call her and give her all the excuses. Lynn finally ran out of patience and told me to find another removal company, so I would point out that I had already given South Park a deposit etc. So it went on and on while, of course Lynn knew nothing of it. Nor will she unless she happens to read this book..... but by now my love, it's too late!

In any case before we actually moved in ourselves something else I ought to mention happened. Ian Yates – he of the yellow Rolls Royce – and I were on a cruise ship to Holland and he was desperate to sell his Roller (not the yellow one) to me. He wanted to buy a new one and, being a pretty good salesman himself stressed how it would improve my credibility in the trade if I turned up at Tesco House driving a Rolls Royce.

This was something I used to do pretty regularly as it happens and in fact the commissionaire there always found me a parking spot next to Sir John Cohen whereas other visitors had to park at the end of the road and walk. As I said Ian was a pretty good salesman but we were arguing about the price, because I had a figure in mind that was £1,000 lower than his.

Actually, to be fair, his asking price was an extremely good one and well below the market price, but there is always a deal to be had so I was trying to get a better one. In the end we decided on a gamble that involved us playing Pontoon (some people call the game 21s) on the ship. The idea was that we started playing after dinner, around 7pm, and continue until midnight assuming neither of us fell asleep before then. The game would end at midnight and whoever was winning at that time got the car for his price.

In fact I was ahead, but only just, when the clock struck midnight and Ian honoured the bet. I got the car for £1,000 less than he wanted, even though he could have got at least double the asking price elsewhere if he'd wanted to – as in fact several years later, I did.

So Lynn and I were soon on our way north to Wilmslow where Ian lived

Lynn, heavily pregnant with Bradley,
as we collect the Rolls Royce I bought from Ian Yates

to collect our first ever Rolls Royce. To my surprise Ian had not only had the car serviced, almost rebuilt to new at the Rolls Royce factory in Crewe but had also bought me a personalised number plate as a present. I still have it – 10JKL (my initials plus the fact we lived at 10 Fairlawns Close then). He'd also put a massive sign on the top reading 'Old Rolls Royce for sale, and Sovereign Sweets 6d a quarter'.

While we were in the north we took the opportunity of visiting friends in Yorkshire and Lancashire, but on the way home we realised we had nowhere to park the car when we got there. We were still in the flat in Hornchurch which had no garage space and very limited parking so we took it to our new home in Emerson Park which was now complete and had a lockable garage. It also gave Lynn a chance to see the new house as well of course (and more opportunities to discuss moving dates), but we now had our new Rolls Royce safely locked into our new garage. It was in before we were.

Well I couldn't keep her waiting any longer and on August 20th, two weeks before Bradley was born, we finally moved in. I remember the night before we did because my secretary Chris and her partner (eventually husband) helped me wipe down cupboards and get the place ready to move in.

Ten days later Lynn was 27 and was getting pretty big, but she was happy to be settled in before the birth. I remember it well too because that day QPR were playing West Ham and I took her dad Bill and some other friends to watch the game, that ended in a 1-1 draw.

Bradley

Bradley was actually due to arrive on Lynn's birthday (August 30th) but he missed it by a few days. She was admitted to hospital to have the baby on September 2nd but it took a while until eventually, at 4.15pm on Wednesday Sept 3rd he was born.

Having already taken Brandon to be looked after by her parents, Ivy and Bill, I was on hand to help out and, as I had with Brandon, helped Mr. Forster deliver our second son. It wasn't Bradley's fault of course but after that Lynn decided that was enough and there would be no more babies. She did change her mind later but as far as I was concerned this birth business never seemed too arduous to me and I wanted a football team of sons.

Anyway Bradley joined the family four years after his big brother, who came to visit his mother and his brother in the hospital the next day. In those days new mothers were kept in hospital to recover for around a week so for that time I was in sole charge of Brandon. That pretty well meant eating out at the White Hart (now the Sugar Hut) in Brentwood and Madame Tussauds.

It seemed odd at the time but Brandon was always asking to visit his brother in hospital. It was clearly a novelty at the time so we were there several times a day although we were also visiting a local fun fair in Upminster that week. I remember Brandon commenting on how pleased he was to have a baby brother and would like some more so we could go to the funfair more often. Harold Wood hospital was very good to us, letting us stay until at least 9pm each night.

A week after he was born Brandon and I went to Harold Wood to collect Lynn and Bradley to take them home for our first day as a family of four. By now Brandon was sleeping through the night but Bradley of course was not, so once again we were, so to speak, open all hours. However we felt we were ready for our very first overnight guest in our new home and that happened to be Stanley Kitts, of Daintee Confectionery.

We had put the boys to bed and Lynn was cooking dinner, but we found ourselves whispering instead of talking and creeping about the house – especially when going upstairs to check on the boys. That night we learned a great deal from Stanley, a man with children and grandchildren, who told us we were going about it the wrong way.

'You are doing it all wrong; you need to make a lot of noise. Get them used to the banging about, the running of baths, the TV and radio otherwise every single time there is a noise or the phone rings they are going to wake up'. Stanley was a wise old guy who always talked a lot of sense – we decided to take his advice and it certainly paid dividends.

We took our new son to Dover to proudly show him off to Nan, had all the photos of our family of four taken and it was almost time for Bradley to have his little snip. Before that happened however I had to spend my own first night (as an adult) in hospital. I just remember severe abdominal pains and being rushed to hospital by Lynn and her brother Tony where they just dumped me and left.

Actually they knew I would do anything not to stay in the hospital so they left me with the staff and went home. I hated being in hospital and checked out again first thing in the morning. No one there had an answer to the problem so I left and took Bradley for his snip later that day. Meanwhile the pool was up and running and I was ready for my first swim in it. It was November 1st and really cold, but it was one of those things that had to be done. Brrr!

Mars to Moscow

Clearly this was, as ever, a busy time with new house, new baby and new Rolls Royce; but business is business and that was what was paying for all these things so all the meetings and greetings went on.

I was having meetings, prior to our taking his company over, with Stephen Docwra of the Docwra Rock Company in Great Yarmouth and introducing my dear friend George Hagon of Palmer & Harvey to the British and Foreign Wharf because P&H was considering wholesaling wine. And then there was Moscow where I took a party of business people on a company trip.

The USSR in 1975 was still a totalitarian communist country of course but, led by an ailing Leonid Brezhnev, was starting to open up a little and tourists were being allowed in more freely. However only twelve years earlier a British 'businessman' called Greville Wynne had been arrested and jailed on charges of spying (which he had been) so there was always a bit of uncertainty and nervousness about going behind the Iron Curtain and especially to its capital.

Now when it comes to meals I am a very plain food and ordinary eater sort of guy and always worry about whether I would eat anything at all (remember the poisonous banana?). So I take a lot of my own and before leaving I packed many Lyons Individual Fruit Pies, McVitie & Price biscuits and lots of Mars bars.

Anyway we arrived and at the Intourist Hotel I was told I was sharing a room with a colleague from EMI, John Mason. Everyone else on the trip were couples but because Lynn had to stay at home with Brandon and the new baby I was a single and so was John. Obviously it seemed sensible to the hotel to put us together, but not to me and, Russia or not, I had such an enormous row with them they even considered evicting me altogether.

I've had a few rows since then but I was not prepared to share a room with another customer who had actually been promised a single and had joined the trip on that basis. I hadn't and while everyone else who'd got their rooms were milling around the bar bringing a beer or two out to us in reception, we were still arguing the point. Eventually reason prevailed and we got our separate rooms but it wasn't the greatest start to our trip.

It was an experience however with some great trips, many of them starting from their magnificent underground system. These had stations decorated with the most magnificent of mosaics and of course, though our hosts didn't like it, we all took plenty of photos.

In fact we took photos everywhere we went and when we got back to the UK and had them developed we all found the same little lady in the background in most of them. It was then that we realised that, because we were a large group from England, we had been unknowingly 'chaperoned'. After we realised some of us did remember spotting that little lady but not as many times as she appeared in the photos.

While in Moscow I took the whole group to see the famous Moscow State Circus. Being the perfect host I made sure to go and buy every guest a programme and, on handing them out, found they were laughing, but good naturedly, at me. Quite naturally they had all been written in Russian so all we had, or at least could understand, were pictures of animals. Great show though.

Back at the hotel one of our party, Jack Davey, decided we should have some champagne – French champagne and not a chance of that in Russia. We called the hotel manager over to explain that we wanted some genuine French champagne and were laughed at. I had to explain to the group that we were just not going to get any French champagne in Moscow – indeed in 1975 we were lucky to even get into the country.

Jack however, was never one to give up and he pulled quite a lot of currency out of his wallet. He flashed it in front of the manager and guess what? In no time at all several bottles of genuine French champagne appeared. I learned a lot that day.

Another man who taught us a lesson was Roy Hall who before coming had realised that while roubles may be the official currency, on the streets it was chewing gum. Knowing that Wrigleys was well sought after in countries where it was not imported he'd raided his warehouse for the stuff. So where the rest of us were buying our souvenirs and Christmas presents etc. from street vendors with money, he'd been swapping chewing gum for them.

As it happened Roy and I were the only ones who had problems leaving Russia for the trip home. Before the Russian trip we had both been to the USA and of course had visas stamped in our passports. At Moscow Airport on departure they were spotted by the duty Immigration Officers and we were invited into another room for a 'chat'. For over an hour we were interrogated as to why we'd been in the USA and what we had been doing there – visions of the Lubyanca floated in my mind.

Eventually we convinced them and they accepted the fact that we'd simply been on holiday, at different times and at different places in America. They finally released us just in time to catch up with the rest of the group and catch the plane, but believe me it was not a pleasant experience.

I got back in time for both Christmas and our 'pretend' Christmas. A couple of Sundays before Christmas Day George and Rina Hagon came, with their son Paul, to lunch and we just pretended it was Christmas, with food, champagne and presents. That actually started a tradition that continued right up to the death, first of Rina and then George, and is one that has continued to this day with Paul, his wife Jane and their children Sally and Michael turning up.

One down side to the season was that I had to dismiss a member of the Sales Team and that led to an Industrial Tribunal. That was a new idea at the time and had become all the rage for people who had lost their jobs and felt they had been treated unfairly. I will have more to say about this Tribunal later in the book.

Still, forget that for the moment because that Christmas (Bradley's first) I was also invited to Keymarkets' Christmas party. That must have said I was doing something right because that event was usually confined just to staff but I did have some good friends there at the time, irrespective of the fact they all seemed to be West Ham supporters.

We had our usual Christmas visit to Dover and I had to attend the Executive Christmas Lunch at Clarks but it was also time for Brandon to see his first pantomime so it was off to the Queens Theatre in Hornchurch. On Boxing Day I went off to see QPR beat Norwich 2-0 – a great win – before going to see them lose 2-0 to the Arsenal the next day – least said etc...

'Were we thinking of getting married?'

Actually the year that followed – 1976 – started with the garage door falling on me and then, on January 8th, Brandon starting proper school, something he found quite different from play or nursery school. I went to a 'do, raided by policemen and I found myself on a plane with Tommy Cooper. Oh yes, and I proposed to Lynn...just like that as that great clown used to say.

Well actually, when I say proposed I am not talking the 'on bended knee' sort of traditional proposal so much as the more modern, 'sorted'. Brandon had started school that day and that evening the RCA (Retail Confectioners Association) had its annual dinner in the Royal Lancaster Hotel. There Lynn and I were, having drinks at the bar before going in for the dinner when I said to George Hagon, 'Would you be my best man?'

Not unnaturally that left Lynn a touch bewildered and asking what it was all about. 'Were we thinking of getting married?' she asked.

I said 'Yes, on the 21st February and by the way I have organised the wedding, the reception, the guests and as it happens I have also organised Bradley's Christening for the following day'.

Unknown to her I had made all the arrangements, booked the Registry Office and a reception and I had had all the guests invited. I had, of course, assumed Lynn would say yes, as of course she did.

George was thrilled. He'd been telling me for years that it was about time that I married Lynn, so I think his feelings of excitement were tinged with relief. In fact I'd always had my reasons, notwithstanding his and other people's pressure, to get married at that time. I always knew we would have at least one more child and had my reasons for waiting until then to get married.

Well it certainly gave the evening an added lift and, although it was a confectionery evening our table, made up of our closest friends were celebrating our own forthcoming event. Coincidentally the following week I was invited to a stag party organised by local police, only for coppers, at the Elm Park Hotel and that turned into quite an experience too.

I would not put down in print here what went on that night but it was an unusual kind of event. The comedian that night was an up and coming youngster who no one had ever heard of but had been booked because his jokes were all about policemen. Jim 'nick nick' Davidson went on to become a top flight comic on TV as well as in the theatre and clubs.

A good night was had by all but as I left the hotel that evening it was to find it surrounded by police cars. It seems that word about this stag party had got out and another constabulary from Essex had decided to raid the place. I was lucky because I needed to be up early the next day to go to Scotland I left just as police officers were going in and was able to walk past them into a car waiting to take me home.

Later on I heard that there had been some rather unusual events taking place after I left. I was 'advised' to lose any tickets I had that may or may not have been printed but of course I knew nothing about all that. I had just happened to call into the place for a quick drink and there happened to be some local coppers there at the same time. Honest Guv! That's all I know about it.

The next day I was off to Scotland, leaving Lynn at home looking after our boys, then it was on to Cologne before coming back down to earth in South Norwood to conclude the take-over talks with Crusader Confectionery. Then I had to dash off to Birmingham and because time was short decided to fly there from Heathrow. There was no other way and I remember getting into one of the smallest planes I'd ever seen. It only seated four or five people but apart from one other passenger I was the only one. He was a big jovial sort of chap and what a journey it turned out to be.

My fellow passenger was the great Tommy Cooper and he was exactly the same person as you see, or used to be before he died on stage while on TV, as he was when performing. Tommy was known in the business to be a bit keen on the alcohol and he did drink an awful lot on that short flight, but what an experience it was. At the end of it he gave me a couple of tickets for his show that night at the Birmingham Night Out club.

I took our Midlands rep, Fred Parker, to see the show and as ever Cooper was absolutely fabulous but took me by surprise by mentioning me. He told his audience he'd had a great flight up there, with a guy who seemed to drink a lot. Well, I ask you. When it came to the booze I could never have kept up with him, yet only a few hours later he was on stage, sober as a judge – not that I am accusing judges of being sober all the time of course.

Back at Clarks we had our first Crusader Board Meeting but then it was our big weekend – our wedding and Bradley's christening. George and Rina Hagon turned up with their son Paul and we all went off to Langtons House, the registry office in Hornchurch.

It was quite a brief ceremony but unfortunately my mother was too unwell but good old Dad made it on his own. All went well until we came out to find that my Rolls Royce had a flat tyre. It was a good job that my best man and Bob (my secretary's husband to be at the time) knew how to change a tyre and they had to do so before we could go off to the Fairlane Hotel for the wedding reception. We had about twenty people there for drinks and a three-course meal, but although it was clearly a big day there were other big events happening that day too.

As I have mentioned before my best man, George Hagon, a director of Palmer & Harvey the largest wholesaler of confectionery in the UK

It's official, signing the register at our wedding

Our wedding day surrounded by the whole family and many friends.

Our wedding day standing in the garden of Langtons

was also clearly a very important customer. It is always important to keep such people happy and, as I have also mentioned before, George was also a fanatical QPR supporter and they were at home to Ipswich that day. Well, business is business and that meant that we, along with Paul, were unable to stay for the whole reception.

We got through as much as we could and then left before the dessert and coffee, leaving the reception in the hands of the bride and others to enjoy. We had to get to Loftus Road and only arrived there at half time to find them losing 0-1 but what I'd forgotten in the rush was that we were not dressed appropriately for a football match. We were all suited and booted but I was also covered with confetti.

Now, we always had the same seats and the same crowd around us. I can still hear the cockney accents around me shouting, 'Well, where's the bloody bride then?' After that day I got that comment every time I went to a game and sat in our regular seats. They never forgot it and in fairness Lynn has only mentioned what happened that day on more than a few occasions as well.

Still at least we won, 3-1 with the Rangers scoring three times in the second half. When we got home the, er wives and children, had gone to bed so George and I sat up half the night celebrating both results – the marriage and the game – and about what a wonderful day it had been.

The following morning we all, with George, Rina and Paul, went to the White Hart in Brentwood, where we'd spent many Sundays, for lunch. Then it was off to St Andrews Church in Hornchurch for Bradley's 4pm christening. That too went well with many friends, most of whom had attended the previous day's nuptials, turning up before going back to our place for drinks and tea. Definitely a weekend to be remembered.

We were that close

After the events of February the year began to pan out in its usual way – trips up and down the UK but we also had another wedding in the family. Well not in ours but Chris, my secretary after Lynn, was almost like one of the family and when she and her fiancé Bob followed us to Langtons House a few weeks after Lynn and me, we couldn't have been happier.

After it we went with her family and other friends to a private hotel in Seven Kings for the reception, where I was surprised to see our South London rep Ron Wood turn up. It turned out that he had brought the couple a present from the sales force so he was forgiven for taking the afternoon off.

We also spent a lot of time visiting Aunt Doll who was ill in King Georges Hospital in Ilford. In fact we visited there most days and I know it helped Uncle Alf to have some company. It was all very obvious that Aunt Doll was not just in discomfort but in a lot of pain and she was in hospital for a long time.

There were some sad days in other directions – like when I had to rush back from Leicester when I heard that another old friend, Dickie Bowes, had passed away. He had been a real good confectionery salesman and I needed to be back to attend his funeral. On the brighter side though we had also been invited to yet another local wedding, that of Arthur Smith's (our company secretary) son.

For emotion however the night of Monday May 4th takes some beating. George Hagon and I were attending a trade show in Maidstone. We were having dinner listening to a football match on the radio and no, QPR were not playing. In fact it was Liverpool who were away to Wolverhampton Wanderers and who were losing 1-0 until the last twenty minutes and we were enjoying our food.

Then, with twenty minutes to go Kevin Keegan scored for Liverpool and that was followed by more goals from John Toshack and Ray Kennedy. It was a win that gave Liverpool the First Division title but if Wolves had kept their lead and won the game it would have been Queens Park Rangers who would have taken the title. Damn you Keegan and Co! We were that close.

It would have been an unbelievable result for such a small club but that season we had names like Gerry Francis, Stan Bowles, Dave Webb, John Hollins and big Phil Parkes wearing the blue hoops and Dave Sexton as manager. It was a feat never likely to be repeated but with the Rangers now back in the top flight of football, who knows.

The other big event that really did happen was an invitation to take part in a Confectionery Exhibition in Earls Court. We were now moving in with the big boys and I stayed in London for the week. One of our customers was Roy Hall – he of the Moscow chewing gum foresight – and he asked if Lynn, the boys and I would like to join him on holiday in Gran Canaria for a week. We did and both our sons developed an unexpected taste for chocolate – mostly because Roy was feeding them daily with chocolate éclairs. He taught me something too – how to ride a motor bike.

I'd always been nervous about motor bikes, refusing to go on them. But he was very persuasive. 'Get on the back and I will take it really easy,' he assured me. So we drove around Gran Canaria at a snails pace and I have to say I enjoyed it enough to allow him to teach me how to ride a bike on my own. I have not been on one since.

I was actually having dinner with Roy in Manchester when I got the message that Aunt Doll had died, so I was straight down to the railway station to get home. I had left my car at Heathrow but Ron Gwinnell met me at Euston and drove me to the airport to collect it. Then of course I went straight to see Uncle Alf who was in a terrible state of course.

The funeral was the next day and I have never seen anyone in such pain as he was that day. The memory of him hanging onto the coffin as they tried to take it away will remain with me forever.

Chapter 9

Man at the top

Dancing at Tiffanys

I think I mentioned in an earlier chapter that the start of seventies heralded the busiest period of my life and, looking back through my diaries (I am an inveterate diary keeper) for the purposes of this book, I can see why. From the moment I started selling Butterkist for Clarks in the mid-sixties my working days had been full and hectic.

The seventies however were more than that. They were probably the most significant years on a personal level too – years, in which I fell in love, got married, started a family and finished up as the man at the top. Yet at the same time they were also spent scurrying around the UK to make speeches, presiding over much of Clarks' expansion or flying off to exotic and dreary parts of the world in a litany of travel. While I always tried to include them, and whatever the circumstances they will always come first but Lynn in particular, and the boys too, must have sometimes felt neglected.

In justification I can claim that they have benefitted from whatever success I had, but I would still like to put it on record how much I have always appreciated their support. That too goes for the many friends I have made and kept over those years, among them Roy Hall, who I'd been having dinner with when I heard the news about Aunt Doll.

After the funeral he, and his girlfriend Reggie, came down to London for a visit. I thought we'd take them to see a West End musical and we went to see one called Itti Tombi. I didn't know that it was an almost naked African dance troupe and it was certainly unusual but we never stayed to the end and finished up dancing in Tiffany's in Piccadilly until 2am.

But it wasn't long before I was up on my travels again, this time to Cardiff to interview for a new sales rep. This particular trip stays in my memory for a ridiculous reason – I ran out of petrol on the way home. It was the sort of reason you gave a girl friend's parents as an excuse when you eventually got them back home, but this was genuine, in the middle of the night and on the M4. I didn't get home until the early morning.

At this time the idea of learning more about wine and selling it was progressing and British & Foreign Wharf's MD Arthur Taylor invited me to join him on trip to Yugoslavia. I agreed but couldn't travel with him so I flew out to Belgrade on my own a few days later, to find myself in a strange place with no foreign currency. I remember walking about five miles to find our hotel where Arthur was waiting with dinner etc. all organised.

The next day however I had an earache and throughout that night was in such severe pain that the hotel called for a doctor. After examining me he gave me an injection and advised me to get back onto a plane and go home straight away, pointing out that if it got worse the eardrum could be severely damaged and I may not be able to fly for several months.

Arthur was brilliant – he got me onto the next flight home and during it the eardrum perforated and there was lots of blood. In fact it carried on bleeding for a couple of weeks.

Future MP claims cash

Signs that Clarks was now a major force in the industry were confirmed when the Observer newspaper came to Dagenham to interview me about what had now become the biggest popcorn plant in the world – yes, we'd made it into the 1976 Guinness Book of Records. The previous year we had produced 60,000,000, yes sixty million, packs of Butterkist.

As our company biographer wrote: *'It was quite a struggle to convince Norris McWhirter of Guinness Superlatives that ours was the world's largest popcorn factory. As McWhirter himself said, one would expect the United States, the home of popcorn and with a population four times the size of ours, to have the largest factory but, after a lengthy correspondence with manufacturers over there, we found it didn't.'*

Like they say any publicity is good publicity especially when it's free like in a newspaper feature article and as General Sales Manager I suppose this all reflected well on me, as would be shown later. It all added to our feelings of confidence in the business and that year's Dagenham Town Show felt all the better for that too.

But there's always a downside to most things and in this case it was the news that my close friend, and best man, George Hagon had been admitted to hospital in Southall. That meant regular visits to that part of the world and because I knew George was partial to his drop of Scotch I discreetly took a bottle into the ward for him.

Unfortunately I was spotted by one of the nurses who wondered what it was I had in the brown paper bag. George tried to explain to her that it was for medical purposes but sadly he never managed to get a drop of it until a few months later when he was discharged, when we both enjoyed it at his place.

In fact by then he was so much better that, at a time when Brandon's school had an open day (our first experience of such an event), Glebelands had its normal fundraising party and the Butterkist Cup was run, he and his family came to stay with us.

In fact 1977 was an eventful year all round, started by the Queen who was celebrating her Silver Jubilee, while in August Bill and Ivy had their 30th wedding anniversary. We had Clarks' AGM in Dagenham, Crusader's one in the Queens Hotel in Crystal Palace and I spent the first day of an industrial tribunal in Nottingham.

Then we had Bradley taken ill and into the Nuffield Hospital overnight, being released the next day which also happened to be Lynn's birthday. A few days later it was Bradley's first birthday so we had a family and friends barbecue after which Bill and Ivy stayed the night to 'babysit' the next day when Lynn and I dashed up to Manchester for Jimmy Yates wedding. It was a quick visit – up in the morning, at the wedding and reception, then home again in time for Match of the Day. Well come on, you have to get your priorities right.

In September that year both Brandon and I started school. Well at least he started his first full time school while I went to night school. Since I was getting involved in the several aspects of the business it was thought it would be helpful for me to understand the financial side a little more. So I enrolled for an accountancy course at the Havering College.

This course was for two nights a week for a year which in itself, and given my busy lifestyle, was difficult but the homework also involved really got to me. I actually did stay the course but understood very little and, reminiscent of my old school days, failed the exam. As a consolation an old family friend Rene Pocket, who had not been well, came to stay with us to convalesce. We actually managed to keep her for six weeks because she was good with the children and it enabled Lynn and me to go out a bit more.

This in a sense was fortunate for me in particular, helping me relax at a time of great stress. Apart from my normally hectic business lifestyle, I had to make continual trips up to Nottingham where the Industrial Tribunal over the unfair dismissal was being held. I had to come back early from a company trip to Gran Canaria to go there. This went on for two full weeks after which there was no conclusion so clearly it would have to continue. It was decided that it would be unfair on the Nottingham ratepayers to have to fund the overall cost of such a long tribunal so it decided that when it reconvened, a year later, it would move to neighbouring Derby.

It lasted three weeks, a record I was told, for an Industrial Tribunal but finally they decided they had heard all they needed to reach a decision. We had to wait for the result and that seemed to be forever until we got the call, from the court originally, to say that the case against us had not been upheld and that full documentation would follow in due course.

This had been quite a harrowing experience but we had proved our point and had won our case against all the odds and against a very powerful trade union. We hoped this would be the end of it all but then we heard there would be an appeal in the High Court in the Strand. Clearly this meant to do little more than financially damage Clarks but we went along for what turned out to be less than a full day to hear that the original decision had been upheld. We were completely and totally exonerated.

On a domestic level we did have a bit of a family 'scandal' involving Brandon, these days the MP for Great Yarmouth, about this time but I don't think it's one for Private Eye or the tabloids. He had joined the Wolf Cubs and one of the conditions of the local pack was that they had to attend Sunday school so it was off to St Andrews on a Sunday morning. All the cubs would go in and sit together so I simply dropped him off and picked him up again after the service.

We weren't sure how he would react to the church thing but after the first time he said it was absolutely wonderful and would definitely go back again… especially since you got paid for going. This took us a bit by surprise of course but apparently he'd been given 10p for attending and that made us a bit unsettled. We didn't think it right to entice, even bribe, young people to go to church by giving them money and we questioned the boy a little closer.

It turned out that a collection bag had been passed down the aisle and, not being a church going family, we'd forgotten this and hadn't given him anything to put into the collection that morning. He'd never experienced this tradition and, quite innocently thinking it was what would be expected of him had taken 10p out of the bag.

Thereupon we hurried back to the church to explain what had happened and to hand back the money. As it happened they thought it was hilarious, but I often wonder how often that happens with young inexperienced children who see a bag of money passing along the aisle.

There's no business like....

About this time Roy Hall had decided to expand his, mainly based in the North, Cash and Carry business by opening one in the South and was looking for premises. Lynn and I took him and his partner Reggie out to look at houses for them to live in while they were down here.

I was always getting invitations to one event or another and receiving one from Cynthia Williams of Rank Theatres to be her guest at the Variety Club awards at the Savoy Hotel in London was clearly one to be taken up. I was in Birmingham on the day but caught a train to London and it was worth the trip. I was approached that night to become a Barker of Variety, a great honour to which I happily agreed. Then, after being proposed and seconded, I was accepted as one of the many volunteers (Barkers) who help this wonderful cause.

For 60 years the Variety Club Children's Charity has been helping sick, disabled and disadvantaged children and young people. The Club has an illustrious history stretching back to the golden age of British entertainment, raising over £200 million in the last 6 decades to improve the lives of more than a million children and young people.

We provide Sunshine Coaches, electric wheelchairs, outings to exciting places, equip children's hospitals and help in many other ways. This is made possible because volunteers from many walks of life, as well as many large companies, give their time and money, supported by a galaxy of celebrities from show-business and sport. To this day I get involved with events including the London Marathon which I ran with Brandon.

I went to collect my new company car, my first and only ever Jaguar, but a few days later Uncle Mick died. He was actually my mum's brother-in-law and owned a glass factory in the East End but he lived in Dagenham just round the corner from the plant so I often saw a lot of him and I liked him. I remember him as a very generous man who never had much money but was always prepared to give it away, especially where family was concerned.

I still grin to myself when I remember calling on him to tell him I was organising a Ruby Wedding party for my mum and Dad but telling him I had run out of money and wanted to borrow some. He was sitting in his very small council house backyard in shorts and boots when I called, and I was just winding him up. He looked up and without hesitation jumped out of his chair and said: 'No problem, son, come upstairs with me.'

Then he saw my face and realised it was me just having a laugh, but the truth was that he really would have helped had it been a genuine request. He was sadly missed by his wife and my two cousins who worked in his factory. We have a few of their 'special pieces' in our home today.

Apart from now being involved in 'show business' with the Variety Club our own business was entering one of its more frantic phases too, especially on TV. In the Glasgow TV studios with our Scottish customers, back down to Manchester for more sessions in Granada TV and then down to the West Country to Westwood TV. The trade always liked receptions but to visit TV studios made them that bit more special.

Not that it was all television. The company trip with staff and customers was to Tenerife that year, getting back just in time for the Confectionery Trade Show in Manchester, followed by the Wholesale Confectioners dinner in London and a Crusader Board Meeting... all in the same week. Phew!

On the subject of dinners we usually had our annual Clarks' Dinner in Dagenham but that year moved it north to benefit those of our staff who lived up there. We had it at the Pinewood Hotel in Wilmslow but had to head straight back down the M1 for the Trade Show at the Excelsior Hotel, Heathrow.

We had time for a quick family holiday to Crete for a week but as soon as I got back I was off again, this time to the Palmer & Harvey Exhibition in Maidenhead, the Confectioners' Benevolent Fund race night at the Connaught Rooms Tottenham Court Road, the CTN exhibition at Olympia, which meant spending a week in London, and then on to 'A Night of a Hundred Stars' at the National Theatre. Like I said – phew! When I look back to those days I wonder how we managed to get around so much.

Added to all this it was the Queen's Silver Jubilee year so there were street parties to attend, and we were invited as a family to join the British & Foreign Wharf families to see the Royal Pageant. The B&F Wharf had a prime position on the Thames by the Thames Barrier an ideal position to celebrate the Jubilee... and they had a lot of wine there too as it happens.

Del-boy... or was it Boycie?

Lynn was 29 that year, just before Bradley's second birthday so to celebrate we went with Bill and Ivy for a week in a holiday camp on Hayling Island in Hampshire, but for me it was hardly a rest. There was a national carrier strike throughout the UK and that gave us problems at work. I had to ensure our customers continued to get their supplies because we could just not afford to stop doing the business.

I had organised with our sales teams for them to hire vans locally and come to Dagenham, daily if necessary but at least a couple of times a week, to collect what product they could and deliver it to the customer direct. This meant that, leaving Lynn and the family to enjoy themselves, I had to be in the factory early every morning.

So I had to leave the camp at 5am every morning in order to be in the factory by 6.30am to supervise getting the vans away, and getting back to the camp (and our holiday) by 1pm in time for lunch. Not the greatest of holidays for me but the kids enjoyed it along with their Nan and Grandad.

On the subject of the sales team at this time we had twenty-two – 20 salesmen and two sales managers and I bought them a fleet of new Datsun cars. They were coming to Dagenham every few weeks to collect them, doing the changeover on our premises. This, of course, meant we had 22 old cars with high mileage on their clocks to sell and for a time I felt a little like Del-Boy, or his car dealer pal Boycie of course, with traders turning up at the factory to price them up and make us an offer.

We were going nuts in other directions as well because while we now had a pretty extensive range of popcorn, pre-packed confectionery and even some drinks, what we did not have was nuts. Since we were now major suppliers of popcorn to cinemas it seemed to be a good idea to sell nuts as well and as a result I was having discussions with Dimitri Marcou who had a company in Dunstable called Q Peanuts. We agreed a range of Crusader Nuts that helped expand our business even more.

At the same time I was also having talks with Ivan Gibson who's company, Impex, specialised in helping small companies like ours export all over the world. They did sell a little popcorn but an enormous amount of our Jellies and Fudge and that turned out to be a good venture for us, especially since they had tremendous experience of global confectionery exports.

On a personal level my Uncle Alf had finally come through his grieving for Aunt Doll and had met a lady called Betty who he felt he could settle down with but for me there was a much more intriguing proposal on the horizon.

The meetings with Impex were still ongoing and we were having meetings with all their staff to promote our products and explain our range more fully. This was all reported when we had a board meeting in Dagenham after which Pitt Junior asked me to give him a lift to Waterloo Station. This was a bit unusual because he usually caught a train from Dagenham but it transpired that he wanted a private chat with me. What he had to tell me made it the best lift I've ever given.

He told me that after discussions with his father and a few other major shareholders it had been decided that when Dick Whitehead retired the following year they were looking to me to take the company forward. I was being considered as the person to be the Group Managing Director

– a substantial move up and what a vote of confidence that represented. Suddenly all the hectic years on the road and in the air were paying off big time.

Only thirteen years after being taken on as a temporary relief Butterkist salesman in1964, I was not only a director but now being considered for the company's top job. Needless to say, I was on a high when I dropped Pitt Junior off at Waterloo that day, but within hours I was deflated.

I had been visiting an old friend Jimmy Grant in St Thomas's Hospital at the time and decided to pop in to see him on my way home to tell Lynn my news. I went straight to his ward and came down with a bang when I found myself staring at an empty bed. A nurse saw me and came over to tell me that Jimmy had died peacefully an hour before I'd arrived. Now I had to go home to Lynn with both good and bad news.

I don't seem to have mentioned football lately but of course being a regular I was quite well-known at QPR's ground so it wasn't a big surprise when their Chief Executive Ron Jones came to see me. The name might not mean so much these day but in the sixties he was one of our leading athletes – a world record holder in fact. In 1963 he was part of the British team that set a new world record for the 4 x 100 yards relay.

Britain's athletics captain at the 1968 Olympics in Mexico Ron won more Welsh sprint titles than anyone else, including Ken Jones, Christian Malcolm and even Colin Jackson. However after his track career he had one of distinction in football. Having spent nine years coaching the team he was appointed Chief Executive of the club where he spent another fourteen years before moving to Cardiff City, becoming the first paid Managing Director of a football club there.

When he arrived in Dagenham to see me however he was selling new boxes then being built at Loftus Road and, of course, it wasn't a hard sell. I remember being the first to place an order for a box which I kept for many years. Talking of boxes that year Clarks took a box at the Royal Albert Hall for the Miss World contest. Bit unusual for us yes, but our male customers certainly enjoyed it. We also sponsored our first match at QPR which resulted in a draw against Manchester United and for which I still have the match ball.

Vote for Lewis and Lewis

Politics is the ability to foretell what is going to happen tomorrow, next week, next month and next year. And to have the ability afterwards to explain why it didn't happen. Winston S Churchill

Well I couldn't keep politics out of the story any longer – particularly since one of our sons is a member of parliament and our daughter a local councillor. Despite the pressures of work, Lynn and I stood for election to Havering Council in May 1978. This was to be our first foray and we were soon out on the hustings.

Notwithstanding the forthcoming election, I was off on my usual January trip to Scotland but this year I had to get back home after a week because Uncle Alf was getting married to Betty and, since I had a Rolls Royce at the time, it fell to me to drive him to his wedding. It was also our own second wedding anniversary and a close friend and our company printer, Laurence Munroe decided to help me to celebrate by taking me to his Squash Club for my first ever game of squash.

Some of you might remember the old Two Ronnies sketch where the 'expert' player, Ronnie Corbett, dressed in trainers etc. and extremely sweated, found himself after the game in the dressing room with the immaculately suited and cool Ronnie Barker who had just had his first ever game and had beaten Corbett. Corbett got more infuriated as Barker insisted on such things as calling the racquet a bat and finished up smashing his racquet to pieces.

Well that did not happen between Munroe and Lewis that day though I do remember that I almost got a point. In fact he did his best to ensure I did get one but I didn't and I have never set foot on a squash court since. I much preferred it when he took me to see West Ham United... and I don't believe I just said that.

On the brighter side I went to the Variety Club Awards at the Savoy again and then to their annual dinner at the Grosvenor House, with a few QPR matches in between. Then, just to emphasise that little had changed, it was off to Stoke for the Ice Cream Alliance Exhibition, back to Derby for the continuance of the Industrial Tribunal, to London for

This picture has been reproduced from local press coverage at the time of when Lynn and I stood for election to Havering Council. Note Lynn with megaphone in hand leaning out the window of the Rolls!

the Royal Film Premier (Close Encounters of the Third Kind) and then back up to Derby.

Then on the very brighter side Lynn and I went on the company trip, this year to Barbados but it was a special occasion for another reason. As we sat on the plane with Ian Yates, drinking champagne, we were celebrating the fact that the day before we had become owners of our own home. We'd completely paid off the mortgage so generously given us by the company. Home owners with friends and family on the way to Barbados – well, who would ever forget such a day?

Back home it was back to the old routine but I will never forget one day before Easter. We often organised tours of the sweet factory for children and this day we had a group from Palmer & Harvey's staff. It was a delight to see their faces even before they got through the factory door – the salivating smell of sweets and popcorn is not one easy to miss.

I was still spending time on the hustings, so to speak. Well not actually making speeches but out on the streets of Emerson Park handing out leaflets for the council elections. I had friends out there helping me and

I was also interviewed by the Romford Recorder as well as attending numerous press conferences so most evenings and weekends we were out electioneering. There is no point in being a candidate if you are not going to put effort into it. Although I can't say I enjoyed it then as much as I would in later years.

Election Day was May 4th 1978 and while both Lynn and I stood neither of us won a seat. We went to the count that night, my first experience of many to come over the years.

After that it was down to the usual round of exhibitions, TV studios, seminars and conferences. On the subject of the TV visits our way was to throw a party at a TV studio for our customers. Then, a few days later, we would go back to meet the local TV sales force and they would go out wearing their uniforms into all the retail shops in their area selling our products and confirming that our TV commercials were about to start. It was a good and proven way of getting distribution prior to the commercials and assisting our wholesale customers.

Bradley joined Brandon at Sunday school – and this time we remembered to give them a few bob for the collection – and Lynn was thinking of changing her car. With a little input from me she finally settled on an imported Mustang, a real sky blue stunner and to be honest I think I enjoyed that car more than any I have driven. We also had an American visitor at that time – Jim Blevins, who grew most of our corn over there and we entertained him for a week or so. We also had Roy and Reggie, who were still looking for a house staying with us for a while.

More significantly perhaps Dick Whitehead finally confirmed he would be retiring which, you will recall raised definite possibilities for me. Pitt Junior, who had raised that possibility in the car to Waterloo, however took me a bit by surprise when he asked me for a 5-year plan.

A five year plan? I never even had a five month plan at that time because I was too busy thinking up how to get next month's business, let alone five years. Still, I managed to wing my way through that and anyway, what on earth was a plan, other than trying to sell product and make money? That had always been my plan for the business anyway.

I went to the Post House Heathrow to brief the Thames TV sales force. Thames was the only company that never let us host a function on their premises so we had to use local hotels. Argentina beat Holland 3-1 to win the World Cup, we attended the Dagenham Town Show and the Clarks' AGM in London with all the shareholders attending.

Then, at the end of July we took the boys to the USA for the first time, first to Florida for the Disney complex and then on a short cruise around the Caribbean. The lads of course were mostly interested in Disney World and even as adults you have to agree that there is something about the place that gives you a sense of adventure. The first sight, standing at the end of 'Main Street USA' and looking down at Cinderella's Castle is a memory that stays with you irrespective of age.

One night, on the cruise, once the children had gone to bed Lynn and I sat down on the deck and I ordered a bottle of champagne. Curious, Lynn asked why and, for the first time I told her that just before we'd left for the States the AGM had voted for me to be the new Managing Director. I'd kept it to myself for the right moment and somehow a warm night under a tropical starlit sky with a glass of champagne in hand, seemed to be that moment.

At last all the hard work over the years, all the meetings, conferences, events and effort, had paid off. I was truly the 'man at the top'.

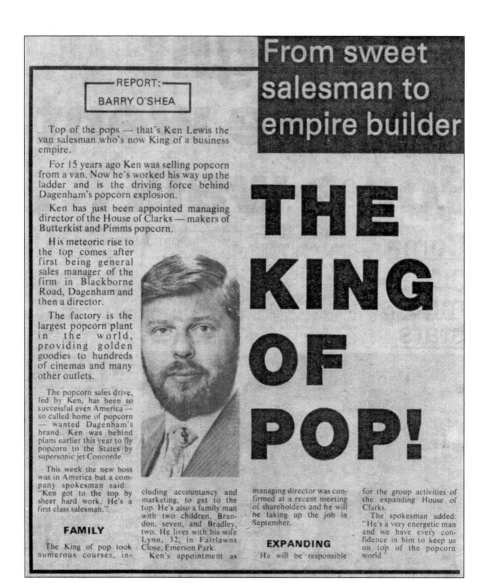

From sweet salesman to empire builder

REPORT:
BARRY O'SHEA

Top of the pops — that's Ken Lewis the van salesman who's now King of a business empire.

For 15 years ago Ken was selling popcorn from a van. Now he's worked his way up the ladder and is the driving force behind Dagenham's popcorn explosion.

Ken has just been appointed managing director of the House of Clarks — makers of Butterkist and Pimms popcorn.

His meteoric rise to the top comes after first being general sales manager of the firm in Blackborne Road, Dagenham and then a director.

The factory is the largest popcorn plant in the world, providing golden goodies to hundreds of cinemas and many other outlets.

The popcorn sales drive, led by Ken, has been so successful even America — so called home of popcorn — wanted Dagenham's brand. Ken was behind plans earlier this year to fly popcorn to the States by supersonic jet Concorde.

This week the new boss was in America but a company spokesman said: "Ken got to the top by sheer hard work. He's a first class salesman."

THE KING OF POP!

FAMILY

The King of pop took numerous courses, including accountancy and marketing, to get to the top. He's also a family man with two children, Brandon, seven, and Bradley, two. He lives with his wife Lynn, 32, in Fairlawns Close, Emerson Park.

Ken's appointment as managing director was confirmed at a recent meeting of shareholders and he will be taking up the job in September.

EXPANDING

He will be responsible for the group activities of the expanding House of Clarks.

The spokesman added: "He's a very energetic man and we have every confidence in him to keep us on top of the popcorn world."

Rather flattering press coverage of my elevation to
Managing Director of House of Clarks.

160

Chapter 9A

The Eighties

And then came Thatcher

History will show just how much Margaret Thatcher influenced the eighties, and beyond. What is beyond doubt is that when she took over, Britain was in a dire state economically and industrially.

Outdated and largely irrelevant industries had been plunged into further decline by the emergence of better technology and competition from the likes of Japan and Germany – countries who may have been defeated in 1945, but who had clearly 'won the peace' as Britain had rested on its laurels.

What Britain of the eighties needed was a 'strong man' and they found it in a woman, for Mrs. Thatcher proved to be no pushover. In her decade in office she stood up to, and defeated, militant unions and left-wing extremists as well as Argentineans on the battlefield and Europeans in the 'Common Market'.

There were early moments of national pride. In May 1980 the SAS cemented their name in history by storming the terrorist-occupied Iranian embassy in London, while in the Moscow Olympics British runners Steve Ovett and Sebastian Coe took prestige gold medals in the 800 and 1500 metres.

But the real tests were to come. Thatcher began to privatise industries like British Aerospace, Gas, Electricity and Telecommunications. She did so in the teeth of fierce opposition from union militants, particularly those such as miners' leader Arthur Scargill. We saw rioting in the streets, mainly in inner-city areas like Brixton, Birmingham and Liverpool where often it was black and white fighting each other, or violently protesting against unemployment. There was great unrest in Northern Ireland, where the nationalists and loyalists did the same by bombing and killing each other and where UK-based terrorism began to take hold.

There was a royal wedding in 1981, but that too was fated to end in divorce and disaster, and, long before things got better, the economic situation got worse with three million unemployed by January 1982. By then Thatcher's unpopularity was increasing and the Conservatives, their medicine not working, were clearly heading for defeat at the next general election. Then, in April the Argentine invaded the Falkland Islands.

Thatcher's response, in sending a task force down into the South Atlantic to do battle to take them back, stirred national pride again and subsequent victory ensured Thatcher's place in both history and in Downing Street for years to come. She became the Iron Lady, respected in Moscow and Washington, if not always in her own country by the defeated militants.

Things were finally getting better in many ways – technology and personal computers were changing not just the face of society, but of industry and commerce. Thatcher took full advantage of all that, and her new found personal strength, to prove the point. In July 1983 she won a second term as Prime Minister.

The following year the confrontations with Scargill and his militants, along with other unions reached a crisis point from which neither would back down. In October she narrowly escaped death when an IRA bomb destroyed a Brighton hotel she was staying in but her spirit remained defiant. In March 1985, after a year-long strike, Scargill finally had to admit defeat and was forced to lead his mineworkers back to work. Thatcher had won again and began to seem invincible. Slowly but surely her methods and medicine began to work, as Britain recognised the problems and took advantage of the new opportunities.

New industries, new car factories (Japanese owned), came into the UK attracted by the rewards Thatcher was offering. She did everything she could to improve business opportunities and in June 1987 set a new record by becoming the first prime minister for a century to win a third term in office – a feat only equalled in 2005 by Tony Blair, who himself has been called a 'Thatcherite' by some of his left wing opponents. In retrospect he has been called a lot worse.

It wasn't an easy transition to prosperity by any means – a few months after her re-election the stock market collapsed in a way that drew comparisons with the 1920's Wall St Crash.

But then, just as another 'Falklands' in the shape of an invasion of Kuwait by Iraq loomed, in 1990 Margaret Thatcher was forced from office, ironically not by the people but by her own party.

She had dominated the eighties, and had dragged the nation back to a position where we were no longer sneered at as the sick man of Europe. She had transformed society, and the business scene. She was never universally popular but today many believe Britain owes her a great debt and that she really had brought hope in place of despair as she had promised in 1979.

Chapter 10

At the coal face

Very little helped

Tesco's have a sales slogan that goes 'every little helps', but for years they had resisted us and did not include Butterkist on their shelves. However I remember a day when little packs of it strategically placed on a particular day certainly did help (us) – but for the moment let's go back to my new job.

I am quite proud of what our company biographer wrote in the House of Clarks '50 Golden Years' book saying it was a 'time recognition, well deserved and well earned'. He went on to say. *'Of the triumvirate of working directors Ken Lewis is architect of the company's growth pattern in the seventies'.*

'His enormous energy, his ability to communicate enthusiasm, his sales-oriented marketing expertise were the catalysts which had lifted the company's turnover from under £300k to over £1.2m in just four years. He may not like us saying this of him but it is true and he deserves a place in this history.' Well I don't mind a bit, but to go back to those early days.

Among the customers was David Trudgill of W H Smiths. He was also a dead ringer for Eric Morecambe and when he turned up a lot of our customers and staff thought it was him and he played up to it with famous dance/walk. WH Smiths in fact took no Butterkist but bought our confectionery from Palmer & Harvey, so I was intrigued a few days later when he rang me to ask me to meet him at the W H Smith bookstall at Charing Cross station. He simply said bring an overnight bag and your passport.

So at 9am there I was standing at the bookstall when I heard my name on the tannoy. 'Would Ken Lewis please report to platform 9'. I walked in that direction and caught a glimpse of David but he was standing with George Hagon and Arthur Perkins, both of whom were Palmer & Harvey. George was a director and Arthur was in charge of the W H Smith account for P&H. They all had big smiles on their faces, said the train to Dover was about to depart and we were to be on it.

Once the train was underway David opened a case, brought out four glasses and a few bottles of champagne before telling me: 'We are going to Bologne for lunch to celebrate the fact that I am opening the account for Butterkist with all our stores'. Wow! What a wonderful way to get a new account, and what an account. A nation-wide chain of stores and bookstalls, in towns and stations up and down the land. Other passengers on the train that morning, and the ones going in the opposite direction, looked on in amazement as we celebrated.

A car was waiting in Dover to take us, still celebrating, to the ferry with another one waiting in France to take us to a posh restaurant. It was a wonderful day out and it didn't finish there because I found out why I needed that overnight bag too. Back in London we went out to dinner and then spent the night at the Russell Hotel – all compliments of W H Smith.

What an introduction to my new job – I cannot think of any other experience in opening an account to beat that one, though thinking about it the Tesco one a couple of years later was a bit, shall we say 'different' as well.

We'd been trying to get into Tesco's for about seven years. They were always welcoming and we always got a wonderful reception but they did not see popcorn as part of their range. I even met Chairman Jack Cohen and executives like Daisy Hyams and Albert Swann but while they always made me welcome it was always 'perhaps one day'.

So on Christmas Eve 1982 Ron Gwinnell and I went to Tesco House in Cheshunt with a couple of white coats. It was the time of year when it was bound to be a party atmosphere, with people wandering around the reception area virtually unsupervised. Ron and I put on the coats and carried a couple of boxes of Butterkist wrapped in Christmas paper into the place.

They were big cases and we marched through reception smiling and waving to go up the stairs into the offices. There we found the Executive

Offices of all the Directors and put a single packet of Butterkist on each desk before leaving and getting out unchallenged.

Early in the New Year I got a call from Albert Swann asking me how this product had found its way into offices not open to anyone but the directors. He asked me to attend his offices immediately and I did. When I walked in he looked very serious, but then broke into a smile and said it had been a pretty clever tactic. Not only that but he went on to say that everyone who'd got the packet had enjoyed the product, so there and then I opened the account.

It had been a gamble but there was nothing to lose and Tesco became a major account selling its own-brand version produced of course by us. In fact not long after that Woolworths began selling its own-brand Butterkist, yes also produced by Clarks. Within a few years (days in one case) of my elevation to MD and Chief Executive, we picked up W H Smith, Tesco's and Woolworths. To paraphrase our company archivist that's the kind of business building architecture I like.

After the Tesco success Woolworths began selling Woolworth's Butterkist as well and with these two giants, and other chains, boosting our sales we'd already introduced shift working and by 1985 we were on round the clock production. Six days a week with Sundays set aside for cleaning and maintenance etc. When you remember we were already hailed as the biggest popcorn plant in the world its clear we had come a long way from the pre-war Butterkist days.

Sticky fingers

One thing that did change was the amount and type of travelling I had to do. There was still a lot of it but nothing like I had to do when I was selling the quality and reputation of the product. Now I had to sell the quality and reputation of the company itself, so in a sense I was at the coal face, having to deal with head office matters and company policies as well as working routines etc., that included crime and punishment.

It was one of those times when, as had happened so often, everything seemed to take place at once. I was at my first marketing exhibition as MD, at Wembley and having a Confectionery Benevolent Fund President's lunch at the Selfridge Hotel when news came through from

Dover that my Nan had died. Then, just after the funeral in Dover we had to travel north to Manchester for the Northern Candy Ball but that wasn't all – suddenly we had another potential tribunal on the cards.

On the face of it, it was a simple disciplinary matter. A male factory worker lost his rag for some reason or another with the factory manager's secretary and, physically holding her up against a wall by the throat threatened her. That meant instant dismissal of course, as it would anywhere else yet he claimed unfair dismissal and took us to an industrial tribunal.

It was clearly ridiculous and we tried, unsuccessfully, to get it sorted through ACAS but even they could not talk any sense into the man. It was another day wasted – well not even a full day because it was all over in a few hours with us winning the case.

There was worse to come but on a more positive note let me explain about Clarks Night because that was another indication on how well the company had progressed. This had started in London because as I said in the last chapter, while we travelled around the UK holding parties in TV studios for our local staff Thames TV never allowed that so we had to hold them in the Royal Lancaster hotel and they had grown somewhat.

Over the years word had spread throughout the UK about these wonderful parties attended by top show-biz stars and big company names and we were getting requests from customers far and wide to attend. So we decided to hold one single party for all our major customers and some of their senior staff who were prepared, at their own expense, to travel and sometimes stay overnight in London. We called the night Clarks Night and it grew from a few hundred guests to, on one occasion, almost 900.

It was always a very special evening with all our sales force attending, wearing blue carnations specially bought in for us at the hotel. They identified Clarks people to other guests and the champagne flowed from 6.30pm. Dinner was at 8pm and a full evening ended with breakfast at 2am with very few guests leaving before then.

On a personal level I had been approached to be a governor of Harrow Lodge School in Hornchurch and attended my first meeting in October. I was attending meetings but never got a word in.... honest. I also attended, with Chris, a seminar organised at the Post House in Brentwood and organised by the local Federation of Small Business. Its subject was 'How

Biggest TV popcorn push ever known

MORE THAN 400 people were lavishly entertained on Friday evening by The House of Clarks, the Dagenham-based makers of Butterkist and Pims popcorn.

The company had organised a slap-up dinner and dance at the Royal Lancaster Hotel, in London, to celebrate their 40th anniversary.

And it was generally regarded as the biggest night in their history.

Guests included top people from wholesale houses, retail groups, the firm's suppliers and their own team of representatives.

During the evening Mr Ken Lewis, the sales director, outlined the background of the company and explained how the goods are made and distributed.

He also disclosed some details of the advertising campaign for the coming year.

For the first time, both Butterkist and Pims are to be promoted on all the television stations. So far, only selected areas have been used.

"This will represent the largest TV campaign that popcorn has ever known in this country," Mr Lewis said.

But the presentation of the company's plans took up very little of the evening.

Most of the time was given over to enjoyment, including a cabaret with comedian Lance Percival, and a draw for 20 prizes, with a colour television set at the top of the list.

EX-INTERNATIONAL football star Bobby Moore, centre, was an "added attraction" at the House of Clarks celebration evening. He is pictured with the firm's sales director Mr Ken Lewis, and Mrs Lewis.

It's all about marketing and good PR. An example of the many press articles which regularly featured the company and its products.

to train your memory' and on one aspect Chris won in a group of 16 who were also attending the course. I forget how I did.

Anyway I had another problem. By that time business had done so well we were operating a 24-hour shift system and we began to realise we were losing too much stock from our warehouse. We had no option but to call in the police and they began to make regular visits by day and night to tour the factory with me. What a revelation that turned out to be.

As they toured the factory with me during the day they were telling me that they recognised some of the people by name – names that did not correspond with the names we had on our payroll. Clearly we had a theft problem but it got worse when they came one night.

Then they recognised a couple of female workers who they knew were single mums and had children at home. An investigation showed that some of the children were being left on their own at night while their mothers were at work.

As far as the thieving was concerned it was suggested that we should operate our own checks on people leaving the factory at the end of their shifts. So one Saturday morning, as the night shift left at 6am we struck. A group of senior staff joined me and we checked out every single member of the night shift. From memory just about every single one of them was taking out souvenirs in the shape of a quantity of various products. We had a lot of sticky fingers working for themselves, as well as for us.

This of course meant instant dismissal. Fortunately there were no tribunals involved this time and the matter was left in the hands of the police. We lost staff, among them one valuable member of our engineering staff who'd been with us for many years.

Our old Tribunal case, the one we'd won, now moved to London to the High Court where in only a few hours, we won the case again. As it happened that turned out to be a nice Christmas present for the firm but it was overshadowed by another more personal sadness, which I'd like to record here.

Our advertising/pr man Reg Powell had been a great friend to the firm, even before my time and especially to me and my career. He'd guided Clarks through its advertising campaigns, helped organise our TV studio receptions and parties. He attended our Christmas conference in 1978 and spoke well to our sales team as he always did. We had a great afternoon and a wonderful evening with him but the next day I was told he'd died in his sleep.

I'd lost a really good friend who'd helped me enormously throughout my Clarks career in so many ways and the company too had lost a good friend and important contributor to its success.

Hey hey, we're the Monkees

When I look back through the diaries that have made this book possible I wonder, not for the first time, how I managed it all. Becoming Chief Executive and MD had not slowed me down as far as travelling and hospitality was concerned and despite all that I still had to ensure I had time for the family.

Thankfully I had the help and support of Lynn, for which I am forever grateful, and so many friends along with colleagues at work and in the industry generally. Mind you Lynn and I did have our moments and disagreements as we did at Christmas 1978 when, apart from the Hagons and their regular visit, the Company Executive Lunch and Crusader Christmas Party, our visit to Wembley for 'Holiday on Ice' and the House of Clarks party, I wanted something more. I wanted to invite Roy and Reggie down from Manchester to stay with us over Christmas and she put her foot down.

We argued about it all through December with Lynn insisting it was too much and we already had people coming for the holiday. Eventually I conceded the point so you can imagine my surprise when, on Christmas Eve a quite small Father Christmas called Roy, with Reggie, turned up at our door. It seems Lynn had been organising this visit for months and winding me up. In fact he came to Loftus Road with me on Boxing Day to watch the Rangers draw 2-2 with Spurs.

There was a lot of snow and ice that Christmas and even on New Year's Eve we were out there with the boys throwing snowballs. In fact January 1st 1979 was so icy and dangerous out that we cancelled our visit to Gravesend to see a pantomime. The following day I was off on my regular UK tour – yes even as MD I did that – starting with the overnight sleeper to Edinburgh, but the journey back at the end of that week was horrendous. Trains were cancelled, no seat reservations were honoured, there was standing room only and thanks to the bad weather it was a ten hour trip.

I did get back for the RTCA (Retail Tobacconists and Confectionery Association) conference, but on 2nd February Lynn's grandad Fred died. This was in the middle of the infamous 'Winter of Discontent' when public sector strikes resulted not just in piles of uncollected rubbish but with the gravediggers on strike too. As a result it took three weeks before Fred could be buried, making it an even more difficult time for the family.

There are many who feel that the only good thing to come out of that dreadful period was the Tory general election victory in May that brought Margaret Thatcher to power. Standing on the steps of 10 Downing Street, she promised to transform Britain's economic and industrial climate. "Where there is discord, may we bring harmony. Where there is despair, may we bring hope," she said to a nation desperate for change, and she did.

In the meantime, following the death of Reg Powell, Clarks was now using a company called Downton Advertising. Tom Clark, who had worked closely with Reg, had joined that company and they were particularly good at producing trailers for cinema screens etc. Lynn and I celebrated our third wedding anniversary with a couple of bottles of champagne.

On the work front we were getting close to a deal with Docwra, the Great Yarmouth rock firm and were having regular meetings with them. One meeting went on quite late, until 2.30am in fact and they stayed overnight so we could continue the next morning. Around that time Keymarkets, who had a lot of West Ham United supporters in their ranks, held a party at the Fairlawns Hotel in Hornchurch and I was invited as a guest. It was quite close to home so I walked home that night with the Hammers current goalkeeper, Bobby Ferguson, who had also had a lot to drink.

He was Scottish so was very difficult to understand (in our condition) but he was very close to being supplanted by what was at the time a goalkeeper for whom West Ham paid a record half a million quid fee whose name I knew very well. He was Phil Parkes and the reason I knew him was because West Ham bought him from Queens Park Rangers.

Back in our own boardroom there were still meetings taking place with regard to salaries and my own future. I was trying to improve salaries of a number of our people but the times were not easy and it was in fact a difficult time. Ultimately I was given a 5-year contract so at least I had some security at last.

Not that it was all doom and gloom – there were some bright spots. We had a stand at the International Food Exhibition at Olympia when I stayed at the Tara Hotel, went to watch the League Cup Final where Brian Clough's Nottingham Forest beat Southampton and then attended the Royal Film Premiere – Californian Suite.

Then Alan Britain (our pool installer) took me to the Starlight Rooms Enfield to watch friends of his called Peters and Lee. Lennie Peters had been blinded in his younger days but was a fine singer/pianist and with his partner Dianne Lee had some chart topping records both here and in America in the seventies. Alan introduced us after the show and Lennie told us his remarkable story. Then not long after that I was in London watching Elton John and even became a bingo caller in the Dorchester. That was following the Confectionery Benevolent Fund (CBF) dinner when I talked the hotel into letting us have a bingo session to raise money for the charity in their ballroom.

Lynn's dad Bill was taken ill and had been hospitalised for about a week. We visited him every day and he was due out on Good Friday, but QPR had a home game that day so I collected him, er on the way home of course.

We were still getting involved in film and TV advertising and a small group had got together to produce a series of films about unusual products, popcorn being one of them. The leader of the group was an American actor and director called Mickey Dolenz whose name might not mean a lot to some people. In the sixties however he was the drummer in an American TV-created pop band called The Monkees.

Modelled on the Beatles they were put together to take advantage of the 'Beatlemania' enthusiasm that existed among teenagers at the time. They starred in some zany films, and they had their musical successes with hit records too. ('Hey hey we're the Monkees'.) He visited Dagenham and caused quite a stir with employees wanting his autograph.

Muddy fields

I also remember visiting the Palladium to see the Neil Sedaka show as part of the company trip but it didn't stop there because the next day we were off to New York and we were flying in Concorde. This was a business trip taking our best customers to see the cornfields that grew our corn.

From the Big Apple we flew on to Evansville in Indiana where a guy who introduced himself to us as Chuck and who managed the cornfields met us with a couple of open-backed trucks. All our luggage went into one of them while the rest of us, about twenty all told, piled into the other one. We had some of our most important customers there, most of them more used to limo or big car travel but they seemed to love this new rough and adventurous style of travel.

We were off on our way to a small town called, would you believe, Muddy. Surrounded by cornfields it had a population of around a hundred most, if not all, of whom worked in the production plant. On the way Chuck asked if we would like to have dinner at his home and, thinking that was a generous gesture, suggested we drop the group off at the hotel first. Well, I say hotel but in fact it turned out to be a rather antiquated motel.

Chuck pointed out that in fact he was inviting all of us and, thinking that was a particularly nice gesture on his part, I agreed. He then said he would stop and phone the wife, when I realised that the lady had no idea that he was inviting over twenty of us to dinner. He stopped the truck, made his phone call and came back to say 'My wife and neighbours are delighted'.

So we carried on with our journey and when we got to Chuck's house found that all the neighbours had come out to help. They'd all brought food, tables that ran from one part of the house through several rooms to the back of the house, and chairs. What a marvellous evening we had – hamburgers, sausages and a wonderful barbecue.

Apparently to have visitors from the UK to such a small place was quite an event and it was a memorable experience and wonderful example of American hospitality for us all. During the visit the local paper – it had been publishing for around 100 years at the time – came and interviewed us to write quite a story about the British visitors to Muddy.

Having arrived in the States on Concorde we had a much more leisurely trip back on the QE2, getting back to Southampton on the very day that Margaret Thatcher became prime minister. My secretary Chris was waiting there with a coach to take us all back to Dagenham.

We got our breath back just in time for the P&H Exhibition in Maidenhead and the Eve of Cup Final banquet in London. The following day we went to Wembley to watch Arsenal beat Manchester United 3-2, after losing a 2-0 lead before getting a last minute winner.

One clear winner so far however was Clarks which was clearly growing and being noticed for its success. A number of big companies were 'chatting us up' and visiting us to see if we wanted to be part of an even bigger group. We had a visit from Beatrice Foods a massive American firm with an array of food and consumer products (even Avis RentaCar) on its books. Very flattering but we decided to soldier on.

We were still looking to the future. For example, I went to Yorkshire with our factory manager to look at new packaging machinery. As yet another example of our busy social networking (which is what they call it these days) we got back just in time to take customers to see Cliff Richard at the Palladium before going off to Epsom the following day to see the Derby.

While we were still negotiating with Docwra in Great Yarmouth our core business however was still, of course, popcorn. We had always dealt with Blevins Popcorn but we were always open to competition and I agreed to see a company called Wyandot from Ohio. The name is that of one of the oldest Indian (Native American these days) tribes in the United States. Their head office was just outside Columbus and they had equally good corn to offer but at more competitive prices, so we decided to buy a small proportion of our requirements from them.

We had a family holiday in America and Canada but when we came back Lynn and I went to a dinner/dance... in London Zoo of all places. I mention it because the catering manager of the zoo, Colin Garland had become a friend and in fact we attended it for a few years. Colin always sat us down at a table of four with Mr. and Mrs. Joe Saphir, whose name will mean a little more later on in the book, but for the moment I had another problem.

I got back from a Granada TV studio lunch to find discontent in the factory because a group of the ladies who wrapped our jellies decided they wanted more money. They were already well paid, in fact they received a higher remuneration than their counterparts in our South Norwood Crusader plant, so we turned them down and they walked out.

Our staff in South Norwood however were very happy and especially with the resulting overtime so we gave it to them. The following Monday all 27 of our Dagenham ladies wanted to come back to work but we said no because we had already committed the extra production for the following month to South Norwood.

Eventually, once that contract had run its course, the staff did come back but we always wondered if there had been any union involvement in that episode. We were a non-union firm and remained that way during my whole time with the company.

Buying our seaside rock

After the 1980 Dagenham Town Show and the House of Clark's AGM I suddenly received an invitation to go to Reading for a meeting with Huntley & Palmer, a part of Associated Biscuits. It was one that intrigued me because, of course Huntley & Palmer was the company who had given me my first experience of selling on the road – until that is they'd discovered I'd been driving one of their cars while not insured because of my age.

Fortunately however there was no connection with that and I'd been invited simply because they were about to produce something that needed a corn filling. They were interested in what we used to clear out as 'wastage'. Oddly enough this meeting came at the same time we were changing some of our rep's cars and had bought nine Volkswagen Passats.

They were delivered on 31st July but not taxed until 1st August, so no one was allowed to leave the factory until after midnight. Unfortunately some of them had long journeys to Scotland, the North and to Wales but at least they were all legal and insured.

On a two wheeled level we bought Bradley his first bike for his 4th birthday while his grandad (Bill) had to go back into hospital for another operation so we are all back to regular hospital visits. In September Brandon had his first day at Gidea Park College so he was moving onto a more senior school.

Remember Trebor whose wrapping machines we'd nicked from under their nose in Italy? Well as I said before, we'd negotiated a deal with them to use the machines to package their products and now they came back for more. About this time Alan Fordham, of a building company with his name, came to see me to discuss my ideas for the refurbishment and expansion of the factory and offices.

We were still expanding the business and it seemed obvious, given the amount of land we had we could build onto the existing factory building and offices. Then we planned cladding for the outside to modernise its appearance and demolish the old offices to make room for more car parking facilities. They were ideas we had discussed with Dagenham Council and they had agreed, giving their consent.

I got a phone call from Pitt Junior saying he wanted to see me the very next day. I did wonder what that was all about but when I went into his office he put a new 10-year contract down in front of me. He said the Board believed it would be to the advantage of all of us to know I was at the helm for the next ten years. Not only did I agree without any hesitation but that contract was honoured by us both.

It was a busy time because, apart from Clarks' Night we were finalising our negotiations with Docwra and on September 27th 1981, in our Boardroom the deal was done. All their legal people, and ours, were there with accountants, executive directors and ourselves. We finally signed the documents that made Docwra part of the House of Clarks. At last we'd got our seaside rock.

In fact the very next day when I attended the Northern Confectionery

Ball in Manchester, I was quite amazed at how many people in the room already knew of the deal. Word spreads rapidly in these associations and it was free advertising with immediate effect. Great!

Another reason I remember that particular weekend in Manchester was because Ian Yates offered Lynn and me the use of his brand new Rolls Royce, suggesting we should take it to see the Blackpool illuminations, stay overnight and bring it back the next day. It was Scottish Week there and a lot of people were drinking, singing and staring meaningfully at the Roller.

We decided not to park it in Blackpool and drove it back to Manchester, checked back into the Piccadilly Hotel and returned the motor to Ian the next day before catching the train home.

But to go back to Docwra, having bought the company we went to Great Yarmouth to meet the staff etc. and also to have talks with a company called Food Brokers who had been handling some of Docwra's products. We waited for them to give us quotes to see if we could continue that business, but it also quickly became apparent that we had much to do there anyway.

Among other things there was a need to get a sensible price list because the firm was not running as profitably as we would have wished. I remember our printer Laurence Munroe (my erstwhile squash instructor) spent a whole day trying to put together a sensible price list that would take in all the products now being produced by the companies owned by the group and the Docwra situation was an important element.

In fact as things would turn out we would soon find that, having taken the company over, cash flow was difficult, turnover was not what we had expected and we were even called in to see the local bank manager. I had to put together a 20-point plan which I presented to him and that bought us sufficient time to move the company on with improved efficiency and sales.

I cannot leave that time of Docwra acquisition and problems without mentioning, that shortly after our visit to Norfolk, it was time for the House of Clarks trip for customers. This time it was on a cruise out of Southampton on the SS Canberra. Why was it so memorable, apart from Lynn and Pat Yates spending a lot of the time feeling bad, while Ian and I staved off seasickness by drinking brandy on the hour every hour?

Well, because a year or so later the ship carried very different passengers after, on April 1st 1982 (all fool's day) Argentina invaded the Falkland Islands and Margaret Thatcher sent her famous 'Task Force' down to the South Atlantic to take them back.

Among the destroyers, aircraft carriers, frigates and naval supply ships the Canberra, then cruising in the Mediterranean, was requisitioned as a troopship. Her captain, Dennis Scott-Masson who'd been skipper when we sailed in her, was told to sail for Southampton where she was quickly refitted as a troopship, sailing for the Falklands on April 9th. This time, instead of seasick and brandy-swilling passengers it was full of Marines and Paras, (some of whom I suspect would have been doing the same).

She arrived to anchor in San Carlos Water in the thick of things where other ships were being bombed and hit with Exocet missiles. Miraculously, or because the Argentine air force was more concerned with attacking the Royal Navy ships, she was relatively unharmed.

She then sailed for South Georgia where 3,000 troops were embarked to be taken back to San Carlos where they went ashore on June 2nd to claim their famous victory. When the war ended the Canberra had yet another different set of passengers, when she was used to repatriate captured Argentine soldiers back to South America before steaming home to a rapturous welcome in July. Captain Scott-Masson was awarded a CBE for his work.

Brandon, aged eleven, presenting a 'thank you' gift on my behalf to Chris Howes who worked so hard every year organising the annual Clarks Night.

David Lodge, the hugely versatile character actor, making a speech on behalf of the Variety Club at a Clarks Night in support of me as a fellow Barker

Max Bygraves performing at a Clarks Night with the Laurie Taylor Band

Myself and the sales team dressed as impoverished beggars touting for business on one of the annual Clarks Nights.

A young Brandon mixing it with the stars aged twelve at a
Clarks Night with me, Lennie Bennett and the much loved Bernie Winters

Lynn and Brandon with 'Diddy' David Hamilton

Chapter 11

Moving on

The better mousetrap

I suppose becoming the biggest popcorn company in the world made it inevitable that we would attract attention from the big American corn producers. Even more significantly, people like Michael Weaver, whose company was also very big in the corn industry in the States, were crossing the Atlantic to talk to me in Dagenham.

After all it was one of their own great writers, Ralph Waldo Emerson, who is reputed to have said 'build a better mousetrap and the world will beat a path to your door', and they were doing just that. We'd been with Blevins for a long time of course and we were also using Wyandot, but it made sense to have as many suppliers as possible so I opened an account with Michael too.

We were now in the strongest possible position as we, the world's biggest popcorn producers, were being supplied by its three biggest corn producers. Indeed the following year, after an exceptionally successful harvest, we were inundated with suppliers – George Brown of Wyandot, Hernan Delgado of Blevins and Mike Weaver all came to see me in Dagenham. It was of course a good market for us.

As far as anything else goes it remained a whirl of 'business with pleasure'. These days they call it 'networking', where socialising is seen as a major factor in actually doing business because of course friends do business with each other much more successfully than with anyone they don't know. Even small firms now have 'business breakfasts' where networking to meet others and do business is the main aim of the game. In our case it was more trips abroad or to places like the Palladium (or

Loftus Road in my case) to either smooth the way for new business or, in the case of staff etc. to encourage them to sell more product.

For me it was certainly a busy time – Tuesday was always Crusader day and Wednesday reserved for Docwra, with the rest of the time spent either in Dagenham, on the road or in the air while always ensuring time for the family. The boys were getting older and more demanding of course so Lynn and I had to ensure we both gave them the attention they needed.

I also included them in the firm's staff activities like our HoC fireworks night when, unfortunately we'd had a burglary and had the police in the factory as well as the staff's children watching the fireworks outside. Actually around that time another fine example of networking happened when someone tipped me off that another old friend of mine, Arthur Perkins, was about to be promoted to the boardroom of Palmer & Harvey.

Arthur had been handling some of its biggest accounts very successfully for a long time so I booked tickets to see the ABBA concert at Wembley. (Where their hit song 'Money Money Money' featured strongly of course). We took the Hagons and Arthur's family as well as other Clarks' members to see the show which was great and it never does any harm to strengthen such friendships.

Then there was a Miss World Contest back at the Albert Hall and the annual National Association of Boxing Clubs dinner at the Royal Lancaster. They were followed by my induction meetings for the Variety Club at the Carlton Hotel, an MCCTA dinner and then another company trip to the USA...er yes on Concorde again.

While on the subject of boxing I remember how Brandon once suggested he might like to take the sport up – an idea Lynn was not exactly enamoured with. At the time my cousins Michael and Steve were managing the Dagenham Working Men's Club and every month they staged a boy's tournament there. They suggested they took Brandon to such a night, which they did and sat him in a ringside seat where he got spattered with blood. To Lynn's relief he then decided that perhaps boxing was not for him and would stick to judo.

As I said above Wednesday was Docwra day and on the one before Christmas after taking the company over I was on my way to Great Yarmouth, having been up to the small hours making Christmas deliveries to customers. I was driving Lynn's Mustang and suddenly became tired, very tired and began to fall asleep at the wheel. I think this is something most of us have been through at some time and will know what an unnerving experience it is.

So I pulled over into a lay-by and fell sound asleep, to be woken up by a frantic knocking on the window. It turned out to be a policeman banging on it to tell me I was apparently breaking the law though I'd probably done the right thing in the circumstances. He was reassured I wasn't simply sleeping off the effects of drink and we both went on our way.

Realising I was going to be a bit late now I cracked on a bit and moved like a Mustang can, but when I got to Great Yarmouth it was to find them in the middle of an emergency anyway. They were all a bit upset because one of their engineers had accidentally cut off one of his fingers. Another member of staff had manage to find it and got it, and him, to the hospital, but it certainly put a damper on things. It also showed me what a close knit family that team was.

In fact I started a tradition that stemmed from our own long-standing one of taking our Clarks' customers to a dinner/dance, by organising one in Carlton Hotel, Great Yarmouth for theirs. Lynn and I celebrated our 4th wedding anniversary at home before taking the boys off for a three-week holiday to the USA and Mexico, getting back in time for, among other things, the Cup Final.

Then I took Lynn to a place she'd always wanted to see, Leeds Castle and no it's not in Yorkshire. It is a beautiful centuries old castle built on an island in a lake not far from Maidstone in Kent. Used in some famous films and also for some very significant (easy to make secure) conferences it has also hosted concerts by Sir Elton John, Sir Cliff Richard and even Meat Loaf. Never saw theirs but we did go to the Albert Hall, after a very nice dinner at the Ritz Hotel in Park Lane, to see Frank Sinatra.

I seemed to spend a lot of time over the Atlantic that year, holidays to the States and Mexico, then a group trip to Florida and another family one to America, this time crossing it both ways in Concorde. In fact we spent Lynn's 32nd birthday in Reno, Nevada at a Hollywood show before getting home in time for Bradley's birthday where he wanted to have his party... in McDonalds. Not a lot has changed.

La Dolce Vita

Speaking of trips abroad I must mention the 'big stag trip' to Thailand – no nothing to do with antlers, but so named because all 37 people on the trip were men. I had just been persuaded to order a Rolls Royce so was feeling good. It was quite an ambitious trip actually, organised by our travel agent Roger Felton in days when Thailand was not such a major tourist attraction as it is these days.

Indeed it was at a time when the Thai government was looking to increase tourism, so the Minister of Tourism in Bangkok was informed and we were treated like royalty. We were collected by private transport and taken to our hotel where some brand new Mercedes were available for any of us who wanted to go out. There were organised trips to the Palace and other sights and one evening we were invited out to dinner at the Number One restaurant in Bangkok, where some of us made a bit of an error of judgement.

The trouble was that we did not understand the food, it looked pretty unappetising to us and some of us, including me, left it although we did our best to explain politely by apologising and telling them it was not for us. Unfortunately they took offence. Oh, they were polite enough about it, waiting until the end of the evening and left our cars ready to take us home, but we never saw or heard from them again – they just vanished. We had obviously been very rude in their eyes, but they had been very generous in their hospitality and we had seen most of the area by then.

We hired a coach and went to Pattaya, on the east coast of the Gulf of Thailand and today one of the most popular holiday resorts in the country. Trying to keep thirty-seven blokes in such a place was not easy and some of them vanished for days at a time. Some of them even fell in love and wanted to bring their happy smiley Thai ladies back to the UK.

It was quite a memorable trip and the start of many such 'stag trips' to Thailand. To this day I am sure that the Thailand trip was a major incentive boost for UK popcorn sales.

It had no connection but after it we organised a competition with Woolworths, offering a brand new Volkswagen Polo as a prize. VW were pushing sales of their vehicles through the UK at the time and were extremely co-operative, agreeing to put a Polo into every Woollies store where it was possible. Its boot would be full of Butterkist packets and people had to buy a Butterkist and send in, to the address on the pack, their estimate of how many such packs you could get into the boot.

The winner was eventually found and the competition a great success, leading us to arrange many more such competitions after that. Clarks, Woolworths and Volkswagen – I call that networking on a grand scale. In Dagenham, where our rebuilding with the Fordham Brothers was progressing well, our staff was increasing so much that we needed a Welfare Officer. Oh yes, and my new Rolls Royce was nearly ready and I managed to get the number plate 50 HOC. (House of Clarks of course).

Just after the Clarks fireworks night and the Miss World Contest I came home to find that Mum had had her first heart attack and was in Southend Hospital, though fortunately she was discharged a few days later. On the subject of health that reminds me that part of my new ten-year contract involved an annual BUPA medical and that followed the annual Christmas Sales Conference so was probably not a good idea.

You see these conferences inevitably became quite a boozy affair. Held in West End 'bier kellers' and restaurants the wine flowed. The last evening was always spent at the Circus Tavern and, irrespective of how many were at the table I would order a bottle wine for each person. Then, everyone who drank their bottle in five minutes got another bottle and no one ever failed. So having a medical the next day was clearly not helpful.

If that was bad enough then just after the start of the New Year (1981) Lynn and I took her parents and our boys out to London for the day. The day? First we saw a film before going for lunch, after which we took them to see a show, had dinner and finished the day seeing another show. That must have been pretty exhausting for Lynn and me, never mind the boys and her elderly parents.

Talking of them just after my annual UK tour and a week in Cologne Lynn had to have a BUPA medical too and came back very upset and worried about a slight problem which needed to be monitored. We managed to buck her up a bit by taking her and the boys, Bill and Ivy, on a trip to Rome for a taste of that fabled sweet life.

We experienced all the wonders of the 'Eternal City', such as the Coliseum, the Trevi Fountains, Vatican City and all those marvellous gardens and water parks. Bill and Ivy certainly enjoyed it but the one thing they remember best of all is when they went back to their hotel room and turned on the TV. Italian TV then was showing the kind of explicit sex programmes that were never seen on British television. Yes, I think they enjoyed their little taste of 'la dolce vita', as much as our male customers had enjoyed theirs in the fleshpots of Thailand.

Even better news after we came back was that Mr. Prinn, our specialist, was seeing Lynn now about her health problem and things were looking better. A little work was needed but it was nothing serious and the worry was starting to slip away.

Houston, we had a problem!

After another family three-week holiday in the States (via Concorde to New York) Lynn and I went to collect my new Silver Spirit roller from Southend. That gave us the chance to pop in to see my parents in Westcliff, before Lynn went into hospital. She had her minor operation and was back home the next day and my hectic life resumed as normal.

One of the events I couldn't miss was Palmer & Harvey's exhibition because that year they held it in Brighton. I took Lynn with me and it was quite like old times because, you will remember, it was there of course that our life together had really begun. It was the next company/family trip however that sticks in my mind the most for a variety of reasons and not just in mine.

It began when I met up in the Post House Gatwick for a cocktail reception with a group of very important people in high profile companies, but whose names will remain a secret here. From there we flew out to Houston and on to a small place way out in the sticks called Banderra to what was called a 'dude ranch' where we planned to spend a few days.

That included going on a pony trek out in the desert and Ian Yates, whose name I can mention, decided to try to get on the right side of one of the horses by bribing it with apples and carrots. Never having been horse riding before he reckoned he would be a lot safer with a friendly horse but, when we all turned up for the trek the next morning, the one he'd been persevering with was given to young Bradley. Ian's mount that day was twice the size of Bradley's and the look on his face that morning stays with me forever, but I wasn't laughing for long.

Before we set out on our trek we were lectured on what to do and what not to do of course. The important thing to remember was that we would be riding through desert areas that are well known for snakes, so on no account should we get off our horses. That seemed reasonable advice but as we were going along one of our important guests, well Paul Hagon, lost his cowboy hat. Then, since I was at the rear of the group, I decided to risk getting off and retrieving the hat.

That was exactly the moment that Bradley's horse (he was in the front) decided to bolt and because every horse on those treks follows the one in front, they all, including mine, took off like mad while I was picking the hat up. There I was, in the middle of Texas in what I'd been told was a snake infested area and with my horse vanishing somewhere over the horizon.

It certainly caused a lot of amusement among the group. The sight of me, running like crazy behind a group of bolting horses, waving a cowboy hat in my hand and screaming 'wait for me'. It must have seemed like one of those old Hollywood Laurel and Hardy comedies or Disney cartoons but in reality this was dead serious. It took a while before the group leader managed to regain control of the horses in a safer part of the desert to come back for me.

In fact everyone except me thought it was funny and members of that group still talk of it, as well as the fact that we travelled internally with what was called then the Love Airline. All the hostesses wore hot pants and low tops while their uniforms, as well as their planes, were emblazoned with a heart. But Texas hadn't finished with us yet by a long chalk.

We eventually reached the Mansion Del Rio in San Antonio, a beautiful place on the River Del Rio where we managed to hire a float and had dinner travelling down the river. It was quite an experience and so was the next day when I took them to see the Alamo and which was very different to what we'd imagined.

We thought we'd be going out into the desert to find the famous 'fort' but when we got there it was to be dropped off outside Woolworths and next to a burger bar. Across the road was in fact the original chapel where the likes of Davy Crockett, Jim Bowie and so many others had died fighting for Texas. It didn't look much to be honest but it was historic and was definitely worth the visit.

Then it was off on 'Interstate 10' back to Houston in a convoy of cars when a tyre on one of them went flat and since we had a Mexican driver who knew nothing about changing tyres we all had to get out. This is the point where there are names I should not mention who, along with George Hagon and Ian Yates, decided they would change the tyre. Me? Well, because I am absolutely useless at doing that kind of manual job, I was standing on the freeway waving cars past while the VIPs were doing the work.

Well eventually we made it after what Ian Yates decided to call that particular adventure the 'Welcome to the Ken Lewis Crap Yourself Tour'. It was one big experience alright and by the end of it we were all very close friends.

On the boards

We did get back in time for the boys' annual medical and our customer's trip to see the Derby but it was also a pretty special time for our friends Roy and Reggie, though she wasn't aware of it at first.

Without telling her Roy had been coming down to London and Lynn had gone to a jewellers with him to advise on an engagement ring. So when we all sat down to dinner in the Piccadilly Hotel in Manchester, which I'd helped him organise and got all the surprise guests together, she was blithely content that it was simply a surprise birthday party.

She'd clearly been expecting to have dinner with someone but not on quite as lavish a scale as this and in those surroundings, but that was Roy for you. It was the way he did things. It wasn't actually until the birthday cake arrived that Reggie noticed an engagement ring on it and at that moment Roy, in front of all of us, proposed marriage. She accepted of course and at the same time I was asked to be best man at the wedding and I accepted too.

Bit more travelling then a CEA conference but back home. Now I'd taken delivery of my new Rolls Royce it was time to get rid of my old one, the one I'd 'nicked' from Ian Yates many years before. As it happened I knew a car salesman quite well – in fact at the time Jim Gregory was

Chairman of QPR and his box at Loftus Road was next to mine. He had a pal in London who dealt in high quality cars and with his help I managed to sell my old Roller at a considerable profit – never disclosed to Ian.

Brandon was ten that year and we bought him his first serious bike, a Raleigh Arena, as well as taking him and Bradley to the Palladium to see Barnum. That was good but the following week I took a group of customers to the Royal Albert Hall to see Sammy Davis Junior and he was of course brilliant. Oh yes, we all stayed at the Ritz that night.

Talking of parties I remember the garden party we had, after the Butterkist Cup final that year. A lot of alcohol was consumed at the Romford Dog Track of course and a lot more when we got home so yes, things did get out of hand a bit. For some reason we decided to throw a teenager, young Paul Hagon to be precise, fully dressed into the pool.

It seemed like a good idea at the time but we forgot that he'd not long been given a rather valuable watch and he was wearing it when he hit the water. I remember his dad standing on the edge of the pool laughing his head off while his mother Rina was screaming, 'the watch, the watch,' in that Italian accent she had. Paul was actually bobbing up and down and often all we could see was a hand, with watch attached, sticking out of the water, just like Excaliber must have looked when they threw it into the lake and the hand of the Lady emerged to clutch it.

Eventually we got him out, completely drenched and with shoes etc. full of water, but the watch was safe and that was all anyone seemed to be worried about never mind Paul. He was seventeen then but in his forties now and has never let me forget it.

It was one of the many such evenings we enjoyed and that people remember, including a lot of senior managers from the company who I think were quite surprised at the behaviour of their MD, perhaps realising he was human after all. That was a fact that would come home very painfully not long after.

Arthur and Gwen Smith's daughter Marianne was getting married and Lynn and I, along with Chris and Bob, were invited to the wedding. This was to take place after the Dagenham Town Show where I'd been moving a lot of product about and had a few twinges in my back which I dismissed as being just aches and pains.

The night before the wedding I went to bed as usual but when I woke up in the morning I found I couldn't move. Suddenly there was the most excruciating pain in my back like you'd never imagine and I found I could not even put my foot on the floor. I knew Chris and Bob were on their way to pick us up and take us to the wedding, so somehow I managed to get washed and dressed but when Bob arrived he had to help me down the stairs and into the car.

He got us to the church in Hornchurch and helped me into the back row of the pews where I managed to sit, very uncomfortably, through the service. The thing was that while the bride and groom were making their pledges all I could think of was how I was going to get back to the car and to Arthur's house for the reception.

Finally the service was over and Bob helped me to the car and, after opening the door, shoehorned me, screaming and shouting in agony into it. It clearly affected some passers-by who, seeing this big bloke manhandling someone who was screaming for help, dashed over to tell him to leave me alone. They thought I was being mugged and as Bob attempted to explain himself I slipped out of his hands and as I fell back into the seat of the car the screams got louder.

It was total pandemonium with me only thinking of the pain rather than explaining to these guys that Bob was a friend helping me out, but eventually we managed to sort everything out and get on our way to the reception. All ok? Like hell it was. By the time we got back to Arthur's house I was desperate for the toilet and of course it was dear old Bob who had to get me there. The other guests were quite bemused about all the shouting, screaming and this big bloke taking me to the toilet.

It was hard enough for Bob to get me through the house in the first place and then all anyone could see was us closing the toilet door behind us with a lot of screaming still going on. I had just about had enough and I'm sure Bob had as well and when we got out of the toilet, thinking it might help deaden the pain, I drank two bottles of white wine as quickly as I could. Whether it did or not I don't know but I certainly felt better after them and knew little about what was going on.

Anyway, with Bob's help, at the end of the evening they got this screaming drunk home. Lynn telephoned for the emergency doctor who diagnosed a slipped disc and should not have been moved at all, let alone go to a wedding. His advice was that I should just lie down on the floor. He gave me an injection for the pain which was wonderful and suggested we get a 'potty', because it would be a while before I'd be able to make it to the toilet.

Now, in those days. (Those?) I was a bit of a workaholic and fanatical about work. I had never missed a day's work and decided I wasn't about to start so I decided Chris would have to find a way of getting me to the office. So, along with the factory manager, a pair of big blokes and a couple of boards it was arranged that I would be picked up (literally) and carried on the boards into the van and then the office.

Lynn was far from amused at this idea and telephoned Arthur Smith who tried to get the whole scheme scrapped, but the cards were stacked against him. I was the MD and his boss and Chris also took her instructions from me so duly turned up with the van and the muscle. Arthur turned up as well and Lynn did her usual 'Don't be ridiculous' stuff but on my orders the guys got out the boards, put me on them and carried me to the van. They did that, carrying me into the office every day for three weeks. I was already on one Board in Dagenham, but getting into the place on two more.

I can remember that in all my working life I only ever had three days off work and two of them were during this period when even I didn't feel up to being manhandled. The other time was due to catching flu and sleeping a day away, thus missing an appointment with Fine Fare but it was ultimately sorted. I am told I was the worst ever patient.

During my time lying on my back I managed to do a lot of work from home, having some important meetings there. In fact I even managed to sell a fleet of our cars from home. It was about six weeks after it all started that I managed the family holiday, to the USA. We had been concerned that I might not get better in time but the disc went back into place and I was able to have a couple of reassuring X-rays.

We did go on the trip but I couldn't handle the luggage of course so had to have some help from porters, though the boys were also there and old enough to give a hand. We went to Palm Springs where Lynn celebrated her 33rd birthday and moved on to Memphis (Gracelands, Elvis Presley Boulevard etc.) where Bradley had his sixth. Then we moved on to that other part of Tennessee, famous for the country music scene Nashville, where we met up with other friends.

The woman in black

When we got home Lynn and I were invited to take a tour of the Rolls Royce factory in Crewe, convenient because the next day, September 12th, was to be Roy Hall and Reggie's wedding day.

As best man of course I had to organise Roy's stag night party and we ended up in a rather unusual Manchester night club where it turned out to be a ladies' 'wet T-shirt' night. This was something quite new to most of us at the time but it was interesting to watch – all I knew was that we were drinking seriously and women in T-shirts were getting soaked. I have no idea how we got back to the hotel but early the next morning I had to be up early to go with Roy to do a few chores, including some at the flower shop.

Now you will remember that I had a new Rolls Royce but Ian Yates who had been designated to drive the bride to the wedding had a brand new one. He decided to refer to mine, which would be taking Roy to the ceremony, as 'the old banger'. So Roy and I had a great day together and of course I got him to the church on time, where we waited for Reggie to arrive. And waited, and waited!

I went back out into the street because we had started to wonder if she had had second thoughts and a change of heart. Well, who would blame her? No, there she was, running down the street in her full bridal outfit carrying her bouquet with Ian running behind her. It appeared that, while the old banger had got the bridegroom to the church on time, Ian's brand spanking new Rolls Royce had broken down.

After all that however it was a lovely wedding. Roy had typically invited all his staff to the wedding, Brandon was a page-boy so of course Bradley had to be dressed up as well but outside afterwards no-one threw confetti. Not because of any church rules but because, like they say, business is business and I'd suggested to Roy's staff that they break into their popcorn stocks in their warehouse and throw that instead of confetti.

Now that really did mean mixing business with pleasure because after the honeymoon I was able to obtain a new order for new stock. I think the vicar wasn't too pleased but Roy sorted that out later and I bet the local pigeons were very happy.

When I got back to Dagenham however the happiness of a wedding

Popcorn, Butterkist of course, being thrown as confetti at Roy and Reggie Hall's wedding! I was honoured and delighted to have been Roy's Best Man

turned to grief at the loss of a friend. Well I say friend, but in truth Cecil Hugh was much more than that because in a sense I owe him everything. The fact that back before the war he actually 'invented' Butterkist, and kept it going through the war proved to be crucial for my own life as well as for the thousands of people who had jobs thanks to his drive. He'd guided the firm through its growth and had given me the chance to build a career from salesman to Managing Director.

History is always full of 'ifs' and if he hadn't done that I might never have met Lynn and we would not have had our lovely family. It was thanks in large part to Cecil Hugh that we owe our lifestyle and our success in life. As a mentor his advice was always sound and sincere and I cannot let this part of the book of my life pass by without acknowledging the huge debt I, and so many others, owe him.

I went to his funeral in Southend of course and remember that it was also the last time I saw Dick Whitehead but saddened to see how few people there were there. Cecil's wife Mary had passed on before him and they had no children or family, but there was a mystery woman there. She was dressed completely in black and I have often regretted not going back to find out who she was, but I never did. The woman in black remains a mystery.

Chapter 12

Capone, Doddy and me

Lynn's luggage went to the Argentine

Perhaps I should start this chapter with one of those riddles we all used to be so fond of at school. What's the difference between Al Capone, Ken Dodd and Ken Lewis? The answer? Doddy got away with it.

I will keep you on the edge of your seats a little longer however because, after Cecil Hugh's death the company he founded continued to go from strength to strength. We were in negotiations with Topps, the big American firm that manufactured chewing gum and candy, while George Brown of Wyandot was back in town determined to do business.

On the home front Lynn and I were still looking for schools for Brandon, this time Brentwood, and we went to Paul Hagon's eighteenth birthday party (I think he got a watch) at the Hagon's favourite Italian restaurant in Notting Hill Gate. Around this time our travel agent Roger Felton invited me to go for a drink with a pal of his called Dennis Day who came from Arizona.

Dennis, a former senior Executive at Fords of Dagenham, had moved out there on business and had found what he called one of the most beautiful areas he'd ever seen. It was a place called Scottsdale that he said was 'up and coming' and that it could be the right time to look for property there. As things turned out later in life this was interesting and proved to be correct.

Then it was time to cross the Atlantic again, a couple of times in quick succession as it turned out. It started out with a company week's tour to Rio de Janeiro, going out to different places each day. On one of them we had a small boat trip to a very small island inhabited by just one family

– husband, wife and three year old son. They were self-sufficient and needed nothing from the mainland but one of our customers happened to have a packet of Butterkist with him.

I still have a picture at home of me handing this packet of popcorn to a young boy who had never seen anything like it in his life. It was an interesting moment and it made a wonderful photo.

We went to jewellery and diamond factories and saw piranha fish in the wild, a really scary sight. Our tour guide threw a piece of meat in and it was quite amazing to see how it vanished in seconds in a feeding frenzy the like of which we'd never seen before.

We did have a problem on that trip however, or at least Lynn did because her case never arrived with us and it had her clothes in it. In those days there was not a lot in the way of dress shops around and we couldn't find much for her, but we did have some good friends – George and Jeanette Lennox from EMI – and Jeanette did have a whole range of spare clothes which did fit Lynn so we got by ok.

Her case arrived back in England a couple of weeks after we did, apparently after doing its own tour of Buenos Aires. The trip itself, our one, was actually very successful and cemented some bonds with customers who became friends, and still are.

We'd hardly got our breath (and our case) back when it was time to jet off again and how we never got jet-lagged I will never know. This time it was back to the self-styled country music capital of the world, Nashville, with a group of customers who had won various company competitions.

There were river boat cruises on the paddle-steamer General Jackson that included dinner and cabaret, and an unforgettable visit to the Grand Ole Opry to see a show there in the old Ryman Auditorium. Lynn and I had a friend, Glennise Perkins (sister of Arthur) who was living in Nashville and working with a lot of Country and Western singers. She

Waiting for a flight at Nashville Airport enjoying a delicious lollypop.

was even able to get us onto the stage – the same stage that the likes of Dolly Parton, the Carter Family and Johnny Cash, whose show we'd seen in London shortly before then, had performed on. Lynn, the boys and I were on stage, with our customers in the audience but no, the Lewis Family never got a record deal out of it.

On that trip we were staying in the famous Opryland Hotel, an experience in itself. A huge resort complex, with nearly three-thousand rooms and a glass atrium that has to be seen to be believed. Rooms with balconies many floors up can look down on this amazing giant glass covered spectacle. The hotel's own brochure speaks the truth when it says: *'Under a majestic climate-controlled atrium you will be surrounded by nine acres of lush indoor gardens, winding rivers, pathways and sparkling waterfalls. Here you can unwind, explore, shop, dine and be entertained to your heart's content.'*

It is truly an amazing place and we had a party there. Jim Blevins (Blevins Popcorn) came to meet us all and took me into the men's shop in the hotel where he bought me a bright red jacket. He felt that as tour

Family and friends pictured at popcorn Village in Ridgeway, Illinois

Learning to fire a gun in the Wild West

leader I should be easy to spot and that jacket went with me on many such tours after that. As it happened I also had a pair of check trousers at the time and the joke was that people thought I was Rupert Bear.

Then, as 1981 drew to a close it was the usual round of parties, conferences and annual dinners. I did try to make my usual Christmas trip to Great Yarmouth but it snowed so badly and the roads were so treacherous that the police were turning us back on the A12 and I never made it that year.

Lynn and I took the boys to London for the New Year, which we spent at the Royal Lancaster hotel and on New Year's Day we all went to the Victoria Palace with John 'I'm free' Inman, before going on to see the Worzel Gummidge Show. Then lo, it was 1982 – a year I am not ever likely to forget.

The Rock

If you go to San Francisco one of the highlights is to visit 'the Rock' and tour the now abandoned prison. That is something we did on a trip to the States and I remember standing outside one of the cells they used to give you the opportunity of being locked in for the experience, and wondering if that was going to happen to me when we got home.

Here, after all, was where they used to lock up some of America's most notorious mobsters, among them Al Capone. Alleged killer, smuggler and all-round gangster the only way they finally managed to cage him was on tax evasion charges and at that moment I was waiting on a decision from the British Inland Revenue that could have easily led to the same result.

It is also the answer to the riddle I set at the start of this chapter because, some years later and in a much more high profile case, Ken Dodd got a result that Capone and Ken Lewis didn't. I guess it would be flippant to add that Capone and me even had something in common because we both had the 'rock' but in my case it was only the sweet one we produced in Great Yarmouth.

In fact joking apart this was a very serious and worrying episode that began with a simple and silly error in filling in a tax form. It came at a particularly busy time (when was it never busy?) because apart from organising my Dad's 80th birthday party we were looking to tie up a deal with a South African company called Beacon Confectionery who also produced goods for Woolworths.

They were looking to get more distribution of their goods in the UK and even seeing if some sort of joint partnership deal could be worked out. However the technicalities and regulations involved made the whole deal prohibitive and, although the proposed deal was an attractive one from the point of view of some of our customers it never really got off the ground. I always regretted that because they had excellent products and was a very nice company to deal with but there was another cloud on the horizon.

I'd become involved with the Inspector of Taxes relating to some of the tax forms I'd been returning for a couple of years. It all began with quite a silly error in filling in a form yet two tax inspectors turned up in Dagenham for a meeting which also involved our Chairman and accountants. I was told off quite severely and then questioned deeply about expenses.

Because I was always very careful about keeping all the documentation relating to expenses I was able to provide them with every piece of information they asked for. As for detail, they asked me how many miles it was from my home to the office and I gave them the exact figure. 'Yes, you are perfectly right – we've just done it', they replied, showing just how much they had already gone into.

I remember them questioning the fact that I had produced a charge for a taxi fare from Bristol Station to the centre of Bristol, but they had noticed in the documentation that I was always collected at the station by my local rep. That meant that, in their eyes, I must have cheated on my expenses.

Now my diaries were (and still are), always explicit and my memory is excellent too so I was able to explain that on that occasion the rep had gone to the wrong station. Bristol does have two railway stations and he had gone to the main one in town, Temple Meads, instead of the out of town station Parkway which is eleven miles away and where I'd asked him to meet me.

You could see the disappointment on their faces when I gave them this obviously very truthful answer. They had discovered an accidental error relating to my marital status in my returns and had decided that it merited a full and detailed investigation of my whole life. It certainly turned my life upside down for about a year and it was not pleasant.

Their investigations led them to following up the question of all the trips abroad and we had to go into detailed explanations of how we organised competitions, chose winners and even taking customers abroad. They asked us for the names of the customers and the companies and we refused point blank. We told them of the danger to our company that this would cause but they retorted that such trips should be on our customers' P11Ds and that they needed to check that they were.

It was pretty evident to us that no one in their right minds would have actually done that because some of them were on the trips as our invited guests because of the positions they held in their companies. In the end we had to come to an agreement which meant we could withhold all names on the understanding that our company paid the full tax, based on estimates of whether they were simply winners on a low income bracket, or senior executives on a high one.

It took a while before we came to an agreement and in fairness the Inland Revenue did give us some time to pay the money. In a sense it was quite helpful to get into discussions about how future competitions could be structured and, although we did not have to we would pay all taxes due for those who we took away.

So we could then reassure our winners, and customers, that their trip was tax paid after coming to an agreement on the percentages of those who would be on lower, middle and higher income brackets. From then on each time we had a trip we kept a note of the value and paid an agreed amount of tax based on numbers to the Inland Revenue.

From the business side of what they termed 'tax evasion' we cleaned up the matter, but my own personal tax investigation was to continue. About that time the Inland Revenue set up a special department and all companies who had been giving incentives had to conform to an agreed structure.

While I was trying to concentrate on them the then MP for Hornchurch, my friend Robin Squire came to Dagenham to formally open our new factory and office block. Among the many guests were the Hagons who stayed with us because Lynn and I were celebrating our wedding anniversary. I was still visiting the offices of our major customers and even managed to open an account with a freezer firm called Bejam, later to become Iceland.

Robin Squire, MP for Hornchurch,
cutting the tape at the opening of the new factory

*Members of staff showering Robin, myself and fellow directors
with popcorn after the cutting of the tape.*

There were a few other bright moments, like having a party in Dagenham
for Thelma Davey to celebrate her forty years with the company, but so
much of my time now was being taken up with my tax problems during
the day and business paperwork etc. at night.

One of the positive things that came out of discussions with the
tax people (who incidentally found it necessary to stay in a hotel in
Hornchurch rather than go back to their offices in London) was that the
box we had at QPR could be a tax benefit. Yes, they must have had a
good night.

We were using the box to entertain customers at the matches but we
were told that if it was being used for business other than on match days,
such as through the working week where we could have meetings with
customers (or anyone relating to business) it could be a tax benefit rather
than a tax liability like the trips. We liked that idea and our customers
loved coming to tour the stadium and have meeting in the box where

excellent food was always on offer. I will return to the tax issue shortly but so much more was happening.

They turned a pony into a monkey

By the time I had my answers ready for the taxman I was also making a lot of changes to the structuring of the company from a sales point of view and that, sadly involved a lot of redundancies. That is never pleasant because loyalty has always meant a lot to me, but it was the result of slashing our customer base from 5,000 accounts to less than 2,000 in order to respond to the market trends and new developments.

Yes it sounds drastic but the accounts that we were closing were the smaller retail ones who only bought a couple of cases of product at a time. That did nothing to help our profit margins but it also helped the small retailers who could buy smaller quantities from wholesalers.

At that time we were gaining massive distribution through supermarket groups and the relatively new 'Cash and Carry' outlets were springing up all over the country. That meant our retailers could just as easily collect our product at competitive prices from their local Cash and Carry warehouse, leading to major reductions in our own overheads.

With the tax issue put to one side for a while as we waited for the meeting things went on very much as usual, socially, business and family. British Home Stores came to Dagenham to check on us and the same day I was invited to John Mitchell's retirement party from Woolworths where he had been a good friend, I had to go to Bristol for a meeting with Gateway Supermarkets. The day after that was Woolworths AGM in the Connaught Rooms.

Then I needed to go up to Sutton Coldfield where we had a stand at the Palmer & Harvey exhibition and that was immediately followed by the Wholesale Confectionery one in the same place so we didn't have to dismantle it.

However there was a much more important diary date coming up – 22nd May – when for the first and only time, Queens Park Rangers were one of the finalists of the FA Cup. The lads, managed by Terry Venables had had a good season having just missed out on promotion from the second division. Unfortunately their opponents that day Spurs, had won the cup the previous year and of course were hot favourites.

The omens were not good to start with because, going home the night before the Final, a car drove straight into the back of my Rolls Royce smashing the rear light. The next day a coach came to my home to collect us with a number of our customers and we were off to Wembley for the best cup final of my life.

Now I should mention that a few days later I was due to lead a trip to Israel and I always remember my friend, and our travel agent Roger Felton who was sitting next to me during the game suddenly said 'What do we do if it's a draw?'.

That would have meant a replay on the following Wednesday by which time I would have been in Israel with the group of customers on the trip Roger had arranged. I told him sadly that in that case I would have to miss the game.

Would you believe that at full time the score was nil-nil? Then in extra time Glenn Hoddle scored the 'winner' for Spurs... except that it wasn't because a few minutes later Terry Fenwick equalised for us. As the final whistle went I looked at Roger and he said: 'You want me to rebook you and the family?' I immediately said 'Yes!' There was no way I could miss QPR at Wembley again.

We all went home, had a garden party and watched the game again on TV. A couple of days later I took the group to the airport and waved them off to Israel. Five days later Hoddle scored a penalty in the sixth minute and that was the last goal of the game but the lads had done well to take the cup holders to a replay.

Getting back with the family to Israel to rejoin the group didn't turn out to be so easy either because we were trying to travel on a Jewish holiday so El Al was not flying. I had to take the family on Swiss Air to Zurich, change planes and fly on to Israel from there, where we rejoined the group and had a very good holiday. When we did get home we had to take the boys home before going straight back to London where Lynn and I were staying at the Royal Lancaster because the next day we were taking another coach load of customers and staff to Epsom to see the Derby (won that year by Pat Eddery on Golden Fleece).

When we got back from there it was to receive an approach from a well-known company called Famous Names of Bristol. They wanted to talk to us about a possible take-over, and they did come up with an offer but we decided we were doing ok on our own. Mind you we were having management meetings in Great Yarmouth where Docwra was struggling a bit and we were considering moving some of the production to our other factories.

Still trying to ignore the tax saga Brandon was eleven and we all went to the Prince of Wales theatre to see a show called 'Underneath the Arches' which was about the Crazy Gang, specifically Bud Flanagan and Chesney Allen. Dad and I had always enjoyed the Crazy Gang when I was growing up. Then the tax ogre struck.

I had my answers ready and our accountant Norman Rees had a friend called Jack Bryant who at the time was Chairman of the Taxpayers Alliance, and they had agreed to represent me. I went up to London the day before, staying at the Royal Lancaster Hotel as I needed to be up early to meet Norman and Jack because we'd been called to the Inland Revenue offices in Oxford Street to continue being questioned.

It was a very long and extremely tiring day with repetitive questions getting repetitive answers. Finally I was told that this would be the final meeting and that all decisions would be made at a later date and you can imagine how that made me feel.

This was such a petty situation and they had found no other errors or mistakes in any way and we could see how disappointed they were. They'd found either an honest man or one with brains who was there simply because of one error. Punishment, they told me, was therefore necessary and they would let me know.

In fact they kept me waiting for months – a truly dreadful period in my life. That was when, on holiday in America I had stood looking at Alcatraz and imagining what life behind bars would be like. You see the Inspector had made it very clear to me that there was the possibility of a jail sentence for any kind of Inland Revenue fraud. Though Norman and Jack tried to reassure me that the threats were over the top and could not happen, they stayed in my mind all that time until the final decision came in. I would like to use this opportunity to thank them both.

It was a fine of, would you believe just £25, but it was to be made up to £500 by what they called lost interest, although they'd found it difficult to present any form of calculation as to how they got to that figure. In

Cockney terms they had turned a 'pony' into a 'monkey' without knowing how or why they did it.

They said that if I was to agree to such a solution there would be no case to bring and thus no record. As annoyed as I was at the time I was probably more relieved so I paid them their cheque to end the whole sorry business. It was clear from the start that there had been no serious intent to defraud on my part, so why the Inland Revenue could not have been more compassionate I will never know.

Seven years later, in 1989, they accused another Ken (Dodd) with tax evasion but he took them to the high court and beat them. After it he opened his act at the Palladium with the immortal line: 'Good evening, my name is Kenneth Arthur Dodd, singer, photographic playboy and failed accountant.'

At least he could get his revenge onstage.

Goodbye Mr. Pitt

It's pretty obvious to any reader now that, apart from being a workaholic, I am also very much a 'sportaholic' too and I don't just mean my lifelong love affair with Queens Park Rangers. Perhaps in a sense it is that aspect of my life that, along with all the theatre and cinema events, that has helped me to relax from the more onerous business world I live in.

There was always the dog racing (and the Butterkist Cup) of course and the failed attempt by our printer to make me a squash enthusiast, but there was much more. I have watched Essex play cricket in Chelmsford, seen the Derby at Epsom, entertained customers at Wimbledon and sat ringside at many boxing promotions. I remember, once the tax business had been sorted, being invited by the Royal Lancaster Hotel, where we spent a lot of time and money, to be its guest at the Henley Regatta.

Naturally I went out and bought the appropriate striped jacket for the event that has been an annual one since 1839 and had a wonderful day by the river. The hotel had its own hospitality marquee sited right by the finishing line just adding to what was a wonderful experience in itself.

Talking of boxing reminds me of the time Frank Bruno asked me to look after his house and I frightened off some possible burglars. Impressed eh? Actually he, his then wife Laura and their children lived directly opposite us at the time and for some reason or other they were away and someone asked me to keep an eye on their place. That led me to doing one of the silliest things ever.

One night I saw a couple of suspicious characters wandering around the back of their house and vanishing down the sideway. It was quite late and pretty dark and without thinking about it I rushed over the road and started to walk round the back. Suddenly these two big guys emerged from the back and started walking towards me. It's quite amazing what happens to you sometimes when confronted with an unexpected situation.

For some reason I just stood there and said 'Hello'. They just said hello back, walked past me to get into their car and drive off. When they'd gone I looked round the back of Frank's house to find that while there had been some disruption it was not serious and nothing had been damaged. I guess I had disturbed them before they could cause any more problems but, whew!

On the subject of intruders, not long after Henley our friend and then local MP Robin Squire invited Lynn and I to be his guests for lunch at the House of Commons. Then we were shown into the public gallery in time for Prime Minister's Questions to watch Margaret Thatcher doing her stuff.

Shortly before that a man called Michael Fagan had made headlines by clambering over the wall into Buckingham Palace's garden one night in July. Then, having managed to elude all kinds of alarms and even staff managed to find his way into the Queen's bedroom. He woke the monarch who must have been alarmed, but who kept him talking for ten minutes until help arrived and she was rescued.

At the PMQ's we watched a lot of questions about that episode and the security levels of Buckingham Palace etc. We found it very interesting, especially as unusually it was non-political. Fagan himself spent six months in a psychiatric hospital before being released.

Back to business, at this time we were having a lot of staff meetings and making a lot of efforts to reduce our overheads. Unfortunately that was always going to lead to redundancies but, having gone through the process of modernising the manufacturing equipment, we were overburdened with staff because improved production had led to lower staff requirements.

It was a difficult time all round, especially of course for the people we had to make redundant. That included some of our sales force and I was back in my motor car trader mode selling off some of their cars, while Lynn took possession of her own new car, a Renault 20.

We had our holiday in America where Lynn spent her 34th birthday in Palm Springs and when we got home Brandon and Bradley both started school at Widford Lodge in Chelmsford. We took the boys for their first visit to the British Museum but, while we were there I got a message from Dad that that Mum had been rushed into Rochford Hospital. We rushed home to find that she'd been admitted with the heart problem again and she was there for around a week.

On the business front all roads were still leading to Dagenham with visits from Rayleigh Crawford who was in charge of selling Blevin's Popcorn and who travelled from Memphis to see us while on his European tour. I was also having meetings with an Esher based company called

Bradley's first day at Widford Lodge

Brandon's first day at Widford Lodge

Food Brokers who specialised in importing and distributing confectionery products throughout the UK.

Then Ed Nypels, Wyandot's export manager came to see us in Dagenham where we were also getting regular visits from Tesco's Quality Controller Yvonne Walker. Her visits always caused some disruption but certainly kept us on our toes and they were such a great company to deal with.

Then a very small American company called Gettlefinger made contact. They produced corn in Kentucky, an unusual area but their owner Mr.

Brandon and Bradley in their first school photo together

Brown asked if he could come and see us. He brought samples of what was the most high quality corn we'd ever seen and invited us to go to see his cornfields, which we did.

They were in a place just outside Louisville on the Indiana border called Palmyra where Mr. Brown was also President of the local bank. It was a very small village with a very small population, all of whom worked in the cornfields. Their production was also small and we could only get a container or two a year, but it was all of extremely high quality and very expensive.

Christmas that year came and went very nicely now there was no Inland Revenue spectre hanging over it and I remember during the New Year we took the boys to see Annie at the Adelphi Theatre in London and then went to St Katherine's dock to see 'the Long Ships' that were there at the time.

The year started as normal with my usual tours round the UK (and to Loftus Road) but then, on February 8th some really bad news arrived – Mr. George Pitt (Senior) and my other great mentor in the company, died. Like Cecil Hugh he had been very kind and supportive to me personally but, also like the founder of the firm, had been crucial to its survival and development.

He'd been involved, as a director of British & Foreign Wharf, when the House of Clarks was being formed, with that company being a major shareholder. It was during the Blitz however that George Pitt really came into his own when, after being 'bombed out' of its East End factory he made alternative premises available in another building he owned. Within days of the Luftwaffe doing its best to put the firm out of business, it was in production again, thanks to Mr. Pitt.

By the time I arrived in Dagenham he was Chairman with Sir Philip Warter his Managing Director and Mr. Hugh as General Manager, the three people who really gave me a vote of confidence and put me onto the promotion ladder as Sales Manager. Mr. Pitt (Senior) was Chairman of many companies including ours and he was particularly good to me during the time he was my Chairman.

He was a strict disciplinarian but he had a heart of gold and whenever I was travelling abroad always told me to take a few days as a holiday there before coming back. He was also a very generous man and losing someone who had been particularly good to me caused me a lot of sadness. I never felt that his replacement (Pitt Junior) was anything like as caring and generous and I would certainly never have the same feeling for him as I had for the man I always called 'the old man'.

I remember to this day, when he called me in to see him and Sir Philip to tell me of my promotion, the advice he gave me. 'You run a business with a fist of iron, in a velvet glove,' he said. It took a few years to fully understand the meaning of what he'd said but it did sink in eventually.

A week later we attended his funeral in the Guildford Cathedral where he was well known and where his name appears on a plaque on a front pew. The very next day was my Dad's 81st birthday and attending Mr. Pitt's funeral the day before made me realise how short life is.

Chapter 13

Chel

Have Phyllosan – will travel

After our wedding anniversary that year, which we celebrated at the Royal Lancaster Hotel with the Hagons, we took up the Inland Revenue's idea of using the box at QPR for business.

We invited a group of our major customers to come to Loftus Road for a 'Think Tank' so we could pick their brains, tell us what they thought and generally give us and our advertising agent some ideas. So it was a very professional business day with great food and plenty of wine – anything to keep the tax man happy. I remember the next day we had lunch in London with our Board of Directors and bankers. They liked to be kept updated with progress in the group, where some areas were doing better than others and I think they were impressed with the Think Tank idea.

In fact all in all it was a very tough time businesswise so when Tesco started looking at selling our product nationally it was good news all round. Yvonne Walker was back at Dagenham for them for a couple of days and this gave us a tremendous boost.

On the subject of boosts I got a personal one around that time. I was in Cheshire with some Palmer & Harvey local managers who invited me to an evening out in the Valley Lodge Hotel. I'd never been there and didn't realise that on certain nights of the week it was turned into a disco club. I'd been visiting a good friend called David Peak at the head office of Makro, a big cash and carry outfit with whom we were working on an own label product.

Now David always had several girlfriends and I'd got to know them, but I was surprised when we got to this club and walked in the door, one of them walked over to us and said to me: 'Hello Ken, how are you?'

It turned out she was the hostess on the door and my credibility among the group went sky-high even though I hadn't even known the club existed until we walked in. As I say it did my credibility no harm and nor did the complimentary drinks she sent over to our table.

Meanwhile back at home Bradley had joined a local football team so Lynn and I spent our weekends watching him but we also had an appointment with Brandon at Felsted School near Chelmsford. We looked at the school but decided against it because at that time it was boarding school only and we were not prepared to lose him from home. (Coincidentally as I write this Brandon's son, our grandson, Henry is about to join Felsted). We then tried Bishops Stortford College but that was boarding as well, so we were still looking for a school for the lad.

I mentioned Bradley's football but of course the real thing was still playing a big part in my life, even the business side because we had a sales meeting in the QPR box. It proved to be a good idea actually because it was easier for our reps to come to London than travel on to Dagenham. Even bigger things were happening at Loftus Road anyway because that was the year that we beat Leeds to win promotion to what was then the First Division.

We took some of our senior management to Wembley to see Liverpool beat Man U 2-1 in the Milk Cup final, but it was the next one that made impact.... at least it did on Lynn. As it happened Manchester United were again in the final but this time against Brighton & Hove Albion who actually drew the game 2-2 after extra time. They did get thrashed 4-0 in the replay, but cup final day itself was also my Mum's 71st birthday – and the day Lynn had her car rear-ended.

If you recall the year before, the day QPR went to Wembley, I'd had my own car, my Rolls Royce, treated in the same way when someone smashed into the back of it. How's that for a bizarre coincidence?

That year we took some major customers, wholesale distributors and some competition winning retailers to the USA and Hawaii. The retailers went direct to Hawaii but the rest of us went to the States first and then followed on to join them. It was where Ian Yates and I had a punch-up in a Pizza.

Well, it was more of a wrestling match in a way but we were arguing about who was going to pay the bill. No, no, don't get it wrong – we both insisted on paying and the argument got out of hand a bit. We fell across a table and onto the floor, causing obvious distress to other customers in the Pizza restaurant and not just to them either. The manager thought it was serious and as our highly embarrassed wives left the place a few 'heavies' were coming in to sort it.

It took some explaining and I cannot remember who eventually paid that bill but it was one of those events that stay with you and to this day the same argument comes up every time we go out with the Yates.

Back home afterwards we were working on an account for Forbuoys and an own label for Bejam but then we had a family birthday, well birthdays really. Brandon hit 12 but that meant that on the same day I hit the big 40.

When I got into the office the following morning there was a variety of presents on my desk – Grecian 2000, Sanatogen Tonic Wine and Phyllosan for the Over Forties.

Just as well because I was still travelling – this time to Kentucky and Tennessee with our works manager David Jones and Chief Engineer Dennis Wheatbread. We met up with the Gettlefinger family in their Kentucky cornfields before moving on to Tennessee where we saw corn silos before going on to see some very modern packaging equipment which would bag our popcorn quicker than our current method of manual labour.

The equipment we eventually bought was to change our company considerably for the better.

Our thriller in Manila

I suppose it was inevitable that, having cleared our name with the taxman he would be quickly followed by the VAT-man because we gave our top staff a cup of tea. Even more unforgivably we were even giving them a slice or two of toast as well.

I mean, you couldn't make this up and you have to wonder (as we did) whether this was coincidental, but the fact was that as the revenue men moved out the VAT-men seemed to move in. They were looking at various aspects of the company's operation and yes, they struck gold.

They caught us out because we were giving our senior staff in the factory tea and toast in the mornings and because we were not charging them for it, as we did with other members of staff, the VAT officers decided they were losing money. Believe it or not we had to estimate how much our senior staff, of which there were not many, would have paid for them had they not been given free. We had to work out how much VAT they would have been paying if they had been charged, and we had to account for that money.

The real cost to us was the amount of work we had to put in to guess what amount was involved rather than the paltry sum itself which we had to pay in the end. The other down side of course was that, like the tax man, once a small error had been uncovered the checks on everything else seemed to go on for ages.

No wonder our family holiday in America and Hawaii, where Lynn spent her 35th birthday and Bradley his 8th, came as a blessed relief. Got back in time to see QPR beat Arsenal 2-0 and that was a blessed relief too of course. The day after that I was off to Paris with the Panto Organisation (of more shortly) for a tour and a day's racing at Longchamps.

I remember that was around the time when George Brown and Ed Nypels of Wyandot came to see us in Dagenham on a day when we were presented with our Hygiene Certificates for the factory. Bradley, now a confirmed QPR fan, wanted to go to away games and we went to Ipswich to see our lads win 2-0.

Now sometime in the sixties, after I'd had to leave Huntley & Palmer and before Butterkist, I got a job with P. Panto, a family-owned wholesale confectionery and tobacco business. At that time Ian Panto, the youngest of the family, was working out of its Brighton depot while I was in the London (Paddington) one. We met now and then but in later years when I was with Butterkist Panto became one of my accounts all over the UK (they had many depots).

Ian and I became good friends – he would invite me on his company trips and I would invite him on mine. We had some great times in places like Thailand and the Phillipines and that reminds me of our own personal 'thriller in Manila'.

Back in 1975 'the greatest', Muhammed Ali, beat Joe Frazier to hold the heavyweight title in what has often been described as the greatest fight ever staged. It ended up being stopped in the 14th round with both men exhausted – some even described them as being close to death. It was Ali himself who had predicted it would be a 'thriller in Manila' and it lived up to its name with both fighters in hospital afterwards.

Now, eight years later I took a group of men, a couple of dozen, on a company trip to Manila where someone had the idea that we should 'ride the falls'. We would all get into boats and be taken by guides on the river run.

The Pagsanjan Falls trip is more of an adventure tour. It takes you south of Manila passing through provincial towns, extensive rice-paddies, coconut plantations and forested mountains until you reach Pagsanjan town of Laguna where the 'fun' of riding the falls starts. It all sounded very nice and when we got there it was to see extremely long and narrow boats waiting for us.

We naturally thought that about twelve of us would get into each boat but it turned out that only two of us at a time would be in them, although there would also be a guide at the front and another one at the back. We paired up, I jumped into mine with Ian Panto and we were off into one of the most horrific and scary rides one can ever imagine.

Just to show how hard it was they only let the guides do two trips a day and by the end of them their arms and legs are bleeding profusely. They have to guide the boat, at very high speeds, through dangerous rocks and you end up being taken straight through and under a massive waterfall.

I don't think any of us would have volunteered for this trip had we known what was involved and I can't remember any of my customers actually thanking me for the experience either. It was a very quiet trip on the coach back to Manila.

Still, the day we got back I managed to get to see QPR beat Birmingham 2-1 so it wasn't all bad that week.

1984

The book, and film, 1984 predicted national misery in a doom and gloom world, but for the Lewis family, apart from one brief moment involving Bradley the real 1984 had much more significance and cause for optimism and happiness. Even Bradley's moment of gloom ended in smiles.

Now a confirmed QPR supporter, he decided we had to go to Anfield to see the team play Liverpool. The club had a coach to Liverpool organized so off we went for the day but by half time the home side was beating us 2-0. This of course was not entirely unexpected – we were after all newly promoted and playing one of the best teams in the land on their own turf.

That expectation did not extend to little Bradley who had expected us to go there and win. By half time he was quite miserable, sitting there looking very forlorn and close to tears but behind us were some kindly Scousers who noticed the problem. QPR in all honesty were getting thrashed off the park and completely outplayed when one of the men behind us leaned over and tapped Bradley on the shoulder.

'Son, you should be very proud of your team and they are very unlucky to be losing because they are probably one of the best teams we've had here all season,' he smiled. As Bradley, now smiling, made a polite comment and turned away to watch the game, the guys behind me gave us a wink. True football fans and the score stayed at 2-0, but I will always be grateful to those Anfield 'fanatics' for the kindness and encouragement they showed to a small boy from London that day.

We'd celebrated Christmas 1983 with the usual round of family visits and lunches for customers and staff while Lynn and I also went to the carol services at Widford Lodge and to see the children perform Oklahoma. Mention of Widford Lodge reminds me that I was also part of the father's football team that played the annual match against the boys. We also bought the family's first computer, a Commodore 64 – however did we all manage our lives before that?

I believe I was chosen partly because I was so bad at the game, but also rather overweight. Most of my life of course was taken up with eating, drinking and entertaining customers but of course the boys, being faster and fitter than us, were always expected to win anyway.

But the real reason we entered 1984 with real optimism was because Lynn was three months pregnant. Yes, despite her previous determination that the two boys were enough and that there would be a big gap – Brandon was now almost 13 and Bradley 8 – Lynn had always wanted a daughter. Now she had decided it was worth another try.

It wasn't just her expanding either because back in Dagenham we were in discussions with United Carriers negotiating better terms because we were getting bigger, as indeed was our business with them. We were also having regular Board meetings because the chairman insisted on being more directly involved and I had to rush back from the Channel Islands where I was completing some advertising deals when our Chief Engineer Denis Wheatbread had a heart attack and was taken to hospital. But I did collect a new Rolls Royce at the end of March and having got it was also testing out a Rolls Royce Turbo which you had to order two or three years in advance.

I seem to remember that we had our first 'break in' and I was called out at 1am. to check it out but all that was missing was a few sweets and some popcorn which seemed hardly worth the guy's effort. We, on the other hand were putting in a lot of effort and I led another company trip to New York, while the Weaver Popcorn company came back to Dagenham for a visit.

We were still doing a lot of exhibitions and trade fairs of course and one that springs to mind was the Palmer & Harvey Exhibition in Sutton Coldfield I went up to after the Weaver lot had left. Clarks was really flying high by this time. Our product had become even more popular

Frank Brough taking an interest in our offerings at the trade fair in London

Michael Parkinson visiting our stand at one of the trade fairs we attended.

and in fact we were selling more than we could produce – clearly a happy state of affairs.

On the day before the exhibition closed we'd sent so many orders back to Dagenham that our Production Director confirmed that although it was only April we'd sold enough product already to keep our manufacturing units going until the end of the year. He was saying that we could not take any more orders for six months so there we were with a large sales force and a product all sold out, so I took action that made me well known in the trade.

I closed our stand down at the end of the day and, although there was another full day to go I put up a huge sign saying: 'Sorry, sold out. Gone racing' and I really did. That lived with me for the rest of my days in the industry. Anyway I went off to Newmarket, as the guest of the British Sugar Corporation, but between races I had a problem to think about – we needed to produce more popcorn.

It was an idea never heard of in the industry before but it was certainly better than having our sales force roaming the country with little or nothing to sell. Sorted!

'What the hell do you do with a girl?'

Apart from the races, night shifts and empty handed reps I also had another little and home based distraction of course. This was the rapidly approaching arrival of the new baby who we were all, especially the boys, eagerly waiting to meet but, with a week to go, was showing few signs of turning up. There was, however, time for a repeat of the Trebor 'coup'.

You will remember that was when we went to Italy on a previous occasion to look at some new packaging machinery and was told that Trebor was already considering buying them. So we immediately bought them ourselves and then signed a deal with Trebor to package their goods with the same machinery we'd 'nicked' from under their nose.

So, keeping my fingers crossed that Lynn and the new baby could hold on a little longer I flew with our Factory Manager to Milan with onward travel to Bologna and the offices of Carle & Montinarie. They were famous for their expertise in the manufacture of wrapping machines and we were aiming to be more competitive with wrapped jellies as we were hoping to supply 'own label' goods to big manufacturers.

We felt that if we could improve the speed of wrapping we could become more competitive than other manufacturers, who would then find it cheaper for us to produce their goods for them. When we arrived at the factory I happened to spot a couple of executives from a major UK confectionery manufacturer who I knew and for whom we were already producing.

I also saw evidence of their produce on the desk of an office we were in and subsequently found that they were considering buying the same machines, we'd come to view. Deja Vu. That would have meant not only that we would have lost our account with them but they would have been more competitive than us. I asked the obvious question – had they purchased any of the machines yet?

To our relief the answer was that they hadn't but had gone back to the UK to report to their board and would be coming back with a decision later. We looked at the machinery ourselves, realised its worth and I instantly ordered a number of the machines on the basis that we would be the only UK company to buy them for a year.

They said it would probably take that long to produce all the machines anyway so, not needing Board approval, I immediately signed a deal on the spot. This deal made a significant difference to us in the wrapped jellies business. We could not only speed up production but reduce our prices and takeover most of the market, which we did. We became famous as a jelly manufacturer, producing for companies far larger than ours.

Got back and dashed home of course but still there was no sign of the new Lewis, so I went straight off to Beccles to visit Europack – another manufacturing machinery company who were making another part that would be needed for our jelly production. Then from there to Great Yarmouth to see Docwra's bank manager, but it was difficult to concentrate with what was happening, or rather not happening, at home.

On June 8th I took Lynn to the hospital where we were told that all was well and the baby should arrive in a day or two. A couple of days later, after having a family lunch and then relaxing in the garden in the afternoon I heard the magic words from Lynn – 'Take me to the hospital'.

At 8.52 that evening a new baby, and this time a girl, joined the family. While once again I helped to deliver her I have to admit I was a bit shocked. I had always wanted boys for the simple reason that I knew, at least I thought I knew, how to handle them. You give them a ball, they kick it around and years later you take them to football matches in places like Loftus Road, but a girl?

'What the hell' I thought, 'Do you do with a girl?' I was truly shocked and concerned about how I would handle a girl in the family. Having said, or rather thought, that it was probably the biggest mistaken thought processes of my life because a girl in the family tempers things down a touch.

Yes ok, she never wanted to kick a ball and sadly showed not the slightest interest in QPR, but she was born at the most perfect time of my life. As you will read later I was able to make the sort of time to spend with her that I never had with the boys. The day after she was born Brandon had to sit his final exams but I picked them up from school and took them to the hospital to meet their new sister.

Of course there were mixed feelings – a little girl was different in many ways and I'm sure they were thinking the same i.e. she will not kick a ball. They were both excited and happy about it however and we never had any problems with a girl entering the family. After it, well... (Sorry Chel, joke honest).

Lynn's favourite photograph of the children

So now we were a family of five and I must say it was definitely fun buying warm and cuddly pink toys. We all integrated very quickly and it wasn't long before it seemed like Cheralyn, the name we'd decided to give her, had always been with us.

Back at the office the next day the staff organised a 'Wet the baby's head' buffet party. Shame Lynn missed it because it was a really good do, but then I picked the boys up again and took them to see their mother and new sister. Then Chris and Bob took me out for a drink or three and Lynn missed that too, but personally I was having a great time.

We, or at least me, were all doing a lot of celebrating during that period of course as well as visiting the hospital. I went for my annual BUPA medical and was told that despite being a new father again, I was fine. Then I took my Mum and Dad to the hospital to see their first (and only) grandaughter before, on the 15th June I brought Lynn and Cheralyn home.

As it happened, a couple of days later it was Father's Day. Then ten days after Chel (as we were already calling her) was born, it was my and Brandon's turn to celebrate our birthdays – his 13th and ...er mine.

It's the way he tells 'em

It was on his birthday (and mine) that Brandon received his exam results and it looked as though he was headed for Bishops Stortford College. Well, at least he had been accepted and we toured the school but it was boarding and that bothered both Lynn and myself, but me more than her. I just couldn't bear the thought of passing one of our children over to others during the week.

It was clearly apparent when we arrived at Widford Lodge for the Father's Cricket Match, when the boys are given a bat and the dads one cut in half. We arrived there straight from the Bishops Stortford College and the headmaster (and owner) Henry Witham could see I was concerned and spoke to me about it.

'You are not the sort of family to board a child and it will not work for you. On Monday morning I will make a call to Forest School, where I am sure Brandon will be accepted and will not have to board,' he said. A good high quality one, Forest School is near Woodford, close to Epping Forest itself and his words changed everything. My whole world changed for the better and we all went home for a barbecue to celebrate the birthdays and Brandon's exam results.

The following week Henry Witham was as good as his word and made the calls. We visited Forest School where Brandon was accepted and in September he started there.

Other than that life went on as normal. We were now regulars at the Essex County Cricket Club, where in June we watched them play the West Indies. The great Viv Richards got 60 in his second innings, while the even greater Graham Gooch scored 101 in his first one in an exciting match that ended in a draw after the three days. Then I flew off to Dusseldorf to see some Bosche equipment we needed in the factory, but I was back the same day to see the new night shift start up.

It was a busy summer that year (when wasn't it?). Mum and Dad had their 49th wedding anniversary, we were visiting the Forest School where Brandon was about to start, and we attended Chelmsford Cathedral for the Widford Lodge Leavers service. When the school restarted Bradley would be going there on his own instead of with his brother, but in the holidays he started at Camp Beaumont in Brentwood.

We also had a new greyhound by then, a bitch called Miss Popcorn so we were visiting the kennels again at weekends. She had her successful third trial at Romford. While we were preparing for our annual Clarks' Night at the Royal Lancaster it was Lynn's 36th birthday. In the years we've been together she's celebrated her birthday in some pretty exotic locations – well this year we did it at the Romford Greyhound Stadium.

Bradley had his ninth birthday weekend that summer so the choices of entertainment that year were his. First it was to the London Dungeon, then to McDonalds, followed by an Indiana Jones film and dinner at the PizzaHut. The next day saw us at the Tower of London, a boat trip on the Thames, back to the PizzaHut for lunch, the Guinness Book of Records Exhibition in London and then another film, Supergirl. Whew!

In September there came a sense of sadness when Bradley went back to Widford Lodge without his big brother – the first time they had been apart. But then, after a quick trip to Manchester for the Northern Candy Ball I was back in time for us to go to Loftus Road. It was a memorable game with plenty of goals that day as well with the result ending up at QPR 5 Newcastle United 5.

Cheralyn was christened on September 23rd and a lot of our friends and customers came to that, after which we partied all afternoon and into the evening. Some of them stayed the night – the Hagons having their usual room – but early the following day I was back in Dagenham for a morning meeting with the Bejam Freezer Company to view our production while in the afternoon I was off to the Trebor head office.

Hernan Delgado from Blevins arrived for a short trip and joined us in the Royal Lancaster for our Clarks Night. He was not used to the sort of evening/morning entertainment we provided and was pleasantly surprised at the tremendous support the company got from the industry. On the Monday he was back in Dagenham discussing terms for future purchasing from his company.

I took a group of our major customers off on a quick trip to New York. We had a few nights in the Big Apple before flying home on Concorde in time to take the boys to the circus in Chelmsford. The Popcorn Institute of the USA was back in Dagenham but we had a bigger problem at home because Bradley began to complain about not being well.

It was the start of a long process of elimination to find out what was actually wrong and what the problem was as initially the doctors could find nothing seriously wrong at all. This was to continue, coming and going, for a while.

I went to stay at the Royal Lancaster for the International Confectionery Exhibition 1984 and in the evening went for dinner and a drink in the bar. In there I was introduced by the manager to a quite famous Irish comedian called Frank Carson. His style was a quick-fire delivery of gags with his infectious catch-phrase, 'It's the way I tell 'em'.

We had a few drinks together and he told me that later he was due to go to the ATV studios on the South Bank to be a guest on the Gloria Hunniford Show. He invited me to go with him because, since I had a car there, it would save him on taxi fares. I rather liked the idea so agreed.

Now off screen Frank was exactly the same as he was is on it and in the car he never stopped talking, mostly all gags. On the way I said I'd phone Lynn and she didn't believe I had Frank Carson in the car so he took the phone off me and started talking to her. He actually went through his act – the same one he was planning to do on the show. It took the whole journey after which he asked her what she thought – I think she was still too busy laughing to tell him.

On arrival we were ushered into a lounge from where I was able to watch the show. I saw him go through the same routines he'd given in the car and, though I'd obviously heard them previously, they were just as funny. It really was 'the way he told them'.

We then went to a pub near the studio and we spent the rest of the evening and into the early hours with a bunch of people who had recognised him before we headed back to the hotel. It was one of those unplanned yet memorable evenings and Frank is sorely missed after passing away, aged 85, in February 2012.

Nicholas Parsons with Mum, Tony Blackburn with Dad at a Clarks Night

Chris Howes and me with Nicholas Parsons at Clarks Night.

Terry Neil, the Arsenal Manager, who generously brought the FA Cup trophy to Clarks Night. He seems more interested with what's under my grass skirt

Clarks Night with Trevor Brooking, Lennie Bennett and Nicholas Parsons

Lynn and I at a Clarks Night. I wore the same style of suit but of different colours for many a Clarks Night!

Bobby Moore, Captain of the England World Cup winning team of 1966 with Lynn

Chapter 14

To buy or not to buy
(That is the question)

Boys will be...

The day after my unforgettable Frank Carson experience I went home to find things not so laughable, especially with the boys. We got a call to say that Brandon had broken his arm at school so I had to go to collect him and take him to hospital. It wasn't a serious break but quite nasty, but then we got home to find that Bradley wasn't too well either and was in bed for reasons we could not understand. He was well enough however to come to see QPR with me at the weekend.

Not that it was an entirely relaxing weekend anyway because, partly to mark our Company Secretary Arthur Smiths' retirement, we took a group of staff and customers to Folkestone... on the Orient Express. We got back to London just in time for me to catch the last train to Manchester for another trip up North.

When I got back from there it was to another meeting, this time in Chelmsford to the Essex Cricket Club ground, where we were negotiating a sponsorship agreement. At home Brandon still needed treatment for his arm but he also had a problem with a toe and had to go into hospital for a minor operation. We got him home just in time to go to Wembley for a Barry Manilow concert.

Bradley, on the other hand, wasn't getting much better with no real improvement in his lethargic manner, just lying in bed with no real evidence of symptoms. We had a good friend, a private doctor called Michael Kehr, and we asked him to take a look at the boy. He agreed and asked to be left alone with Bradley for an hour and he cracked it. He found that Bradley was struggling, trying to cope with being at a different school from his brother.

Since he'd started school they had always been together and it appeared that the separation was affecting him. That seemed to be the outcome of all the worries we were having with him at that difficult time and we decided that we would have to see what could be done about changing his school. That opportunity came quicker than we'd expected.

It was getting near Christmas and the usual round of lunches, dinners and other events were soon in full swing. I remember one unusual one when a friend of father-in-law Bill, Arthur Green, took me to what was called the Eccentric Club, and it was all of that. There were lots of celebrities present and you are always asked not to talk about it, but I had a Bishop on one side of me and comedian Les Dawson on the other.

More to the point re Bradley however I'd setup a meeting with Henry Witham, the head of Widford Lodge, his school. I had intended explaining Bradley's situation to him but as it turned out there was no need. Henry was a very astute and charming headmaster who straight away said to me: 'I know why you are here'.

'We had an agreement that if I took Brandon into my school you would bring Bradley. Brandon has gone and now you are going to ask me to release you from the deal and my answer is absolutely yes. I think it is the right thing for him to move to Forest and I will give him a glowing reference.'

There are times in life when people sometimes shock you and this was one because it was obviously not to Henry's financial advantage. However he did have a strong feeling for children and while this wasn't an easy thing for him to do it was his natural instinct to help a child and a family. As things turned out he was as good as his word and early in the New Year we took Bradley to Forest School to sit his entrance exam – after on New Year's Day he'd seen QPR beat West Ham 1-3 at Upton Park. That cheered him up a bit too.

Then it was back to business and the 1985 annual UK tour, popping back from it for the Retail Confectionery dinner/dance at the Royal Lancaster and to take Bradley for his interview at Forest School. That done it was up to Leeds to the ASDA head office to open an account with them before back to London for my Dad's 83rd birthday and our wedding anniversary when I took the family out to dinner locally.

Our Irish agent had retired and the new one, John Peadon came to Dagenham for a meeting and to pick up all the items he needed to do the job. Clarks was now recognised in the USA as a major importer and to prove it I was invited to a party in the U.S. Embassy in Grosvenor Square. In fact one of our American suppliers, Ed Nypels of Wyandot, was back in Dagenham. At the time I was also having a lot of meetings with various TV companies, including TV AM, Central TV, Anglia and Yorkshire, with whom we were planning major TV advertising campaigns.

All that pressure might have been the reason I was forced to take my one and only 'sickie'. We had been exhibiting at the International Food Exhibition at the Olympia but I had to rush back because Mum had been taken ill again and was back in hospital. Then it was my turn to go down with a temperature of 102 degrees and that day off sick – but just the one, because I was up the next day to complete the ASDA deal in Leeds, followed by the Royal Film Premier of the latest James Bond film, 'A view to a kill'.

The good news was hearing that Bradley had been accepted at the Forest School so we were off to get him fitted for his uniform. Then, after attending the Essex Cricket Club dinner at the Heybridge Hotel in Ingatestone (a lovely old building now demolished and replaced by a housing estate), it was off to the USA again for the family holiday and, boy did I need it.

We didn't cross the line

We were back by April 29th, just in time for Bradley's first day at his new school, and now reunited with his brother of course. Then it was back into the usual routine of visits, dinners and events – first a dash to Sutton Coldfield for a week at the Palmer & Harvey and Wholesale Confectionery Association Exhibition, followed by a more relaxing weekend with the Hagons visiting. We had a pleasant day watching Essex playing in Chelmsford.

We were building up for the next company trip because this time we were doing something different – we were going to South Africa, a very different country from the one we have now.

When we went there Nelson Mandela the man who would, without bloodshed, ultimately take the country from apartheid to what he called a 'rainbow nation' had been in prison for many years. Things would not change for another ten years and until then the black population was still being suppressed, often brutally. There had been many riots, particularly in Soweto, over the years and when we touched down in Johannesburg that danger still existed and it didn't take us long to fall foul of apartheid.

Our coach collected us at the airport and, after a short while, everyone decided they needed a drink so we stopped off at a bar and walked through... the wrong door. There were two doors and it was quickly apparent that we'd come through the wrong one, because we were the only white people on that side of the bar. Incongruously, to those of us more used to ordinary bars and pubs, the only other white thing there, apart from ourselves, was a white line down the middle of the place.

There was no one at all on the other side and we were quickly redirected to it but not by simply crossing the line. No, we had to go out of the bar into the street and go back in through the other door where we found ourselves in the same bar but on the right side of the line. I think that for the first time we realised how difficult it must have been to be living in South Africa, whatever your colour, at the time.

We were actually on our way to Sun City, sometimes called the South African Las Vegas because of its casinos, gambling and revue shows which had often attracted major stars even of the calibre of Sinatra, Queen and Rod Stewart. Termed a 'resort city' it's in Bophuthatswana, which had been set aside as a 'black homeland' under apartheid and was allowed to set up the gambling casinos etc., not allowed in other parts of the Republic.

I have no idea why but on the way we were taken to see Soweto, a real hotbed of anti-apartheid activity. Then, as if to demonstrate the fact, a brick came through the window and we left rather hurriedly.

One of the problems was that we were seen as white South Africans at a time when there were a lot of problems and that happened several times but, as soon as we spoke with British accents, they were sorted. In fact on one occasion I even had to deliberately lapse into the Cockney vernacular of my youth and that worked too.

Eventually we arrived at our destination, a major golfing hotel in Sun City and were able to relax, even getting in some days on safari. Some of the areas in that part of the world, with wild animals roaming the plains and its picturesque landscapes, are absolutely stunning. To see leopards, lions, elephants, rhinos and buffaloes in their natural habitats along with herds of zebra, wildebeest and antelope is about as moving and as exciting an experience as you will get anywhere in the world.

I have been back there since and know why so many other people get drawn back to the plains of South Africa, especially now that apartheid no longer applies there. It was a wonderful experience and we all got back safe and sound.

In fact we got back just in time for Bradley's first Forest School Parents Evening where everything was good and where the boy himself was clearly happier than he had been. I remember that the MP for the area, Norman Tebbit, was there to open the new Pavilion and Sixth Form Centre.

Then, after some meetings with Central TV about an advertising campaign I was in the Royal Albert Hall for a boxing tournament before going to Loftus Road. No not this time to see QPR, because it was in June and the season was over of course. On this night the place was packed with Irishmen to watch an Irishman become a world champion.

On a warm summer evening Barry McGuigan took on the Panamanian world featherweight champion, Eusebio Pedroza and after what were described as 'fifteen pulsating rounds' (fifteen rounds was the usual length for a title fight in those days), took the decision. At one stage in the fight Barry even had the world champion on the canvas and at the end of it there was no doubting who would get the decision.

He held the title for three fights before losing it but twenty years later was recognised as one of the greats by being inducted into the Boxing Hall of Fame. To this day McGuigan is still at the fights but ringside usually commenting on the big ones, but I was there the night he became the best in the world. In a sense he crossed his own line.

Actually quite a sporting summer that year with Wimbledon and The Ashes tour but it was also Cheralyn's first birthday, my Uncle Alf's 65th, Brandon's 14th... and mine. We took our senior staff to Wimbledon in the year Boris Becker won his first and Martina Navratilova won her twelfth titles.

Then I went with George Hagon to Essex to see them play (and draw with) the Australians, to Newmarket Races with the Williams & Glyns Bank. We were more involved with Essex, who got through to the Benson

& Hedges Cup Final at Lords that year but were beaten by Leicestershire. Let's not forget the Butterkist Cup at Romford dog track either.

Oh yes I also fitted in another trip to the USA to see the cornfields and machinery suppliers that summer so I needed our family holiday in Bermuda, albeit being a disappointing one. It was wet, windy, pretty dull and very expensive. Our room was damp and we were very uncomfortable so I was racing around local travel agents very quickly.

Eventually they got us onto a flight to Florida which suited everyone, especially the kids as we were based at Disneyworld. Much better and we got back to watch the first game of the soccer season when QPR beat Brian Clough's Nottingham Forest 2-1. (This was to be the season when we not only beat Liverpool and even Manchester United but lost the Milk Cup Final 3-0 to Oxford United).

Still, it was nice to sit down to a quiet dinner at home to mark Lynn's 37th birthday.

Hi Bali!

A much more cheerful Bradley had his tenth birthday, so we all went for a day in London – Wendy's for lunch, Police Academy 2 and then to Loftus Road to see QPR play Arsenal. Unfortunately we lost 1-0 but Bradley was given presents from the club as well as a birthday cake so that made up for losing the game.

I remember it mainly because of what happened the following day. Because we were now a club sponsor we were allowed one, or two, days to actually use the ground to play a cricket match. We did have a company football team but not a cricket one but I was allowed to 'guest' for the Palmer & Harvey team when they played Britvic Drinks who were also sponsors.

So it came to be that I actually walked out on the 'hallowed turf' that, even apart from visiting English and foreign captains had been trodden by some great England captains. The legendary Trevor Bailey, Keith Fletcher and Graham Gooch, while still to come after me were the likes of Nasser Hussain and Alastair Cook.

All of them great batsmen, in Bailey's case an all-rounder, so I had some pretty impressive records to live up to and it was a wonderful experience. Sadly, for me, it only lasted a couple of minutes.

Not to worry because the following week Miss Popcorn won a race at Romford Stadium and I was home in time from Manchester where I attended the Confectionery Benevolent Fund dinner dance, to see QPR beat Birmingham 3-1. The following week I was there to see them beat Liverpool 2-1.

We had a company trip to Barbados for our major accounts and that was memorable for what never happened. First one of our rep's wives got so badly burned on her foot that Ian Yates had to rush her to hospital while Brandon suffered as well because he refused to keep his T-shirt on. We'd actually taken Lynn's mum Ivy on the trip to babysit but she was having such a good time dancing to the hotel band with our customers that we had to do our own babysitting. Lynn, aware that on our return she would be going into hospital decided to take a daredevil dive into the Caribbean from the deck of the Jolly Roger tour boat.

In fact on our return she went into Hartswood Hospital for a hysterectomy and was there for ten days, coming out again just in time for Christmas – that time of the year when all wives and mothers can relax of course. Seriously she recovered sufficiently enough to enjoy dinner dances and to see Freddie Starr at the Circus Tavern. We also took the children to the Palladium to see Cinderella with Des O'Connor and Dame Anna Neagle.

Ian and Pat Yates spent the New Year at the Carlton Towers but came to us for New Year's Eve to see 1986 arrive. We saw Aladdin at the Cliffs Pavilion in Southend and went off to Cologne for a week to attend the ISM exhibition, getting back in time to see QPR beat Liverpool (again – they were the days) and for Lynn to pick up her new car.

It wasn't all fun and laughter at that time however because I'd been working very hard to get the Iceland account and at home Brandon and Cheralyn both went down with German measles. Then, although we beat Chelsea 6-0 on Easter Monday we went on to lose the Milk Cup final 3-0 to Oxford United. Even worse we then went on to lose 0-5 at home to Spurs and Brandon needed a hernia operation – it never rains but it pours eh?

At the time I had to be in Birmingham for the Palmer & Harvey exhibition so I was in Penns Hall for that by day before driving back home to visit the boy in hospital and then back up the M1 to Birmingham again. I did that for a few days but thankfully the operation all went well and he recovered well.

Domestically I suppose what helped cheer him, and the others, up was the visits we were getting from companies about satellite TV, something fairly new in 1986. We ended up with a great big dish at the end of our garden and a remote control almost as big in the lounge, but it did let us watch a few channels that we'd never seen before.

Mum had her 87th birthday and I was also invited to the retirement party of my good friend in Tesco's Albert Swann. He'd been a leading member of the Tesco team from its earliest days and was an absolute gentleman who I was going to miss working with.

My passport was taking its usual regular airing of course and we flew out to Singapore on a company trip. All went well and we stayed there for a few days before flying out to Bali, that magical island made famous by the musical South Pacific. We were all looking forward to arriving there when, on the plane, one of our guests – Julian Soundy, a Palmer & Harvey manager suddenly noticed an article in a flight magazine that caused problems.

It said that if you did not have six months left on your passport you needed a visa to get into Bali. Julian did not have six months left on his and let's not forget we were in the air already en route to the island. We were all confident that, with a dozen men on board, no one would notice and we would just go through unquestioned. Certainly our travel agent, Roger Felton, who was with us, was sure there would be no problem, so we relaxed a bit and when we landed we tried to sail through Immigration. Unfortunately there was one very bright and intelligent immigration officer on duty that day.

He spotted that Julian only had a few months on his passport and therefore would not be allowed in and he was taken to a separate room. Then a loud voice called out asking who our tour leader was and I told him it was me, whereupon I was told to go to another room, which Roger and I did.

There it was explained that it was necessary for Julian to have a visa to get into Bali and since he did not have one the whole group would have to go back to Singapore. It would not be right, proper, or exactly clever, to explain what happened then but we did manage to get Julian a temporary visa and we all went on to enjoy our stay in Bali.

'For a Chairman, you seem to know nothing.'

In recent years, with all the banking problems and issues making the headlines, the Royal Bank of Scotland (RBS) has been taking some stick. As far as I am concerned however it played a major and very positive part in the lives of me and my family and I will always be grateful to it.

Thanks to its advice and help – indeed to its initial push – I bought the company I'd started with as a salesman, selling Butterkist off vans (in the City as it happens) for a shilling a box commission. It's a long story but ironically it does have some similarities with a Burns Night celebration when, awash with booze, I was encouraged to apply for the job of Sales Manager. This one did have Scottish connections (RBS) though had nothing, apart from the drinking aspect, to do with Burns Night except that this time I was urged to buy the firm, of which I eventually became MD.

At the time I, along with some of my senior management, was getting a little frustrated at the way the company was progressing but I only owned around 17percent of the shares. It came to a head when our Chairman George Pitt (Junior), Company Secretary Arthur Smith and I were invited to an annual lunch meeting with some RBS directors.

We spent the morning discussing new plans for the business and then had a very nice lunch in the boardroom where we drank far too much. One of the RBS directors was a very good friend (then and now) called John Dickson, a man I have mentioned before. John could hold his drink and in that sense he won't mind me saying nothing has changed but he'd also realised I'd been running the business while the Chairman was getting all the credit.

To be honest I'd never had a problem with that, even though Pitt Junior and I had never been over friendly. I had always been quite happy for him to take the plaudits as long as I was taking the money but towards the end of the meal John started asking Pitt some serious questions about the running of the business.

'What sort of turnover do you have with certain major customers?'

he asked, whereupon the Chairman referred him back to me for the answer. John asked a few more similar questions and the same thing kept happening. In fact he was being a bit mischievous and started asking questions about the manufacturing process, which I also had knowledge of and was again needed to answer them.

He moved on to questions about where we got our corn from and how the cornfields worked. Same thing and now John used the 'killer' question. 'For a Chairman you seem to know nothing,' he said quite rudely and, since then I have realised, clearly deliberately.

Pitt was more than a bit upset and decided it was time to leave so he stood up and with Arthur (always an ally of his) stalked out. That left me sitting there, slightly embarrassed but still drinking, with John Dickson. He turned to me and said: 'Look here Ken this is really your business, for God's sake why don't you just buy it'.

He explained that since I'd been mainly responsible for the growth and profitability of the company since becoming Managing Director, whereas other members of our board had not played a significant part. I began to get the feeling that this had been at the heart of things during the whole meeting and that Pitt Junior had been deliberately provoked by our bankers.

Staggered at the suggestion, I told John that I had no funds for that sort of thing whereupon he said 'We will deal with that.'

That set in motion the extraordinary events that would lead me to becoming the owner, or at least the major shareholder, of the House of Clarks. In a drunken stupor it seemed like a good idea – well what's a couple of million quid or so between friends – and it was felt that Charterhouse, the investment arm of RBS, might be able to help.

Sidney

As things stood at that moment I held just 17percent of the House of Clarks share while my other senior management held none but over the next few weeks John Dickson took me to some financial institutions in the City. First of course we went to Charterhouse, but they did not see a popcorn company as being worth their investing a couple of million pounds.

Chris and Bob Howes at a Wimbledon day out

But George Pitt, the major shareholder, decided the company was worth £3m – an absolutely ridiculous assessment and definitely over the odds. In fact he did not want to sell anyway and was not best pleased with me at the turn of events. Now I had the bit between my teeth but could not see anyone lending us that sort of cash.

I did try Charterhouse with the new figure but, as I thought they would, they confirmed they would not be progressing with the deal. That was a shame because it had been RBS who had come up with the idea in the first place.

There was a lot going on outside Clarks – it was birthday time again for Brandon who was 15 (and me, who was older) while my parents celebrated their 51st wedding anniversary. On the down side we had to watch England being beaten 2-1 by Argentina (who went on to beat West Germany 3-2 in the final) in the World Cup, but we did manage to get a group onto the Centre Court at Wimbledon.

Obviously though the situation at Clarks was now taking up most of my time, even though Pitt's figure of £3m was a major setback to getting the cash. Hence I was feeling pretty low when I went to Essex County Cricket club one day and someone told me about a man called Alan Reagan who managed a NatWest bank in Brentwood. I was a bit sceptical because managers of local branches were not really the sort to be dishing out the millions of pounds I needed, but I had nothing to lose so went to see him just the same and what a good job I did.

He shook me somewhat by telling me that he not only knew the company and had been alerted to the situation but could see serious potential. He confirmed a local bank would not be financing it but NatWest did have an investment arm called County NatWest. Even better he knew the man heading it up, Sidney Donald, and was prepared to give him a ring.

To be honest I'd heard it all before because at that time I was literally going around the City with a begging bowl and getting nowhere. Then, out of the blue, Sidney rang me. He said he liked popcorn and Butterkist in particular and thought it was quite an unusual venture so was sending 'a young lad' as he described Alastair Gibbins down to Dagenham to see me.

We struck lucky because Alastair came out of the Heathway railway station and as he walked down Blackbourne Road he could smell the popcorn. Something about his visit (and we'd said he was a potential customer) clicked and he suddenly liked the idea of his bank investing in popcorn. It was easy to see that he was excited about it all but he was still just a junior and though his report to Sidney was going to be favourable I didn't hold my breath.

Yet early the next day I got a call from Sidney saying: 'We like the idea, we want some figures, another meeting and one with your lawyers.'

Now that last request did present a problem because obviously I could not use the company's lawyers who were all loyal to my Chairman and the Pitt family. I asked John Dickson and also Tony May who used to handle deals on behalf of RBS. He told me I needed a top flight lawyer skilled in handling management buy-outs. He recommended one called Peter Wayte because RBS had lost a few major deals to other companies thanks to this man.

Peter worked for a company called Wilkinson Kimbers and Tony May urged me to contact him. Eventually, and it did take some time, but on July 16th 1986 we met and it proved to be one of the luckiest days of my life. He was interested in what I had to say and was actually specialising in the kind of deal I was looking for, so he agreed to handle it for me. It also resulted in my gaining a lifelong friend because Peter has been that now for over 25 years and has helped me through many ventures, some of which you will read about.

Speaking of friends, back in the real world around that time I lost a close one in Ray Hancock. A golfing fanatic he always said he would die on the 18th hole and he did exactly that, dropping down dead on the 18th hole of a golf course and I had to attend his funeral in Loughborough. Then I went to Wembley to watch a neighbour of ours, Frank Bruno, fight American Tim Witherspoon for the WBA version of the world heavyweight title. Frank put up a great fight but in the 11th caught one on the chin and went down in a corner, needing the referee to step in and save him further punishment.

Back to Clarks and by this time three other senior members of the management team – Chris Standing my PA, factory manager David Jones and his deputy Chris Day, were all involved with me. They didn't have money sitting in the bank but wanted to be part of the deal. Chris Day borrowed everything he could from his dear old Mum while the other two took out mortgages, or second mortgages, on their homes. I did have a little money in the bank and was prepared to take out a mortgage too but we needed to come up with 10% of the money to get 70% of the business.

A friend indeed

It was a mountain to climb but this was too good a deal to miss out on, so the thought of borrowing was already in my head when I got a call from my bank to say that a quarter of a million pounds had been lodged into my account. Very fortuitous and I was tempted to say thanks, but this must be a mistake. I told the bank it could not possibly be me and that they must have another Ken Lewis account holder. They asked me if I knew any one called Ian Yates and that stopped me in my tracks.

I said that I did and that he was one of my closest friends but what had he got to do with it. It turned out that Ian had put that money into my account without any discussion or reference to me or anyone whatsoever. Not unnaturally I called him to find out what he was doing. His reply will live with me forever.

'There is no way you are going to risk the family home, because I don't

think Lynn would be very good on the streets. The money is yours and I
don't wish to discuss it. One day you will pay me back, but it will be as
and when you are ready. Now go and buy the company.' Just how do you
describe a friend like that?

It made things possible and we now had the 10% of the £3m required,
a top lawyer working on our behalf and a great investment company in
County NatWest behind us. Battle commenced and meetings were going
on all the time now, many of them in Dagenham of course with others in
the City, for this was now seen as a hostile management buy-out.

At the same time it was necessary to keep the company not just
running but doing so profitably because the bank wanted to see figures
on an almost weekly basis. It was a never-ending series of producing sets
of paperwork and I would be off to the City at 8pm to 9pm at night and
on many occasions working through the night. I can see from my diary
how many times I was ending up back in Dagenham at 5am/6am, going
home for breakfast and then back again for a normal day's work.

There were many times when I was left wondering whether or not it
was worth it but Pitt was putting up a fight and I could never resist that.
For us it was win or bust. We either had to win this deal and buy the
company or we were all probably going to be looking for new jobs. It was
a big risk for all four of us.

By then of course the atmosphere in the Dagenham boardroom was
pretty bad as you would expect and some shareholders were sticking
together and they had a higher share ownership than I had. At one point
Ian Yates was even threatening to fly out to the Bahamas, where one of
our shareholders lived, in an effort to help us gain share advantage but in
the end it was decided to simply make the offer.

Charterhouse reappeared, now clearly interested in the deal, but while
warning me that it was a lot of money to be repaid for a small popcorn
house. They were absolutely right of course but we were now in a major
battle for our own futures as well as the company's.

In fact we were getting closer to a deal all the time and our buy-out
group had an all-day meeting at Wilkinson Kimbers before going back
to County NatWest for a late lunch. I remember that day having to rush
back for Bill and Ivy's 40th wedding anniversary at the Cherry Tree in
Rainham. Meanwhile Bradley had joined the Essex Cricket Club School

in Chelmsford but I was in need of a break and we decided to go to Minehead for a week with the family to celebrate Lynn's 38th birthday.

We were still there for Bradley's 11th but it wasn't much of a break for me because I was continually making calls to the lawyers and banks, partly for more information but also to keep in touch with the business. I needed to get back and on the Saturday we did – just in time to see QPR lose at home to West Ham and for the Butterkist Cup that night. It wasn't much fun for the others because all we four could talk about, even at the garden party afterwards, was the buy-out.

The Hagons stayed overnight and George and I sat up half the night talking about it and when he was telling me how much his company would support us if we were successful.

More figures were needed and since none of us was particularly good at that some meetings were set up with Touche Ross the accountancy firm. Now we were meeting with some pretty serious financial people who were trying to put together some future projections based on our figures – figures best described as being, as they say, on the back of a fag packet.

I remember leaving a meeting in the City to go to the Royal Lancaster just around the corner for a meeting on Clarks Night but most of our time was taken up with Wilkinson Kimbers, County NatWest and Touche Ross. I broke away one day for a BUPA medical but then went straight back to the City for another all-night meeting.

By this time our Chairman had taken on his own lawyer Charles Good, I think from Slaughter & May. My God they were tough to deal with, so we had some serious opposition always arguing about money and the best deal available for the shareholders, particularly the Chairman of course. But at last we were clearly now moving in the right direction and we had a Board meeting in Dagenham to discuss the deal.

I had to break away for the Northern Confectioners Ball in Manchester and then back to the Clarks Night 86 when over 800 guests attended. Finally however, we had reached the stage where the Chairman and his family had agreed to sell their shares and it was time for them to pull out.

It looked as if we had fulfilled all their requests relating to what I consider was the over-value of the company but at least the Chairman felt he'd obtained the best possible deal for his shareholders. It had been a long and hard year and we were all exhausted but on October 16th 1986 the day came.

An enormous room filled with bankers, accountants and lawyers, along with us was where the deal was signed, sealed and delivered. The House of Clarks was ours and at long last we were the masters of our own fate. We owned 70.1% of the company with County NatWest holding the remaining 29.9%.

I thought it had been hard enough getting a deal with the bankers, who of course wanted to earn out of it, but then trying to buy the company off the owners had been a killer and between them they'd nearly killed us all. But now, at last and with the help of some very good friends (one in particular of course) and the patience and support of my family it was ours. I owned the major share in the company I'd joined as a van salesman selling popcorn in the City (as well as East and West London) in 1964.

We celebrated on the Hispaniola, a riverboat on the Thames near Westminster that night and then I took the family off to Orlando.

Presenting flowers to Lynn Lodge. Her actor husband David, a fellow Barker, attended many Clarks Nights

Lennie Bennett with Mum and Dad

Lynn and myself with Bobby Moore at one of the Clarks Nights.

In the latter years the annual Clarks Night would see 800+ guests

What an honour to have Henry Cooper attend one of our Clarks Nights.

Bobby Moore with Lynn and me

Clarks night with Terry Neill and Tony Blackburn

Henry Cooper with Lynn and myself at Clarks Night

At Clarks night appearing with Roxy Rollers
and congratulating Trevor Brooking on his wedding anniversary

Chapter 15

The sweet smell of success

All roads led to Dagenham

What followed our, now well publicised in the City, management buyout was perhaps, in many ways more astonishing than the events that had led up to my three colleagues and I actually buying the House of Clarks. For months I had struggled, fought, pleaded and begged for help with the financial institutions to raise the £3m price figure that Pitt Junior had put on the value of the firm.

Until the intervention of County NatWest had made the deal possible all those efforts had been frustrating and unsuccessful; but now all roads seemed to lead to Dagenham and they were packed with eager buyers brandishing cheque-books and goodwill.

Possibly the fact that we were in the Guinness Book of Records as the world's biggest popcorn plant had been forgotten by those who turned a deaf ear to our pleas for the cash. Perhaps we'd been seen as just a scruffy and tiny 'backyard' operation in East London by those who could not be bothered to properly explore the opportunities we were offering at the time. Suddenly the buyout seemed to be a wake-up call for a lot of people.

Frankly I don't know, but after the buyout I took Lynn and the children off to Orlando for a well-earned rest and to get away from it all. Fat chance – Fedex and DHL parcels were arriving there for me every day, but it was all good news. Then, when we got back I went off to Leeds to tell ASDA and Poundstretcher that it was now my business and it was amazing how attitudes had changed.

Suddenly they were talking to the actual owner and in those days the trade in general appreciated being able to do business with an individual who could make immediate and on-the-spot decisions. It was also good to be able to talk to the staff back in Dagenham to enlighten them on what had been happening. They'd been aware for a long time that something was going on, because of the consistent movement of strangers in and out of the building and our own long absences.

The bad atmosphere and hostility that had existed in the boardroom between the Directors by then, was pretty apparent in the workplace. There was even one occasion when Pitt Junior tried to get a colleague of his to come in and run the business in my place, but the staff had turned out at the gates and I had to warn him not to enter the premises. It became quite a nasty situation but it would not be fair to go further here, other than to say that it demonstrated that the staff were behind us and trusted us to look after their best interests.

Now we were back to normal, or so we thought. In fact news in the financial and industrial world of our deal had alerted a lot of people and suddenly all roads seemed to lead to Dagenham for those who wanted to buy us out. I spotted one local competitor, who had a number of businesses including one producing popcorn, sitting in his Jaguar outside our gates spying on us. I went out to see them but, realising they had been rumbled, they drove quickly away. Then they invited me to the Savoy for lunch.

I was a touch excited by that because I assumed they were going to ask me to take over their popcorn business. They had a lot of companies and popcorn was just a small part of their group and the possibility arose in my mind that we at Clarks could instantly get bigger, so I went to lunch with three of their directors. Contrary to what I'd thought however, they were not interested in selling their popcorn business to us, but to buy ours.

Admittedly they would have given us a good, almost immediate, return on our investment, but then I told them how much we'd actually paid for Clarks. They quickly dropped their offer and backed away. They implied I must have been looking through rose tinted glasses to have parted with such a large amount of cash for such a small company. However that did not prevent their leading investor coming quietly to my home to try to persuade me to be part of his group, offering me a slight profit on my own share of the investment and it had been a nice lunch.

Back in the real world Lynn's Auntie Ethel had died so we had another funeral to attend. Then I remember a meeting with Peter Wayte (Wilkinson Kimbers), Sidney Donald (County Natwest) and Touche Ross to wind up the final details of our deal, when I left early to go to Forest School to watch Bradley play football. Family things were just what I needed at that time to bring me back down to earth.

In the meantime we now had to establish a new Board of course and on November 6th 1986 I officially became Chairman of the House of Clarks – the 'van boy had done good'. That night my cousin Michael took me as his guest to the House of Commons for dinner with his local MP. The new board directors, along with their partners/wives/husband etc., had a party at our home to celebrate our owning the company.

There was one lesson in Chairmanship I learned about that time. Sidney Donald, now a director on behalf of County NatWest of course, was late for our first meeting so I delayed it until he arrived. Far from grateful he said: 'You never start a board meeting late, no matter who is not there. You always start on time'. It was a lesson taken note of and well learned. Sidney was never there when we started meetings after that but he was an absolute gentleman who helped us in every possible way.

One last memory of that time is when, just before Christmas, former chairman George Pitt (Junior) invited us to

Ken Lewis, Chairman and Managing Director, House of Clarks

dinner for a farewell drink. We'd never really hit it off as much as I had with his father but it was probably the right thing to do. After all we'd made him, and his family, a lot richer so I suppose he felt pretty good and perhaps a little triumphant knowing what he'd achieved for the shareholders. For our part we still felt we'd had to pay too much but we'd done so knowingly and the drinks that evening were short, but it ended on a more reasonable note.

It didn't last!

Roots and Krugerrands?

Actually even apart from what had happened in Dagenham I was having a pretty successful time in other areas too. Miss Popcorn, for example – the best greyhound I ever owned – won me my first (and only) trophy and that stands in my snooker room to this day.

We went off to Forest School for drinks and to see Brandon on stage in a play and then took all the staff's children to a pantomime. I was even being wined and dine by Touche Ross at the Dorchester and, it being

Here I am collecting the winners trophy at Romford Dog Track when my Greyhound, Miss Popcorn, came home in 1st place

Christmas, we had the Hagons visit, the Executive Christmas Lunch and my first Clarks AGM as company chairman. Not a Christmas and New Year I will easily forget.

Being Chairman never altered one thing however, and that was my annual UK tour and heading off to Scotland. Then, on the way home I stopped off to pick Bradley up from Sammy Lee's house where he'd been staying for a few nights. Sammy, one of England's greatest footballers with 14 caps at senior level, left his home town club Liverpool to join QPR and we'd got to meet, and like, him through our club.

He had a son the same age as Bradley and since they knew almost no one in the South of England, Bradley would often go and stay with them. It was exciting, especially for Bradley of course to be on such good terms with such a great footballer and his very nice family. I have a feeling these days that Sammy is on the England coaching staff.

In fact the day after I picked Bradley up was the Football Writers Award dinner and we always had tables for this event at the Savoy. Then I had an RCTA dinner at the Royal Lancaster before going to Cologne for a week – a very special week – at the IFE (International Food Exhibition). That year Cologne was very different from usual, thanks to 'Cotton Candy'.

I had been contacted by an American firm in Chicago called Stacey International who had developed a product they called Cotton Candy but which we knew better in the UK as Candy Floss, that wonderful sugary pink confection 'spun' onto a stick. No fairground or seaside resort was complete without someone selling candy floss and I suppose in one way we would be going back to our roots because of course it was in Southend – a real candy floss 'kingdom' – before the war that Cecil Hugh had first launched Butterkist.

But I digress. Stacey International had developed a process through which their Cotton Candy could be supplied in an airtight aluminium bag. It kept fresh and could be sold on the counter, taken home and when you opened it, you were eating candy floss. This form of it had never been seen in the UK and there was something about the product that intrigued me, so I'd agreed to take a few sample cases and put them on our Cologne stand. We were amazed at the response.

Almost immediately the Hancock 'cash and carry' organisation ordered a container load and that was followed up with a massive order from Woolworths – then still a global phenomenon and a fixture on every

British High Street. The problem was that I had no idea whether or not I could tie up supplies from Stacey, because all I had agreed to was a few sample cases for the Cologne show to gauge reaction. We had no agreement or contract with them and definitely no right to sell, but here we were flooded with orders for the product.

I had to think very seriously about our next steps and, while I was with the family watching the Sootie Show, my mind was not exactly on the puppets.

The IFE moved to Olympia in London and again we showed the Cotton Candy. Once again the response was unbelievable, confirming that we had an opportunity to move into a totally new area, if we could only be appointed sole UK agents for the product.

I contacted Stacey International to find I would need to deal with a man called Bill Daniels but he was tied up for a week at the Candy Convention in Las Vegas. As it happened, Ivan Gibson, MD of Impex who handled our exports was also heading out to Las Vegas for the same event. One of his colleagues, David Green who was particularly helpful to us in Cologne had also spotted the response we were getting to Cotton Candy there.

We had agreed that if we got the rights to import the product into Britain, Impex could handle further exports into Europe and even worldwide. I was on our stand at Olympia discussing the extraordinary response we'd got from the product and the Impex potential with some of our board members when they urged me to leave, pack and get on a plane for Nevada that day.

Before doing so I made contact with another friend, a coin dealer, and bought two gold Kruggerands from him. I also had a document, on our official paper, typed up which simply said 'Contract between the House of Clarks and Stacey International' at the top, with a space at the bottom for signatures.

Then, armed with my 'contract', coins and an overnight bag I took off on the first available flight I could get onto. It was an Air New Zealand flight to Los Angeles where I transferred onto another plane for Las Vegas. There I checked into Caesar's Palace and headed immediately for the MGM Convention Centre where I found Ivan Gibson who pointed me in the direction of Stacey International. Finally I met with Bill Daniels, and his partner Mike Hornton and we agreed to meet up and have a drink that evening.

So, sitting in the bar of the MGM later, I explained that I had put their product on show in Cologne and London and believed we had an opportunity, with the help of Impex, to sell a lot of their product in the UK, Europe and the wider world. I told them I would do so if the House of Clarks was the sole agent to import their product into the UK. To my surprise they didn't bite my hand off.

They had realised we were quite a small company and that all they had done was ask us to show their product as a favour. My explanation about the type of companies, especially Woolworth which of course did mean something to them, who had shown tremendous interest and had offered me vast quantities of orders persuaded them to take us seriously.

A few drinks later and we'd agreed a deal when I said we would need a contract. They looked a bit surprised and asked what I had in mind and I confirmed I had actually brought a contract with me and that if they wished they could sign up to it there and then. They still hesitated but of course they had to open the envelope to look at the contract, only to find it totally blank apart from the heading and space for signatures. They looked at each other and up at me.

I offered them my hand and said: 'The only contract I'm prepared to make is for you to shake my hand as gentlemen and we have a deal.' They were stunned, for it was not their usual way of conducting business, but understood that was how we act when we trust each other across the pond. We shook hands, the deal was struck and to commemorate it I handed each of them a Kruggerand as a thank you from our Company for their trust.

It was the beginning of a long and quite fruitful relationship though it did take me a while to get home that time. I managed to get a flight out of Las Vegas to Dallas and then one on to New York. Bill and Mike both flew with me on those flights so we had time to get to know each other and to share a few drinks in the sky. Then I flew on to Heathrow, landing very early in the morning but as it happened the Hagons lived nearby so I finished up there for breakfast and with a deal for Cotton Candy that I knew Palmer & Harvey would go for.

In fact Cotton Candy was on its way up before it even left the States and within a day or so David Green was in Dagenham discussing how Impex would be handling the work.

Unfortunately the product proved not to have as long a life as we had hoped. The UK legislation stated 'minimum weight' had to be put onto packets and the production of this product was such that that could not be guaranteed in every single packet. Although, as foreseen, we had massive orders which we completed in a month or so, about a year later a local Trading Standards Officer somewhere weighed a packet and found it to be slightly underweight and that was that. Sadly the production unit in Chicago had no way of dealing with the problem that did not exist in the USA where no such legislation existed.

We'd had a good run though and even though we did have to take some product back, with the help of our good friends at George Heley & Co we managed to clear the product. It had been a wonderful period that had earned Clarks a significant profit and I still see it on sale in the States when I go there.

Offers

As I have said previously in this chapter it was odd that, having had so many problems raising the money to buy the company, once we'd done so we began to be inundated with offers to buy it from us. As a result while business continued as usual we were having a lot of meetings with Touche Ross, County NatWest and Peter Wayte to discuss these offers and to really establish the true worth of the House of Clarks.

Nor should I forget the family either because it was this time that Chel was starting playschool and my Mum was celebrating her 75th birthday. Brandon had to have a minor hernia operation so we took him to the Highgate Clinic where he needed to stay overnight. We stayed with him 'til 11pm and Lynn and I popped back there the following day when he was having the operation. Then we went to Nottingham for a wedding and collected the boy on the way home.

I had always told Brandon that when he was 18 I would take him to the American Bar in the Savoy for drinks and dinner. I'd been telling him that for years but he took me by surprise the day before his sixteenth birthday (once again I was older) when he took me to the American Bar himself.

He just thought he would turn the tables two years early. We were sitting there having a drink when, after hiding behind a pillar, George Hagon popped out to help us celebrate. He and his wife came out with us all the following day to have dinner at the Dick Turpin. Then John Dickson, to whom we owed so much thanks to his initiating the idea of buying the company out and helping make it possible, had his 25th wedding anniversary and we were off to Danbury to celebrate that as well.

On the subject of celebrations I think that at this point I would like to mention Thelma Davey, our 'tea lady'. Thelma, who had looked after our food and drink needs for over forty years, decided it was time to retire. A lovely lady who was always polite, quiet and calm had taken care of all the Board Room requirements as well as the office and factory, wandering around with her little trolley. She'd been there since the start and we threw an all-day party for all departments for her.

We were starting to have some serious meetings about selling now because it was becoming clear that we all had a real opportunity to safeguard our futures. County NatWest gave us Alastair Gibbins – the young man who had helped us with them in the first place – to carry out some of the work. Along with Peter Wayte we had a meeting with some of the companies, like Appletree and its boss Tom Angear, who were showing a real interest in buying us.

Another company showing interest was Hazelwoods and Peter Barr, who had visited with Barrs Popcorn, came with Dennis Jones and they were making advances for our group. We even had an approach from Beatrice Foods, an American company. I remember getting a phone call from Peter asking directions to our home so that he could land his helicopter in our garden. I don't think he realised that we lived in a normal house without a garden big enough for a helicopter to land. We found him a local hotel which had enough space and a helicopter landing pad.

The meeting took place at home but, although there were some sensible discussions, we were now getting close to a deal with Hunter Saphir. Of all the people looking at Clarks Hunter Saphir, who owned a number of companies from British Pepper and Spice, Matthew Walker Christmas Puddings, Emile Tizzot frozen foods, Hunter Fresh Veg to Hunter distribution who owned and worked the distribution warehouses for Tesco and Sainsbury, seemed keener than most. We began to get the feeling that this could be the best deal for us, the business and the staff.

As one of our senior partners County NatWest was very involved and, along with Sidney Donald, Alastair Gibbins was doing a lot of background work, but business had to go on as usual. I remember Tesco's Quality Controller visiting us in Dagenham and having to keep different visitors apart so there was no suspicion as to what was going on.

Bruce Daly, the MD of one of the Hunter Saphir group turned up and at the time we were busy working on organising Clarks Night 87. Negotiations had progressed so far that we were asked to have meetings with Stoy Hayward, the international financial accountants who were acting on behalf of HS. I remember having to leave that meeting early to go to the funeral of a great friend, George Freeman. He'd been a manager of Palmer & Harvey for many years and had been an absolute gentleman and it was a sad loss to us all.

Our printer, Laurence Munroe, took me and the boys to Upton Park where West Ham was playing QPR and we beat them 3-0. We had a quick break in Folkestone with Lynn's mum and dad but things back in London were hotting up and the phone was ringing all the time about the deal.

Brandon got his O level results and did so well he was able to stay on at school to complete his A levels and then, to make the day complete we went on to see QPR beat Arsenal 2-0. We had a staff party in Dagenham to mark the retirements of our Company Secretary Arthur Smith and our Midlands rep Fred Parker. A couple of days later Lynn is 39 and we celebrate at the Dick Turpin. Happy days all round.

Ta mate, deal done!

By now we had discarded most of the offers we were getting and concentrating on the approach from Hunter Saphir who had made a generous offer I was trying to fine tune a little. Their MD John Saphir came to Dagenham, bringing his financial director Brian Dudley with him obviously to look us over and test our resolve.

Although I didn't get on with all the HS directors I did get on with Brian, who became Chairman of Clarks when the deal was completed. He, and the MD of Hunter Distribution Mike Cannon, have remained good friends to this day and with our wives we get together every Christmas to celebrate the old days.

It was a very serious moment in the negotiations with a lot of meetings between lawyers, bankers and accountants going on. Peter Wayte was working hard on contracts etc., and I was spending a lot of time with John Saphir and Brian Dudley thrashing out the best deal I could and then reporting back to the Board. We'd also now got to the stage where we were having meetings with Oppenheimer (the financial advisers handling the deal for HS). Meetings were going on to the early hours and I remember taking Peter home to St Albans at 3am.

At home we were looking for the next stage of schooling for Cheralyn and went to look at Woodlands in Warley, where she started on September 28th. In Dagenham however we were very close to a deal and a few weeks later I was to meet Hunter Saphir's Chairman Nick Saphir. He proved to be a charming man who probably wanted to finalise the deal in his own mind. That was on October 8th and the next day it all happened.

We were holding Clarks Night 87 in the Royal Lancaster hotel so I had checked in the previous night before meeting Peter at 6pm and arriving at Oppenheimer's at 7pm. The meeting between me, our lawyers and theirs, went on and on and to be honest I was reaching the stage where I'd had enough.

Suddenly I said: 'Look if this deal is not concluded tonight it's off and I walk away.' I told them that we had Clarks Night 87 the next night and either I break the news to our customers and staff that we were joining Hunter Saphir, or I say nothing and I will be carrying on business as usual.

Cheralyn ready and waiting for her first day at Woodlands School

I could see Peter looking at me in stunned amazement because, being a far more patient man than me he would not have been so blunt but, as he said later, it had some effect. We signed the deal at 1.25am.

I remember walking back to the Royal Lancaster in a rainy street with a young lawyer who'd been working on our behalf and getting back there at 3am. By then of course Ian and Pat Yates had already checked in and were in bed so I slipped a note under their door saying: 'Ta mate, deal done, going to bed'.

As for the deal itself, well I have to admit that during all those approaches from other firms I'd been playing one off against the other to bump up the price. In the end it was Hunter Saphir who came up with the best offer of, would you believe, £6.67m – more than twice as much as we'd paid for it only months before. That, however, was not the end of the story by a long shot.

Indeed not – because they also offered a two-year 'overage' deal of 4.5times on a two-year profit scheme, keeping us on to achieve it. This was a deal whereby a company takes you over for a price plus overage which means you get extra if you achieve better profits than before. Apart from anything else of course it meant we all still had jobs for two years to supervise it. As consultant they did send me round to some of their other companies but of course when they realised my absence from Dagenham could cost them money in profits I was left alone.

During that two years we were kept on to maintain and/or raise profits and we worked like mad. Some good friends in the business gave us some good orders, with improved commissions our reps did great things and we sold a lot of old unused machinery. Chris Standing, by then a director herself of course, reminds me that Sothebys even sold the old painting in the Board Room for us. We all felt that our final two years of employment by Clarks was the most successful time of all.

You do not actually get the overage money until the two years is up of course because it is based on the two years. So at the end of the first year we made a profit of £1m – £500k more than the previous year so we got 4.5 times £500k (£2.250m). Not bad but at the end of the second year we'd made a £2.1m profit which was £1.6m over the original profit. That gave us £7.2m so in the two years we'd made £9.45m on the overage deal.

It almost broke them and was the biggest overage ever given and made a lot of national business press headlines. Their shareholders went mad having paid us £19m for a company we'd bought for £3m. Shortly afterwards I think that kind of overage deal was outlawed on the basis that shareholders were being asked to agree to open ended deals.

County Natwest only got their 29% share of the original £7.5m Hunter Saphir paid and we shared the overage money. In the end we took some of our money in shares which was a mistake because they almost went bust and sold out to Albert Fisher cheaply. We had to sell our shares at a loss but it only meant a few bottles of bubbly less.

I don't think I slept much that night we signed the deal, I was so excited about it. It was one that would secure the future of the Board of Directors who had all risked their money and could now look forward to some rewards and a significant profit.

The next day was our big Clarks Night and there was a table set aside for the directors of the Hunter Saphir Group, because we thought they should see how we operated. On the stage I had to announce that our deal had been concluded and we were now part of a much bigger group.

THE INDEPENDENT Tuesday 13 October 1987

Hunter Saphir snaps up popcorn leader

By Clare Dobie

HUNTER SAPHIR, a food company, is acquiring the world's largest popcorn company, The House of Clarks, which makes Butterkist and Pims Popcorn.

Hunter, which came to the Unlisted Securities Market in 1984 and plans to join the main market next month, is paying £6.3m in shares for Clarks. Further payments may become payable, depending on profits.

The sale price means that Ken Lewis, Clarks' managing director, and other managers have more than doubled their money in the year since a management buyout.

The acquisition takes Hunter into sweets for the first time and will provide a platform for ex-panding in snacks, according to John Saphir, deputy chairman.

Hunter is at the same time raising £1.9m by issuing a further 740,000 shares. In all 2.6 million shares are being offered in a one-for-eight rights issue at 265p.

S & W Berisford, the commodities company, has agreed to take up its rights, leaving its shareholding at 19.9 per cent. Berisford acquired the stake in payment for four companies it sold to Hunter last December.

In the year to 31 March Clarks made profits of £595,000 before tax on sales of £5.51m. This sug-gests that Hunter is paying 16 times earnings for Clarks.

This multiple may look high, but it is lower than Hunter's own. Hunter's shares at 302p, down 2p yesterday, are trading on 29 times historic earnings.

Clarks' net assets stood at £400,000 at the end of March, suggesting that Hunter will have to write off £5.9m.

If profits exceed £540,000 in the current year or next Hunter will issue further shares, worth 4.5 times the pre-tax excess.

The Saphir Brothers — John, Nick and Joe — are not taking up all their rights. As a result 891,000 shares will be placed with institutions.

Press coverage of the sale of House of Clarks to Hunter Saphir.

Then I introduced both Nick and John Saphir who came on stage and said a few words.

On the lighter side all three of us had beards and I remember Nick saying that they'd had to grow theirs in order to conclude the deal. He always had a great sense of humour. That night the brothers entered into the spirit of the occasion and were both generous in the auction we held every year to raise funds for the Variety Club of Great Britain. The evening ended at 5am. when we were all totally exhausted.

We'd owned the company for ten months, had well-paid jobs for the next two years working on what would be our extra money thanks to the overage. I understand Mr. Pitt (Junior) was unhappy and though I never heard from him again, I did hear from the lawyers that he had had an investigation carried out on whether we'd had anyone waiting in the wings to buy us out while negotiating with him in the first place.

In fact nothing could have been further from the truth. We'd bought the company to have security for the rest of our working lives and had then been stunned at the offers that came in. The one we achieved was too good to turn down of course.

The full range of products of the House of Clarks

Chapter 16

Goodbye Clarks

A very formal affair

One way or another 1987 had been a pretty frenetic year and, with the sale of the House of Clarks now complete, I took off for California with a small stag group. Chris Day (our Deputy Works Manager) George Heley, Nick Daunt, John Wood and I landed at Palm Springs and I drove us on to Las Vegas.

There we were, in brilliant sunshine and enjoying the bright lights in Nevada, when George phoned home to find that the UK had 'enjoyed' a major storm that had uprooted trees, including one that had fallen right across the middle of his Porsche. Whoops! Meanwhile of course, at home the children were growing up fast – Brandon was into squash, Bradley football and Chel was having ballet lessons.

Hunter Saphir started to send their people in to deal with the accounts and finances etc. and we met their Company Secretary Barry Homer and accountant Ken Payne. They were there of course to evaluate the company they had just bought. We held our first AGM with the new owners in the QPR box, so they could see and enjoy part of their assets. Then the original board, along with wives and partners were all invited to dinner at the offices of County NatWest to celebrate the conclusion of the deal.

Part of that deal of course was that I had to stay on, as a consultant, along with my team, for two more years to head up the business as we were all on an 'earn out' thanks to the overage part of the sale. I was having a lot of meetings with Nick Saphir but around this time I also received a call from one of the Hunter Saphir secretaries to say that their Directors would like to hold a Board Meeting in Dagenham.

I agreed and set our boardroom up accordingly but then Barry Homer rang to ask if we understood what board meetings were about and that this would be a formal one. In fact he said a 'very formal' one and I realised that somehow they thought they had bought a company in the back streets of Dagenham and wondered if they thought we worked out of the bike sheds. But I played along with them and said: 'Oh, right – I think we can manage that.'

They had clearly not appreciated that we'd been having formal board meetings for many years, but then we were just a little firm in Dagenham. I arranged for the meeting to be held at 9.00am when David Jones, Chris Day and I turned up in black tie and dinner jackets while Chris wore a ball gown. We had balloons on the back of chairs and made the room look formal but mixed up with a party atmosphere.

So, when Barry, Brian Dudley (the new Chairman) and Bruce Daly walked in with a couple of others they found us sitting there in full evening dress. They looked a bit stunned and asked why we were dressed like that at 9am and, keeping a straight face' I said we'd been told it was a formal affair so we'd dressed appropriately. Brian Dudley, who'd spotted the joke smiled slightly and said: 'Ken, you bastard'. It relieved the atmosphere and the first 'formal' meeting – though no more formal than any others we'd had over the years, took place.

John Saphir asked me to set up a meeting with Michael Land of Playtime Popcorn, so we all had lunch together at the Connaught in London. I think John wanted to talk to our opposition to see if there was any possibility of a future merger, but nothing happened.

In fact I was now being asked to go to all sorts of meetings within the group and that did not make me too happy because my job was to run our factory and business as efficiently as possible (and get the best earn out). One day, for example, I was at British Pepper & Spice in Northampton and then at Hunter Distribution in London. I think they simply wanted me to give the benefit of my sales and marketing knowledge/experience, but you can imagine how I was welcomed by their own sales and marketing teams. At that time we were the shining light in the group as far as profits etc. went and I would guess that that caused a little resentment in some quarters.

Over Christmas that year I was invited to many functions – like the Rolls Royce Christmas party at SMAC's in Thorpe Bay who obviously wanted to sell me another Roller. We had the Christmas Conference, the Hagon's Christmas visit, our Executive Christmas Lunch and on December 23rd, the day the firm shut down for the holiday, Nick and John Saphir, along with Brian and Jan Dudley came to Dagenham to join us for our buffet and drinks. That also gave them the chance to meet both office and factory staff.

We went to Great Danes near Maidstone as usual for Christmas and, also as usual, I took my Santa Claus outfit, which I've done every Christmas Eve since the children were born. So once again I was pottering around the hotel that night as the man himself. In fact even in the days we never went away I would be out in the street at night putting boxes of popcorn on the doorsteps of other houses in the street. That was a tradition I kept going throughout all my popcorn days.

It was soon 1988 and we took the children to the Palladium to see Babes in the Wood, while our staff night that year was held at the Circus Tavern where Bobby Davro was the star turn. On New Year's Day I took Brandon and Bradley to Loftus Road for breakfast and to see QPR beat Southampton 3-0. After that it was back to the old routine, heading up to Glasgow to start the annual UK tour.

Dad

It was around this time that I became aware that both my parents were of an age where they needed to be cared for in a retirement home, so Lynn and I were spending a lot of time looking at various homes in and around the Westcliff area where they were living. Then towards the end of January my dad was taken ill and rushed into Rochford Hospital and I was taking Mum to visit him whenever she felt able to travel.

I managed to get to see the QPR versus West Ham United fourth round FA Cup game which I was delighted to see us win 3-1. Then I was straight off to meet my partners at the airport for our annual week to the ISM Cologne show, but as soon as I was back I was visiting Dad again.

In fact I was visiting him most evenings for several weeks, often taking Mum with me, though she wasn't too well herself at the time. Dad spent his 86th birthday in Rochford hospital and Lynn and the boys would often come with me as well. He actually came out of hospital on February 23rd, two days after our wedding anniversary.

At work I was now onto some very serious visits to every customer's head office in order to push sales, and therefore profits because of course of our two-year 'earn out'. In fact during those two years we never stopped working and of course there many House of Clarks board meetings, chaired by Brian Dudley. On a lighter side John Dickson of RBS took us to see a new show opening in the West End followed by dinner at Covent Garden. The show was 'Les Miserables' and of course is still playing to packed houses.

Sadly however, on March 21st Dad was taken back into hospital and, though I managed to visit him several times, three days later he passed away. I was actually there with him as he died at 5.10am. There was a lot of paperwork to do but my first thought was to go to wake up my Mum, who didn't live far away, to tell her the sad news – news which I think came as little surprise. Then, having already phoned Lynn with the news I had to go home to tell the children.

Dad had had a pretty good life and a reasonable retirement so we were pleased he never suffered in any way. I was left with so many memories of course – how he'd got me into a decent school, the St Marylebone Grammar School – because as a waiter he'd struck up a friendship with an influential diner who happened to be the school's headmaster.

I remember how he used to get me up early in the morning to go out and do my paper round and, when I'd lost my wages – a ten shillings (50p) note – he quietly refunded it against Mum's wishes. It was Dad who introduced me to greyhound racing, swearing me to secrecy about his going to the ten-shilling Tote window 'Your Mum thinks I only use the two-shilling window...' he grinned.

I have told how he once joined one of my uncles in betting on a 'dead cert', raising £125 (an enormous amount of money for working people then) to put it on the nose and the dog lost. His reaction? He shrugged his shoulders, laughed and said 'Oh dear, well we came close.' That's the kind of guy he was, as he showed again in 1972 when Lynn and I took Brandon, Mum and Dad to Majorca for a few days and this is what happened (as I have already written in this book)

Dad was a great character, one of those lovely guys who never missed a trick and he thought it wonderful that there was such a thing as Duty

Free. This was something he'd never experienced before and the thought that abroad you could buy cheap alcohol and tobacco, and I do mean cheap, set him thinking.

So on the return flight and unbeknown to me of course, he took full advantage with more packets of the latter than he was legally allowed. He had them stuffed into his pockets, socks, underwear and any other place he could think of, but of course hiding alcohol is a lot different and much harder.

We reached Customs and guess who was stopped and whose luggage was searched. What alerted the Customs man to Dad was finding a bottle of Schweppes tonic water on him. Why on earth would anyone be bringing tonic water back with them? They took the cap off the bottle and guess what? They found it was pure gin.

He did like his drop of gin and he'd had his full allowance but he couldn't resist taking the chance. I think that, after they also found the fags in odd places and looked at this lovely old man, they realised he wasn't a big time smuggler. They just smiled, gave him a ticking off and sent us on our way but he loved thinking he'd got away with something.

'You see son, if you don't try you will never know,' he said, with a twinkle in his eye. The fact that we could all have finished up with criminal records didn't seem to matter. That was my dad.

On March 28th George and Rina Hagon arrived and with Bill, Ivy and Brandon, Lynn and I collected Mum and we all went to Dad's funeral. It was just a small group and Lynn organised some refreshments for afterwards in Mum's house. It was hard leaving Mum on her own afterwards, but she stood up pretty well.

We had the internment in Southend on the 30th with just myself, Brandon and my closest other relative Uncle Alf, who has himself since passed away, present. I took Mum to a care home in Westcliff, Tudor Lodge, for some respite which I think she appreciated although she still hankered to get back to her own home, which she did.

I cannot leave this section without a final memory that Dad left me with. When he knew the end was in sight he told me that when he was dead he did not need a rabbi to carry out the funeral. I thought that would have been appropriate so I asked him why not and he said that they charged too much and he did not want me to have to spend more money than was necessary.

He'd never fully appreciated that I was financially secure, so I said for him not to worry about that but he insisted and to satisfy him I agreed. The way he smiled and held my hand when I did told me all I needed to know, so of course when he passed away I went out and found a local rabbi. I told him the story and he laughed before quoting me a price.

He conducted such a fine and kind funeral that I actually paid him twice the amount he'd asked for, telling him it was a donation to the synagogue. I will always remember his comments on that. He said how generous I was and that the generosity of my father would stay with me forever. I hope it has.

The Good Life

After going to see Dame Edna Everidge at the Strand Theatre I took a group of those who had helped the buy and sell outs to Florida. It was a way of saying thank you, so we took Ian and Pat Yates, Peter Wayte and his family and a few others to Disneyworld. For a week we reminisced about the long days and nights that had been necessary to come through a really hectic time and we all had a great and really relaxing time with the kids.

That was just as well really because once I was back in Dagenham it was back to the old 'nose to the grindstone' routine with meetings, visits and events and now not all connected with popcorn of course. For instance I had some meetings with National Amusements of the U.S.A. which was considering moving into the British entertainments industry. I had regular meetings with Impex and with Bruce Daly of Hunter Saphir. Then it was time to go off to Penns Hall in Sutton Coldfield for the P&H and WCA exhibition.

I went off to Portugal for a few days, partly to attend the Landmark Conference I'd been invited to by Geoff Purdy but also to look at properties there because Lynn and I were considering buying one on the Algarve. Then it was home for a day before leaving for New York on Concorde for a 4-day trip to attend the USA Confectionery Exhibition. Got back just in time for the cup final when, shock on shock, Wimbledon (the Crazy Gang) beat Liverpool 1-0.

Talking of Concorde, I was a pretty regular traveller on that remarkable aircraft when it was in service. It was a quick method of getting to New York, but it also meant you could get back to London on the same day without having to spend the night on the plane. I went to many other places on Concorde as well and before it was taken out of commission I had actually flown in it 84 times – once even landing on ice.

Not to Cyprus however which is where we went on our next group trip, with Ian and Pat Yates. That was great but I suspect that for Bradley the most important moment at that time was getting a trophy for being part of the football team that won the league in a local contest.

I was contacted by London Weekend Television which was intending to do a show about companies who used hospitality to get closer to their clients and since a great deal of our success had been based on that philosophy they came Dagenham. Then, shortly after Brandon's 17th birthday (when once again I was a little older) Lynn and I went to their studios for the filming.

The documentary was called 'The Good Life' but had nothing to do with the Richard Briers sitcom, and we were filmed being driven from the studios to Drury Lane which was staging a show called 42nd Street. They filmed us in the theatre enjoying the show and then having dinner afterwards. We weren't the only ones of course – they filmed a number of people from companies living it up and the show was aired a few months later. I guess that, with our future secured now, it could be said that we were really enjoying the 'good life'.

The Hunter Saphir big meetings in their head office were something special too. We all went to Northfleet to make a presentation to the Gateway Supermarket Group. We all sat round a big table with all the Gateway executives and each of us MDs had to introduce and present our product, explaining what opportunities each would have in their stores. Then I was off to Q Peanuts to continue our relationship because the nuts were doing well in our range, before shooting off to Lords to see England play the West Indies.

Speaking of cricket I was now in the Forest School Dad's team though to be honest I was not a cricketer of any real note. I found it a little unnerving to be facing young men throwing a very hard red ball at me, but I did get one run (I think it was a bye) before they declared so yet again I was one, not out. Brandon was on stage at Forest School in their production of 'Grease' while Chel was a princess in her school play.

I was really getting fed up with all the meetings, presentations and board meetings Hunter Saphir was so keen on, and I wanted to get on with our own business. I was also getting increasingly irritated and frustrated with the way meetings often went with MDs coming up with ideas that were never approved by the Board. So I did a deal with Geoff Purdy at Landmark under which, as soon as I heard another board meeting was being called I phoned him to ask if I could come and see him for lunch.

He'd laugh and say, 'another board meeting eh?', but he'd always say yes. I always had to apologise to Hunter Saphir and explain that I couldn't make the meeting because I'd been summoned to Landmark. It was such a good account that they knew I could never say no and Geoff and I had a lot of lunches, a lot of laughs and did a lot of business too.

Chris was helping me with meetings at the Inn on the Park in Park Lane where we were organising a surprise birthday party for Lynn, but more of that shortly. There was a moment of sadness because in July for the first time in 53 years Mum could not celebrate her wedding anniversary with Dad, so Bradley and I went to collect her to take her to his grave.

Other than that life was still hectic. Hunter Saphir had another Board meeting organised but sadly this time Geoff was away so I had to go to it. It went on until 10pm and the next morning I was in the office at 5.30am and then on the 7.20am from Paddington to Bristol for yet another Gateway head office presentation. Nick Saphir gave me a lift home from Bristol in his new BMW and I did start to get to know him better.

For a brief rest I took the family to Portugal, where we were still looking at properties. I was interested in an area called Dunas Durados and their rep was now visiting my office so we could negotiate. In those days we did all the hospitality and it was rare for customers to return the compliment but that could not be said of George Heley, who took my whole family to Legoland in Denmark with his family.

Bradley celebrates, Brandon fails and Chel screams

What with the demands of the new business consultancy and the continuing efforts to boost our earn-out in Dagenham it might have been easy to overlook the demands of the family but they have always taken top billing. Whenever and wherever possible they have been included in events, trips etc. and both Lynn and I were always as supportive as we could be for them at school.

In fact shortly after our short holiday in Portugal I took them all on our month's holiday to America. We all had a great time during which Lynn celebrated her 40th birthday and we had dinner at the Hyatt Hotel in Cambridge just outside Boston. She didn't know it but she had more to come on that score.

We actually got home the next day, just in time for Bradley's 13th birthday which we spent in our box at QPR where the birthday celebrations were ruined a touch by Southampton who beat us 1-0. The next day, with the Hagons, we all went for lunch at the Dick Turpin pub in Ilford.

The day after that however we hit a really major problem because a Royal Mail strike had just started and we had to organise a meeting of our sales force to re-arrange things. For companies like ours of course the problem a postal strike brings is almost totally concerned with money. There is the worry of getting invoices out to customers but, even worse perhaps, that of getting cheques back in return.

There were of course no e-mails and since public telephone boxes were mostly vandalised, we decided to use our sales force as our back-up personal postal force, delivering invoices and collecting cheques by hand. We, or perhaps rather they, did a remarkable job because the strike, which went on for two weeks not only disrupted things for that period but for a while after which the backlog was cleared.

Brandon was due to take his driving test until he got a letter cancelling it for that day, but we'd also been busy in Dagenham with meetings with Peter Wayte and with Nick Saphir. We were desperately trying to maintain a ring fence around our part of the business because of course the 'earn out' that meant so much to us meant we needed to retain as much as possible.

I was working with Chris organising Lynn's surprise 40th birthday party. Since hers had been at that Boston hotel and Bradley's had been celebrated in Loftus Road we thought we would combine the two with a joint party at the Inn on the Park.

Lynn thought she was just going out for dinner but walked into a room to be greeted by a great number of people singing Happy Birthday. We all had a great evening and stayed the night there. Around that time we were

*Lynn showing a bit of leg at her 40th birthday party
sitting on the bonnet of the new car I bought her*

also having initial talks about Brandon's 18th birthday which would be the following year (when of course I would again be a little older).

Our friend Alan Britain, who'd built our swimming pool, decided to go into the retail business and opened up a new supermarket in Harold Hill. I prevailed on our neighbour, the ever-obliging Frank Bruno, to go there to open his shop and sign autographs. He stayed there for several hours and did a great job for Alan.

Apart from making visits to Dad's grave and popping in to see Mum who lived nearby, I was also invited (by our local dealer SMAC) to spend the day at the Rolls Royce factory in Crewe. Chris Day, David Jones, Chris and I went to Leeds to see how another popcorn factory worked, Pierre Folari from Portugal came for more meetings over the property and my old friend Gareth Thompson also came home for a visit from Australia to stay with us for a while.

We had another short holiday in Cyprus but I was having some pains and went to see Rodney Burnham for some tests. Bit scary of course but all you can do is have them and then wait for the results. As it turned out they proved to be ok, thank goodness. In Brandon's case however the test did not turn out so well because he failed it – his driving test that is.

Obviously there was a need to relax a bit so, with Christmas coming, after the Christmas conferences and seeing Freddie Starr at the Circus Tavern, we took off on Concorde again....on ice. I did mention it before but we took the kids to Lapland and that was some experience. After landing on the ice, Father Christmas greets you, his reindeers take you to your hotel and you spend the rest of the day on snow-mobiles. Then it was home by Concorde (still on the ice) again so in a sense it was several experiences all in one.

In January 1989 I started off again with the usual UK tour, though I did have to come back to see QPR draw 2-2 with Man United. We took Cheralyn to the pantomime and Brandon has another driving test and this time he passed. Both Bradley and Chel have to have medicals and this time they involved a blood test but she did not like that idea.

We remember how she screamed the house down. There was no way she wanted a needle anywhere near her and there was no way anyone was getting any of her blood. It took a doctor and several nurses to calm her down and hold her long enough to get the blood.

If I say its fudge, its....

By now we former owners had become aware of just how valuable our 'earn out' had become. Based on the previous year's profit, we were to get four and a half times any profit we made over and above that figure over the next two years, so the more we made and saved, the more we would get. Who was it spoke about a licence to print money?

I remember discussing it with an incredulous Michael Land at Playtime and he said that if he'd been on earn out like that he would be issuing his staff with just two pieces of toilet paper and no more, every time they went to the loo. We didn't go that far but we did do some strange things nevertheless to save a few pennies.

For example we cancelled all the periodicals, newspapers and trade magazines that we'd had for years. Yes it only came to a few pounds a week but that times four and a half times over two years adds up a lot. We looked around to see what we didn't need any more and spotted a rather tatty looking old picture in the board room that had been there for years. We thought it might be worth a few hundred pounds so we took it down and sent it to Sotheby's and asked for an opinion.

To our surprise they said it might be worth a couple of thousand pounds so we told them to sell it for us. To our amazement, and probably theirs, it actually sold for around £10k and since this was pure profit it added up to four and a half times that for us.

We looked around the factory and offices for anything that was no longer in use, such as the old equipment that had been taking up room at the back of the factory. We sold all that, sometimes just for scrap money but every penny counted, and that wasn't all. We even sold imperfect product that had always gone for pig fodder before – like the famous fudge.

Our confectionery department had decided to experiment with toffee and we produced ten tons of the stuff. That was a lot but after it had been left standing for a few days we found it had gone too soft, almost like fudge and I decided to call it that. I telephoned my old friend Ian Yates. I told him we had ten tons of over produced fudge to sell off cheaply and we did a deal.

We delivered it to his Manchester warehouse and since he also had warehouses in the Midlands, Scotland and Wales he could distribute it fairly easily. A few days later however I got a call from Ian saying 'This is not fudge, it is toffee gone soft.'

I said, 'No, this is definitely a new type of fudge we are producing,' but I could not convince Ian of this and to make matters worse his customers were bringing the goods back. However Ian is a good salesman and found a good market for the stuff – literally a good market.

People who buy confectionery off market stalls tend not to take the product back if they are unhappy with it. I suppose you never know if the actual market stall holder will be but that turned out not to be a problem thanks to the relationship between myself and Ian. The story did create a lot of humour though and provoke a lot of after-dinner conversations.

It was one of those family stories that became legends and led Chel, our daughter who pushed me into writing this book to suggest that it be called 'It's not fudge, its toffee' but at this stage of writing it I have not finally decided on a name.

Apart from that, over the two years we were contracted to, we came up with every legal plan and scheme to increase Clarks' profits and it was amazing what we did and how much we achieved. In fact the turn round in the Company's fortunes was so significant we made it to the pages of the Financial Times. During the earn-out time company cars were not changed and we did everything we could to encourage our reps to keep their expenses down.

Unless there was a guaranteed result at the end of the meal entertaining came to an end and of course we pushed harder than usual for our money from our customers. Our suppliers, however, were kept waiting for their money longer than usual although in fairness we always told them why and that their money was safe. After all on both accounts we had been dealing with most of these people for years and that honesty and our reputation for it clearly paid off.

Every £1 of profit was worth £4.50 to us of course and on our annual trip to ISM Cologne we managed to negotiate for a bigger stand at no extra cost and we were very careful about who we wined and dined in Germany. Then, on getting back to Heathrow I never went home but met up with Lynn and the children and we all flew (yes Concorde again) to Barbados for a week's holiday, getting back just in time to celebrate our wedding anniversary.

Hunter Saphir told me I had to start having meetings with their new MD Ken Duberry. I had to introduce him to major clients around the country, update him about the business in general and explain how the company was run. Again we did not get on very well, even though he was a charming man. He was 'one of them' and not 'one of us'. I was in fact by then being called upon to carry out far more than the duties I was prepared to as it was of course taking me away from earning the money with Clarks.

On that subject again we had economised to such an extent that we only had two reps covering the entire country – John Walker covered Scotland and the North, while Ken (my life is full of Kens) Richards handled the South. These two were also part of the pension committee and were having meetings related to dispersing the pension fund That was something I could not do on my own, because it had to be agreed with the Trustees.

It turned out that there were significant funds available in the scheme and I was coming to the end of my time in control of the company. There were several choices of course. The cash could simply sit in the scheme which would eventually become part of the Hunter Saphir pension fund or, according to our advisors, it could be dispersed among members of the scheme, many of whom had already retired.

We decided it would be in the best interests to dispense the majority of the fund to those who were already on pension or would be at some time in the future. It made absolute sense. They had all been loyal members of staff for several decades, it was their money and we were advised of their right to it.

That meant there were no further payments to be made into the fund and on a personal note, I did not benefit as I had chosen not to join the scheme until much later in the day.

Chapter 17

Business Consultant

That's a lot of Rolex

All through this story, or at least since that part relating to June 1971, I have been highlighting Brandon's birthday rather than my own, which falls on the same day. But on his birthday in 1989 – the one on which he became an adult – it was me who got the biggest 'birthday present'.

For some months we four former owners had been winding down our relationship with Clarks, having come to the end of our two year 'earn out'. Life was looking good of course because we had become aware of just how much that two-years had been worth to us. I took them all, along with good old Sidney Donald of County NatWest, to the Variety Club dinner at the Grosvenor House hotel. The following week we took Chris and Bob to Langans to celebrate their wedding anniversary.

It was a kind of 'La Dolce Vita' period when we'd been building an extension to the house that also included a new indoor swimming pool. We decided to have an 'official' opening on Easter Sunday, calling it a 'Pool Extension Fish & Chip Party' and to which a lot of friends and family arrived. Then, the following week, Nick Saphir invited me to dinner at the Savoy. Evenings never took up working time so that was fine and it proved to be an evening of conversation about my personal feelings on the group and I think it was the last time he invited me out.

I also remember it as a time when I experienced my first 'Chinese'. Geoff Purdy had his 40th birthday and we all had dinner in a Chinese restaurant in Southend. I had no real idea of what I was ordering, or what I was eating so – surprise surprise – I tended to keep to the wine. Then we took the family to Miami (on Concorde of course) for a family holiday in America.

When I got back from the States I had a call from a couple of guys called Peter Woodman and Howard Reece. They were directors of the Tarmac Company which had ended up with a South Wales confectionery company called Lovells of Newport within their group. They'd heard I was coming to the end of my time with Clarks and Hunter Saphir and wanted to know if I would be interested in a position with them, but more of that later.

Still enjoying life I took a group of senior executives to see 'The Ultimate Event' – a show at the Royal Albert Hall featuring Sinatra, Sammy Davis Jr and Liza Minelli. Wow! How ultimate can you get? Then I took a group of customers on yet another trip – a ten day cruise in the Caribbean – fortunately met on our return at the airport by the Hagons. I say fortunate because of a rather unusual experience I'd had.

We'd been to a small island called St Marteen where Geoff Purdy and I decided to have a rest on the beach while the others went off touring the island. On the way to it we passed a very nice looking little store called Little Switzerland and, having received my payout (not all) from the company I was feeling a bit flush. Now I had always wanted a Rolex watch so Geoff and I popped in to look at one in this shop.

I was shown one that looked quite interesting – more than I would normally pay for a watch but in my mind it represented a reward for all those years in the company. I was just about to buy it when Geoff asked the manager if that was the best Rolex he had. He said that he did have another one in the vault and when he brought it out to show us Geoff insisted that was the one I should buy.

To be honest I was a bit uncertain myself whether I wanted to go that far but the Manager asked me to leave my credit card number and other information with him and come back later. I did that and he said he'd had approval for me to have it so, what the hell, I bought it.

In fact since Geoff and I had spent that afternoon drinking on the beach by the time we did get back I would have bought the whole store, but I bought the watch without giving any thought to possible duty implications. I tried to declare it in America where their rates of duty were lower but they said that since I was in transit back to the UK I should declare it there.

I was a bit worried that they would forward the information on, so when we got back to Heathrow I declared it only to find I did not have enough cash on me to pay the duty. That's why it was fortunate that George Hagon was there to meet us because he was able to lend me the extra money I needed and the watch became legal. To celebrate we all went off to watch Essex playing cricket.

About this time Chris was looking for offices in the Hornchurch area, or at least reasonably close to where we both lived at the time. We were coming to the end of our days in Dagenham and had both agreed that it was not retirement time for either of us. We would continue working together from offices somewhere in the locality.

Part of the deal with Hunter Saphir was that after my retirement in August 1989 I would remain as a consultant to the company for another two years. I was also being approached by other firms (like the guys from Tarmac re Lovells) to consider giving them help and advice based on my experience, contacts and success. So we'd started a company called Ken Lewis Business Consultancy, which was why Chris was out looking for office space.

Two very happy birthdays

I suppose the real highlight of that period was going, with Laurence Munroe and the boys, to see QPR beat Manchester United 3-2 – always the kind of memory to treasure – but to be honest a lot more was happening on the business and family front too. I was having a lot of meetings with various people, such as Michael Land who was considering building up his own company prior to selling it.

That particular lunch meeting took place in the Inn on the Park and I remember staying on afterwards to discuss Brandon's forthcoming 18th birthday celebration with the hotel. Yet another meeting with Hunter Saphir at their head office in Northfleet, where Ken Duberry and I discussed the eventual handover and how I would introduce him to our major accounts.

We also had a surprise lunch in Ginos with the Hagons – well it was intended to be a surprise for George as we'd decided to have his retirement lunch there. I would like to stress again how much I valued our relationship and how much he enjoyed having his two families – the Hagons and the Lewis's – around him.

George had been our best man and he and Rina were Godparents to Bradley and to say we were close is an understatement. So much so that even our kids grew up believing they had two families. George retiring was a good thing because it meant he and Rina would have more time together but he went on well past retirement age. In fact I would jokingly call him a 'money grabbing swine' and he would laugh and say he just loved going to work.

I had meetings with Chris Nash and Howard Reece about Lovells of Newport and on the same day Ian and Pat Yates came to London. We had lunch in Langans followed by a visit to an auction in the Cafe Royal where Ian was selling some of his premises. Then I took the family to Portugal where we were still looking at properties on Dunas Douradas, before flying off again to the States on a business trip to tie up final details with colleagues there who we needed to know would still be supporting Clarks after I left.

Suddenly it was Brandon's birthday when, once again, I was a bit older as well but this time was a bit different. Brandon would be getting a new car when we had his party but that day Brian Dudley, Hunter Saphir's Financial Director turned up in Dagenham at 9am and he brought money. He arrived with the cheques to pay for the shares that the four Directors of the House of Clarks had sold and did I say cheques? I had never seen one like it, it was so stunning. I know how national lottery big winners feel when they celebrate, because we felt the same that morning.

Brian, one of the 'good guys' at Hunter Saphir, was always welcome and of course we were all very keen to celebrate and have lunch, but the only thing on our minds was to get to the bank as soon as he left. We were all very conscious that the banks closed at 4p.m. and while we were trying to be polite and friendly, we couldn't wait for him to go. Anyway finally he did and we all left early that day, paid the money in and had a little party at home that evening.

The next day it was back to reality when a major UK company which we dealt with wanted to see our production. Their buyer, and I will not mention either the company or his name, arrived and we put him up in a local hotel. As was our custom we usually tried to persuade our friendly customers to come home for dinner, rather than in hotels or restaurants. I went to the hotel to collect him to find that he had a young lady with him.

'This is not my wife,' he whispered to me, although she was apparently a member of the company. That never mattered to me and they came home and had dinner with us – a great couple and a lot of fun so it was a good evening. Then, after a particularly long drinking session, they asked if they could use our sauna. No problem but I had not mentioned to Lynn that she was not his wife so she got out some towels; we put the sauna on and left them to it.

Then they also wanted to use our swimming pool but without using costumes and we were both a bit shocked to see them moving from the sauna to the pool in the nude. We had to make sure the boys stayed up in their bedrooms and it was the early hours of the morning before they were ready to go back to their hotel.

I remember discussing with other companies in our industry about the different things we did for our customers, even walking their dogs for them in the West End. You always went the extra mile and, for what it's worth, the sauna deal turned out to be a pretty good one.

The next day I went to the Cumberland Hotel for another meeting with Lovells, who were really keen for me to do some work for them. That meeting went on a bit too and I was there until 1.30am. Then it was the Saturday and time to celebrate Brandon's 18th in the Inn on the Park. These were always very special events with a couple of hundred family and friends present and there was always a special surprise at the end for whoever's birthday it was. Brandon got a Volvo 340GL.

As my last few weeks with Clarks progressed they were not exactly winding down in the accepted sense, so much as handing over. After a few more celebratory lunches and dinners, discussing how the company would progress after Chris and I left, I flew out to America again with Chris Day, our works manager, to deal with machine and corn suppliers as well as a general 'farewell' tour. I got back just in time to take the family (on Concorde of course) off to New York and Miami where we took a cruise and visited Disneyworld. We also went to Scottsdale in Arizona to look at properties there too.

Back home my new Rolls Royce arrived in time for me to drive Lynn and myself to Alan and Sue Britain's wedding, followed by my new

Porsche 944 and we also ordered a new Renault for Lynn. There was a little more business to do with County NatWest however.

I was busy discussing how the 'earn out' was progressing and negotiating on behalf of the four House of Clarks directors to see if we could buy County NatWest out of it. It was a bit of a gamble but we felt that if we could get a reasonable deal, and we did, the full earn-out would be ours. I seem to recall that this was the only time we had heated discussions with them. Alastair was particularly tough but he was balanced by a slightly softer and more amenable Sidney Donald and the deal was finally concluded.

We four used our money to buy them out and take the risk on the eventual earn-out – which proved to be most successful.

The last goodbye

On August 25th (Liberation Day in France) 1989 I said my last goodbye to the House of Clarks, exactly 25 years almost to the day since I'd arrived there in 1964 as a youthful 21 year-old relief van salesman. It had been a spectacular career in which I had seen so much happen, both to the development of the company and in my own life, that I could be happy and even a little proud about.

For a large part of that quarter of a century I had been instrumental in helping to steer the company to great success, helping to create many jobs for a lot of people and that made me happy too. Even more importantly I had met so many people within the industry as well as outside it and made some lifelong friends too, all through Clarks and I am so grateful for that.

I may have been retiring from Clarks but of course not retiring completely. In fact I had even negotiated a deal with Hunter Saphir under which I would remain as a consultant for a couple of years. Lovells of Newport however were in no way competitive with the House of Clarks and Nick Saphir agreed that there was no reason I should not join it in some capacity or other.

It was almost inevitable that the run-up to that retirement date would be a busy time. I went with Chris Day to the head office of the Popcorn Institute and other areas to make my goodbyes before, ensuring I still had my priorities right taking the boys to see QPR beat Crystal Palace 2-0 and the next day taking customers and friends to see Essex play Australia in Chelmsford.

In those last days I was also having a lot of meetings with our own staff and managers, including reps Ken Richards and John Walker, explaining what the takeover meant and thanking them all for their help to me personally. Then the House of Clark directors went off to Langans for a farewell dinner. On my penultimate day in Dagenham it seemed that everyone wanted me out of the way because we had a party on retirement day that started at 12noon and ended at 11pm.

It is always difficult leaving a job, and a company, after so many years, especially having been in charge of it for so long as well. Lynn, bless her, knew this and had made plans to take me away to the North where we stayed with Roy and Reggie Hall for a few days.

The day we got back was Lynn's 41st birthday but I spent most of the day and the next, with Chris looking for furniture for our new office. She had found some excellent offices on a trading estate in Upminster where they loaned us a desk and chairs but we decided to fully furnish it ourselves and that took a day or two. In fact on her 50th birthday, because the furniture had not yet been delivered, we were still working from my home.

We were out looking for more when Ken Duberry arrived for yet another meeting on how the company should progress now. While I no longer had a position there I, or at least the Ken Lewis Business Consultancy, had still been retained as a consultant and they were looking for continuing help. I also had a more formal request from Lovells to visit their head office at Tipton in the Midlands. I had got an agreement from Nick Saphir for this and spent the day with them finalising details of my association with them.

As part of that deal I was out and about a lot with Ken Duberry, introducing him to our major clients, like Rank etc. but on September 13th Chris and I moved into our new offices... and Lynn's new Renault arrived. Back in Dagenham David Jones was now in charge and he asked me to a boardroom meeting to discuss new designs for some of the products. That was a strange sort of meeting in the sense that I was now the 'visitor' rather than the man in charge but it was something I now had to get used to I guess.

I also had more time to spend with the family too of course and I remember Lynn treating me to dinner at the Pandora in Hornchurch before springing another surprise – she had tickets for the Queens Theatre where one of my favourite performers, Joe Brown, was topping the bill. In return I took her to the Royal Albert Hall for the Neil Sedaka concert.

Then I spent the day with Bradley in hospital when he had his adenoids and tonsils removed. The next day I took Cherlyn with me to see him before she went off to school. He came home a couple of days later. We also took her and the boys to the Victoria Palace to see the opening night of Buddy (the Buddy Holly story) so, as you can see we were enjoying a lot of 'family time'. That also included going to shows featuring country and western stars like Don Williams and Randy Travis.

Hunter Saphir was also still asking me to do some work under our agreement, mainly making reports and recommendations. They'd also been interviewing for a new Sales Manager and had taken Alan Simpson on and I was asked to take him round to introduce him to our major customers. This wasn't long after I'd taken Ken Duberry around on the same mission so of course explanations were needed but that wasn't too hard because most of them were friends anyway. At this time I was also very busy writing reports for Hunter Saphir, very quickly using up the number of days of the 30 a year I'd been employed for.

I was also now fairly heavily involved in meetings with the board of Lovells, trying to work out a way forward while Ken Duberry was also needing to know more about the workings of the House of Clarks. I left all that behind me one day to go to Wembley to see the Neil Diamond concert. We saw QPR draw 0-0 with Millwall before going on to dinner at Wheelers and then to see Connie Francis at the London Palladium and that was a disaster.

We became totally convinced that she was drunk. Rolling around the stage she slurred and forgot her words and the performance was cancelled. We were told by the stage manager that she was unwell but we surrounded him demanding our money back. We went home and sent a letter to the theatre management but never did get recompensed. A year or so later Connie collapsed onstage in America and was finally diagnosed with the 'toxic illness' now seen as 'bipolar disorder' she'd apparently suffered from for years. A great singer but unlucky in her private life because, apart from several failed marriages, in 1974 she was raped in a motel and in 1981 her brother was murdered.

KEN2, KEN3 and Diana

On January 4th 1990 I started my first official day with Lovells, but it had been a busy four or five weeks leading up to Christmas before that. We took Chris and Bob, with Roger and Pat Felton on a two-day trip to Portugal, then I had to have my BUPA medical before flying out to Las Vegas to see Nigel Benn (the Dark Destroyer) knock American Jose Quinones out in the first round. The following year he would win his first world title.

As Chris had now sorted out our new offices in Upminster – the furniture was in and it all looked fine – so we decided to throw a KLBC party. It started at midday and went on 'til 11pm. During it, at 6pm to be exact, I announced that we had the Lovells deal wrapped up and that the company would be responsible for running its factory in South Wales.

There were more meetings with Hunter Saphir people, like Mike Cannon who came to explain how the Clarks' distribution systems might be changed. Mike was in fact the MD of Hunter Distribution, a guy I got on particularly well with and who remains a friend to this day.

Hunter Saphir then sent Bruce Daly to Dagenham to meet me as they were not certain whether they wanted to continue with Q Peanuts, or indeed selling nuts at all. In that case I had to have even more meetings to make sure Clarks honoured all the commitments relating to using up any cellophane that had been purchased on our behalf.

I took Alan Simpson to Hancocks to introduce him and then to Langans for lunch with Arthur and Thelma Perkins – he was a Director of Palmer & Harvey – before on another merry-go-round of introductions to as many top clients as we could possibly get in. In fact customers were getting quite used to me by now, having first been round to say goodbye, introducing them to Nick and John Saphir at our Clarks Night. Then I'd been taking Ken Duberry on the rounds and now Alan Simpson.

On the family front we went to the Savoy Grill for dinner and on to the Paul Daniels Magic Show, before visiting Dad's grave and going on to see Mum. Then it was off to Great Danes for Christmas, the Palladium to see 'Allo Allo', the movies to see 'Back to the Future 2' before seeing the real icing on the Christmas cake – watching QPR beat Everton 2-1. A few days later we got an even better result when we were at Old Trafford to see our team draw 0-0 with Man United.

After that first day in my new job at Lovells, I stayed the night in a local hotel before going home to take Lynn to the Widford Lodge School Ball and then flying out on what was my last trip for Clarks to the USA. Not my last association with Clarks however because at the Football Writers Dinner that month we took Ken and Norma Duberry as our guests. He was trying to find out how we dealt with the social side of our business and of course how important that was.

I spent a full week at Lovells, with lots of organised meetings but as an aside I can reveal another stroke of luck. I had recently purchased a number plate with KEN2 on it but then found that KEN3 was also available, well providing I bought the car it was attached to. I agreed and a couple came down from the Midlands to deliver it so now I had two cars in the garage that I didn't need but each bearing number plates that I still own to this day.

I went back to Lovells head office in Tipton to report on my findings about my recent trip to Newport then, a few days later, flew out for the ISM Cologne. Now this was a bit of an unusual year because not only did Lovells have a stand there, but the House of Clarks had its usual one as well. I had to find ways of working both stands at the same time.

While I was there Lynn phoned me to tell me we'd been invited to the wedding of our neighbour, Frank Bruno who was marrying his longtime girlfriend Laura. It had all been organised very quickly so I flew back to London, went to the wedding and reception and then flew back to Germany.

When I got back Lynn and I took Bradley and Chel to Portugal and on our return attended the Relate Awards luncheon at the Inn on the Park. Over the years I have met many celebrities but this particular one turned out to be a real highlight.

Relate was the new name for the charity, formerly the Marriage Guidance Council, that tried to help broken families and Lynn and I had been invited to be part of a fundraising team headed up by none other than Diana, Princess of Wales. At the Inn on the Park we were presented to Diana for the first of what would become many times.

Lynn and I being presented to Princess Diana at the
Four Seasons Hotel in Park Lane, London

In fact we did attend quite a few committee meetings with her. One of the interesting points about Diana was that, though she was a famous name and obviously pictured everywhere, there was another side of her that we were fortunate enough and privileged to see. We would have evening meeting in a hotel in Hendon that she attended and about which no one knew. That told us that she was not the publicity seeker that she was often accused of being.

Back to business, I was travelling to Newport every week for a few days at a time and reporting back to Tipton. Peter Wayte came down for a meeting with me and Neil Jenkinson, Lovells' Sales Director because we were trying to put a Management Buy-out – one I was not intending to be part of – together. The Hagons took Lynn and me to Ginos to celebrate our wedding anniversary, after which Lynn went into hospital for one day for a small minor operation.

Meanwhile I had to go back to Newport because one of the things I had discovered was that the stock rotation did not seem to be in order. It was pretty clear that thefts were prevalent and I had a meeting with a special investigation company, recommended to me by Andrew Hancock, who specialised in this sort of thing.

It didn't take long to find out that more goods were being loaded onto vans than were being invoiced for, so it was quite a difficult situation which meant the sacking of a number of company employees. Needless to say, the result certainly helped Lovells' profits. Then we had lots of meetings with the MD of the Lovells Group where Peter Wayte was involved. There had been agreement with the Lovells Board that a buy-out could take place if the deal was right.

I was out at lunch with Ken Duberry after introducing him to Woolworths when I got a phone call to say that Uncle Alf, who had been very close to Lynn and me during our earliest days had been taken ill. He had been our saviour on many occasions and I was particularly fond of him but he'd been rushed into Epping Hospital.

After a few days when I was still rushing about around the country I went back to see him in the hospital and, although he had a private room, it was clear he was not happy. He and his new wife Betty were both aware that he was not likely to live much longer and he wanted to go home to Redbridge to spend his last days or weeks there.

I agreed to deal with that and also to get them some home help and plans were well underway with it all to happen in a few days. I was in Harrogate however when I got the news that he'd died on 13th March and I headed home for the funeral which took place on the same day and which I attended with Lynn and Brandon.

Later that week, after Cheralyn's Parents Evening where all was well, and going to the opening of our architect friend Tony Harding's new tea-room in Burnham on Crouch I spent a day 'sitting shiver'. For those not acquainted with Jewish customs this is a seven day grieving process following a funeral.

There was one lighter moment in that period (apart from going with George Heley to see QPR beat Spurs 3-1) when the Evening Standard came to take photographs of our house and pool. They did that along with other properties in Emerson Park and as a result we appeared in the paper the following day.

Chapter 18

House of Clarks, RIP

I tried to buy it back

In April 1990 I took the family for a week to Portugal, getting back just in time to see QPR lose 1-2 to Manchester United. Then we went, with Bill and Ivy to the Wembley Arena to see a Country and Western show featuring Jerry Lee Lewis, but work was still predominant in my life and I had a couple of meetings with Ken Duberry one of them during what I call a 'blitz day'.

I went to the Hunter Saphir office to collect him to take him to lunch at the Rank head office, and then in the evening I took Lynn to see QPR beat Sheffield Wednesday 1-0. After that we went on to the Lyric Theatre to see 'Bus Stop' before going on to the Apollo to see 'Geoffrey Barnwell is unwell'. Then it was off to an Italian dinner before going to the Odeon to see 'War of the Roses', arriving home at 2.30am.

We often had a 'blitz' like that – going out for a long day seeing films and shows and we were lucky to have Bill and Ivy, who were always good at looking after their grandchildren. The modern way is to talk of a 'work-life' balance but I'm not sure that applies to the kind of life I was living at that time because, despite now being financially secure, I was still working hard and playing hard. For example, apart from all the cinemas and theatres we visited, one day I took Chris to see the P&H exhibition at Penns Hall before going on to a meeting with Peter Woodman, the MD of Lovells at his head office in Tipton.

I was asked to set up a meeting in Dagenham where Mike Cannon of Hunter Distribution could meet Neil Jenkinson of Lovells. The idea was to try to put some of Lovell's business through Hunter Saphir's distribution company but I had also been invited to look at some new designs for Butterkist, when I learned that they had changed the company name to Butterkist Limited.

One of the things I had noticed on my return to Dagenham was the dramatic changes that had taken place. We'd sold popcorn in a couple of different sizes in our own way quite successfully, but the new owners had gone computer mad. Where we'd had a really nice board room, which had always impressed visitors for meetings, now there were banks of people sitting at computers and I was not impressed.

Certainly the ordering process was taking longer and it didn't appear to me that more business was taking place. I remember Chris Day, who was still working there, telling me that now they had become a big organisation, giving plenty of work to computer experts and designers, but were still selling Butterkist in a couple of sizes. The change was quite significant and it was clear that modernisation was taking place but, needless to say, profits were down.

I felt, and still do feel, that that was a great shame. So many people, apart from me, had worked long and hard to build up a company with around £5m sales and £2m profits. Changes however are always made under new owners and the old ones, like me, seldom approve, but I was still on a retainer as a consultant so I said what I thought and my views were constantly disapproved and ignored.

I remember predicting the company would not last too long and as far as I can remember it didn't go beyond a couple of years. In fact it became obvious that sales had dropped, expenses had increased and the company was making losses. Later I heard that the company was up for sale and it was likely that in that event a lot of people who had spent their lives working for the company would be losing their jobs.

After thinking about it I made a significant offer for it, one I believed and still believe, to be one higher than that made by the company it was sold to. I had a lot of support from the local MP Brian Gould and the Dagenham Post, all of whom helped me in my quest to keep the company open. I even employed lawyers to fight the owners in an effort to force them to sell the company back to me on the basis that mine was the best offer and in the best interests of the shareholders.

However the Directors didn't have to conform to that kind of pressure and I did not succeed in buying it back. The company was sold to another group as a business although it was moved to Barking, the Dagenham site was sold to a developer and a lot of people did lose their jobs.

In fairness the local council could not have supported me any more than they did but to no

Millionaire's hope for firm he started out at

'I want to buy back popcorn factory'

'Firm not closing down'

Butterkist factory for sale

The national, local and trade press ran several stories on my attempts to buy back the business, its eventual sale and subsequent closure.

Hunter Saphir disposes of Butterkist

By Peggy Hollinger

HUNTER SAPHIR, the herb, spice and food produce group, has disposed of Butterkist, the loss-making toffee popcorn business, for £2.9m. Hunter purchased the company for more than £15m four years ago.

Butterkist has been sold to Portfolio Foods, formed 18 months ago through a management buy-out of Hazlewood Foods' confectionery and snack foods business. It now claims to have 80 per cent of the £25m UK market.

Mr Nicholas Saphir, chairman of Hunter, said yesterday that write-downs in recent years had already negated the loss over the original purchase price and no additional expense would be incurred this year. The cost of 100 redundancies at the Butterkist factory – announced late on Friday – would be taken off the proceeds.

Mr Philip Courtenay-Luck, chief executive of Portfolio, said Butterkist's production would be transferred to the group's existing popcorn factory in Dagenham, thus wiping out "large overheads". Portfolio plans to invest a further £700,000 in combining Butterkist with Bard Brothers, its own popcorn business.

Hunter will retain the Butterkist factory and site – valued at £700,000 – while Portfolio has taken the fixed assets and brand name. The Butterkist brand accounted for £1.5m of the purchase price.

Mr Courtenay-Luck said he expected Butterkist, which incurred a loss of £500,000 in the first three quarters of the year, to return to profit this year. "Next year it will make a considerable contribution," he added.

Butterkist is one of three businesses which Hunter was determined to sell as it refocuses on herbs and spices. The other two are Matthew Walker and Emile Tissot.

Butterkist site set for housing estate?

AS HOPES rose that some Butterkist workers may get new jobs, speculation grew over the future of the now defunct factory site.

Machinery and stock is being moved out of the Blackborne Road, Dagenham site, while the future of the three-acre plot is considered.

Sweet makers Portfolio Foods bought out the popcorn and fudge makers for £2.9 million after the 100 plus workers were made redundant.

Director of Hayes-based Portfolio, Philip Courtnay-Luck, said: "We will be moving production to one of our plants just 15 minutes away. The last thing we would want to do is completely get rid of all those experienced workers for good."

Factory staff were told they were being given the sack during their Christmas party on the Friday before Christmas.

"Butterkist is the best brand of toffee popcorn in the country and we will still be producing, only at our Forest Gate factory," said Mr. Courtnay Luck.

Butterkist's former owners Hunter Saphir, still possess the buildings and land on the site, and are currently looking at the best use for it.

Owner Nicholas Saphir, said: "We are keeping all options open. Our agents are looking into all possibilities."

The land is valued at £700,000 but experts at Glenny, in Longbridge Road, Barking, reckon the cost could be nudged nearer to £1 million if flats were built on it.

Up to 100 one and two-bedroom flats could easily fit on the land.

avail. One compensation was that, when the new estate was built, they did name it Lewis Way and I went back there on a quick visit and took a photo of the signpost. After that the product moved through several different companies over the last few decades but is still on sale in the UK.

Thinking about it later I had mixed feelings. I was really happy when we sold of course because we guaranteed the future for our families and that was what really mattered to us all. But I did get pretty frustrated with Hunter Saphir who seemed (perhaps not deliberately) to be undoing all the good work we had worked so hard for.

We were a small business in size compared to their other companies, but we were the most profitable; yet they just seemed to want to go for turnover hoping profit would follow, putting in systems that were operating in their other, but less profitable, companies. I spent my two year consultancy frustrated as I watched all we had achieved slipping away for no good reason. I was pretty sad and I had friends still in the company telling me horror stories and that didn't help much either.

When it was finally over I adapted to life without Clarks much better than anyone around me thought I could. Most of them thought I would be lost without Clarks, but other opportunities such as Lovells came along and then the schools that keep me very busy, so never quite got to a full retirement.

I watched the Butterkist side of the business sold several times, from one company to another till it almost faded away, but I have never really looked back myself. I have to say that my years there must have been the most important part of my life, as most of my night dreams are about them. Even today I sometimes wake up thinking I have a decision to make or a trip to go on, or someone to see. All the people's faces from those days are so clear in my dreams.

Yes I would go back, with the same team, and do it all over again. It was hard, tough, crazy, but above all, so much fun and so very rewarding and I don't just mean in terms of financial security. To have been able to employ, work with and provide jobs for so many wonderful people in Dagenham, South Norwood, Wembley and Great Yarmouth was a reward in itself.

The customers we had in those days are mostly still around. Many of them still keep in contact and remain friends today, but sadly the House of Clarks is no more. RIP.

Brandon's poor old gran

We bought a villa in Dunas Dourades in Portugal (and later also an apartment) and after I took a group to Wembley to see the Cup Final between Manchester United and Crystal Palace that finished up 3-3 with Man U winning the replay 1-0 the following week we took the children, with Bradley's friend Mark, there. It was our first trip to the new villa that we had for eight years.

I was still busy helping a small group in Lovells who wanted to buy the company from Albrighton, the holding company but generally speaking life was a mix of Lovells, birthday celebrations and seeing shows like the Kenny Rogers Concert at Wembley.

On Sunday June 17th, Father's Day and just before my 47th birthday, Lynn sprang a bit of a surprise on me with the help of Peter and Liz Wayte. They came down for the day and I thought we were just going out for lunch. We sat around the garden drinking and chatting when suddenly Peter said he'd take us out for dinner. Apparently he'd booked a surprise and though we went in Lynn's car they blindfolded me so I couldn't see where I was going.

About twenty minutes later we arrived at the Warley Park Golf Club in Brentwood where I knew they did Sunday evening meals, so I wasn't suspicious when we walked in. Then I spotted a lot of familiar faces like Ian and Pat Yates along with Roy and Reggie Hall who had all travelled down from the North. There was also a tall guy who seemed familiar but who I couldn't place at first. Then he laughed and said 'Hello' in an American accent and I recognised him. Lynn had actually persuaded Mike Weaver of Weaver Popcorn in the States to come and surprise me.

That was all great but perhaps the biggest surprise of all was to see comedian Bernie Winters and his wife Ziggi. I was also shocked because Bernie, an old friend who used to top many a bill with his brother Mike, was very ill and had in fact retired. However Lynn had asked him if he would come to my surprise party and he'd said he would. It was a truly wonderful night and one of the few times I have been genuinely surprised.

Bernie persuaded Brandon to go on stage with him to help him perform the old Flanagan and Allen tribute act he used to do with Leslie Crowther. They were a great success that night, but it was a hell of an effort for Bernie who died at the age of 58 from stomach cancer the following year. I will always be grateful to his memory for helping to make my birthday such a wonderful night that year.

In fact I owe Bernie a great deal more than that. Many years earlier he had been on a trip to the States with Ziggi (who still stays in touch) where he'd stayed with a friend who had a hotel in Scottsdale, Arizona. He told us about a dude ranch they'd visited in Tucson and, being the cowboy fan I am, we went to stay there too. While there we also visited Scottsdale and fell in love with the place, promising ourselves that one day we'd have a house there. When we sold the company that is what I did and we've holidayed there every year since.

What a wonderful investment that proved to be. All our kids holidayed there while they were growing up and when Cheralyn gets married in 2012 that is where it will be happening. She always said she'd like to have a wedding surrounded by mountains and with guaranteed sunshine. There we have mountains and desert all around us, its peaceful, clean and pretty well crime free, thanks to the famous Sheriff Joe Arpio, who is reputed to be the toughest sheriff in America.

Anyway back to Brandon, he'd been caught speeding up in Macclesfield while we were up there for the New Year celebration. Peter Wayte got one of his local lawyers to represent him in court but my abiding memory is watching my 18-year old son in the witness box.

He made one of the speeches for which he has since become famous in his political life, explaining that he was not only unfamiliar with the local area but that to lose his licence would cause his 80-year old grandmother a problem. He explained how she lived alone, down in Southend where she couldn't get to the shops, so he had to go there every weekend to take her shopping.

It was a lovely story and to be honest, never mind the magistrates, I was quite impressed with my young son's oratory. It seemed they were too, because he got the minimum three points and a £30 fine – the lawyers of course cost more than that, but wow! The next day we celebrated by going racing at Ascot.

After going back to Newport with Chris and Chris (Day) to work on the administration of the company and the factory, I took a group to the Guild Hall in London for the Variety Club Lunch. We'd raised enough funds for a new Sunshine Coach and I was presented to the Duchess of Kent, a gracious lady.

It was also World Cup time and on the big day the final in Rome was going to be between Germany and Argentina who had Maradona in their team. Now in England we resented that man so much because of his 'Hand of God' moment that he cheated us out of a world cup victory with the previous time. So, just for a change most of us in this country were supporting Germany.

Now Bobby Moore, England's great world cup winning captain and his then wife Tina, had organised a special trip to Rome for the game. They'd persuaded BA to allow them a Concorde for two days for 100 people and I bought two tickets and took Bradley. We were met by a coach which

Bradley and Bobby Moore on our way to the 1990 World Cup final in Rome

took us on a tour of Rome before taking us to the stadium where Bradley and I sat alongside Bobby and Tina to cheer Germany on.

They won and after the game the coach was waiting outside to take us to a hotel on the outskirts of Rome for dinner. That went on until 3am and the following day we were back on the coach to the airport where the Concorde was waiting to take us home. A few years later Bobby, by then divorced and married to someone else, sadly died, but what a wonderful experience.

Gareth and Betty Thompson, with young Gareth visited us from Australia but then I took the family and Justine, to Los Angeles. From there we moved on to Palm Springs, then to Scottsdale in Arizona – where, after falling in love with the place, we signed up to have a house built – Vegas and the Hawaiian islands before going back to San Francisco and home. Justine? Oh yes. Well, she was a school friend of Brandon's at Forest School at the time, though she was two years younger than him.

She will appear again in this story because it was a teenage romance that resulted in marriage and, up to the time of writing, they've been married for fourteen years. While on the subject, it's worth mentioning that Bradley, who also went to Forest School of course, met Lisette there and they have now been married for eight years.

Oh yes, Forest School has a lot to answer for, but in the nicest possible way because Lynn and I have two great daughters-in-law and some wonderful grandchildren.

A royal welcome

When we got back from the States we went through one of those sad and happy, up and down, periods that always seem to happen once in a while where everything seems to happen at once. Chris had been in hospital for an operation, but we also learned that John Saphir was dead. Apparently, shortly after his best friend had been killed in a motor racing accident, he dropped down dead while exercising in a London gym. At the same time Toby, a friend of Brandon's, had been involved in a bad car crash and we were visiting him in hospital.

Then, after celebrating Alan and Sue Britain's wedding anniversary, I flew out to Jersey to update our customers on what was happening at Lovells before going out to Portugal with the family. On our return we had to attend yet another funeral, that of June Dickson whose husband John had set the ball rolling that enabled us to buy Clarks.

Back on the happy side, after a trip on the QE2 to the Norwegian Fiords – a gesture of thanks to those who'd helped us buy, and then sell, Clarks – we celebrated Lynn's 42nd birthday, her parent's 44th wedding anniversary and Bradley's 15th birthday. In fact just before the lad's birthday we went with the Hagons to Loftus Road where we beat Chelsea 1-0 but for Bradley it was even more special than that. We had a party in the box, then he had a tour of the club, was given a QPR football and presented with a cake – blue and white of course.

Bradley was always one for stretching out his birthday so the next day we had a party in Madisons with friends before going home to continue it in the garden. Then we had a coach full of family and friends to the Beefeater at the Tower to complete the celebrations. Well almost, because Bradley and Tony had decided to earn a few bob for themselves, so we booked a stand at a car boot sale in Rainham for them.

RBS had a financial arm called Charterhouse who, as I mentioned at the time, were unable to help in my original quest to purchase Clarks, but they had followed my activities and what had happened. They asked me if I would go and lecture some of their employees at their college in Stoke Poges. They wanted me to talk about management buy outs, and mine in particular. Apparently you don't get paid for this but you do get a free case of champagne – and in my case a certain degree of satisfaction of course.

Still living a hectic lifestyle I took a group of family and friends to Wembley to see England beat Hungary 1-0 before we took off for Portugal with the Heley family. Then Lynn and I went with Laurence and Joan Munroe to Wembley to see Tina Turner. George Heley took Brandon and me to see his new box at Spurs, and the following week to the New London Arena to see George Foreman on his comeback trail years after losing his world title to Ali in 1975. George won the fight knocking out fellow American, Terry Anderson, in the first round!

Michael Land invited me to breakfast at Claridges to discuss some elements of his business but the dominating factor at that time was Rina Hagon being taken ill and being diagnosed with a serious form of cancer. She was rushed into Ealing Hospital and of course we rushed there to visit her. The following week I took the family to the Palladium to see Ken Dodd but I don't think we lasted to the end (who does last to the end of a Ken Dodd show?), going straight to the hospital to visit Rina.

Not one of the happy times but one spark of 'amusement' sticks in my mind. We'd gone home from the hospital to get ready to go to Bob's 50th birthday party. When we got there it was to find one of Brandon's girl friends of the moment actually trying Lynn's clothes on and she was not best pleased.

In fact she was so annoyed that when we did get to the party the first thing she did was to have a very large drink, and then a few more. I think it was the first, and only, time I have ever seen Lynn so drunk and I do mean drunk. Laurence managed to get a taxi home and then came back with it so we could get Lynn home. She remembers nothing of this, other than that she spent the whole of the next day in bed.

Actually not long after that another incident cheered her up somewhat. We'd been seeing a lot of shows in London theatres – 'Woman in Black' at the Fortune, 'Man of the Moment' at the Globe and 'Having a Ball' at the Comedy Theatre. I was also spending some time in London with Bruce

Daly and Mike Cannon of Hunter Saphir, but I was also getting close to the delivery of my new car – an Aston Martin Virage.

Because of that we were invited to tour the factory at Newport Pagnall and to arrive there at 11am. We did that and, to our astonishment as we drove into the place in the Bentley, found what seemed to be every member of staff lined up there to greet us, waving and smiling. It was a wonderful experience, nothing like we'd ever experienced before and of course we waved back to them. I remember saying to Lynn 'This is really something. I know an Aston Martin is a bit special but to get a welcome like this is so professional.'

We pulled into the car park, just in front of an Aston Martin which had actually been following us for a couple of miles and as we got out of the Bentley out stepped the Duke and Duchess of Kent from the Aston Martin. That's when we realised that the 'royal' welcome had not actually been for us – but at least we got to tour the plant, with them close behind us.

A kitchen for No.10?

Brandon, having left school, was working for George Heley in Grays and could not take a holiday. That gave us a bit of a problem because I was about to take the rest of the family to America and we didn't feel comfortable about leaving him at home, or perhaps leaving our home with him. So we booked him into a room at the Hilton Hotel in Hornchurch in the belief that whatever happened in the room would not be a problem for us, though I did feel a twinge or two of guilt in thinking our home would be safer that way.

I remember going out to buy a lot of chocolate bars, packets of biscuits and bottles of water – though I think by that stage my eldest son was drinking something a bit stronger. I left him with the words 'Don't knock up too much of a bill' – fat chance.

The rest of us flew out on Concorde to Washington, then on to Miami for a cruise before going back home, collecting Brandon from the hotel – after signing a bill that took some time to go through and a lot of explaining on his part. Still, with the winter and Christmas approaching the rest did us good and prepared us for our usual busy, at that time of year, social life.

I noticed that my father-in-law's car was not only getting on a bit but was also slightly dangerous. In fact he was driving what I would call 'an old banger', so I thought it would be nice to get him a new one for Christmas. We were all planning to go to Great Danes in Kent again for the holiday so we bought him a Suzuki and arranged for it to be delivered to the car park there on Christmas Eve so we could give it to him on Christmas Day.

In the run up to Christmas we took a group to the Circus Tavern to see Hale and Pace, Brandon and Justine to see 'Observed Person Singular' at the Whitehall Theatre and then took friends to the Palladium to see Gene Pitney. We saw 'Gasping' at the Theatre Royal, 'Hidden Laughter' at the Vaudeville, took Lynn's brother Tony and his wife to the Royal Albert Hall to see The Shadows and the next day we went to the Dominion to see Shaking Stevens. Whew!

After pausing for breath we saw 'The Boys Next Door' at the Comedy theatre with our friend from the Circus Tavern, Colin Stevens, to Wembley with Arthur and Thelma Perkins to see Charlie Pride, with the family to the Queens in Hornchurch to see 'South Pacific' and then with more friends to see Cliff Richard at the Wembley Arena. During all this Lynn found the time to go into hospital for a minor operation – oh and yes, QPR lost 0-3 to Leeds.

That Christmas the Hagons made their usual visit but one difference this year was that I took a large group of family, friends and staff of Cheralyn's school, Woodlands, to Leeds Castle. I will go into the growing relationship between myself and the school later, but by then I had 'bought into' the school and was a director and it was in that capacity, as well as a gesture of thanks for what they had done for Chel, that I included them in the Leeds trip. She, by the way was now having skiing lessons.

Then we heard that our new home being built in Scottsdale was ready to be furnished. Well in the main it had been as far as furniture was concerned, but needed the smaller items – the pots and pans, kettles, bedding etc. – so it was back onto Concorde and off to New York where we caught another plane to Arizona. Brandon was still working so it was back to the Hilton with his biscuits and mini-bar again for him. The rest of us spent six days completing our purchases before coming home again to pick up Brandon and pay his hotel bill again.

We did have a Country and Western party in Upminster before, first going to visit Dad's grave, heading off with Bill and Ivy to Great Danes for the actual Christmas holiday. This one was a bit special because we had been a bit coy about Bill's Christmas present and he was clearly wondering when we opened the curtain. We'd placed his new car in a position that could be clearly seen from our window and I remember pointing it out in the car park saying there was a new Suzuki down there.

'What a lovely little car', he commented and at that moment I put a box with a bow on it into his hands. Inside the box were the keys to that car and while they rattled inside the box he still didn't connect it with the car, until he opened it to find them. Then the penny dropped and we suggested that we all – Chris and Bob as well as the Hagons of course – went down to the car park to see the car.

Bill was quite an emotional man at the best of times and this made for a very emotional Christmas morning. He kept that car in perfect condition and it was his pride and joy until the day he died many years later. There was nothing anyone could do after that to persuade him to change that car because of its emotional attachment, while for Lynn and I the sight of his face and his reaction that morning made it all worth it.

The New Year started busily as far as our regular social round was concerned – I even managed to take the boys to Wembley to see England beat Cameroon 2-0, but that winter we had some very bad snow. It was so bad that we couldn't even get out of the street so no school for Bradley or Cheralyn, while Brandon couldn't get to work. In fact we were about to go to Portugal but all flights were cancelled for a few days. Eventually Lynn and I, along with Bradley and Chel were able to get there for a few days.

We did get to the Relate lunch at the Inn on the Park with Princess Diana who, while rumours of a rift between her and the Prince of Wales persisted (and would result in an official announcement of separation the following year), I recall her as being as charming and dedicated as ever. She would not be the last public figure we would have lunch with that year as we will show shortly.

Before then however we were visiting a lot of places with a view to finding a new home for mum. She was, as ever, very independent and

Lynn and myself with John and Norma Major at 10 Downing Street

resisted any suggestions of going into a home where she could be better cared for and in the end we gave up trying.

The previous year, Margaret Thatcher having left Downing St, John Major had taken over as prime minister and on April 11th Lynn and I were invited to a special dinner there. This was largely due to the Lords Taverners and I was delighted to be invited – in fact I was so enchanted by the place that I didn't want to go home and they found it difficult to get rid of us at the end of the evening.

I'd had a few drinks (of course) and that made me a bit bold I suppose because when everyone else had gone I remember saying to our host: 'Is the bar open upstairs and are you important enough to get another drink?' He said he was and as a result Lynn and I stayed around a bit longer with John and Norma who, it turned out, had a friend who was teaching Bradley at Forest School.

I particularly remember what a dreadful kitchen Norma had to put up with and, having had another drink or three, I offered to buy a new one for 10 Downing St. Norma thought it a good idea and the following day I confirmed it in writing. Then, and I still have it to this day, I got a charming letter from the Prime Minister explaining that the kitchen was not theirs, that it belonged to the state and there was no way that any gift of that magnitude could be accepted.

John was (and I expect still is) a very exact and honest guy who was very easy to talk to. At the time I was wearing a rather flashy evening jacket and I remember his commenting that, unlike him, I was obviously not a Chelsea supporter. I told him about my history with QPR and the evening continued even longer.

I was amazed at his knowledge of both cricket and football – he was a really interesting guy and they were a very nice couple who made us feel very much at home. He took us into the Cabinet Room where I managed to find a piece of 10 Downing Street notepaper which I still have in my personal collection.

John Major, who as you will see later does figure in our lives in the future, had other things on his mind at the time with the first Gulf War, but he was very charming to us that day.

Ian and Pat Yates with Lynn and me.
Here we are on board ship before having dinner at the Captain's table.

Chapter 19

Woodlands

I bought a school by mistake

In the previous chapter I mentioned Woodlands and that my association with the school had gone beyond just being a parent. The school will now be playing an increasingly important part in the whole story so perhaps now is the moment to expand on that. I need to explain how it happened and how a 'failure' of the St Marylebone Grammar School – the only boy in its history to fail every exam – came to own a school.

Cheralyn had been going to the school for a few years by then and both Lynn and I had been impressed with her progress and with the school itself. In Great Warley, a very historic and rural part of Brentwood, the primary school had been opened after the war and was being run by Linda Tingle, its owner and headmistress.

Originally known at "Wareleia", the village of Great Warley is Anglo-Saxon in origin and was mentioned in the Doomsday book in 1086, when the population was just 38. Even its 'woodland' is mentioned as having 200 pigs, while in pasture there were 100 sheep, eight cattle and a beehive. The village is the third highest point in Essex at 368 feet above sea level and is surrounded by parks with many scenic walks within the village itself.

Up to the early and middle part of the last century Great Warley was very much a 'big house' village – a part of Brentwood. Many local celebrities and wealthy people, including Ellen Willmott the famous hor-ticulturalist, lived in some splendour there employing villagers to work in their farms, gardens and houses. Going back even further there are suggestions that Elizabeth 1st may well have passed along Great Warley

Street, on her way to Tilbury to make her inspirational speech to the troops waiting for the Armada that of course never arrived anyway.

In fact the Common at Great Warley had been an assembly or mustering point for her troops at that time and had then gone on to become a full scale army barracks that was only closed in the fifties. Over the centuries men had marched out from that barracks to build (and lose) empires – in the Americas and then in India, when it was used by the East India Company to train its private army.

Anyway back to the story, there came a day during Cheralyn's time at the school that it was going under financially. Linda Tingle knew me as a parent but that I was also a business consultant and she asked me to go and see her. She explained that the school was having financial difficulties and that her bank had given her fourteen days to pay them what she owed. If she failed to do so they would close the school and sell it, with the land it owned around it, to recover their money.

Now it was at this moment there was a total misunderstanding between us – one that led to me one day owning Woodlands. I thought she was asking me to lend her the money to pay off the debt, but in fact her purpose had been only to seek my advice. I looked at the papers and immediately realised that seven of the fourteen days had already come and gone. I pointed that out to her, saying that I would help and that I could get the money in that time.

That genuinely shook her rigid because of course actually asking me for the money had not been in her mind. 'Do you mean you will help us?' she said.

I told her I would and would contact my friend and lawyer Peter Wayte, which I did. Within the seven days the debt, loan and overdraft had been cleared, the school (and Cheralyn's primary education) had been saved and I'd become a director with 25.1% of the company. That gave me some control over finances and, in particular, over Directors salaries.

The deal was that I put in £25K and held shares at £1 each for five years. After the five years I was to get my money back and they got the shares back. It took a year to bring the company to a break-even point but from then on we made substantial profits and the value of the shares rose as a result.

At the end of the five years we duly offered them their shares back in return for my £25K – shares which by that time were worth £500K – but they said they wanted me to keep them and stay on with the company. We did point out how much they would be giving away and advised them that they should talk to their lawyers about it first. They said they fully understood that but it had been my intervention that had saved the school and enabled it to prosper which was why they were asking me if I would stay on.

To be honest by that time I had rather fallen in love with the idea of helping children through their early years, and it didn't take a lot of thinking about it to agree. Initially my only interest had been in ensuring that Cheralyn was able to continue at the school, but during those five years I had fallen in love with Woodlands and stayed that way even after Chel had moved on three years later.

Then the day came when Linda and Alan, her husband, wanted to retire to their homes in France and Croatia. Linda had often mentioned selling the school but not to anyone but me and now she asked if I would buy their shares too. I agreed to do that and that made me a majority shareholder.

There were eleven other BES (Business Expansion Scheme) shareholders and since then most of them have dropped out so the company, which of course since then has expanded with another school (Hutton Manor) at the other end of Brentwood, is now 99% owned by the Lewis family.

I was a chauffeur

If life is to mean anything at all, it is to have friends. I have had more than my fair share of them and I do not mean just passing acquaintances or working colleagues. Some of my closest friends have been so for many years and I will always be grateful for their friendship. That also includes of course many who also worked for, as well as with, Lynn and me.

There was, for example, a married couple called Linda and Martin Bevan who we employed for many years to help us in so many ways. Linda helped Lynn around the house and Martin, who is still with us after all these years, looked after the garden and our cars. We once took them both to London, to the Queens Theatre to see 'Matador' and on to Bentleys for dinner afterwards. The following day we went to the Queen's

Theatre again, this time the one in Hornchurch, to see 'Risky Kisses' with Laurence and Joan Munroe.

Then Roy and Reggie came down from the north to stay with us when we all went to the Grosvenor House for the Candy Ball, and the following night we all went with another group of friends to the Ambassador Theatre to see 'Shoyna Maidelel'. So you see that while we were still enjoying a great social life, doing so with friends was the best thing about it.

May 5th that year (1991) proved to be a special day simply because of a friendship – that with Peter and Liz Wayte – who asked me to be Godfather to their new son John Henry. Peter of course was more than just a friend, because he'd been so instrumental in my business success so I was more than delighted to agree.

They'd already had a couple of children but I was honoured to do this. In fact he is now twenty-one and I can honestly say that I have really enjoyed being his Godfather and the special bond that exists between us. He and I have always kept in touch and these days of course with e-mails it is even easier to do so.

He kept in touch while at school and then when he went on to university. I went to Uppingham to see him play rugby and then followed his progress through all his tours abroad – tours that included a prolonged stay in Brazil. He would send me videos of all the special times he enjoyed in Brazil and of course we are still in touch – another example of a great relationship resulting from a great friendship.

As I say, friends are very important in life, but of course family even more so and Mum came to stay with us for a few days on her 79th birthday. Around the same time I was lucky enough to get tickets for the Monaco Grand Prix and, leaving the women at home, went with Brandon and Bradley to see British driver Eddie Irvine come third to the winner Mika Hakkinen and Giancolo Fishichella.

As it happened Irvine was driving a Ferrari while the winner Hakkinen was in a Mclaren-Mercedes. Another British driver, David Coultard retired half way through the race but it was an unforgettable day.

Brandon and I were, at the time, still looking for a property he could move into and we had been negotiating for a flat at the new development on Hutton Poplars. In retrospect it was a little ironic because at the time we had not been aware of Mum's childhood connection with Hutton Poplars when it had been a children's home. You will remember that she had spent some time there and had had the awful experience of waking up one morning to find her five year old sister had died in the next bed. We completed the deal in June and our eldest son moved out of the family home (always an emotive moment) into his first flat.

Not long afterwards I was offered the chance of a table at the celebration of the Duke of Edinburgh's 70th birthday party at the Royal Naval College Greenwich. We took some friends and found our table was next to that of the Duke's so we could see and hear everything that night. Great experience!

We had another 'friends' experience at that time as well. We were still living in Fairlawns Close in Emerson Park when one of our neighbours (the Wood family) were organising a family wedding. Lisa Wood was getting married and we were invited to the evening reception which we were delighted to attend.

Then, half an hour before the wedding, in a church in Hornchurch, there was a knock on the door and it proved to be a desperate neighbour. It seemed that their chauffeur driven car had broken down at the last minute and no replacement could be found. They knew of course that I had a Rolls Royce in the garage and wondered if I could drive the bride to the wedding.

What Lisa didn't know was that I also had a chauffeur's cap, so I put that on and drove her to her wedding in real style. Actually it was all quite fun and is another reminder that friendship is a two-way street. As it happened, a couple of days later my own birthday present to myself – the Aston Martin – arrived.

Not that our friends are all British either. Next door to us at our new home in Scottsdale we had a couple called Kal and Liz Rubin. Both of them have since passed away but they were great neighbours and very special friends.

Kal, already in his seventies, would poke his head over our garden fence and call out to Cheralyn. 'Let's run away to Disneyland together – I'll pick you up later tonight' he would tease her. He had a special affection for her and always said he'd be around for her wedding which, of course he no longer is able to attend when she does get married later this year (2012).

Kal and Liz often came to London for any special family events, but he was very connected in Arizona. He actually owned a street in Tucson, where he grew up, along with all the shops in it, but his influence went much further than that.

Bradley and I were sitting in his house one day when my son was talking about going to university and mentioned Arizona State University, which is in Tempe just south of Scottsdale, saying he would have liked to have gone there. Kal promptly picked up the phone and explained to someone that he had a friend from England whose son wanted to go to the Arizona University. The message came back 'no problem Kal – whenever he's ready'.

It turned out that he'd been talking to Barry Goldwater, Governor of the state and who he'd grown up with. In fact Kal had Governor, Senator and many political friends and connections all over the United States but never boasted about them. A generally quiet and shy man he called himself a wealthy Republican and I learned a lot from him, particularly about the American banking system. Indeed, until he educated me on that score I was at risk there for a while.

Liz, his wife, was equally ebullient – a charming red-haired and friendly woman – and we were lucky to have them literally as both friends and neighbours. On that score we lost another neighbour back home when Pat Greaves, who had been a particularly good friend to Lynn, died of a heart attack. Sadly, that year, she would not be the last friend we'd lose.

Rina

We watched proudly as Cheralyn won her first gold medal at the Woodlands School sports day before taking the family off to Scottsdale for a month. When we got back Woodlands had reopened after the holiday and a new girl, Elizabeth Buttie (or Liz as everyone called her) had joined the school.

Now at the school we did everything we could to help children with learning and/or physical disabilities but Liz was blind and that was something we had not catered for. Chel, because of her kind and loving nature, was given the job of sitting with Liz and talking to her at playtimes etc. and they became very good friends.

Liz was with the school for a few terms but then it got to the stage where she needed far more help than we could give her and she went to the blind school at Dunton House in Kent. By then she and Cheralyn had bonded with each other and Chel was missing her lovely kind nature and was a bit upset that her friend had gone so far away. So, from time to time I would take her to Kent to visit Liz, who was being extremely well looked after in her new surroundings.

Socially it was another busy period with theatres and football taking up a lot of our time, though Brandon did have to go into Holly House for a small operation on his throat. It was also time for another Relate meeting. There were nine of us, including Princess Diana, at the Hendon Hill Hotel that day. She was always very relaxed at these meetings and very passionate about helping children in particular.

Although she always had a driver and security of course, there was never any press involved and no one other than us knew she was there. She came, she helped and then quietly went back home to Charles (then) and her normal life. A genuine person and that is surely why there was such an outpouring of national grief when she died so tragically seven years later.

In October that year Lynn took delivery of her new BMW850i and then as Christmas started to approach we were into our usual round of theatres, concerts and dinners as well as, of course, watching QPR. The boys and I, sometimes the whole family, still attended the games frequently and in fact I still have all the programmes of the matches I ever attended.

By this time I was also very involved in helping the Conservative Party, becoming a member of its 'Team 1000' and was invited to an evening in Smith Square, the party's HQ at the time. After that we all went to Scottsdale for a couple of weeks at half term.

Brandon went into Hartswood Hospital in Brentwood for a small operation on his knee and somehow his pain must have affected me as well, because we had to call out an emergency doctor at 2am for myself. I can't remember much except that I was in a lot of pain but fine the next day. After visiting Brandon in the morning Lynn and I went to see 'It's Ralph' at the Comedy Theatre. On our way home we collected Brandon who was using crutches. He had spent a total of five days in hospital.

I decided it was time I bonded further with my daughter, well that was always an excuse to take her out to London for the day. We started out of course with a trip to Hamley's Toy Shop, the play BFG (Big Friendly Giant) at the Aldwych Theatre, lunch at Bentley's and then, of course, a trip to Harrods before going home.

Not that I was ignoring work – far from it, because I was having some serious meetings with an investigating company to get help relating to some of the problems at Lovells. We had been experiencing some that had been adding to the company's losses.

At this time Rina Hagon, who had been diagnosed with cancer, was still in hospital and some of her relations from Italy came over. George and their son Paul took them, and us, to dinner after which we all went to Ealing Hospital to visit her. I took the staff of Woodlands and some friends to Leeds Castle for a Christmas dinner party.

I paid a Christmas visit to Dad's grave and then Lynn and I went with her brother and his wife to the Savoy Grill. I remember this evening particularly well because when we got home it was to find Bradley there, drunk. He never could remember where he'd been other than it had just been a night out with the boys but I don't remember his mother being too impressed.

It had been a normal sort of Christmas, apart of course from the fact that this time we did not have the regular visit from the Hagons, though Rina was never far from our thoughts. Then, on December 29th, at 3.55am, she died and we lost a good friend, with Bradley losing his Godmother and I would like to take a moment here to think of her.

A very wonderful and unusual lady who spoke Italian with a Cockney accent and English with an Italian one – depending on how many drinks we'd got down her. I have so many memories of her, like seeing her standing on a Grosvenor House chair at a Variety Club Ball singing Land of Hope and Glory.

George had met her during the war when he was in the army in Italy and his tale of how they met and decided immediately she would be his wife was one he often told. He'd told her that when the war was over he would be going back to take her home, but in fact he went back and married her in Italy before bringing her home.

We'd known of course how seriously ill she was and that it was only a matter of time but, when it happened, it was still very painful. The Hagons and the Lewis family had, over the years practically become one family and it was the first time we had lost one of its members.

I got the call from George and Paul that Rina had passed away and, after a brief chat and putting the phone down, wondered what the hell I was doing still sitting at home. I told Lynn what had happened and got into my car to drive over to Southall to spend some time with George and his son. I do remember that I couldn't get there fast enough, but of course all I could do then was sit and talk about her. George was lucky, at that time of his life, to have Paul with him to give him his support and strength.

In fact he was not terribly well himself and though he had been realistic enough to know that Rina was coming to the end of her days, it still came as a terrible shock. It probably helped bring his own life to a premature end because he was never quite the same again. Life without Rina was never going to be easy but having Paul there telling him he had to go on, did help a great deal.

It did not make for a 'happy new year' of course (well apart perhaps from seeing QPR beat Manchester United 4-1, yes 4-1, at Old Trafford being the one bright spot. We finished 11th in the 1st division that year and qualified for the new Premiership league starting the following season). Ian Yates came down to stay with us and then we all went to Rina's funeral.

Sadly, not long after hers, Ian and I had another funeral to attend – that of Stanley Kitts who had owned the Daintee Confectionery Company in Blackpool and who had been such a great help in the production of confectionery in Clarks. Stanley, a really charming man and a good friend as well as being a trusted business colleague, had been our first guest in our new home in Emerson Park. It had in fact been Stanley, a father himself, who had given us such good advice about how to act when we'd put the kids to bed and were creeping around the house trying not to wake them.

Chel is taken to the Tower

By 1992, despite my own 'failings' at school as referred to earlier in this chapter, I have always been keen to ensure that my own children did not follow in those particular footsteps. Brandon was at Buckingham University, Bradley was still doing well at Forest School and Cheralyn was proving to be a good and in some areas gifted student at Woodlands. Then a marvellous opportunity for her to learn more about the history of our country presented itself.

As a Lords Taverner I was allowed a couple of tickets for a special dinner in the Tower of London. This was to be held in the Officers Mess with Lieut. Colonel George Pettifar, the Lord Lieutenant of the Tower at the time and offered a marvellous opportunity to see more of the Tower which, of course, I had known all my life. Once the home of the English kings and queens it had of course seen some notable executions and held some equally notable prisoners – in the 20th century from Nazi Rudolph Hess and traitor William Joyce (Lord Haw Haw) to the Kray twins who were taken there for a few days after not turning up for their national service.

I was fortunate enough to fall into conversation with Col Pettifar, a fanatical Arsenal fan and I offered to take him to see his club play QPR in my box. In return he agreed that we could return with Cheralyn to show her around the Tower.

So it was that a month later we were there for a very special tour, seeing some very interesting areas that the public generally do not get to see. That included the Governor's House, the cellar where the murdered young princes had been kept and to the top of the battlements. Cheralyn learned a lot which I know she has remembered to this day. It was one of those very special days out for all of us.

Not long after that Bradley and I had a sort of special day as well when I took him to see Lennox Lewis (no relation of course) win the Commonwealth heavyweight crown by beating Derek Williams. The following year, in October, Lewis beat our old neighbour Frank Bruno on a technical knockout in the 7th round.

Actually around this time we took Chel and Bradley on another treat – a couple of days in Euro-Disney, when it rained all the time. As a result it was pretty quiet and I guess that Bradley, at his most mischievous at the time, got bored as we waited for a ride, and decided to pull my shorts down to reveal my underpants.

Clearly he was trying to impress his sister and thought it was hilarious, though the French sense of humour was quite different and I don't recall me falling around laughing either.

It does seem that a lot of this chapter has been as much to do with the loss of good friends as anything else and not long after Chel's 8th birthday I had another funeral to go to. If you remember in Chapter 2 I was taken in by Flo and Ed Barret in Alperton after I had to leave home in 1959. They'd looked after me for a few days, helped me find a bed and breakfast place and fed me in the evenings on my way home to my lodgings. They'd also maintained my morality in somewhat difficult times and were always a special couple to me as a result.

After Ed died I had stayed in touch with Flo who was living in Bletchley when she died too and it was yet another funeral I had to go to. After it I picked Brandon up from his University and took him out to dinner. Not long after that I had yet another funeral to go to.

This time it was for Alf Finch – a builder who had done a lot of extra work for us on our old house in Hornchurch. In fact, apart from a couple of week's holiday, he'd worked non-stop every day for two years, turning up early every morning and never left early. He was an absolutely charming man, a brilliant, fair and honest worker who, over time, had become a very close friend. We are still in touch with Babs, his widow to this day and I suppose that while I am sad to be recording the death of so many friends writing this book does give me the opportunity of paying them the tributes I believe they deserve.

It also means I can do the same with the friends we still have with us. In them I must include Steve and Anne Marie Taylor and it would be nice to lighten this sometimes sorrowful chapter with their very uplifting story.

When Lynn and I had moved to Emerson Park back in 1975 some neighbours recommended a restaurant they'd discovered in Old Harlow. It was some distance from our house of course but it was a small, discreet and upmarket place called The Gables. We found the place and had enjoyed it so much we became regulars, along with a number of Spurs and Arsenal footballers, and that was a draw too.

It was owned by a very nice elderly lady and we had regular bookings there when our orders were taken by a waitress called Anne Marie, who took them out to the chef who was Steve Taylor.

The lady who owned it decided to retire and wanted to sell out to Steve and Anne Marie because of their long service and also because they were getting attached to each other. In fact she was not happy about anyone else getting it but they couldn't afford it so she lent them the money herself to be paid back over ten years. What a magnificent gesture of thanks for loyalty.

Well they took the deal, got married, had children and still own The Gables to this day. I even went to the party they held to celebrate the last payment and we booked the place ourselves for the Millennium Party in 1999 when we shared it with their family and ours. We've holiday in Dubai with Steve and Anne Marie and, if I can put in a personal 'advert' here The Gables still does well under their ownership and is always worth a visit.

As I have just indicated the other end of the scale to losing friends is to make them and perhaps this is a chance to introduce another name that may become familiar later in the book. I had a new car, a Shogun, delivered to me by a young man working for Nelmes Motors. His name was Russell Quirk and at that time he was around 20 years old.

Well it didn't mean much at the time but about twenty years later Brandon became prominent in local politics, as Leader of the Council in fact, and the name Russell Quirk appeared again. It rang a bell and I emailed him to see if he had worked for Nelmes Motors and indeed he had. In fact his father, a local publican, had also been a friend of mine for years as have now I become with his son who is an estate agent. In fact I have even helped in his campaign to become a Brentwood Councillor and as members of the local Conservative party have worked together (and played) on many occasions.

Again on happier times I should include my Mum's 80th birthday in this chapter when we took her, and fifteen others, for a private birthday dinner in the Savoy Hotel, after which she spent the weekend with us.

Chapter 20

Oh, Bradley!

Bradley goes on the run

We went to see the New Year in at Claridges – well most of us did. Medically speaking it had already been a bit of an emotional lead up to Christmas that year, so Claridges had been intended to be a new start in a way.

Brandon had been suffering with a knee problem, visiting the Wellington Hospital two or three times a week while, shortly after the Woodlands Christmas Carol event, Bradley had been rushed into Whipps Cross Hospital. Fortunately that turned out to be nothing much and he was home again the next day but even Brandon's basset hound Bertie had been taken to the vet after being taken ill. He too had recovered and was with us all in Claridges.

Now, health issues apart, we were also having a lot of 'teenager' related problems with Bradley, who was more interested in spending the time with his pals from school than with 'the old fogies'. He played up quite a bit in fact but we laid down the law and finally, albeit grudgingly, he came with us. We all checked in and went to our rooms to unpack etc., but that was the last we saw of our youngest son that year.

What he did was to pick up his rucksack and vanish from the hotel as soon as our backs were turned. It made for a particularly dreadful New Year's Eve for us without him of course but we tried to enjoy it. We had no idea where he'd gone to, although I did have my suspicions that he'd gone to see the New Year in with his pals. Needless to say his mother was frantic and I even got the police involved in looking for him without success.

We were pretty sure that he would be with his friends somewhere but at that stage we had no real idea where that could be and there wasn't much more we could do about it. The next morning we all – Brandon, Bob, Laurence and me – spent New Year's Day out looking for him until finally we – well it was Brandon and Bob as far as I can remember – found him. While we'd been desperately worried, he'd been having a wonderful new year's eve at a friend's house. We were not impressed and, needless to say, words were said.

When it came to going back to school after the holiday Lynn and I decided it would be in all our best interests for our somewhat rebellious son to be boarded at Forest School. He did and by all accounts had a wonderful time. As far as I can remember he regularly stayed out later than we would have allowed him to at home. He was going to local pubs and not just with friends but in some where teachers also went. He'd not been keen to go there as a boarder but somehow the life did suit him and definitely did help him to grow up.

In retrospect perhaps Bradley wasn't the only rebel in or around the family because it was about this time that I got thrown out of Downing Street – well it was Ian and Pat Yates who got us thrown out and at least it wasn't Number 10. Both strong Tories, I'd taken them to a meeting of the Team 1000 at 12 Downing St. Ian is quite vociferous at the best of times and was pushing, asking so many detailed questions that finally we were asked to leave. I've been thrown out of a few places in my time but surely none as prestigious as Downing Street and we went on to have a few more drinks in the Grill Room at the Cafe Royal.

I have mentioned Team 1000 before but I should explain that it was a Tory Party group of supporters who had donated a minimum of £1000 to the party. I had long been a committed Tory of course. That activity has increased over the years, including in Brentwood after we moved there, and of course these days Brandon is currently a Tory MP.

Cheralyn of course was still at Woodlands where I was increasing my investment and had become a Director, but she had ambitions to go to Brentwood Girls School when she was old enough. We took her there so we could see around it ourselves. This ancient school went back many centuries to pre-Elizabethan times and had produced many great achievers, from politicians and soldiers to sportsmen and show business successes. For all those centuries it had been a boy's school only, but five years earlier it had taken a decision to admit girls as well and wanting to go there was a pretty positive desire on Chel's part.

We were visiting Bradley at Forest School a lot, because to be honest we were missing him, but we were also going to see Brandon who was playing for the Forest Old Boys. I was also getting more involved with Woodlands and trying to bring a little more business expertise into it.

They had not been used to having any kind of formal meetings, including Board Meetings so, now a director with 25.1% of the shares (at that stage) I introduced them to that practice with their first one. From then on we agreed to have regular monthly meetings to discuss all aspects of the business.

It made sense to try to get the business, for that was what the school was after all, onto a more secure footing. A successful private school has to be a successful business too and until then nobody there seemed to be talking to anyone. As a result, outside of the educational side which was always excellent, no one knew what was happening in the business. I'd learned a lot with Clarks of course and that kind of knowledge, expertise and experience was clearly going to be essential in Warley in turning the school round. In fact at some stage that year the Woodlands directors decided to hold a dinner at the Romford Dog Track and I couldn't possibly imagine whose idea that was.

Talking of Clarks, at the end of February that year I decided it was time to hold a reunion with all the original House of Clarks staff. I invited them all to the Palms Hotel in Hornchurch where we put them up from Friday to Sunday and had a wonderful long weekend of meals, drinks and generally talking over many memories. Sadly today so many of those old friends are no longer with us of course, but I owed them so much and as far as I am concerned this was more than just a gratuitous gesture.

I still look back over that particular weekend with happy memories. It still gives me a warm feeling that I did something worthwhile in bringing us all together again for what turned out to be the last time. I'd started there as a young man on what was probably the lowest rung of the ladder and had not only risen to the top (and gained a wife from it) but had finished up actually owning the firm.

Yes, I like to think that that had largely been as a result of my own energy and endeavour, but that would not have been enough without the equally hard work and support of so many other people – from the shop floor and tea trolley to the boardroom. That wonderful weekend in the Palms was my way of saying a final, in some cases, thank you to all those people.

The last time I saw Laurence

It must be pretty clear by now that friends and family mean a lot to me and have always played a very important part in my life. Family first of course but I have had some friends for many years – some even going back to my school days, as teachers Bosley and McNeill had predicted back in 1954 when I started at the SMGS.

There have been others like George and Rina Hagon and of course Ian and Pat Yates, along with so many more I am proud to call, or have called, friends. Take Tony Betts, for example, who I first met when he joined Woodlands School. A fully qualified sports physiotherapist he was taken on to teach the older children exercise and physical training but in a sense he taught me a lot about personal health too.

We became great friends and I decided to take him on as my own personal trainer. He came to my house a couple of times a week, but I would also go to his gym in Rayleigh (Essex) a few times a week in return. In fact to the best of my memory I never missed a training session in over sixteen years and this being a particularly stressful period of my life staying fit was, and remains, very important.

After he retired I stayed on the correct path by joining a local gym, but Tony had become yet another of those close friends who helped not just me but other members of the family too, and remains a friend to this day. Then there was Bradley.

No, in this case I am not talking of my second son but of footballer Bradley Allen, another personal and family friend who I'd watched playing for QPR on March 6th 1993 when we beat Norwich 3-1. I know I have the date right, because that day I drove him home – he lived in Essex too.

In fact we'd also known him for a while under very different circumstances because Lynn and Bradley's mum Pat were together in Harold Wood hospital going through labour – Lynn with Brandon and

Pat with Bradley – so the families had known each other for a while. Fifteen years or so after I drove him home, Bradley Allen began working for Woodland Schools as a sports master

Ten days after I drove Bradley Allen home, I went to Fulham's Craven Cottage then under the control of Jimmy Hill, but not to see Fulham. Jimmy had donated the ground for the final of the Independent Schools Cup and one of the teams was Forest School which had a lot of Bradley's (our Bradley) friends on the team sheet.

Forest School had reached the final for what I believe was the first time and were seen as the underdogs against Charterhouse. Our school did have a fine team at that time and a lot of support – we had thirty coaches of parents etc. at the game, while Charterhouse had over fifty. By any school standards it was a massive game and I do remember thinking – and don't forget, I had been watching professional football for most of my life – it was one of the most exciting games I'd ever seen.

The team, which actually won the game 5-2 – included Tony Lawlor and David Pratt whose father played for Spurs, but Forest School also included a young man from Soweto who stood out among all the players that day. His name was Quintin Fortune and he'd been 'discovered' by the then Spurs manager Terry Venables. He had persuaded Quintin's parents to let him bring him to England (don't forget apartheid was at its height in South Africa then), where he'd enrolled him at Forest School.

Bradley, my Bradley, had been helping the young South African to learn more about the English way of life in the playground etc. and they became great friends. In fact they remained friends for many years and we were all pleased when Quintin went on to make a career out of professional football, including at Atletico Madrid, Manchester United and Bolton Wanderers, let's face it, you have to be pretty good to get a contract at Old Trafford, or with Atletico Madrid for that matter. He also won 53 caps with South Africa.

In May that same year however a different kind of problem developed when I found myself in the middle of two friends I'd fallen out with. On the fifth of that month Laurence Munroe left his wife Joan and their sons Simon and Russell for no apparent (at the time) reason. One of my oldest friends Laurence part owned a printing company which did all the printing for me at Clarks.

I have to admit I'd known there had been problems there for a while and that he was considering such a step but I never thought he'd actually do it. In fact I was totally shocked when he left Joan to go to live with another woman he'd known as a business colleague for a long time. We had always been close as families and I read from my diary at the time how often I had been going to visit Joan and the boys. I wouldn't call it counselling because I don't have that kind of qualification, but I was a good friend who could sit and listen as well as talk and so help in that way.

I did phone Laurence after he left Joan and he did promise to come to my 50th birthday party the following month, but he never did. There was another down side in a way as well because he asked me to take care of his wife and make sure she was alright by looking after her to the best of my ability. That was always going to put a strain on our friendship because it meant I had to take her to the solicitors and get the best deal possible for her with regard to her home, pension and finances etc. I did that but of course it soured the relationship between Laurence and me for a long time, because the only way I could live up to my promise to him was at the detriment of our relationship.

That was almost twenty years ago and time is a great healer and we have stayed just in touch, although the birthday cards seem to have stopped. Although we were the closest of friends and are still in contact, via Christmas cards with an extra little note in them, I have never seen or spoken to Laurence since. I've been to West Ham and sat close to his seat but never caught so much as a glimpse of him again, which I always believe was a great shame. Losing friends in that kind of way was a new and unwelcome experience for me.

Eventually Joan managed to move from Upminster to Shenfield, not far from where we live now, so we do still see her from time to time. We do hear about Simon but Russell, who is now a gardener, looks after all the family's gardens as well as those of some of our friends. I still get comments from Laurence thanking me for keeping an eye on them all, but sadly he has never seen his sons since the day he left. I still think that this particular time was and remains one of my unhappiest moments.

A surprise from Oz and problems in Portugal

By this time I was getting more and more involved with Woodlands and felt that we were lacking a little expertise in one area in particular – one that I happened to be personally interested in. Cricket was the only sport we were not covering and that didn't seem right.

I managed to find the Ilford Cricket Club, then being run by a man called Joe Hussein who had a son who'd been at Forest School a couple of years ahead of Brandon. The son had gone on to Durham University before ending up playing cricket, first for Essex and then for England, following in the footsteps of Graham Gooch and Keith Fletcher by captaining both. His name is Nasser Hussein and from 1999 to 2003 he captained England for 45 tests and remains a highly respected name as a journalist and pundit in the game today.

With that kind of track record in training cricketers I was confident in Joe Hussein's ability and keen to get him. He started working for Woodlands, training our own school teams for a few years. Not long after that I persuaded a neighbour and ex-professional footballer, Mike Flanagan who'd played for Charlton and QPR, to help us out at Woodlands too. He took on a part time job to do so, meaning that by then we had real professional expertise out there on our cricket and football pitches.

It was Cheralyn's 9th birthday so George and Paul Hagon came over to stay the night while Joan Munroe, with whose solicitor I was still negotiating regarding the marital split, joined us at home for the party. Now Chel has always been one to want to spread her birthday about a bit so, apart from the party at home she insisted on dinner at Madisons and then lunch at the Gables the next day, but the party that sticks in my mind at that time was thrown by our local MP Robin Squire.

He wanted to celebrate his son Nick's 21st birthday and his wife Susan's 50th, so he hired a boat for a trip on the Thames. I remember very clearly how worried he and a few other Conservative MPs on the trip were that, because the party was going through a bad time, they wouldn't get re-elected. In the end some of them didn't, but he did and remained a good constituency MP for 18 years.

Celebrating another election victory for good friend Robin Squire MP for Hornchurch whom I worked with when living in his constituency.

Then, of course, there was my own 50th birthday party. Thinking about it, I must have been getting younger because, with Brandon only 22 that day, I was only just over twice his age when some years earlier I'd been four times that. Joking aside we had a party at the Royal Lancaster Hotel in London for 200 guests – in fact the only person who never turned up was my own doctor who, ironically, was unwell at the time.

Anyway it was a really great party and was perhaps one of the few times that Lynn, with Brandon's help, caught me out. I was suddenly called to the phone because they had set up a surprise phone call from Australia where my old pal Gareth Thompson was living. I was handed the phone and there on the other end of the line was Gareth's wife Betty, singing 'Happy Birthday' to me all the way from Australia.

Then she said 'I suppose you want to talk to your buddy as well,' and called Gareth to the phone. Suddenly I heard his voice and the reception on the line was so clear it was just as though he was in the same room as I was. Then I felt a tap on the shoulder, turned round and found that he was standing behind me.

Brandon had taken care of him the night before after he'd arrived in the UK and had smuggled him into the hotel, keeping him out of sight until that very moment. My first reaction was to have someone save a meal for him but it had all been taken care of as part of what had been a really wonderfully organised and fantastic surprise.

Gareth stayed with us of course and when we went off for a week in Portugal he came along too, so we had a wonderful week before he had to go home to Oz.

Up to now I have not mentioned Peter Ives, a photographer who over the years became another close family friend. In fact he has consistently taken photos of us and the children over the years. Even our children are now using Peter to take photos of their children, our grandchildren. He is now not just the official photographer for Woodlands Schools, but also for so many of our friends and their families too.

He would have also been taking the photos at the Woodlands Speech day which that year was followed by a concert and a football match which I refereed. I am uniquely unqualified to referee any kind of football match, which is why I suspect I was always asked to do so for the annual Fathers versus Sons match. I would never admit it of course but it was almost mandatory for the boys to beat the dads and always did, but it was a great opportunity for the Dads and Sons to get together. That led to the annual Mums versus Daughters netball matches.

The Woodlands School Football Team.
A very proud dad to be playing alongside both the boys: Bradley top right with his brother Brandon, top row, fourth from the right and me top left.

Bradley was coming to his 18th birthday and also the end of his time at Forest School of course when it was customary for the boys and girls to go off on a trip together. Bradley asked us if he could use our flat in Portugal for a group of around four so they could fly out together. This did make us think a little of course, especially in view of his New Year antics and we had a meeting with them to discuss their behaviour. We were assured there would be no problem and that there would be just the four of them travelling together.

They never thought to mention that at different times seven or eight more would be joining them in our very small two-bed roomed apartment so, oblivious to all this, we took Chel away on a trip to Canada, the U.S.A. and to board a ship on a cruise to Alaska. Then, just as the ship was sailing out of Vancouver, Brandon phoned to report that there had been problems in Portugal. He told us he had to buy a ticket home for Bradley and quick.

The rest of that cruise was not as relaxing as we'd hoped it would be. That was largely thanks to the calls between us and our neighbours in Portugal who were telling us about dozens of boys and girls flooding our apartment.

Eventually we got back to Scottsdale where we found that Bradley's group had been chatting up some Portuguese girls who 'belonged' to Portuguese boys who'd chased them back to our flat where they'd been under siege all night. The boys had decided to get out quickly and while I never found out how the others got home, Bradley had done so on the ticket his brother had bought for him.

The apartment in Portugal was never quite the same for us after that. We put in new doors, mended a few broken items of furniture and changed the locks but we decided it was time to sell it rather than have any repeat and eventually that's what we did.

Spurs is not my team

We were getting close to Bradley's 18th birthday but it looked for a while as though I would be celebrating it on crutches, thanks to a spot of mountaineering in Arizona. A friend and I had decided to climb the mountain and run down it again, but unfortunately the effort seemed to damage my back, so I was having some daily physio sessions for it.

At the time it really did look as though I'd be very limited in what I could do and having been active all my life that was very frustrating. Fortunately the physio worked and that, along with the help of some good painkillers I was able to hold everything together.

More of our friends from Arizona, Lee and Rita Wilson arrived for their first (of many) visits to the UK. They look after our house in Scottsdale and had become close friends so Bradley's event provided a good opportunity to invite them over to stay with us. They came to stay in London for a week and for people from Arizona that was quite an experience. We didn't have the time to give them a full UK tour but we did show them around Essex and its beautiful countryside. (Their President at that time, George Bush and later his son of course, had ancestral roots who'd come from Messing, near Colchester).

Anyway the big day came and we all went to the Inn on the Park for our younger son's birthday celebration where a couple of hundred friends etc. turned up to help us mark the day. My back was still a problem but with the help of some painkillers, and some alcohol of course, it was a wonderful evening enjoyed by all. That especially applied to Bradley of course who got his new BMW3 series with a personalised number plate.

Then we all went off to Portugal for a short break and on our return found another Scottsdale friend, Richard Gilbert, was in London so we had dinner with him in the Savoy Grill. Then one day I arrived home from work to find another old friend, Gerry Robinson, sitting in our lounge having tea with Lynn. Gerry was Jean's (my ex-wife) uncle and I hadn't seen him for years but in the old days we used to spend a lot of time together and it was nice to see him again.

Lynn and I had decided to take Chel on a special Christmas treat – to Australia – so after Bradley's big day we spent some time in Australia House organising our visas. Bradley however had to go into hospital for a minor operation but was home the following day.

I was invited by Daniel Sugar (Lord Sugar's son) to have a look at the boxes at Spurs where at the time his father was Chairman. In fact he offered me a very favourable deal and I have to admit that I was tempted. Then I remembered Tottenham was not my team and while it was closer to home of course I'd been a QPR man for a long time and never felt that Spurs would be as exciting so I declined. I have since then enjoyed some nice occasions at White Hart Lane but my loyalties remain at Loftus Road.

Lynn and I went to see 'Time of my Life' at the Vaudeville Theatre and went on to Simpsons afterwards, getting home to find Brandon had invited some of his friends round to see our old neighbour Frank Bruno fight Lennox Lewis on TV. The fight, called by some newspapers the 'Battle of Britons' because it was the first time two British boxers had fought for the world heavyweight crown, was won by Lennox on a technical knockout in the 7th round.

I seem to remember that the fight, held at Cardiff Arms Park, was brought forward by an hour because rain was expected and there was a story that Lennox was asleep in his changing room at the time. He certainly took some time to warm up but when he did he soon had Frank in trouble.

Generally speaking at this time things were still looking pretty good. The regular board meetings at Woodlands that I'd instituted were proving worthwhile and were helping to improve the general running of the business by putting it onto a proper business footing. Doing so well in fact that by Christmas that year I had to take the children and staff to the Queens Theatre to see the pantomime as usual but this year over two days because the school was growing so quickly.

Actually Lynn and I, along with various members of the family, were still doing a lot of theatre going as 1993 began winding down to a close. We'd even been to the Tory party conference in Blackpool with Ian and Pat Yates, but seen a lot of legitimate theatre too. We'd seen 'Lysistrata' at the Wyndhams, 'Carousel' at the Shaftesbury, Lloyd Webbers 'Sunset Boulevard' at the Adelphi, 'City of Angels' at the Prince of Wales, 'Hot Stuff' at the Cambridge Theatre and 'An Inspector Calls' at the Aldwych.

Speaking of socialising I remember having drinks at the time in what was called the highest placed pub in England. I'd grown up thinking that a relative called Sylvia was a cousin but in fact she was the grandaughter of my 'Nan Salmon', and she invited us to her daughter Leanne's wedding in the Derbyshire Hills. The next day we went to Portugal for half term.

Then, after a firework party at home in November we saw 'Eurovision' at the Vaudeville Theatre before taking Chel to the Palladium to see

Sylvia and John Grainger's wedding in Dover.
Sylvia is the only surviving 'relative' to have known me since birth.

Bobby Vee. After that we took the whole family, including Bill and Ivy, to the Prince Edward Theatre to see 'Crazy for you', following that with dinner at Simpsons – Bill particularly likes eating there because of the roast beef they carved at the trolley.

We took Joan Munroe, who we were still keeping an eye on, to The Gables to celebrate her 50th birthday and there were a lot of Christmas lunches and dinners around that time of course. We intended spending Christmas in Australia so we had a lot of early events here with friends and family before then. We did a pre-Christmas lunch at home and had the Woodlands Christmas lunch at the Palms hotel, then Lynn, Chel and I flew out to Bangkok for a few days before moving on to Hong Kong and then to Australia.

Brandon and Bradley had both decided they wanted to stay in England for Christmas. In fact Brandon and Justine had flown out to Australia before us and we did meet up there for a few days before Christmas before they flew home in time for Christmas Eve. On the day itself they had lunch with Justine's parents who also kindly fed and looked after Bradley over the holiday.

Lynn, Chel and I spent Christmas in Australia before flying on to Singapore, arriving home on New Year's Eve when we had our normal party for family and friends at the Gables. Now we had 1994 to look forward to.

Chapter 21

Brentwood

"Brentwood has always been a much sought after place
to live, boasting the best of urban and suburban living..."
(Gareth Jacob, Sales Director Linden Homes Eastern 2012)

Honouring the legends

At the time of writing this Lynn and I live in a very nice home in an exclusive part of Brentwood – an Essex town recently described as one of the five best in the UK to live in. Our house faces, across a lake, the one in the same small group of houses that Brandon lives in and is within easy reach of the rest of our family, but it has been a long and winding road.

For me of course that road began in a small flat in Hendon before going on to a motel in Stratford, rooms in a house owned by friends in Gidea Park and then to our (Lynn and I were together by then) first house in Hornchurch. After that we moved to Emerson Park, where at one time world heavyweight boxing champion Frank Bruno was a neighbour (and friend) and where we lived for many happy years before coming to Roundwood Lake. How we got here is a story in itself, one that began in February 1994 when Brandon, who was still living in his Hutton Poplars flat, began looking for another place.

We'd started the New Year in our usual way with friends and family, theatre and football. That included a family dinner at the Savoy with Ian Yates who was in London as usual for the Boat Show. I'd also taken Brandon back to Buckingham University to get his results and we were all delighted to find he'd been given a B.Sc. It's always nice for parents to see that their investment in their children have paid off and we're no exception, being proud of all our children and what they have achieved so far.

Bradley and I were taken, as guests of LJK Garages who we'd been buying cars from, to watch Spurs beaten 1-0 by Manchester United. It was a good game with the winning goal scored by Mark Hughes a Welshman, but it was also the first time we watched another exciting young Welsh player called Ryan Giggs. Even then he looked a cut above the others, a real prospect and of course, since then he has become one of the most famous players ever to come out of the Man U stable playing over 800 games for them.

Coincidentally at the time of writing Hughes, now an established and successful football club manager has been appointed as manager of Queens Park Rangers. I saw someone else in the crowd that day – my cousin Michael Harris – and we had a chat, but it was the last time I ever saw or heard from him again.

Actually a week or so after that I went to help honour another Man U (and Man City) legend, Denis Law, who was the guest of honour at a Football Writers Association annual tribute dinner. Now I have referred several times in this book to the FWA, having been to every one of their annual dinners, so perhaps should explain my relationship with it. So how did it come about that I, not a journalist or football writer, should be involved with the FWA?

Well it actually all began back in 1982 when journalist Denis Signy OBE was chief executive of QPR, where of course I had a box. He was also a famed Fleet Street sports journalist and, sitting with me having a drink in the box one day, he mentioned that he and other writers were thinking of setting up an award to honour someone playing or otherwise involved in football.

He was trying to organise a dinner at the Savoy for the following year and asked if I would take some tickets. I agreed to take a table for the House of Clarks but then, seeing he was struggling a little said I'd take tickets for two tables, i.e. 20 tickets. In fact I seem to remember taking 80 tickets in all, around half the number that actually turned up for the event which in that inaugural year honoured the then recently appointed England manager Ron Greenwood C.B.E.

The following year when Liverpool manager Bob Paisley was honoured we managed to get a couple of hundred people there and I took my usual number of tickets. Then, as the event began to become more prestigious I was able to reduce the number of tickets I had to buy. Over the years we have honoured the legends and real knights of the game like Stanley Matthews, Tom Finney, Bobby Robson, Bobby Charlton, Alex Ferguson and Trevor Brooking as well as so many other giants. That included, incidentally, in 2007 the same Ryan Giggs who had impressed us so many years earlier

In fact the event became so successful that they brought a rule in that only people in the football world itself would be able to buy tickets. It is now regularly sold out at 500 and because of my earlier support for the event I am still allowed to buy enough tickets for a table of 12 guests even though not being connected with the game I was not entitled to do so.

Until two years ago Denis Signy and I were the only two to have been at every event since that first one, but then he became ill and missed a couple of years. So I am the only one now who has been to every one of the dinners which this year 2012 is set to honour two more Manchester United legends Gary Neville and Paul Scholes.

Anyway back to 1994 one of my guests, George Hagon, came to us for the day of the dinner and went with me to LJK Garages when I took a car there to be serviced. While we were waiting he spotted a BMW 7 series – not new, but just what he'd been looking for. Even better as far as he was concerned the number plate included the letters BFG – the initials of one of his favourite books, The Big Friendly Giant. He bought it and kept that car to the end of his days.

Mr. Stone

As I said at the start of this chapter Brandon, who had been living in his flat in Hutton Poplars, had started looking to buy a house. One area he had been scouting was Hutton Mount, only a mile or so from the Poplars and in a very exclusive part of Brentwood in Essex.

Strictly speaking our own home in Hornchurch then had been in Essex (and in postal terms still was), until a great reorganisation had taken place in the early sixties that had resulted in Hornchurch becoming part of the London Borough of Havering. Brentwood was still part of the county of Essex and was an ancient and historic small country market town surrounded by charming villages. It has since grown to become a much bigger place, a borough in its own right with its own mayor, and we did not know then that one day Brandon would become a very significant figure on its council.

We had heard of a new development on Hutton Mount called Roundwood Lake, but at the time we also had a bit of a worry with Bradley who needed two operations. He had a throat problem but also a hernia lower down and wanted both problems dealt with at the same time so he persuaded two different surgeons to use the same operating theatre in Brentwood's Hartswood Hospital at the same time.

Fortunately the two surgeons knew each other petty well and they agreed to his request. As a result it meant that Bradley only had to have one lot of anaesthetics and was out of hospital in three days and we could get on with our search, one that led us to Countryside Properties and an odd coincidence.

For several years every Saturday morning I'd been taking Cheralyn to her drama club in Woodlands Schools. While I was waiting for her I often chatted with another father, also waiting for his daughters and although he knew who I was I did not know his name. Lynn and I had been in a Shenfield estate agency, Beresfords, where we'd spotted an advertisement for eight houses about to be built around a lake on Hutton Mount.

Further investigation showed that the houses to be built were no bigger than the one we already had in Hornchurch, so I asked if I could buy two of the plots available and have one house on them. The agent decided to phone Countryside Properties, who were building the houses, and managed to speak to the Managing Director of the project. His name was Stephen Stone and he said he actually knew me, but to be honest his name meant nothing to me then.

We were invited to go to their offices there and then, which we did and were shown into the Board Room. Shortly after we arrived the door opened and in walked Mr. Stone, who I instantly recognised as the other father who'd been waiting for his daughters at Woodlands every Saturday with me.

Perhaps that helped because Countryside agreed I could have the two plots, 6 and 7; but then later while away in Scottsdale, I got to thinking that if I bought plot 8 as well it would give us 1.2 acres of land to build our dream house on. It also meant we would have the last plot on the

development, so over the phone on the other side of the Atlantic I negotiated successfully with Stephen Stone and bought the plot.

The Roundwood Lake development had been planned as a group of eight houses but now had just six, with us living at the end of it. At the same time I also bought one of the other five plots for Brandon who now lives on the other side of the lake at the start of this nice and peaceful 'Close'.

This was just as well because it was around this time that Brandon and Justine decided to get married. They'd been together a long time, having met at Forest School and decided they wanted to spend the rest of their lives together. So, at the same time discussions about the properties were going on, wedding plans were also being made and everything was starting to fall into place. In fact shortly after that Justine came with us to Buckingham University to see Brandon get his degree.

Brandon's Graduation Day - Now a Bachelor of Science in Economics

333

There was a lot of romance in the air at that time when, for one thing, Lynn and I celebrated our wedding anniversary before going up to Scotland to attend another wedding – that of James Shaw. James is the son of Derek and Gloria Shaw and Derek had been my factory manager, after joining us from Crusader Confectionery, for many years and we'd kept in touch.

We were only in Scotland for the day because the following one I had been invited by the Royal Bank of Scotland to a dinner at the Carlton Club. At the time I had no idea that the club, in St James Street in London had any political affiliations and had just gone there for the dinner. Now of course I know much more – Brandon and I are both members and it has played an important part in his political career for you have to be a Tory Party supporter to become a member.

Then we had George and Paul Hagon coming to us for dinner and with them they brought a young lady called Jane who Paul had been dating for a while. We took them to a restaurant overlooking Shenfield Common in Brentwood, called Ye Olde Logge. At one time celebrity chef Anthony Worral-Thompson ran the kitchen there though I have no idea whether he cooked for us that night. Later the centuries old building itself burned to the ground to be replaced by a modern block of flats.

As we will see later Paul and Jane are still together – in fact they were married in Kent and asked Cheralyn to be a bridesmaid. We were all excited by that – Chel especially of course because the wedding was going to be on her tenth birthday, but before she could walk behind Jane down the aisle she had a little more walking to do – along the Great Wall of China.

Going for a 'Chinese'

Looking over my notes that particular travel episode had us circum-navigating the globe, but first Lynn, Bradley and I had drinks and dinner with 'Pippa' and then with the Prime Minister of the day. Pippa, I should explain is actually Philippa Jessell, a criminal barrister in London where she lives and who had been extremely helpful to me in business when we needed advice on criminal law. She had become, and remains, a very good friend.

The next day Lynn, Cheralyn and I went to the Chinese Embassy to obtain the visas for our trip to China, and that night I took Lynn to Newmarket for dinner at the Jockey Club with John and Norma Major. Then, on Mother's Day we took Mum to The Gables after which she stayed with us overnight. Then we were up and away.

The People's Republic of China had gone through enormous changes since being established in 1949 by Mao Tse Tung and by the time we arrived there in 1994 the man in power was Deng Xiaping. He had been busily transforming the bleak and hard line Communist state into a much more, even 'capitalist based' one and indeed at the time of writing China has become one of the leading economic power houses in the world.

Deng died three years after we were there but the very fact of tourism being encouraged by that time was a sign of his influence on party thinking. He opened China up, not just to tourists like us but to industry and the business world in general. The country we visited was just getting used to the relative freedoms that Mao had denied them and it was an extraordinary and interesting experience.

The Great Wall of China for example is an obvious target for tourists and we were no exception. Well Lynn actually preferred to see it from below but a 9-year old girl was a lot more adventurous than her mother and insisted that I went with her to walk several stages. Then we came back to a typical Chinese meal which, as I have said before, is not my favourite kind of cuisine but I had a few Mars bars in my pockets.

From there we flew on to Japan where Chel had another experience she will never forget. We attended an evening where Japanese girls who danced on the stage invited members of the audience to join them and our girl needs no more encouragement than that. Then we had yet another culture change when we arrived in Taiwan, expecting it to be very much like China. It probably is now because then Taiwan was full of factories manufacturing goods for export all over the world, much as the mainland does now.

We flew on to New Zealand, a different and new area for us, where we met up with an old friend, Jo Leathley who we knew from the North of England. She'd left there to join her family who'd previously emigrated to New Zealand and it gave us the chance to take her to dinner. We went on a wine tour of that lovely country before taking the longest flight, across the Pacific, to Los Angeles from where we flew on to Scottsdale where we spent a couple of weeks recovering.

Then we completed our global circumnavigation by flying home – arriving there twenty-four hours before our suitcases did. I had to go back to the airport the next night to collect them.

At least we got back in time to have dinner at 10 Downing Street with John and Norma Major who organised it on behalf of the Water Rats, but we also had our AGM at Woodlands Schools where I was getting more deeply involved. I was also still having meetings with Countryside Properties over the plots I was buying for Brandon and myself. At most of the meetings we included Tony Harding, an architect and our friend who had helped us build, and with various extensions, our first home. Like so many others he remains a friend to this day.

We did have some other problems around that time because Brandon was having some pretty serious back problems. They eventually led to a big operation carried out in Hartswood Hospital in Brentwood. He was there for around five days and we were constantly going backwards and forward to see him. Then, when he did get home to his flat he was stuck there for weeks, needing constant attention with wound dressings that needed changing.

Fortunately 'Nurse' Justine Rappolt, as she was then, was on hand to help, which was just as well. He did have a real nurse for a period of time but after then they expect you to get it dealt with yourself. Justine, as I remember, was absolutely tremendous – always going round changing his dressings and making sure he behaved himself. Well, nothing's changed there!

We celebrated George Hagon's 70th birthday with a dinner at the Inn on the Park after which he came to us the next day for lunch, but a couple of days later we got the sad news that we lost another old friend.

David Peak had been a good friend, both personally and in business, for many years and had been ill for some time, during which we'd been visiting him frequently. He was a confectionery buyer I'd met years ago when he was working for Makro, a big cash and carry outfit in Eccles near Manchester. He would often come and stay with us – very popular with the boys, because he always brought them presents. (This was before Chel was born).

He had an office in the north, in Eccles, and was one of those friends and business colleagues, always good company, who came on many of the company trips abroad. A bachelor, he was a lovely man and one with an eye for the girls, often having one on each arm and was the sort of person who would help anyone.

He'd been diagnosed with a cancer that, while incurable had been treated in Christies in Manchester successfully enough for him to enjoy his last few years doing what he liked most. That was travelling the world to see countries he'd never seen but had often wanted to visit. As I say he was a great lad with plenty of girlfriends, many of whom felt close enough to him to come to his funeral – one which Roy Hall and I also attended.

Back on the brighter side Woodlands produced the Wizard of Oz in which Cheralyn had a part and which we attended on both nights; but the big news was that it was Justine's 21st birthday and we had a party in Brandon's flat. The next night we had another, bigger, party at the Royal Lancaster Hotel at which she and Brandon got engaged.

So now we were having meetings with Countryside Properties and at the same time some with Peter and Marion Rappolt, Justine's parents, about a wedding.

Back to Forest Green

While Brandon was now looking forward to his big day with Justine, his little sister was looking forward to her own – another wedding on her tenth birthday – that of Paul and Jane Hagon, at which she was set to be a bridesmaid. It took place in Kent of course and we all arrived for dinner at the Burford Bridge Hotel in Dorking, on June 9th so the guests could all get to know each other.

Dinner and a few drinks of course – well perhaps more than a few, as was our custom where George Hagon and I were concerned. Despite that I do remember, I think, the jokes and pranks played on people that night, especially on Paul after someone got a key to his room while he was still downstairs.

At the same time I remember deciding that guests were considering going to bed too early so, while a few more drinks were ordered, the boys and I managed to move some of the hotel's big items like pot plants in front of all the doors of rooms being used by the guests. We ourselves had a few more drinks and then went to bed, taking the precaution of locking our doors.

It was all taken in good fun and when the big day arrived it was a wonderful wedding in a glorious church with Chel especially enjoying her tenth birthday as a bridesmaid. There is now a standard joke in the 'Lewis-Hagon' family about this day because George and I, with other members of the family, had been discussing how some people took advantage of the free drinks at weddings and drank too much as a result. Disgraceful!

In fact George and I had been discussing that over six or seven bottles of wine and a couple of bottles of whiskey. In fact, unlike all the other and better behaved guests who had not taken advantage of the free booze we ended up quite paralytic. We would dearly have loved to deny this afterwards but unfortunately it had all been captured on video.

The only real argument George and I had over this episode was whether he was holding me up, or I was holding him up but neither of us could ever make up our minds, or how we got to bed for that matter. Though George is sadly no longer with us, the Hagons have continued to hold me to account on every occasion they can. My only defence is that it was a great wedding that we'd set out to enjoy, and we did.

While we were in that part of the world, the next day I took Lynn and Chel to an area nearby called Forest Green, where I'd spent a lot of time when I was at the St Marylebone Grammar School. One Wednesday morning in the summer we'd be picked up by coach outside SMGS, who owned the camp thanks to a cash gift from newspaper baron Lord Rothemere. We'd be taken down to deepest Surrey to spend the next seven days there, living in tents and digging ditches apparently learning to be surveyors.

It was a great part of the school year when we experienced life under canvas, cooked over open fires, dug our own swimming pool and laid out a concrete cricket strip. I hadn't been back there since but it was where I'd gone every year from the age of 11 to 15. Now, at 50, the place did seem somewhat different, but in the old barn where we sometimes used to sleep I even found a picture of my year group with me in it. Wonderful memories I was able to share with my wife and daughter that day.

Around that time Cheralyn was very much in our thoughts because apart from her day as a bridesmaid, she was becoming an accomplished musician. She had already passed an oboe examination and was sitting for a piano one. By the time she left Woodlands she had learned to play the piano and had certificates not just for the oboe but for the saxophone, recorder and cor anglaise. All these instruments are still in our home, along with a didgeridoo which she is the only person able to get any kind of sound from. When she calls in these days she just plays the piano, which helps keep the grandchildren amused.

Shortly after we got back George, Paul and Jane came over with the wedding video and, as usual, George and I had a few tipples – too many for him to drive his car so he stayed the night. Then a few days later I took Lynn and Chel to Montreal for a few days, before flying on to Scottsdale where we spent the next eight weeks.

Bradley flew out there to join us when we celebrated Lynn's 46th birthday at the Ruth Steak House in Scottsdale and the next day he left for home. It was coming up to his 19th birthday and in fact we got home the day after and celebrated at a small family party with him, Brandon, Justine and Cheralyn at the Peking Garden in Hornchurch. At the weekend, after I'd taken Mum to visit Dad's grave and Lynn and I had visited the new site in Hutton, we celebrated properly with a party evening with family and friends at the Joy Fook.

Speaking of birthdays, Brandon and I shared our birthdays as usual of course – that year he was 23 and me a mere 51, who celebrated it by spending more time at the Countryside Properties office in Warley. Then it was Ivy's 70th birthday which we celebrated at home with a family dinner. The next evening I took the family for a meal at Wheelers before seeing Copacobana at the Prince of Wales theatre. At the weekend Steve and Anne-Marie who owned the Gables entertained us to lunch at Hanbury Manor. Then there was the golf – ah, now there's a story.

Drowned rats on the 7th

It is pretty obvious now to any reader that sport has always played a big part in my life – football, cricket, boxing and racing (dogs and horses), you name it. One sport that has never appealed to me however, perhaps surprising for a businessman, is golf. Yes a lot of business deals are done on and around a golf course but I guess I was too busy in my business life for all that.

Brandon and Bradley however thought otherwise and were constantly telling me I should take the game up so eventually I agreed. My friend Alan Britain took me to a golf shop in Brentwood where we bought a cheap set of clubs and a bag to carry them in. Then the boys, with one of Brandon's friends, took me to the Epping Forest Golf Club near Chigwell, and it rained.

Did I say it rained? Well, the moment we arrived at the first tee the heavens opened and it dropped out of the sky, cats and dogs, stair-rods, call it what you will but we pressed on. By the time we reached the second tee we were pretty well soaked and by the time we got to the third tee most people had fled for cover in the clubhouse. Brandon and I however, decided to carry on mainly because he still felt I might get the flavour of the game and enjoy it.

As far as I can remember we were called in off the course at the 7th tee by which time we were like drowned and mud-covered rats. I decided then that the game was definitely not for me, at least in the UK, so I took the clubs home and stood the soaking wet bag, dripping with water, in the garage. There it stayed for weeks and weeks, never to be used again.

I know lots of bits of it went rusty but I'm not sure whatever happened to that set of clubs – probably still hidden away somewhere at the bottom of a cupboard but I am just too scared to look. It wasn't the end of my golfing 'career' however, because I did join another club but a long way from the rains of Essex.

This time it was back in Arizona because, it seemed that when you bought a home on the Gainey Ranch in Scottsdale the thing to do was take out a membership of the golf club, so I did but it was a business decision. Apparently you could only be a member of the club if you had a home there and they said it added great value to the property.

Anyway I had literally hundreds of lessons and I can remember standing on a tee with a golf professional in August sunshine with the temperature at 120 degrees. The only water then was that dripping off my nose onto the golf ball and into my eyes so I couldn't see properly while trying to hit that little ball as far as I could. After several years of this and having only once managed to get par 3 on a par 3 hole and not even being excited about that I decided that enough was enough.

Yet for some crazy reason I kept the membership for eight years before, realising I hadn't even been out on the course for four years, I wrote in to resign my membership. Well my house was never going to be worth any less and I could always call in there for a meal, but the game itself was definitely not for me.

To my surprise I was actually given back far more money than it had cost me to join. That was because membership fees had increased considerably and they gave you back an amount accordingly. I don't think I actually made a profit because there was always an annual fee to pay even when you are not playing but it was a pleasant surprise. I no longer go onto golf courses.

Still into other sports though and on Sept 24th I went with the boys to see Lennox Lewis fight Oliver McCall at Wembley. Lennox, the world WBC champion, was the out and out favourite but McCall shook the world by knocking the champion down in the second round. Lewis got up but the referee decreed he wasn't fit to carry on and gave the fight to McCall. A year later McCall lost it to our old neighbour Frank Bruno.

Shortly after that Bradley had to go into Hartswood Hospital for a minor operation, so minor he was home the same day, but Cheralyn's future was occupying a lot of our thoughts by then.

What with the school and our new home being built, Brentwood was playing an increasingly large part in our lives and would be even more so in the years to come.

Chapter 22

Globetrotting

A knight to remember

Cheralyn, rapidly approaching the end of her time at Woodlands in 1994 and was looking for her next school, attending a number of open evenings at different ones. Forest, of course, where her brothers had gone was an obvious option but she also looked at Chelmsford County High, St Martins in Brentwood, Cooper Coburn in Havering and Brentwood School which as we will see was where she finally ended up.

Bradley had not been terribly well however and I decided to take him on a break to see if that would help. We flew to Singapore, toured Asia and went on to Australia before coming home via Hong Kong. In fact we were doing a lot of globetrotting that winter as we headed into December and on towards Christmas – a lot of Christmases, almost frantic at times in terms of party time.

First of all, early in December, we had the Hilton Meats Christmas party at the Rodings and on the following day I took the family and some friends out to the Gables for a Christmas lunch. We took all the Woodlands children to the Queens Theatre Hornchurch for their annual pantomime treat and that evening took staff and friends to the Leeds Castle Christmas party. I visited Dad's grave and then took a group to the Albert Hall to see Elton John before having the Woodlands Schools Christmas lunch at the Palms Hotel in Hornchurch and a Christmas lunch at home – and it wasn't even Christmas yet.

Lynn, Cheralyn and I flew out to New York to do a spot of Christmas shopping and then went on to Scottsdale where we actually spent the holiday. We had some English friends, Tom and Frances Hindley (sadly

Frances is no longer with us), for lunch along with neighbours Kal and Liz Rubin who I have mentioned before and who have also passed away since.

It was a reasonably quiet Christmas after that but we really missed the family – Chel especially missed her brothers, so we flew back home again in time for New Year's Eve and to welcome 1995. That was when Roy and Reggie arrived from Cheshire and we all went to the Gables for our New Year's Eve party. Then on New Year's Day (1995) we took family and friends to the Heybridge Hotel in Ingatestone (no longer there) for dinner. During those early days of the year we even managed a spot of culture by squeezing in trips to see the Nutcracker Suite at the Festival Hall with Chel and her friend Anna, following that with going to see Peter Pan at the Cambridge Theatre.

In the last chapter I mentioned the Football Writers Association annual dinner which occurs in January and the one that year in the Savoy stands out in my memory, for it was to honour a true knight of the game and a personal boyhood hero. Having been part of the first one and attended every one since then, none was quite like that of the one held in 1995 to salute Sir Stanley Matthews CBE as he approached his 70th birthday that year.

That night he looked every bit a footballer of his day. In his playing days Sir Stan had been a role model that many of today's expensive and highly paid 'stars' could learn from. Silver-haired, he was smart, elegant and an absolute gentleman who had represented both of his clubs (he only had two – Stoke City and Blackpool) – and country with distinction. He was the only footballer to have ever been knighted while he was still playing – which, incredibly, he was up to the age of 50.

Dubbed the 'Wizard of Dribble, he had never fallen foul of referees and had never been known to retaliate when fouled, other than in terms of making opponents look foolish. It was even jokingly claimed that, when he crossed a ball from the right wing to his centre or inside forward's head, he made sure the lace was facing away from his team-mate's forehead. A very friendly man, albeit a little shy, he had no inhibitions about talking to people or signing autographs and it was one of the most memorable of all the dinners I've ever been to.

From when I was about 7 or 8 years old until Sir Stan retired my uncle, a season ticket holder at Spurs, would take me once a year to see my hero come down from Blackpool. Although I was a regular at QPR by then, Stan was the man of those days and what a yearly treat that was.

I had to get myself across London to Bethnal Green station from Shepherds Bush and my Uncle Alf would collect me from the corner of Mile End Road and I was off to see Spurs, well Stan really, play. At 10 years old I was glued to the wireless on that famous cup final day in 1953 but I did get to actually speak with him on the night of that FWA dinner. He was so quietly spoken you really had to concentrate to hear him, but at least I got close to the real footballer for a minute or two.

In his later years, after managing Port Vale for a while, he toured the world and in apartheid South Africa, formed a team of young black schoolboys called 'Stan's Men' who he took on a tour of Brazil – the first black team to play outside South Africa. It may well have been on that trip that he met Pele, the Brazilian legend, who wrote in his own biography that Matthews was *'The man who taught us the way football should be played'.*

A tribute on his statue in Stoke reads: *'His name is symbolic of the beauty of the game, his fame timeless and international, his sportsmanship and modesty universally acclaimed. A magical player, of the people, for the people.'* It's a sentiment I whole-heartedly agree with.

Dodgy films in the Eternal City

Brandon was back at Buckingham Uni while Chel was sitting exams for Chelmsford County High and for Brentwood School as well as playing home and away games for the Woodlands Netball Team and singing in the Brentwood Choir. Bradley was now also at Buckingham University where Lynn, Chel and I visited him occasionally.

On January 24th Cheralyn was informed she had been accepted at Brentwood School, which was where she had really wanted to go. We were having Woodlands Schools Board meetings in The Shoes restaurant in High Ongar, and more meetings with Tony Harding in the Countryside Properties HQ in Warley.

Lynn and I spent our wedding anniversary in Portugal and after a week there got home for a couple of days in time to fly off on Concorde to Barbados with Cheralyn. A very enjoyable start to the year really but a downside was coming and it arrived with the sad loss of another great friend, Ron Wood.

A long serving and loyal member of my old sales team Ron had been ill with lung cancer for some years. He'd often boasted that he used to smoke sixty Capstan full strength cigarettes a day at a time when that particular brand was noted for its strength. When someone speaks of 60 a day you are never sure if they actually mean that but Ron always knew it was a risk anyway and he was happy to take it. He was one of the happiest and jolliest guys I have ever met – always laughing and I never saw him when he wasn't smiling.

That was probably what helped make him the good salesman he was, but sadly at the end of March we lost him and found ourselves attending another funeral. Even worse, at the same time, my closest friend of all and my best man, George Hagon was taken into Chelsea Hospital. I'd known George since the 60s when we were both selling on the streets of London – me selling popcorn and him Van Houten chocolate.

Then, when I became Sales Manager, he went to work for Palmer & Harvey where he became confectionery buyer and our paths crossed again. It also helped when I invited him to our QPR box and learned that he too had been a lifelong supporter of the club and asked if he could bring his six year old son Paul as well. Our families had become lifelong friends after that, always spending Christmas together for example.

George had never really recovered from the loss of his beloved Rina and that was obvious when we went to see him on March 15th.

We had the feeling that he would not be coming out of hospital, but I felt that if I called him regularly on the phone, as I did, it kept him informed and interested in what was going on. I knew I had to balance visiting against phoning, which would enable me to keep in touch more regularly. I will explain later in this chapter the reasons for not making too many visits.

Chris and Bob celebrated their wedding anniversary and we took them to Shepherds, while over in the Gables it was Steve Taylor's 40th birthday so there was a party there too, in his own restaurant. There was another trip around that time that sticks in my mind – taking Lynn to the Ideal Home Exhibition in Earls Court, never a good idea. It's truly amazing that before you go to a show like that you need absolutely nothing – but when you get there you find there are lots of things we desperately need. It is definitely an exhibition for husbands to avoid.

To be fair we were spending a lot of time by then visiting the Roundwood Lake site in Hutton where we were having our new house built so we probably did need a lot of new stuff. At Woodlands Lynn and I were still attending Parent's Evenings and I had to organise the Dads versus Sons football match for early on a Saturday morning. It had to be early because we were booked onto a flight to Boston in the afternoon, from where we went to Scottsdale for a five-week stay.

We got back home at the end of April just in time for me to be Best Man at my friend John Lawson's wedding and, in May, to attend Peter and Ingrid Ives wedding at the Woodford Moat House. No photographer problems there because Peter was and still is a professional photographer. A personal friend for many years, he has also been the family photographer for a long time. After going to see West Ham draw 0-0 with QPR I decided to have a few days in Rome and we took Bill and Ivy, who had always wanted to see that city, with us.

We did the lot – the Coliseum, Vatican City, the Spanish Steps, the Fountain de Trevi and of course enjoyed the beautiful streets, attractive shops and friendly people, but my in-laws did get a bit of a shock. It came when they turned on the TV at night and saw films of the type that were not allowed at that time in the UK. They were both absolutely shocked and spent breakfast times telling us what dreadful TV they had in Italy.

Thinking on it we had already 'done' America and Italy that year but after my Mum's 83rd birthday, when we had a nice family dinner at home, we picked up our passports again and flew out to Portugal for a week. Then, a few days after we came back we decided to take another trip, but to a place neither we or our passports had seen before – Dubai.

We weren't quite sure whether this would suit us actually, but a lot of people were starting to talk about Dubai which was then starting to plan one of the most imaginative projects ever, the Palm Islands. This was the construction of an artificially created archipelago in the shape of a palm tree but at the time we went that was for the future.

Anyway, we caught an evening flight and I remember that when we landed at midnight even the smell of the place was different. Everyone we saw was in long white robes and it was quickly apparent we were in a foreign land. A car met us and drove us through streets that were very different from what they are today and to be honest we did not feel that comfortable.

All we could see around us was sand and the odd building and it was very dark. Then we arrived at the Forte Grand Hotel Jumeria (today it's called the Meriden Hotel) and suddenly found ourselves walking into bright light and a very friendly atmosphere. Since that 'on spec' trip we have been to Dubai many times because it has become one of our favourite hotels and places in the world and we've made many friends in that hotel.

Thanks Ron

The project at Roundwood Lake was still progressing and we were having lots of meetings with people like BAC Windows, carpenters and electricians etc. because we were determined that our new home would be as perfect as we could make it. There was also, of course, a lot of family stuff going on.

Cheralyn was celebrating her 11th birthday with a party in the Courage Hall – significantly part of Brentwood School whose Open Day we took her to shortly after – while the following day I took family and friends to lunch at the Heybridge. Then it was off again to Buckingham University, this time for Brandon whose 24th birthday (and my birthday of course) came shortly after.

Among the friends who came to dinner around that time was Ron and Pearl Gwinnell and that pleased us especially because it showed there were no hard feelings. I make the point because Ron had been a very loyal member of staff and a good friend, in fact much more than that because he may well have saved Brandon's life after he had swallowed a coin.

Ron had come through the House of Clarks ranks, first as our Salesman in the South of England to become our Southern Sales Manager. Things changed at Clarks however and we decided that we only needed one Sales Manager for the whole of the UK. Naturally we offered that first to Ron, but he decided he could not take up that challenge, one that would mean him spending more time away from home.

Sadly that left us with no option other than to make him redundant and that was a very painful decision, not taken lightly. I did everything in my power to persuade him to take the promotion and he did have a lot of discussions with his family. Finally he decided it would be better to take the redundancy and we lost a good member of staff, but by coming to dinner that night all those years later he showed that our true friendship had stood the test of time and still shone through.

July 4th in our Scottsdale home is celebrated as Independence Day of course and that year in Brentwood it represented independence for Brandon and Justine, who moved into their new Roundwood Lake home. I am unsure where Brandon was that day but my diary, and Justine's memory, seems to confirm that it was me and her who did most of the actual moving.

I do remember that later that same day Lynn and I had a meeting with Richard Cherry, Chairman of Countryside Properties and whose father had founded the firm, and Tony Harding. It was the day we finally got all the points about our own house on that site and which we'd been arguing about for months, sorted.

On Cheralyn's last day, after eight years, at Woodlands, the same day she took her LAMDA (London Academy for Music, Drama and Art) exams and we had the prize giving day at the school. It is a day I remember because it was one I had to get my skates on... literally.

People, and the children in particular, tend to do crazy things on such days and I just felt like joining in. I put on some roller blades and skated around the playground. There was another, more family based, reason that I remember Chel's last day at Woodlands.

I'd driven her to school most days that I could and that was most of the time. I'd realised that because of my work schedules and the amount of time I had spent away from home I hadn't seen too much of the boys as they were growing up. I'd resolved that I would at least try to see my daughter a little more and in any case taking her to school was always a joy. Like me she had a love of Country and Western music so we had that playing out loud, and singing with it, on the radio during the journey.

We also had a little game where I would tend to forget how to get to the school and threaten to turn left when I should be turning right. She on the other hand would shout out that I was going the wrong way and would put me right. We seem to have done that for many years, but there was another story about her I treasure.

There was a lollypop lady in the Upminster area showing children across a crossing and of course we always made a point of stopping, to let them do so. At that point Chel would always open the window and shout 'good morning' to the lady and that went on for years. The same lady was always on duty and at Easter time we would stop and Chel would hand her an Easter egg and at Christmas a box of chocolates.

It had become a ritual and on her very last day we stopped to say goodbye and Chel handed her a present. I don't remember what it was but I will always remember the look on that lady's face as she thanked her and said how disappointed she was to know she would not be seeing her little friend on a daily basis again. She said how much she had enjoyed those little waves and smiles and what a polite and friendly young lady Chel was. It's amazing how you can build a relationship with someone you don't really know, whose name you don't even know and yet somehow it happens. Of course it's also nice for any father to hear his daughter praised so much by someone like that.

Cheralyn herself of course was going to start her new school, Brentwood School, that year and we all celebrated by taking not just her to Wimbledon but also Linda Tingle (the Woodlands head) and her husband Alan and also John and Deanne Kelsall – John then being the head of Brentwood School and who eleven years later joined Woodlands and is now a main board director. It was like saying thank-you to one and 'here we come' to the other. It all went well and we are all still friends. Then it was off to Scottsdale and the USA again for seven weeks – whew!

Santa doesn't wear Rolex

We got back from America the day before Lynn's 47th birthday when we had a surprise party for her but perhaps the best thing about that time was to find that George Hagon was home from hospital and we went to see him.

Talking of birthdays Bradley reached the ripe old age of 20, so we held a birthday party for twenty people on Tower Bridge – well at least in a private room at the Pont de la Tour there. I also took him on a tour of Buckingham Palace, but then Cheralyn took centre stage again because she had her first day at Brentwood School – one with a centuries old history.

Established in 1557 as The Grammar School of Anthony Browne under a licence given to him by Queen Mary it had mainly catered for boys, but in 1986 the Girls School there was opened. It is a school that, apart from its high standards in most areas of education, also has a rich tradition for its drama, art and music department having produced great musicians and performers like Griff Rhys Jones.

It's also a school that over those years produced many national and international names – politicians and judges, sports and show business stars etc. Even dress designers like Hardy Amies and writers like Douglas Adams and many others have emerged from that school.

Don Williams, on the other hand didn't go there of course but I have to include him in this chapter because we went to the Brentwood Centre to see him, not for the first time, around that time. Famous on the Country and Western music scene Don has been touring the UK for over twenty-five years.

Having seen him perform in Arizona I always make a point of going to see him when he's over here and two days after seeing him in Brentwood he was at the London Palladium so Lynn and I took Cheralyn. In fact she got quite excited to find herself standing next to him. It was then that we realised just how big a man he was – six-foot six inches and of course wearing the cowboy hat made him look even bigger and probably resulted in his being the 'Gentle Giant of Country Music'.

A Texan he made his name as a songwriter originally but in 1974 signed up with JMI Records as a solo artist and went on to have a string of top-ten hits. In America only four of his 46 singles failed to make it to the top ten.

Apart from more meetings with Richard Cherry at Countryside we were still having site meetings with suppliers – electricians, kitchen manufacturers and fitters along with bathroom suppliers. The new house was starting to take shape! Soon it was time for another eight day holiday in Dubai and making preparations for Christmas as early as November.

That was when we had the Woodlands Schools Christmas Fayre, where Father Christmas makes an early appearance in his grotto, listening to children and giving them small presents. That was not the time for him to catch the flu but that year he did and I was 'volunteered'. I was called in early, gowned up and ready to go in the grotto by the time the Fayre started where I spent some hours talking to the children.

After the grotto closed and we were all circulating with food and drink etc. the children were explaining how they'd seen through my disguise and that I wasn't the real Father Christmas but Mr. Lewis. I had been fully bearded, cloaked and hooded with everything down to the Wellington boots but I had not reckoned with the brightness of the kids at Woodlands. They'd spotted the gold Rolex on my wrist and definitely did not believe that Father Christmas had one exactly like it as well.

Actually at the time I had another job too. Bradley had started his first job that was something to do with brokering but it had an early start. That involved him getting up at 5.30am every morning to catch the 6.15am train from Gidea Park, some ten minutes away. Trouble was that I was the 'designated driver' for this job at that ridiculous hour of the morning and thus became the breakfast cook too.

I would get up just after 5am, wake Bradley, get dressed, go downstairs and, once I'd learned how, cook eggs and bacon or anything easy to do so he at least had some breakfast before I drove him to the station. I have to admit that I wasn't too disappointed when he found another job, which he has worked at for nearly sixteen years since then.

Woodlands Schools was holding its Board Meetings at our house by then, followed by dinner at the Tingles who still actually owned the business at the time. Shortly after that however we had an EGM which, if memory serves me right, was the one that gave me full control of the business. I took the staff to Leeds Castle for their Christmas lunch that year, but we went to Scottsdale for our Christmas break after it, getting back in time for New Year's Eve and a Gables party with friends.

Bradley 'celebrated' the start of 1996 by spending an afternoon in Hartswood Hospital. Lynn, on the other hand, picked up a virus and took to her bed for four days. That left me in charge of catering as well as getting Cheralyn to school and Bradley to the station every morning. I see from my diary just how well I did during that 'family emergency' – or at least how well our local chippie did, because we seem to have had fish and chips every day.

I should mention Chris, my 'right hand woman' at this stage because she too had a medical problem and had to go into Rodings Hospital for an operation. I phoned her on the day of the op and she was clearly very nervous. Lynn and I visited her in the hospital where she stayed for a few days and then at home. I probably helped to relax her there by taking some paperwork for her to do, but in any case I collected her when we got back from our latest trip and took her to the office so she could get back to work. Well, I learned a long time ago to look after the staff – but seriously we were all happy when she made a full recovery.

We were also still into our globetrotting mode because we'd decided to take Chel on a quick trip before going back to school. She was also involved in some plans of her own as I recall because, though she was now at Brentwood School she was busy organising a Woodlands Reunion for her old classmates. She also went to her first Brentwood School Disco before we packed up the cases and passports again.

The idea was to take her to some interesting places and we actually did a four-country trip in a week. We caught a flight to Cairo where we stayed for a couple of nights (more than enough), then on to Madrid, staying at the Ritz for the night before going to the George V hotel in Paris where we celebrated our wedding anniversary. We came back to Heathrow, changed planes and flew off to Portugal for a couple of days. Whew again! Later on, at half term, we took her to Dubai. Her passport was looking as dog-eared as ours were by then.

There plenty of the usual lunches, dinners and theatre trips in the early part of that year, including the Silver Wedding anniversary of our friends Barry and Tina Waite who I've not mentioned here before. I was flying back to the UK from America one trip and got talking to the guy next to me about football, well what else? His name was Barry Waite and he came from Austin in Texas, but he was President of Motorola which had, as it happens, a plant in Scottsdale so we had that in common. Our families stayed in touch and we have often visited their home.

However the most important family landmark that happened in the early part of that year was Brandon who got his final results and was called to the bar – the first Barrister in our family. He was also of course the great grandson of a Polish refugee who had arrived in this country all those years ago penniless and is now an MP. He'd come a long way from Forest School and then getting a degree in economics at Buckingham Uni followed by his LLB at the same place. He'd won an LLM with merit at Kings College and had then been called to the bar by the Inner Temple.

Should we be surprised? Not really, thinking back to the time when he was eighteen and he'd been done for speeding in Macclesfield. He'd waxed eloquent about needing his licence to take his poor old 80-year old Gran shopping in Southend, and we should have known then. He got off with three points, a thirty pounds fine and the admiration of everyone in the court that day so no, we were not surprised but very proud of our oldest son, as we are of course of all our children and their individual achievements in life.

While all this was going on, we were still visiting the Roundwood Lake project on almost a daily basis. Brandon, already in residence in his house there, had had his new Range Rover delivered and mine arrived a week or so afterwards. My friend Paul Weinberg, a partner in insurance brokers Heath Crawford & Foster, came over to advise me on security there. At the same time Tony Betts was also visiting there to help design the gym I was having installed in the new house and were also having regular visits from Tony Harding as well as meeting joinery and bathroom shops.

There were a few other issues regarding the site which I will come to in the next chapter.

Chapter 23

George and the 'BBC'

Trees

Although I may not be known for allowing a lot of grass to grow under my feet, metaphorically speaking, I am a lover of nature and that includes trees. After all where would we be without them? But not when they cause me grief and/or cost me money, which they did – first in Hornchurch and then in Brentwood. In Brentwood for example the site of our new home on Roundwood Lake was full of trees that would present great problems later. However all will come out, but one thing at a time and overwhelmingly at this particular period of my life that year was the fact of losing one of my best friends, but more of that later.

Perhaps the first low point of the year, particularly for my younger son, came in June at the Euro 96 semi-finals at Wembley. That was when Bradley and I saw the Germans beat Terry Venables' England team after a hard-fought 1-1 draw at full time. Alan Shearer got our first goal after only three minutes but a quarter of an hour later the Germans equalised. The teams fought out an extra time duel but despite close attempts by Paul Gascoigne and Darren Anderton that finished up all square too, so it went to penalties.

After both sides had survived their first five penalties Gareth Southgate, one of our finest players, had his one saved. It goes without saying that, inevitably, the next penalty taker, the German, scored. It was a moment that hit the nation but perhaps not quite as hard as it did Bradley Lewis.

I have never known him to be so upset at the result of a football match, any football match. Neither his brother Brandon, or even people like Rodney Marsh who was at a party with us afterwards could get him to talk. The result put Germany into the final with Czechoslovakia when once again the game finished 1-1 at full time, after which the Germans won with a 'golden goal' five minutes into extra time. That hardly helped to cheer Bradley up either and I don't think that really happened until his 21st birthday party a few months later.

That year however, on the bright side, British Airways did us a favour by starting a direct flight from Heathrow to Phoenix (Arizona) which meant we did not have to fly to Los Angeles first if we went to Scottsdale. Lynn and I took Chel when we flew out to our American home for an eight week break. We got back just in time to celebrate Lynn's birthday with a surprise party at the Gables and a new Jaguar, then it was Bradley's 21st. We celebrated that at the Four Seasons hotel in London where a couple of hundred guests even included my old friend Gareth Thompson who flew in from Australia for a few days to help us celebrate.

While we were away Chris and Bob, who had sold their home in Chadwell Heath and were waiting to move to their new one in Hutton 'house sat' in our Hornchurch home for a few weeks until they could move. I mention that at this time because, while it had nothing to do with our friends using our house, in September we were actually in the High Court in London over an insurance dispute involving the house. The problem was about a tree that was long gone before we'd even moved to Fairlawns Close 22 years earlier.

We'd been suffering from what is called 'heavage' which was causing a problem when it came to selling the place and/or claiming insurance. We'd never experienced a problem before but it turned out to be caused by the roots of a very old tree which had been taken down during the building of our home, and well before we'd seen the site. For some reason or other the roots of this tree seemed to have come to life again and we lodged an insurance claim.

The problem was that seven or eight years earlier we'd decided to change our insurance company and the current one refused on the grounds that we must have had knowledge of this heaverage when we'd moved over to them. That of course was totally ridiculous because if you did know of such a problem you'd hardly change insurance companies. We took them to the High Court.

Our 'in family barrister' Brandon came with us of course to the four days the hearing lasted before the insurance company made us an out-of-court offer. It looked to be a fair offer and they even allowed us to keep the house so, the day before the Judge was due to hand down his decision we took it. We were all pleased and Brandon said that our star witness had been our friend Alan Britain who had even invested in buying a suit for the occasion and we took him to dinner to celebrate.

Now, with the case over, and the house still ours with our new one in Brentwood nearing completion, I started to have meetings with John Allerton of estate agency Hilbery Chaplin to start the process of selling it. We were already getting prospective buyers visiting us and of course we still had the problem resulting from the roots of that tree to deal with. He felt that the best way of doing that was to put in a full and detailed report and its heaverage problems of the house with the sale particulars and ask for sealed bids. That is what we did and was how we sold the place.

We were still some months from actually moving and little did I realise then how many more problems, and another legal battle, the trees there would bring us. Before that would happen however we, and I mean the whole family, would suffer the loss of perhaps our greatest, if not certainly one of our greatest, friend.

MATE

Almost the first thing I did when the trial finished was rush off to the Chelsea & Westminster Hospital to see George Hagon, who'd been there for some weeks. It was a visit I'd put off for some time after he'd gone into hospital, though I had visited him at home and phoned him almost daily at the hospital.

Perhaps it was psychological, but we knew that George was coming to the end of his days and I kept feeling that if I visited him I would not see him again. I felt he was hanging on, but on the phone he was always so full of life and we were able to have some wonderful long conversations, reminiscing a lot about the old days. We talked a lot about Rina of course and recalled the trips and Christmases we'd all had together as families. He'd always called my lot the 'BBC' (Brandon, Bradley and Chel) and of course we were (and are still) close to his son Paul and his family.

The last time we'd spoken he'd not sounded so good and at the time I'd been locked away in a London courtroom for four days, so as soon as it was over I rushed over to see him. I felt I would never see him again, but he knew who I was and we were able to communicate easily. I knew the visit was important to him, well to both of us I guess, as we were about to go off to Arizona for a few weeks again.

We'd only been in Scottsdale for a couple of days when Paul rang and almost before he spoke I knew what he was going to tell me. His father, my best man and lifelong friend – my mate – had passed away. We were supposed to be in Arizona for a few weeks but, after some haggling with airlines, we were back within seven days.

Paul had delayed the funeral until we got back and I didn't know until we got there that I was being asked to be one of the pall-bearers along with him and two of his cousins. I was very honoured to do so but it was a very sad day of course, as it always is when you lose a special friend and George Hagon was all of that.

George and I had met back in the sixties when we were both selling on the streets of London – me selling popcorn of course, while he was selling Van Houten chocolate. I ended up as Butterkist's Sales Manager while he went to work for P&H (Palmer & Harvey) as its confectionery buyer so our paths crossed again because I had to go and see him to sell popcorn.

Our friendship deepened, especially when I invited him to come to Loftus Road in our box to see QPR. He not only accepted but revealed that, like me, he'd been a lifelong supporter of the club and could he bring his six-year old son Paul. That was forty years ago and it strengthened the bond between the Hagons and the Lewis family. Although, sad to say, Paul went off the rails somewhere along the line to become a Chelsea supporter, we are still close.

In fact the two families did a lot together with regular trips abroad and visits to each other's homes. As our sons and then our daughter came along the relationship thrived even more and still does.

George himself I suppose I could describe as the typical English bulldog who, in appearance looked very much like that other old English 'bulldog' Winston Churchill. In fact he could have been his double who could have taken him off to a tee and in fun frequently did so. He could put the fear of God into all who walked into his office, but it was all part of the act. In fact he was a very kind man at heart and he and Rina seldom failed to call on us almost weekly, as much to see the 'BBC' as Lynn and me and we felt the same about them. I have already written about the great love that existed between Rina and George and he never really recovered from losing her.

The last Sunday before Christmas was always our private and separate Lewis/Hagon Christmas Day which we'd always spent together as two families and still often do. Indeed whatever we did as a family he was part of it and vice-versa and I still get a little emotional thinking about him, especially o that first one after we lost him when Paul and Jane came to us.

He was always very supportive of me and very defensive too. I remember him once actually threatening one of my co-directors that if he got nasty with me, he (George) would close his account with us. At the time he was our biggest account customer next to Woolworths. He'd worked his way up through P&H, much as I had at Clarks, to becoming a main board director who'd helped build the company up from a 10-warehouse one to having over 60 branches in the UK.

As I said I hadn't expected to be a pallbearer but the big floral tribute from us in front of his coffin was just the four letter word – MATE, for that is what we always called each other.

George had worked like a Trojan in my view retiring too late, and recently Paul reminded me that I'd said that and assured me he would not be making the same mistake. In fact like his dad he too is now a main board director of P&H because many years ago, when he was about to leave Rowntrees to join Mars, I advised him to go to P&H. He took my advice then and I hope and think he will do so again.

My lady of the lake

We could not have opened 1997 in a more spectacular place. Immediately after Christmas I flew out with Lynn and Chel to Cape Town where we spent New Year's Eve, but then flew on to Zimbabwe and the amazing Victoria Falls. What an absolutely fantastic sight.

Discovered by David Livingstone, locally the falls are called 'the smoke that thunders' – a far more descriptive name than his one. I do not use words like 'awesome' lightly but other words cannot come close. In parts of the Victoria Falls National Park there is an abundance of hippos, crocodiles and elephants as well as many varieties of birds in all shapes and colours but surely even these cannot compete with the Falls themselves. Chel of course was only twelve at the time and what an experience it is for a child seeing them – for any of us come to that.

We also took her to Europe that year, to Berlin, Frankfurt and Venice, where we found ourselves during their Mardi Gras week when everyone dresses up in colourful outfits.

But I suppose the most important event of the year was always going to be moving to our new home in Hutton in March when we began moving small bits and pieces from Emerson Park. We were still having a lot of meetings both on site and in Countryside's offices in Warley and had been having discussions with South Park Removals but before we did we had a 'Fish & Chip and Champers' garden party in our old place. Roy and Reggie turned up for the event that went down well and is still talked about in the family.

I met up with E J Equipment at the house to see them install my new gym and then the alarm company turned up, to be followed by a variety of tradesmen because a lot of work still needed to be done before we could actually move in properly. That happened on March 12th when the vans arrived and we began to settle in. We did that with a touch of Scottish flair because I'd arranged for a lone piper to greet us and pipe us into the new house. Style eh?

We spent the day unpacking and rearranging, in fact we were up to 2am, but all in all it took us a couple of weeks to get organised properly including setting up my office. Then over the next few weeks we had people working on the trees (more on that shortly), the alarms and swimming pool, BT and insurers turned up as well so it was a pretty hectic spell as we moved into Roundwood Lake.

In fact it would take us five years or so before all the work we needed done on the house was completed to our satisfaction. In the meantime I took the family off to Scottsdale for a three week break. A month or so later all the Roundwood Lake residents, including Brandon and Justine who had moved in several years earlier of course, were invited to Countryside Properties head office for a meeting about taking over the lake and surrounding areas. That eventually happened and now we, the residents, own the lake.

Then, on May 1st Tony Blair led 'New Labour' to a near landslide victory in the General Election and life for all of us began to change, quite dramatically and especially politically. When a new government takes office, whichever the party, there is always a period of uncertainty as it settles down and usually starts to look for ways to avoid carrying out its manifesto pledges. History is already making its own judgements on Blair, and then Brown's, governments so I won't do so here.

Before (for the moment) I leave talking about the house, there is one memory that we all have – the day we locked Lynn's mum in it. That was on Father's day, when we'd planned to take her and Bill to dinner at the Gables. We also had some other special guests from Arizona staying with us.

They were Don and Jeannie Doody, the very first people we'd met in Scottsdale many years earlier. We'd been there looking over the area where our new home was being built and we'd gone into the swimming pool area. As we had the gate had shut behind us and since we had no key we had no way out. Bradley had managed to climb over some high railings and knocked at the first house he came to, which happened to be that of Don and Jeannie. He'd asked them to get us out, which they did and a friendship formed there and then.

Anyway, I digress – on that Father's day, what with them, us and Lynn's parents, getting them all organised into cars for the ride to the Gables had been hard work. However, after we'd all been to the toilet etc. we managed to get them all settled into the cars, I'd locked the house and set the alarm, when suddenly Bill realised Ivy wasn't there. We checked all the cars but couldn't find her anywhere and realised she must still be in the house where the alarm had been set.

In fact she'd got herself locked in a toilet – a new house, a new door with a dodgy lock and the alarm going off. Eventually we managed to get Ivy out, apologised to her for not noticing we'd forgotten her and then made our way to the Gables.

As we began to settle in there was little change in our lifestyle. Friends we'd met back in our early Christmas days together at the Buck in Bungay made contact to say they'd taken over the Ship pub in Burnham on Crouch so we went to the opening. Then Alan and Sue Britain arrived and we were able to show off our new home to them and then it was my Mum's 85th birthday and she came for a visit too. We all celebrated that with a family party at the Marygreen Manor hotel in Brentwood.

As a sure sign we were settling in to Brentwood, this was also about the time when Lynn, Chel, Justine and her neighbour – our 'ladies of the lake' so to speak – took up Line Dancing at Warley Hall. Then, another surprise I'd been quietly working on for some time, along came Joey.

'Dream on, dream on, teenage queen'

Country music legend Johnny Cash had a hit in 1958 with his 'Ballard of a Teenage Queen', which has a chorus of *dream on, dream on, teenage queen*. Well in June 1997 we had our own new teenage queen in the family as Cheralyn reached the grand old age of thirteen. That's always a special landmark for a youngster and I had a special 'dream' gift in mind.

Her birthday was actually on the 10th June but she was celebrating as early as the 7th when Roy and Reggie arrived and we took the Gables over for a special family party. I had been quietly working behind the scenes for weeks without anyone else, even Lynn, knowing what I had in mind. That was to buy Chel a horse and I'd asked a local stable owner, once a Horse of the Year Show winner, to keep an eye out for me.

He heard about a gelding that sounded right in Ireland so he went over to look and brought him back for me. Then I had to let the secret out, but to only one person – Peter Ives our photographer, who I needed to go to the stables and take a photo of Joey, for that was the horse's name. He took a beautiful photo of Joey and had it specially framed for the event. In fact it was even remarkable that Peter kept the secret because he is not always good at that.

Anyway back to the Gables where I called everyone's attention to make a small speech to our daughter. 'Cheralyn we have a very special present for you tonight because you are about to become a teenager', I told her, presenting her with this lovely framed picture of Joey. She assumed that the picture was actually the present and it took a while before the penny dropped that it was the horse in the picture that was her present. Chel was ecstatic and still has Joey to this day.

That was on the Saturday night of course and the next day, immediately after breakfast, we all trooped off to the stables to meet Joey. That night the new teenager had a small party at home for her friends and then on the 10th June, her actual birthday we all went, with Don and Jeannie from Arizona who Chel was particularly fond of, to London for a celebration dinner.

A few weeks later we were invited to another special day but before I go into that I have to mention taking the family and some friends on the Orient Express to Ascot for Ladies Day. I'd been to Ascot before but never to Ladies Day and to be frank, never again. It's quite amazing how much ladies on a day out can drink and I must say that the behaviour of some of them that day, made me swear never to go on another one.

A far more pleasant day out was spent at the Oxfordshire home of the, now Sir Richard, Branson on July 6th and I know the date exactly because it was Finals Day at Wimbledon. It had been Sir Richard's custom to open up his home for a party for his Virgin Airways regular passengers and we had been invited because of that. He is an absolute gentleman who met everyone to welcome them personally at his garden gate.

We found him leaning casually on his garden gate and thanking us for supporting his airline. Lynn, of course, headed straight for his lounge to watch the finals on his TV, while I had a quick chat with our host who I'd never met but in a way he did know me. 'I'm the guy who is always sending you letters which end up fly to Phoenix', I told him.

Since purchasing a house in Scottsdale I'd been sending letters to him and to the Chairman of British Airways urging them to start direct flights to Phoenix, a fast growing city which is now the fifth largest in the U.S.A. As it happens, BA got in first and do indeed now have regular flights that are very handy for us of course and was just as well since shortly after that we flew out there for a seven-week stay in our American home.

We got home to celebrate Lynn's 49th birthday in the Café Royal and it was a brilliant evening all round. Little did we know that in Paris that night a tragedy that would touch us all was unfolding. We got into bed around 2am. that night and were sound asleep when the phone rang. It was Bradley, and the news he was telling us didn't quite sink in at first, I was that tired.

'Have you heard, Dad? Diana's dead', he told me. I was still half asleep when I picked up the phone and to be honest the words never really registered. I had friends and relatives with that name and was having problems co-ordinating my thoughts and Bradley finally put the phone down so I could go back to sleep. Lynn, herself still half asleep, had been woken by the conversation and asked me what it had been about.

When I told her, it registered with her even before me and she shot up in bed saying for us to switch the TV on and then it hit me. Diana, the Princess of Wales who I'd worked with, with Relate, had been killed in a car crash.

Like most of the nation that dreadful day, we all had problems taking in what had happened. One of the most popular members of the royal family, even after the divorce, losing her in the way we did overwhelmed the nation in grief. In the days following the tragedy it responded with flowers, tributes and tears. Her funeral was one of the most emotional since that of Churchill and, for the first time I can remember, after she left the Cathedral on her way to her last resting place, the crowds applauded her for what she'd done. Even Sir Winston had not been paid that compliment.

Personally I remembered the many times she'd turned up for what was then the Marriage Guidance Council – in fact it was thanks to her help that we changed the name to Relate. As I have said before in this book a lot of her detractors claim she only did things for the publicity but I know that she turned up at our meetings without any kind of publicity.

There is no doubt that Diana was followed everywhere by the paparazzi but on some of the serious meetings where we were trying to help families, she was always there without publicity. In such cases very often no one was aware that she was even on the hotel property.

Of course however when we had Award ceremonies or public fundraising events in posh London hotels, it was inevitable that she would be photographed and everyone would know about her being there to support the cause. It was her high profile and willingness to use it in that way that allowed us to raise the necessary funds for Relate to become that.

There were no airs and graces about that woman, who I met many times. Her concern for children and the victims of mines etc. in Africa was totally genuine and at the time she died we were working on the problems caused to the children of parents who were breaking up. I have worked, and come into contact with other royalty, raising money for such things as the Variety Club, the Princes Trust, the Lords Taverners and the Water Rats, as well as being invited to the Duke of Edinburgh's 70th birthday party at the Royal Naval College in Greenwich, but Diana will always have a special place in the hearts of Lynn and I.

Thank you for being Gold Hearted

February 14th 1997
with children at heart

Presented to

Mr J K Lewis

in recognition and with heartfelt thanks for your kind support

The Greatest Children's Charity in the World

_____
(Chief Barker)

Certificate of appreciation from the Variety Club of Great Britain awarded for our support over the year.

More trees

I did start this chapter sounding off about trees and here we go again because, shortly after we moved in, Brentwood Council introduced itself to us in a very negative way, several times in fact. First its officers made contact to tell us we had a problem with some trees on our Roundwood Lake site. I had no problem because there were 144 of them on our 1.2 acre site and I wanted to take at least 20 of them down. It was them who had the problem.

There was a Town Hall planning committee meeting where I was accompanied by Dr Frank Hope, a leading specialist on trees and James Martin of Trees Plus who was felling them for me. By October he was doing that under my instructions when someone from the Town Hall turned up. They took a quick look and vanished, coming back the next day with photos. It seems they had gained cooperation from a neighbour by going into his house and taking the pictures of James and his team up different trees, and cutting them down, from a bedroom window.

Dr Hope was there too, preparing a full report on every single tree for me, but in the meantime Bradley took centre stage on October 15th by arriving with his girlfriend Lisette to announce their engagement. That was great too because, like Brandon and Justine, they'd known each other from school (Forest) and had been an item ever since.

Then, in November after we'd come back from a couple of weeks in Scottsdale, Chel came home from a local church youth club in a bit of a state. She'd got into a fracas and had been hit by a bigger, stronger and older boy. Bradley, who we'd never seen in a serious temper loss before went flying round there to sort things out. It was a great demonstration of brotherly love to a little sister.

Meanwhile we had another problem with Brentwood Council, but this one was related to Woodlands School rather than our own back garden 'woodland'. We'd been trying to extend and improve the Warley School, including the installation of CCTV to help protect the children's safety. We had put in a planning application which contained eight additions, but it had been turned down by the Planning Committee and so we'd gone to Appeal.

That was held in early December in the Town Hall and went on for three days. At the end of it we'd won a few points, but no extensions and no more building. In fact they were pretty hard all round and made it clear they were not keen to see us improve the school in any way. Because of some dreadful events that had taken place in schools around the country where shootings had occurred we did get permission to install CCTV, but perhaps one positive thing did happen. The Council suggested that since we were expanding at such a fast rate we should perhaps be looking for further premises. That single comment would one day lead us to Hutton Manor and more of that to come.

As Christmas approached I was working, with Dr Hope, a lawyer and a barrister on the tree felling issue and we'd been told the case would be heard at Grays Magistrates Court (Brentwood Magistrates Court had long been closed down). The Council had decided, in its wisdom and despite the advice given by their own tree expert Andrew Laing, I should not have taken down the number of trees I'd had removed. They decided to bring a case against me and to make matters worse sent someone round to serve me with the papers only a few days before Christmas. Jamie Martin also got his papers at the same time, so both our families headed into the festive season knowing we would be appearing in court in the New Year.

Even that didn't start well thanks to a tree because Lynn and I took Cheralyn to the Virgin Islands on December 29th and were in St John's for New Year's Eve. Unwittingly Chel had stood under a particular type of tree that gave her a very unusual rash. In fact it burned her skin, giving her blotches and then scars for a long time afterwards. The hotel hadn't been equipped for a New Year's Eve event, then, coming back on the plane we were split up with Chel and me at the back and Lynn at the front, and of course we got home before our luggage did.

When we did get back Jamie and I went to London to see a barrister, Geoffrey Stephens in his chambers. He would be acting for us in court and that happened on February 25th. Our solicitor, Daren Allen, QC Geoffrey Stephens, Jamie and I went to Grays for a hearing on the case brought against us by Brentwood Council. According to the council what we'd done amounted to a criminal offence which, if we were found guilty, would leave us with a criminal record and they were pretty tough on us.

The lawyers acting for the Council asked that both Jamie and I should be put on bail and that we should surrender our passports. Our QC pointed out calmly that we were hardly likely to abscond over a case involving trees and that I had already booked flights to the U.S.A. for our Easter holiday.

Somewhat reluctantly the Council agreed to our keeping the passports but we were both put on bail until the case, scheduled for June could be heard. When that was over we all went home to Roundwood Lake to meet Dr Hope for a site meeting.

Chapter 24

Hutton Manor

In the dock

Our appearance in court for the actual hearing into the case brought against us by Brentwood Council involving our felled trees was set for June 2nd 1998. Before that happened however we had another personal and civic issue to resolve – getting Brandon elected to it.

Brandon, who had moved into Brentwood some years before we had, had political ambitions and had felt he could not only get experience as a member of his local council but do some good too.

Brentwood had traditionally been a Tory stronghold but in fact had been held by the Liberal Democrats who had held it since 1991, largely thanks to the Tories losing support nationally thanks to the poll tax issue. By 1998 the LibDems had 25 seats against the Conservatives 11 and Brandon had been selected to fight for the 'safe' seat of Hutton South, so clearly the family was going to help. As a result I was spending a lot of time out on the streets handing out leaflets and going to meetings in the 'Secret Bunker'.

This was a relic of the Cold War when the government was making plans to continue running the nation if London was bombed and also needed to ensure our air defences could be maintained in the event of nuclear war. In 1952 it took over some farmland in Kelvedon Hatch and, 125 feet below it, dug out and created this vast underground complex. In 1992 it had been decommissioned and the land sold back to the original Parrish family who'd owned it.

Michael Parrish, an active local Tory, set the place up as a unique local tourist attraction and also as one for meetings – including for local party members of course. It was in that unusual venue, deep underground, that we planned our tactics to get more Tory councillors, Brandon included, elected and we succeeded. On May 7th 1998 our eldest son Brandon was elected to Brentwood Borough Council, and I broke a toe.

Somehow, getting out of the bath, I'd damaged my toe to an extent that I had to visit hospital. I couldn't actually walk the streets as I'd been doing throughout the campaign and had to settle for 'telling' outside the voting station. Six months later a regular medical revealed I'd actually broken the toe and it had healed itself. Anyway the bright spot was Brandon's success and, knowing it was the start of his political career, we celebrated back at his place. Then we had a bigger garden party at the weekend

Ten days or so later, on Cup Final day when Arsenal beat Newcastle 2-0 and my Mum was 86, we found ourselves celebrating another Brandon moment. We went to their house in the evening for drinks and he and Justine took the moment to announce that they were getting married.

It all helped to make May 1998 a wonderful month for us, but hanging over us all the time was the appearance in court. The week before we were due to do that, Lynn and I went to Dubai for a week to try and take our minds off it, but we were back the day before the court hearing. Jamie Martin, Tony (our architect) and I had breakfast together at home and then left for Grays. There Jamie and I had to stand in the dock, waiting to give our own evidence as we listened to all the legal arguments.

That wasn't easy – far from it, because if the case didn't go our way we could finish up with criminal records, so standing there listening to our fate being decided wasn't funny. During the morning various witnesses, from Brentwood Council and who included Andrew Laing, gave their evidence, a lot of which our barrister was showing up to be false.

Astonishingly Laing proved to be absolutely forthright and honest, giving his opinion that we had been right to chop the trees down. His professional view was that they were either already dead or were dying, dangerous and/or diseased. He said that in all the years he'd worked for the Council (not then a Tory controlled one, as I've said previously in this chapter) the councillors had listened to his advice but had not done so on this occasion.

By that time we could see the case was going strongly in our favour and Jamie and I were biting at the bit to give our evidence. We wanted to tell the bench how difficult the Council had been and how they had waited until it was almost Christmas before serving us with the summons with a smile. We needed to emphasise just how much time and money this had cost, with all the visits they had made.

During the lunch break our barrister told us that, much as we were dying to get at them, we would not be going into the box. He wanted to put the point that there was no case to answer to the bench and he was sure the magistrates would see it that way too. While we were keen to vent our feelings and tell them how badly we'd been treated, we agreed to do it his way and when we went back into court he made his speech.

He said that in his view there was no case to answer in view of some of the testimony given by some of the Council witnesses. To my recollection one of them even admitted lying on oath. The Bench immediately took a five minute recess and were back very quickly saying not only that they fully agreed but were surprised that the case had even been brought before them in the first place. At the time there was a limit on the amount of costs that could be awarded in such cases against Councils and ours had gone into tens of thousands of pounds, so he asked for the lot.

They readily agreed and by 3.30pm that day we were all back home in the garden celebrating with champagne. Obviously we were pleased that the whole nightmare was over, and we were no longer on bail of course, but perhaps a little annoyed at the same time. Not having to go into the box meant we could not give our own personal side of both the story and the way the council had acted towards us.

Jamie Martin especially had been great, putting himself at risk during it all by standing by us, and has become a valued family friend ever since. He has also been tremendous in supporting Brandon in his political campaign and in fairness has always been there for us whenever needed.

Not that we had finished with tree controversy that day because the following evening we were due to appear in the Town Hall again seeking permission to fell more trees. Knowing that local reporters were covering the meeting I took the opportunity to remind councillors (and the press) that only the previous day we had been awarded tremendous costs. We emphasised that if permission was again denied we would not hesitate to take the same course of action.

Brandon, now a member of the council, could not take part in the discussions of course but Dr Frank Hope, who'd originally presented the most detailed document on every tree, was. He spoke in our support again but this time the outcome was very different and we were given permission to continue. Apart from his testimony, I am sure my recital of what had happened the previous day helped and it got me onto the front page of the Brentwood Gazette that week, embarrassing the council still further.

I have often wondered whether the LibDem-controlled (at the time) council had made their decision on political grounds, knowing I was an active Tory supporter. Another group who'd spoken against us over the original application was the Hutton Mount Association, but how things change – these days I am one of its committee members.

The following day we had a visit from Andrew Laing, the council's arboriculturist, to check that all was well and, thankfully, the whole story is now over. Of the 144 trees we originally had in our garden we still have three healthy ones, which in fact we had permission to chop down but chose not to.

Lynn thought the vicar was a stripper

We had a lot of celebrating to do once the woodland saga had ended, starting in June when I took Brandon and Bradley to Marseilles to see England beat Tunisia 2-0 in the world cup finals. We managed to avoid the trouble between the local gendarmes and some soccer fans and got home safely. The final that year was won by France who beat Brazil 3-0.

At home I had been electioneering for the Tories because a by-election had been called in Hutton South and I'd been out leafleting and on July 9th Frank Kenny was elected to serve alongside Brandon. He won with a majority of only 36 in what is locally seen as a rock solid Tory seat. That was mainly because there was a lot of internal strife going on in the local party at the time and, as well as the Liberal Democrat and Labour candidates, there was an Independent Conservative Party one as well and he took almost half the Tory vote.

Frank and Brandon went on to play a huge part in the Tories regaining control of the council a few years later, with Brandon becoming its Leader and Frank would later become its Mayor. At home however we had other things to celebrate, or at least prepare to celebrate.

Before flying off to Arizona for six weeks I had started to secretly prepare for Lynn's 50th birthday party and while we were in Scottsdale those plans continued with Chris's help. We were back by the end of August with plans laid and guests, including Lee and Rita, along with Kal and Liz Rubin, all from Scottsdale, arriving to help us celebrate at the Four Seasons Hotel.

In fact their appearance shook Lynn quite a lot and for a minute or so she was stunned to suddenly bump into friends from across the Atlantic. She didn't know the half of it because she thought she was going to have dinner with a few friends on the night before her birthday, not the couple of hundred that turned up. That was because this was not going to be just a birthday party.

We had had quite a small wedding, and as you know even that had been cut short so I could go and see QPR. I thought that it would be nice if Lynn and I could use the occasion to retake our vows so, without her knowing of course, I'd made arrangements. I had arranged for a man called Jonathan Blake, who carried out what could safely be called 'unusual' wedding services.

He'd married people up in the Himalayas, under water and even jumping out of planes with parachutes. I asked him if he would do a blessing for us at the stroke of midnight which would herald her actual birthday. I had arranged for her dad, Bill, who was also in on the secret, to walk her to the front of the room with our children acting as ushers.

Jonathan turned up, in full Bishop's (which he has now become) regalia and I stood up to announce to the party that Lynn and I were going to get married again. My 'bride' was sitting just behind me and grinning, thinking it was just another of my jokes. Bill, sitting behind her stood up to escort her, the children came down too and suddenly Jonathan, in full regalia and clutching a bible, appeared.

Lynn, still only half believing was totally convinced that the 'vicar' was a stripper who was just about to shed his clothes. In fact we were well

Lynn and I renewing our vows at Lynn's 50th birthday party with the kids.

Gerry Marsden of The Pacemakers.
He came down from Liverpool to celebrate Lynn's 50th birthday.

into the service before she realised it was all for real and it was actually happening. Jonathan said a few words, we said a few words and coming from a Jewish background we stamped on a glass, signed a document and it was all done in front of 200 people.

Even today Lynn admits she was absolutely convinced that she was about to be faced with a male stripper. The next day we took 17 people, including our four American guests who were staying with us, to Marygreen Manor to dinner for yet another of Lynn's birthday celebrations.

We were having a great year that's for sure but it wasn't all politics, partying and travel – I was, and remain still a businessman and there was still plenty of that going on too. Woodlands, for example, was taking up an increasing amount of time and I even got back into the popcorn business for a while.

That happened when I was approached by a small popcorn company in the Midlands. Called Cornpoppers they asked me if I could help them build up their company, much as I had Butterkist of course. They asked if they could come to my home for quick chat – in fact their quick chat of an hour or so, actually lasted eight hours.

They were very keen but at that time my mother had gone back into hospital and she had to have priority of course so I told them I would think about it before rushing off to Southend Hospital. Eventually I did agree to join them on a six month agreement and, like their 'quick chat' concept had, that lasted for over two years.

I suppose that apart from our usual round of dinners, theatres and politics the other big family thing that year was when, in November, Brandon heard that he'd passed his Masters in Law. Oh yes and then Bradley also distinguished himself in a very different way – and he might not thank me for reminding him of this.

Just after Christmas Lynn and I took the family to Gleneagles in Scotland for a few days and for 'hogmanay'. The Scots know how to celebrate the end of the year of course and it turned out to be the first time we'd seen our younger son on stage in public.

Bradley has always liked 'Kiss' a Tom Jones favourite and on New Year's Eve in Gleneagles they were playing it. There we were, all dressed up to the nines in evening dress, when Bradley jumps up onto the stage and gives it everything – the full treatment, the Tom Jones movements and gestures, as he mimed every word. I think we all had a bit too much to drink that night, because I remember us ending up dancing by the reception desk in the foyer of the hotel, to the obvious disapproval of the hotel staff.

Hutton House

After his Tom Jones gyrations in Scotland Bradley had to go into Hartswood hospital again for a small operation but only for a few days. What really marked the early months of 1999 was a deepening interest in Tory politics and meeting Rudy Capildeo.

More of Rudy shortly, but I did have lunch on successive days in some fairly unique venues around that time. First I had lunch in the House of Lords with Michael Ancram and the next day Alan Tingle and I were invited by Brentwood MP Eric Pickles to have lunch with him in the Commons, followed by watching Prime Minister's Question Time later. Not long afterwards I was back in the House of Commons again but this time with Brandon, who was working for Tory MP John Redwood at the time, and Justine.

Then I was invited to the Conservative Central Office for a meeting with the party's then leader William Hague, who was having meetings with people 'from different walks of life'. I also went to the Brentwood and Ongar Conservative Association (BOCA) AGM, where Brandon was installed as Chairman.

Now it was also about this time that I had been meeting Rudy Capildeo who is a consultant neurologist in Hartswood and had an idea for what he called a 'one-stop medical centre'. He always believed there was a place for such a venture, especially in the Brentwood area, a place where patients could come, be seen, dealt with and possibly even have all their test results before they left.

He asked me to consider being the business end of the venture, leaving him to set up all the medical implications. We went to his home in Fryerning to discuss the idea in more details and agreed that we'd look for suitable premises. So the following week I was out looking at sites while he was working on the plan. He also took me on a tour of local hospitals to give me an insight into the workings of such places and where

A Conservative function when David Davies became Party Chairman

*I'm pictured here at the Conservative Party Conference in Bournemouth
with William Hague and Councillor Jean McGinley*

we met medical staff who might, or might not, be interested in the idea if we could set it up and get it going. I also involved our architect Tony Harding and lawyer Peter Wayte in those initial sessions.

Speaking of lawyers I was also involved in a court action with American Airlines around this time. That dated back to our fairly disastrous New Year trip to St Johns in the Virgin Islands when I had first class tickets to fly back to the States but we were then told there were not enough seats for us on the plane. After keeping us hanging around at the very last minute they said that if we wanted to get back to Miami we had to accept two economy class seats and one first class.

We had to get back so we could catch our connecting flight back to London so we had no choice. That day Lynn had a comfortable flight while Chel and I had to go 'steerage' at the back of the plane. When we did get back AA apologised and offered me a derisory sum in settlement and I took proceedings against the airline. As things turned out on the day of the court hearing the airline's solicitors agreed a settlement and I was able to rush back to Brentwood for a Woodlands board meeting.

Back on the political scene local party agent Andrew Varney, who had been so helpful to Brandon in particular had decided to retire and we held a party for him. Then Lynn, Chel and I flew out to Scottsdale for an intended three weeks break. For the first time we were able to fly into Phoenix direct, thanks to British Airways, but just after we got there I had a call from Rudy saying he'd found the ideal premises for our venture.

He said that there was a considerable number of people showing interest in the place so I decided to come home again. After arriving back in Gatwick we had dinner at Brandon's house to discuss the meeting the next day that was set to take place in a property called Hutton House, in the Rayleigh Road between Brentwood and Billericay.

The property, which stood in 30 acres of ground, had been the Hambros Bank sports and social club and not only had football and cricket pitches, tennis courts and a gymnasium/function room, it even had a small golf course, there was even a small bar in the house. It was a listed building that had sat empty for about three years with just one family, caretaking, living on a top floor.

We inspected it carefully and came to the conclusion it could not function as a medical centre, purely because of the amount of land involved that would cost a lot to maintain. It was also a very old building,

Grade II listed, and we could not see planning consent for change of use being granted. The cost would have been exorbitant and a lot more than doctors and specialists were already paying to hire facilities at local hospitals.

This was clearly not going to be the right kind of property for what we had in mind. Then Lynn, who was with us that day, made a quiet observation that some would say was stating the obvious – but it was her who realised it first.

'This would make another Woodlands School', she said. My mind went into immediate overdrive.

We'd recently lost our appeal to extend our facilities at the Warley site and the Chairman's comments were still ringing in my ears. His advice had been for us to look for another property in the borough to cope with our ever increasing numbers and at that moment his words struck home. I immediately phoned my partners, Barbara Young and Alan and Linda Tingle and explained the situation. They arrived in less than half an hour, saw what we'd been talking about, and Hutton Manor was born in our minds.

I say Hutton Manor because, while the place was then called Hutton House according to the deeds, which I had the opportunity of looking at, it had originally been the area's manor house. At that stage the concept of the one-stop medical centre had gone but a completely new idea was now in our minds. Hutton Manor would be our next major venture.

Thatcher told me not to trust the Russians

Hambros Bank had pulled out of the site because it had been taken over by Societe General (commonly known as Soc-Gen) of Paris and the site had been on the market for over a year. In fact they'd already had an interested party but the deal had fallen through and the property had been put back on the market using a local estate agency.

By that time there had already been 147 parties interested and we were clearly way down the line. I was told, though I didn't believe it because they all say that, that no bid short of the asking price would be considered. Nevertheless, I made my offer well short of that asking price and was turned down. There were various reasons why other parties were looking at the property but quitting is not in my nature.

Some were planning to knock the house down and rebuilding in the middle of the 30-acre site, but since it was Grade II listed that got them nowhere. Another bidder wanted to turn it into a night-club or restaurant, but that got shot down by Brentwood Council on the basis of too much noise and cars, at night.

Other offers were from football clubs looking to use the site for training purposes but one of them wanted to put floodlights up there for night time and that could have affected traffic on the Rayleigh Road. There were many similar ideas but one by one most of them were turned down. One club that did not require the floodlights looked to have landed the property but, literally on the day the deal was about to be signed up its Chairman passed away and it all fell through.

The Council was aware of our interest in creating another school there and was supportive so we gradually moved up the line until eventually we were number one on the list. I increased my offer several times, turned down each time, and there was one occasion when Brandon and I, along with Tony Harding our architect and our lawyer were invited to Soc-Gen's London offices.

We found ourselves in a very nice room with tea, coffee and biscuits on offer and it was at this stage we were told about an overage. I have mentioned this before in connection with selling Clarks but this time the overage was to be on us. We said 'no' and the chairman of the meeting who was with Soc-Gen of course stood up and said 'meeting over'.

Our lawyer pointed out that we hadn't started the meeting or negotiating but he simply said 'No deal, goodbye' and we were shown the door, just as the tea lady was arriving. It was a very strange meeting indeed but talks continued until, after fourteen months of negotiations I finally capitulated, gave in to their demands and price and agreed the overage.

There are times in life when you have to do a deal and that was one of them. If I am asked today was it the right decision I just have to reply, 'walk into Hutton Manor and you decide.' I'm not saying that it was the best financial decision I've ever made but it was certainly one of the best, and so Hutton Manor was born.

Well, not just like that of course. We knew from the start that as it stood the place was not fit for a school and needed a lot of work. That included working with the Council on building regulations and planning consents, and with National Heritage on preserving the buildings etc.

We actually did a deal with National Heritage. For example we needed to change some of the rooms in the house along with some of the windows so we compromised with National Heritage to the effect that if we did other things to improve the property they would go along with some of our requests. They had noticed that a beautiful staircase handrail had been painted over several times over the years, and I was asked if we could restore it to its original condition. We agreed to do that and in fact it was one of the most expensive pieces of work done during the year and it took a lot more to get the place ready to open as a school.

I suppose the most expensive outlay at Hutton Manor however was the brand new indoor swimming pool. We went the whole nine yards – CCTV, top of the range security etc. Since we were doing it from scratch, we thought we'd do it right and as a result council and fire brigade officers, as well as National Heritage – the lot – were all involved and continually visiting until the day finally came when we were certified and ready to open.

That was all still to come, but in the meantime life went on as usual – lunches, dinners and events etc. as well as some business. In fact in that latter context I suddenly got an intriguing invitation from Coutts Bank in the Strand to attend what they called an 'entrepreneur's dinner'. Apparently it was intended for a lot of people like me, getting together talking and exchanging ideas with a lot of the bank's executives. It sounded all very laudable but I found out quite quickly that there was no one else like me there and I never really felt part of it. Still the food was good and the wine excellent.

Speaking of wine, with their forthcoming wedding in mind, Lynn and I went with Brandon and Justine on another 'booze cruise' to Calais where we loaded the Range Rover up with champagne. Not just for his wedding either because we were all still leafleting and working hard for Brandon's forthcoming Council Election date on May 6th. That is also probably why I decided to get fit, training and jogging most days.

On that subject I was getting deeper into local politics myself because I had been elected as Deputy Chairman of the Hutton branch of the Brentwood Conservative Party. It was a post I held for three years, later becoming Chairman for a further three.

As I've said before we'd already known a lot of senior Tory MPs, even up to the level of John Major when he was living in No 10, but I suppose the ultimate has to be the 'Iron Lady'. I had been helping the Oxford college (Somerville) that Margaret Thatcher had attended, to raise funds for the Margaret Thatcher Centre. As a result she invited me to dinner in the House of Lords and I took Brandon and Justine along.

Margaret that night was absolutely charming, bright as a button and, while she was slowing down in her speech a little, she still commanded attention and respect. Such an intelligent and friendly woman. I remember being introduced to her and, not wishing to take up too much of her time, felt it was time to move on. We were on the terrace at the time and it was a beautiful June evening, but she made it clear she had not finished with me.

'I need to give you some advice' she said, adding 'Never trust the Russians.' What a lady! As it happens while I was writing this part of the book I have just been to see the film 'The Iron Lady' which won Meryl Streep, who played her in it, an Oscar. A brilliant film yes and Streep was wonderful but the film, which is based on her being sick and old but has flashbacks to her past does focus too much on her being old.

I think I have mentioned Pippa (Philippa Jessel) before. A close friend and a barrister by profession, she'd been very helpful to Brandon when he was studying law. She'd taken him to prisons and to the Old Bailey, giving him an insight into the workings of the law. Once married to an MP, she met and had formed a friendship with a highly decorated army officer called Bill MacDonald – an absolute gentleman, who we loved from the minute we were introduced and they stayed with us for a weekend.

Lynn and I took Chel away for a quick 3-day trip to the Czech Republic. As it happened our hotel in Prague was directly opposite the Opera House and we decided we'd give culture a shot so in we went.

None of us had ever been to an opera before but we still should have known the problem. It never occurred to us at that moment that of course most operas are in Italian, a language which of course we do not speak. Still they do have sub-titles on a screen so that people like us know what is happening, and they did here too. In Czech! An Italian opera with Czech sub-titles. We left during the interval.

In 1935 it was the Marx Brothers who made the film 'A Night at the Opera' – in 1999 in Prague the Lewis's had half a night at one.

Standing on the Terrace of the House of Lords
with the indomitable Baroness Margaret Thatcher

Chapter 25

Cornpoppers and Eightacres

Thanks Chris and Bob

Ask our daughter-in-law Justine where her new husband Brandon actually spent his honeymoon and she will probably grimace, grin and then say with a laugh, 'Blackpool'! What's more he left the bride at home after the wedding while he travelled to Lancashire with me.

I'll come to that later in this chapter but, not long after he and Justine had joined me for the Margaret Thatcher dinner date Ron Wenn, who'd been the first person outside the family to see Brandon after he was born, contacted me. When we'd first met, Ron had been a Key Markets buyer and we'd become friends who'd remained in contact over the years ever since.

He was by now however working for a Basildon based company called Eightacres, which specialised in selling 'end of line' and 'close to sell by date', products – a whole new 'shelf life' industry that developed since Marks and Spencer led the way in the 70s. Ron asked me to meet up with him and his directors with a view to my joining them as a consultant and salesman in relation to certain commodities, one of which was popcorn.

I agreed to do that so now, apart from Cornpoppers in the Midlands, I was also working for a company in Basildon, as well as Woodlands School of course. Oh yes, around that time I was also helping fundraise for a new swimming pool for Brentwood School. A lot of hard work of course, but I think my record since leaving school shows that I've never been afraid of that. Perhaps I owe that work ethic to my Polish/Jewish ancestry, for later in this chapter I will bring in yet another company who sought my help.

It's also always been a source of pride to both Lynn and I that when it comes to hard work our children are not lacking either. By that time the boys were both working in their own spheres and Cheralyn, while only 16 and still at school, had ideas of her own. She felt she wanted to do something for Brentwood's young people, so she went along to a local Ongar Road nightclub called Sam's to talk to its manager Kevin Springham.

The nightclub has now gone but the building had for many years been a popular Brentwood venue called the Meads Ballroom owned by a Mrs. Elsie Pepperall. When she sold it to the Bartella family for a nightclub she insisted on it being called Sam's after her long dead husband and it really did become a popular club in its day.

Chel wanted to ask Kevin to consider handing over the night club to under-18s when once a month, on Tuesdays, they would be able to safely enjoy all the facilities of a real night club. Well, not all because there would be no alcohol on sale of course and anyone going in would be thoroughly checked out for drugs or anything else. The event turned out to be a big hit with youngsters in the town with all 650 tickets being sold out before the actual night. There was a nominal charge for the hire of the club and only soft drinks were sold.

All the profits from each evening went to local charities and other good causes like the Endeavour School which catered for young people with learning or other difficulties. (Coincidentally the Endeavour School headmaster, Peter Pryke later became the principal, and at the time of writing is also a director of Woodland Schools). In fact all the local schools supported the idea, which Chel christened Funk Productions because it gave Brentwood's young people a safe and well regulated place to go. It was a tremendous success and very popular in the town for two years.

After that Chel, who had organised everything from tickets to advertising and publicity, had to give it up because she was going to Essex University. Before she did so, just to show she wasn't all 'goody goody', I would like to remind her of a Brentwood School trip she took to see Les Miserables in London – a show she'd seen before with us.

Knowing the coach, with the teachers, wouldn't be leaving for Brentwood before the end of the show, she and her friend Anna decided that the interval would provide a convenient moment to slip out for a few drinks. They found a small bar not far from the theatre and forgot the time. When the show ended the teachers found they had two of their theatre-goers missing. After a search they found them and got them back onto the coach. That happened the day before I was due to help out at another Brentwood School Appeal evening, where of course we were told about the two who had done a runner.

We had many of these appeal meetings to raise money for the pool and in fact at the end of it all we'd raised the best part of three-quarters of a million pounds. The rest of the cash was provided by the school itself and as a result it now has a well-used indoor swimming pool.

We had the usual outbreak of birthdays that autumn but one in particular I have to mention, because it gives me the opportunity to pay tribute to a couple I owe a great deal to. Chris, my 'Girl Friday' for so many years, was celebrating her 60th birthday and had decided, or more likely her husband Bob had decided, to do so with a big family party and we all went to their house.as well as being a trusted business colleague

Bob Howes, who retired as a fireman in 1987, has supported, and still does, Chris in every way and all through the House of Clarks years, waiting patiently for her to get home, sometimes very late in the evening. He often helped us out during the Dagenham Town Shows and various Conferences at which he often hosted the wives of our sales teams while Chris was working for me.

They are both of course close family friends and he has been at every party, dinner, barbecue etc. that we have arranged over the years and he still puts up with Chris continuing to work (for me). Indeed she has played an important part in helping to put this book together by typing out my handwritten notes and then checking out the chapters for accuracy etc. I would like to thank both Chris and Bob for the valuable part they have played in my business career, as well as that of being valued family friends.

Of course by that time both Lynn and I were getting fittings for our wedding outfits for Brandon and Justine's big day – me for a morning suit and waistcoat with her visiting Alfrene's dress shop in Westcliff. Brandon and I also went on another 'booze cruise' to Calais for wine for the wedding. Not that their wedding was the only one on the horizon, because Pippa and Bill also did the deed in Maida Vale and we went to that as well.

In the meantime on the business front I had another eight-hour meeting, at home with the Cornpoppers people, to agree my fee and starting date, while having similar meetings with Eightacres in Basildon.

In fact I went to the Cornpoppers' factory in the Midlands and attended my first board meeting there. The big event of the Lewis year however, was always going to be Brandon's and Justine's big day.

Brandon's Blackpool 'honeymoon'

The wedding itself was fixed for Saturday 2nd October but Brandon not only decided to have his 'stag do' a couple of weeks before that but to have it in a county, Norfolk, where one day fate would have a bigger role for him to play as one of its MPs. It also gave me a chance to relax from business for a couple of days.

It was a three-day event in Norwich which I, along with Bradley and Brandon's friends attended. At one point I was shoved into a go-cart and had all different coloured pellets shot at me, during a War Games event. All in all though, it was a great trip with lots of drinking and good food with good friends. In her turn Justine went off with Lynn and some friends, to Five Lakes for a couple of days.

Friday 1st October 1999, the big weekend had arrived and we helped Brandon and Justine load up their car with all they would need before they set off to London. The actual venue for the wedding was the Inner Temple in the Inns of Court, the ancient centre of legal advocacy for barristers. It was of course where Brandon had been Called to the Bar and it was that which entitled him to have his wedding there.

Justine had managed to get an apartment for the girls in the Inner Temple, while the chaps going to the wedding were all booked into the St James Club. We quickly unpacked there before going off to the Inner Temple for the wedding rehearsal, after which we returned to the club for dinner. Justine and her friends were 'champagne-ing' it up and having a good time (we hear) in their apartment.

The next morning we had breakfast as a group in the St James Club and then, all dressed up for the occasion, went off to the wedding. It was obviously a special one for us, in a special place that most people never get to see. It was very special for Brandon in particular of course, because it was exactly the place where he'd been Called to the Bar. Somehow he'd even managed to get a Westminster choir that guests remember to this day.

Based in the heart of London's legal quarter, the Inner Temple is one of the four ancient Inns of Court and has been home, workplace, school and library as well as a place of worship. It was there, in the 12th century 'Round' Temple Church, that the great grandson of a Polish immigrant refugee made his marital vows.

It was a great wedding with a reception afterwards in the hall attached to the church. Then those of us staying at the St James went back there for a few more drinks into the early hours. The following day, after breakfast,

Brandon and Justine's wedding day

we all went home with the family coming to us for tea (or was it an Indian takeaway?).

The next day, October 4th, one would have thought that the happy couple would be off on their honeymoon. In fact Brandon was up at 5.30am, as was I, and we went off to the Conservative Party Conference in Blackpool, via Wednesbury where I took him on a quick tour of the Cornpoppers factory, arriving at midday.

As I have written earlier, when anyone asks Justine these days where she went after the wedding, she grins and says: 'Well my husband's honeymoon was at the Party Conference in Blackpool'. They actually went off to the Caribbean for their real honeymoon a little while later, but only after I'd attended an East End funeral in Dagenham. We'd got back from Conference to find my cousin, Mickey Newman, had passed away and the turnout was enormous. To me it was a traditional East End funeral with many people, most of whom I didn't know, attending to pay their respects.

After a brief holiday in Dubai and the Maldives I held a Cornpoppers Conference for all the members of the company involved in sales. By then I'd organised a team made up of Agents, many of whom were already known to me from previous companies. I'd also shown Geoff Purdy round the factory and as a result he became one of their best customers ordering container after container for the group of shops of which he was a director.

The rest of that final year of the millennium was taken up with a mix of work and relaxation of course but perhaps the biggest moment of our year, apart from the wedding of course, came on December 8th when we got through more champers. Well most of us did but probably not Justine because that was the day that she and Brandon told Lynn and I we were to become grandparents. Very exciting day and while not everyone likes to be reminded they are getting older both Lynn and I were thrilled and excited.

From our point of view we'd always wanted to be grandparents and we just couldn't wait and what a fantastic start to the new century, and the next thousand years, that would be.

In fact we ended the old one, and started the new, in some style as a family with so many of our friends. Unfortunately Mum was still in the St Martins Nursing Home but on that last Christmas day of the old century

Bradley with Nanny Ivy and Grandad Bill

Lynn's parents, Bill and Ivy, both came to lunch with all the family. Howeve on New Year's Eve we had something really special planned.

We had Gareth and Betty with Gareth Junior over from Australia while Roy and Reggie made their way down from frozen Cheshire to stay the night. We'd hired a coach to take us to our favourite restaurant, The Gables, where Steve and Anne Marie opened it up just for their own and our families and friends and not to the public.

That is what happened – between us we had the entire restaurant to ourselves for the whole of the Millennium Eve. What a memorable way to spend such a significant night. The coach got us all back to Hutton at around 3am.

George and Peter

Two great people in particular dominate the first few years of the Millennium in my life – one a footballer and the other a teacher – but before that, those who were around at the time will remember all the predictions of disaster.

Computers, allegedly unable to cope with the change in dates, were going to crash worldwide, even bringing down aeroplanes in transit and all the regular harbingers of global doom were out in force. Then after all that nothing happened, apart from some very spectacular global televised celebrations and I started it with my first jog of the New Year.

As I've mentioned before, I have been to all the annual Football Writer's Dinners since helping kick-start them and as a result I've met and dined with many 'legends' of the game. I haven't mentioned them all, but 2000 was a special year and that year we honoured, in my view, a special guest. This was a man about whom Pele himself once said: 'When people ask me if I am the greatest I disagree. I say no, because it's Best and I genuinely believe he is,' the great Brazilian praised. I could not agree more.

Yes he had his critics, but as a footballer in his prime George Best had it all. He didn't just play with the greats at Old Trafford like Law and Charlton, he was one of them – but it's said that one of Sir Matt Busby's favourite expressions before a game was 'Where's Georgie?'.

Most people there would assume he was having a tipple before the game but I have a very different view. I remember going to Loftus Road on a day the Rangers were playing Manchester United and seeing him, surrounded by fans at a hot-dog stand, having a hot-dog and happily chatting with supporters of both clubs.

On another occasion I had taken the family to Wembley for a concert, and we always got there early so we could have dinner in a hotel opposite. This time the only other person there was George, who was with a rather attractive young lady and, not wishing to intrude, we kept our distance while we couldn't help looking. There was a buffet and when I went to get mine from it he'd appreciated the situation and just said hello before starting to chat.

It wasn't the first time we'd met because we'd done that when I took the boys to Old Trafford to see Man Utd play QPR. By that time George had retired and we were all having lunch in one of the restaurants when their current first team squad came in. They were introduced by Wilf McGuinness and everyone got excited, clapping and cheering with the press taking photos.

Then, in the other corner of the room a small door opened and George walked in quietly. Suddenly there was uproar with everyone, press included, switching their attention away from the first team squad, most of whom were famous in their own right, to him. You could see that he was embarrassed by the attention but he came through it all nicely. To honour him at that dinner in 2000 was an added bonus but sadly a few months later he was diagnosed with liver disease and though he had a successful liver transplant five years later he died from a condition brought on by alcohol.

It had been a great career that sadly, once he left Man Utd and perhaps the stabilising influence of Sir Matt, went steadily downhill. I won't go into that but the final picture in the newspapers was of him lying in his hospital bed and leaving a final message saying: 'Don't die like me'. That, for me, says a lot about the man I'd admired so much.

I think this is also the time to introduce Peter Pryke into this narrative. At this time he was head of the Endeavour School in Brentwood that catered for youngsters with learning and other difficulties. The Endeavour was one of the schools that Cheralyn's Funk Productions had been helping out with the proceeds of the Sam's nights, and he invited her and me to visit it. In future years Peter would play a much bigger part in my life in the sense of running Woodlands Schools, but at that time he had a growing local reputation as a man dedicated to his school.

As part of that, the following year (2001) he stood as an Independent candidate in the General Election against Eric Pickles and for the story behind that I will hand over to Brian Lynch who is editing this book for me.

(Editors note: Peter Pryke had a dream to provide a sports college for children with learning difficulties and I'd been helping him campaign for that in a variety of ways. When the General Election was announced he asked me to be his agent because he wanted to stand as an Independent candidate. There was no realistic chance of his ever being elected, but the publicity attached to being a candidate was potentially enormous, particularly since at the time Eric Pickles, the sitting MP was being challenged by a nationally well-known Independent – a former journalist and MP, called Martin Bell.

In the event Bell did well but, thanks to internal local party frictions over a situation I won't go into here, there was a national press focus on the Brentwood election that year. The Pickles vote held up and while his majority was slashed that time, he was re-elected and remains our MP to this *day. From my point of view however as Peter's agent what was nice was that, during the campaign and despite his being a candidate too, both Eric Pickles and Martin Bell invited Peter to speak at their election meetings where he was able to push his sports college message.*

We were both grateful to them for that and while we only got the expected few hundred votes the local publicity we achieved for Peter's campaign, thanks to their kindness and support, was cost effective and well worth Peter losing his deposit. B.L.)

Peter, as you will see later, will play an increasing part in this book and particularly in the running of Woodlands Schools.

Mad cow disease

Still always responsive to business ventures my next one was, like Cornpoppers and Eightacres, food related. In America Arby's is still one of the biggest take-away food groups and sells hamburgers with a difference. That's because they are made with shredded beef rather than the normal burger mince.

Some people I knew had negotiated the UK franchise for Arby's and approached me with the opportunity to invest by joining in their new venture. We had several meetings at my home, some of which went on late into the night. In fact I was having a lot of business meetings at that time – in one 48-hour period I was involved in meetings at Hutton House, Woodlands School and the Brentwood School Appeal – and several more were related to Arby's.

One of the other people involved in the project was Keith Brown, a former Brentwood Council chairman and highly respected financial expert, who chaired some of the meetings. We were all trying to put a plan to raise the money for the investment and to obtain the franchise, as well as starting to look for our first premises. Cornpoppers, where I introduced Mike Cannon of Hunter Saphir Distribution, was also taking up some of my time.

A lot of work had been done on Hutton House and by the end of March we were ready to exchange contracts for its purchase which we finalised on March 31st. We continued having meetings about the place with Council and Fire Brigade officers, National Heritage and a variety of tradesmen, including Alan Britain about a swimming pool.

As far as Arby's was concerned I agreed to become a shareholder and we opened our first outlet in Southampton, swiftly followed by another one in Sutton. That all seemed to be going to plan and we were making preparations to open a third one in Romford when tragedy in the shape of mad cow disease struck.

Bovine Spongiform Encephalopathy (BSE) is a disease that mainly affects cattle but from it developed a human form called vCJD, or variant Creutzfeldt-Jakob disease. BSE had been around for many years but it wasn't until the late 1990s that it was fully realised that it could be passed to humans through eating infected beef.

There was immediate panic during which British beef couldn't even be exported to the continent and many firms dealing in it collapsed. People stopped eating burgers and, while the big groups with hundreds of outlets – the McDonalds and Burger Kings etc. – managed to survive, we hadn't had the chance to get that big.

It was a great shame because we had been going well up to then but we had no option but to pull out of Romford and close the other outlets down. In America the company survived and still does well, so it's a pity the timing was all wrong for us, but having said that, my other business activities were progressing well and keeping me on my toes.

I'd introduced Neil Jenkinson, of Lovells, to Cornpoppers and that had proved to be helpful. I also had meetings with T & S Stores – a large group of retail confectioners and they became Cornpoppers biggest customer. I also remember attending one Cornpoppers meeting, particularly because it ended with me getting home in a recovery vehicle.

I'd had lunch in the House of Lords with Lord Basil Feldman, who I'd known for years when he was fundraising for the Conservatives. The next day I had two meetings to do with Cornpoppers – the first in nd then another in the East Midlands Airport Hotel. Then, having waved off Lord Feldman, I found my own car wouldn't start. I finished up with having it towed away with me getting home courtesy of the AA.

Things at Hutton House were also moving well with new fittings and carpets etc. as we moved towards our planned opening day. During a chat with a Brentwood Gazette journalist I happened to remember that, according to the deeds, the place had once been the local manor house. I switched into marketing mode and realised that it could sound a lot better as Hutton Manor. The other board members agreed and Hutton House officially became Hutton Manor which it has been ever since.

We were looking to improve facilities at both there and at the Warley school so issued some Rights Issue shares to raise the cash, but we also had other 'teething problems', and not just in Hutton. One of them resulted in yet another court appearance after the Woodlands School in Warley contacted a neighbour to say water from his pool was running onto our property and damaging classrooms.

He took exception to this and launched an action against Woodlands Schools claiming that as a result of our complaint to him we had put a blight on his property. More visits to court, plenty of time wasted sitting around talking and arguing, with the end result of the case being thrown out of court. Then we had more distractions as we fought to get our costs paid.

However after that we pressed on, with projects like the new swimming pool that Alan Britain was installing and lots of new fencing being erected. As a social club the chicken wire around the place was fine but not for children and that needed replacing with suitable fencing. We also invested in a more protective barrier between the school and the Rayleigh Road as we prepared for our opening.

It was around this time that Lynn had a nasty accident at home. On one Sunday, while in the kitchen, she burnt her hand and arm pretty badly. We rushed her off to Highwood Hospital and they did what they could, but it was too serious an injury for them so we had to go on to Harold Wood hospital. She needed regular visits there for weeks to have the dressings changed, but thank God she made a full recovery. Speaking of hospitals we had another event, of a very different kind, to look forward to then.

Henry

Brandon, now set on a wider political career than just Brentwood Town Hall could provide, had got himself onto the official Conservative candidates list and, with a General Election looming for 2001, found himself a seat – in Robin Hood territory. He'd been selected to fight the Sherwood seat and, while it was not seen as a winnable one, we all threw ourselves into it on his behalf.

The seat was held then by a popular Labour MP Paddy Tipping, whose previous majority had been over 16,000 and of course in 2001 Tony Blair's Labour government was riding high so it was a daunting challenge. We'd already had several meetings with local Tories and were also looking for a property to rent.

We had a dinner up there when our own MP Eric Pickles came along to help support Brandon's cause. We got home after 2.30am, but would have been earlier had Brandon and Eric not discovered a McDonalds on the way home. There is something about these two – they cannot seem to be able to pass one and if they don't then they set out to find one.

On Saturday August 12th Lynn and I were expecting a very special delivery – our first grandchild. He however proved to be a bit laid back and never turned up on time. A few days later however we got the message that Justine had gone into labour and, at 5.15am on the 16th in Harold Wood Hospital, where his father, uncle and auntie had been born, Henry arrived. He weighed in at 8lbs 14oz and of course never had a name at that time, but when we arrived to be introduced we were told he was to be called Henry – the same name as my father.

Lynn and I had always wanted to be grandparents and of course we were both overjoyed with the 'gift' Brandon and Justine had given us and still are. I'd always wanted to be a grandad and I've loved every minute of it since, and not because of all the old jokes about them going home afterwards. The new grandmother and I stayed as long as we were allowed and then went off to the River Room at the Savoy to celebrate.

The new Henry Lewis came home the next day and Bill and Ivy came over to see their new great grandson. Everyone turned up to be introduced of course and I remember Linda Tingle's words 'Ah, we have another child for Woodlands'. She was of course right and the lad spent eight years there and, as I write this, has gone on to Felsted.

Lynn and I of course became fully qualified babysitters very quickly but it was a good period for the Lewis's generally. Cheralyn got GCSE good enough to allow her to stay on at Brentwood to go into the 6th form and take her A levels. In the meantime the new dad was still working in Sherwood for the following year's election.

Taking things generally, what with all the business interests, the schools and then being capped with the event of the year, Henry's arrival, the new millennium had begun pretty well for the Lewis family. Perhaps the only 'down' side as we approached Christmas was Mum being kept in Wellesley Hospital for a few weeks so we were often having to visit her.

The New Year began with as much promise as the last one had left behind. Indeed we started it in real style by having young Henry on the evening of New Year's Day. How wonderful to have a baby in the house again and re-learning all the skills we'd learned the hard way all those years earlier.

On January 4th 2001 we opened Hutton Manor School – with eight children. I well remember our first assembly which we held in the hallway with a few children on the bottom of the stairs and the rest further up. It wasn't until two weeks later that we got our ninth pupil. Yes, we must have been absolutely mad to open a new school at that time with just a handful of children and I wasn't the only one to think so.

I remember talking to Teresa May (currently the Home Secretary but Shadow Secretary of State for Education then) saying we were opening a new school and inviting her to come and open it when we were ready. She agreed but asked me why we were opening a new school when, at that time, so many others were closing down. I really had no sensible answer to that other than to point out we already had one successful school which was full and we didn't want to deny any child the chance of a Woodlands education. Thank goodness I had never discussed this with my financial advisors because I believe if I had it would not have happened.

In fact a year later we had 26 children and a year after that we'd reached fifty. It was absolutely crazy and we'd struggled to keep it going but it proved to be worthwhile because now, in 2012, we have a full school, with some wonderful children and a great staff.

In fact when it came to the actual opening day Teresa May was suddenly not available so Eric Pickles stepped into the breach to cut the tape. We had the Brentwood mayor, some councillors and local newspapers for a photo shoot and a bit of a party with more guests than students.

Back at Woodlands itself we started to hold Management meetings.

These gave senior members of the staff the chance to have a say in how the school would be progressing in the future and what they wanted from Directors. We held these meetings, and still do, in advance of the Board meetings. It offers teachers more chances to have their input into their school than they would normally get in State schools.

A few weeks after that we were having meetings with Linda and Alan Tingle about their forthcoming retirement from Woodlands – a school they'd started, almost lost, and had seen rise again from the ashes. In fact, with Hutton Manor now part of the group it was even bigger than ever.

brentwoodweeklynews.co.uk

NEWS WWW.BRENTWOODWEEKLYNEWS.CO.UK

MP opens Little Acorns with songs

MP Eric Pickles cut the ribbon at a pre-school which opened in the grounds of Woodlands School in Great Warley. The Conservative MP did the honours at Little Acorns nursery before taking a look around and joining in with songs.
Mr Pickles said: "I had a great time playing Lego and singing songs with the children."

Officially open: Eric Pickles cuts the ribbon

Chapter 26

Sixty

The secret of staying young is to live
honestly, eat slowly, and lie about your age.
Lucille Ball

Brandon in Sherwood

Today, as a family, we are very proud that our eldest son, the great grandson of a penniless Polish immigrant refugee, sits on the government benches in the House of Commons. Brandon Lewis MP has proved that we still live in a land of opportunity – a country where those who work hard can achieve and make progress; but of course it didn't come easy. In fact, as I said in the previous chapter, his Westminster career began in a place made famous by a legendary 'hero', a man who stood up for the rights of his neighbours and famously looked after the poorer ones.

Whether Robin Hood actually existed or not, he certainly left his mark on history, and of course in Sherwood from where he sallied forth to defend the people. In his own small way Brandon did that too for a while. Against all the odds, in a General Election where Tony Blair's Labour was still getting landslide majorities, he slashed the majority of a popular sitting Labour MP and achieved a swing from Labour to the Conservatives.

Brandon, having cut his teeth in Brentwood's Council Chamber where he'd helped lead the Conservative party back into power after many years, had long been looking to widen his political horizons. He'd managed to get himself onto the Conservative 'A' list of national candidates and had been offered the 'unwinnable' seat of Sherwood. Whatever their party, most new candidates need to go through that kind of experience and he jumped at the chance.

The seat had been held for many years by a popular Labour MP called Paddy Tipping who in 2001 would be defending a majority of 16,812. However before him, and since its creation in 1983, it had been held by a local Tory farmer but, with mine closures then dominating the local scene, Tipping had won it in 1992 and held it in 1997.

So clearly it was a challenge and not just for Brandon but for the whole family and we rented a property in the ancient Nottinghamshire village of Epperstone, so we had somewhere to stay while we helped out. During the year or so before the election was due we all spent some time up there. I remember one incident in a village store where Justine was buying some groceries and the assistant got a bit heavy handed, resulting in a bag breaking and spilling sugar everywhere.

Asked whether she needed a new bag for it, Justine was quite emphatic in saying that of course she did. Brandon, clearly not wanting to create some unfavourable local publicity, asked her to speak quietly. I will never forget the look on her face, for our daughter-in-law is quite a forthright lady.

'Did you shush me?' she demanded to my son's obvious embarrassment, but the moment passed quickly and they both dissolved in laughter. Whenever she feels the need to put him in his place, she often reminds her husband of the incident. Talking about Justine, on March 25th 2001 the other 'man' in her life, Henry, was christened in the same place she and Brandon had married – the Inner Temple.

Apart from electioneering I was still also working hard for Cornpoppers, pushing their product with Palmer & Harvey and with T & S Stores, as well as for the schools of course. Lynn and I also had another milestone moment that year when, on May 5th, our second son flew the nest. Bradley left home to move into his own place in Booths Court, leaving us with just Chel at home.

Politics however, both in Brentwood and in Sherwood, was keeping us all busy and I'd be out leafleting in one area for Eric Pickles and in the other for Brandon for much of that year. Brentwood was easy enough of course (though that year Eric did for reasons already explained in the previous chapter have a tough one) while for Sherwood of course we had to travel up and down the M1 on a regular basis.

Nor was it all a choice between Brentwood and Sherwood, because my old friend Robin Squire, who'd been the MP (and ours when we lived there) for Hornchurch for eighteen years, also needed my help. In fact I had been the first person Robin had met when he'd arrived from Surrey for selection and we'd been friends ever since. I'd worked for him in all his elections and so had Brandon and Bradley when, as children, they'd been on the streets of Hornchurch with me.

Now Brandon had his own cause to fight and that of course had to take precedence. It was a period when my whole life seemed to be fighting for the Conservatives and of course our son. Leafleting, public meetings, canvassing and, a week before Election Day, taking part in a cavalcade in Sherwood. That was composed of a dozen cars with loudspeakers, all decorated with Brandon's banners and slogans, driving all around the constituency seeking support.

On the night before the election we were out in the early hours replacing many of the 'vote for Lewis' boards that had somehow vanished in the night. On Election Day itself, May 7th, it was non-stop action all day from morning up to the time the polls closed. Then it was off to a meal in Epperstone before going off to the count.

It was a year the party generally was doing badly in the national polls with Blair leading his troops to their third result yet, against the odds and all the trends, Brandon got a 5.0 percent swing from Labour to the Conservatives. He had reduced Tipping's majority from its previous 16,812 to less than ten thousand and had turned a previously unwinnable seat into a more winnable one. Indeed Sherwood does now return a Conservative MP, partly due I am sure to the inroads we made in 2001.

For Brandon, apart from earning his political spurs it was a result that stood him in good stead next time round. Certainly it played a major part in him getting the Great Yarmouth seat he won in 2010 (with another swing from Labour to the Conservatives) and now holds. Sherwood launched a career that, as I am confident time will show, still has great potential.

What a circus!

With all the election stuff over for the moment and with Eric Pickles safely re-elected, he came to Hutton Manor to formally open the school for business. As I have said we only had around eight pupils then but it was a start and Eric did the tape cutting bit with style. A month later we had our Woodlands Open Day in Warley and then opened our new office in Ingatestone.

A couple of days after that I had a health problem myself in the shape of a hernia operation, but it wasn't long before I was back on my feet and back in training, jogging etc., with Tony Betts keeping an eye on me. It had been predicted as only a minor operation i.e. in and out the same day so after we arrived and I checked in at 7am. Lynn and Tony wandered off to the nearby Brent Cross Shopping Mall, expecting to spend the day there while waiting for me.

As it happened I had the op early and, on waking up called Lynn on her mobile phone to 'get me out of here'. I was back home by noon and at 4.30pm walked down to the surgery to see my GP who was not only surprised to see me but shaken to learn that I'd actually walked that sort of distance on the same day as I'd had the op.

We were involved in a lot of political activity then and, although Brandon had lost the election, we had promised to keep in touch with our new friends in Sherwood and they invited us to join them on a trip to both the Commons and the Lords. Following the 2001 election a lot of Conservatives had lost their seats and as a result party leader William Hague had decided to stand down and Sir Paul Judge threw a party for him at his Millbank home. As it happened I'd known him when he was simply Paul Judge and working for Cadburys and he invited Lynn and me to the party.

William, a recognised Tory orator since he'd been a schoolboy of course, made a brilliant speech thanking the party for its efforts. He is of course still around and doing a great job as Foreign Secretary in the Cameron government.

One of the Conservatives to lose his seat in 2001 was my old friend Robin Squire who we'd also tried to help in Hornchurch. The Hornchurch Conservatives decided to thank Robin for his service over eighteen years by giving him a retirement party at the Conservative Club there. It was a sad occasion in more ways than one because as well as Robin losing the seat it marked the end of a 22-year era for me.

During that time we'd got to know Robin very well and he remains a good friend to this day. It will have been realised by now that I tend to not just make friends, but to keep them long term as well. Like John Dickson of course who had made friends with a lady called Barbara Kirk and had decided it was time we met her so we all went to dinner in Brentwood. They are still together.

Eric Pickles, having survived his toughest campaign and seen off the challenge of Martin Bell, held a party at the Heybridge in Ingatestone (no longer there) to say thanks. I suppose on reflection the 2001 election was my busiest ever having worked for Robin and Eric as well as of course for Brandon, but I was getting deeper into politics anyway.

I was also getting deeper into West Ham United as well, but without wholly dropping the club of my childhood, QPR. Bradley and I went to Upton Park to order some season tickets because we both loved football and the Hammers were opening a new stand, the Doctor Martens stand – then the club sponsors – but at the time of writing it is the Alpari Stand.

Apart from being closer than Loftus Road of course our main reason was that with West Ham being in the Premiership then England's top clubs would be playing there in the following seasons so we bought some tickets for a couple of years. Incidentally by then we were getting deeper into 'Henry watching', often taking him for walks that inevitably ended up in a Shenfield sweetshop.

We had a bit of a fright on the day before his first birthday though when Justine phoned me, in a terrible state, to tell me that Brandon had been in a car accident in Ingatestone. I rushed to the scene to find that in fact he'd been shaken but was fine other than that – the car on the other hand was not. Life always seems to be going well for long periods of time when suddenly there's a hiccup. That was just the time for a hiccup and I can still remember the feelings I was going through as I drove, well above the speed limit, to reach the scene. Thankfully all was ok and Henry had his first birthday party with no problems.

The real problem with Henry actually happened months later when Lynn and I took our grandson to see his first circus, just down the road from us in Hutton. We had the best seats down the front and Henry was loving it, well at least he was until all the lights went down and the band started playing. Suddenly it is black and noisy; he grips my hand and starts screaming 'Go Go Grandad' at the top of his voice. He was petrified.

I picked him up and rushed him outside, noticing that Lynn was not behind me. Gradually I made him calm down and persuaded him to go back in, albeit only for short periods. It seems there was all these nasty and funny looking people – of course they were the clowns but he didn't like them either, so I took him out again and we walked around looking at all the animals in their cages and pens. Lynn? Well she stayed to watch the show and came out with the rest of the crowd when it all finished.

Henry and the Scorpion

As I have just mentioned 2001 was proving to be a very busy year and was not without its hiccups! It was during a break with the family at our home in Scottsdale when the young Henry picked something up in our garden and screamed. Bradley, who was there, very quickly realised that a scorpion had bitten him. We rushed him to the local hospital who instantly recognised it was a scorpion bite but said that before they could do anything with such a young child they needed the scorpion that bit him. I left Henry and Justine at the hospital and rushed back home to find our neighbours, Don and Jeannie Doody, were at the house. They had come to see the young Henry and say goodbye to the family before returning home to the UK later that day.

Don was brilliant, he immediately knew what to do and went in search of the scorpion. He caught it, put it in a jar and I then rushed back to the hospital with it. Thankfully, it turned out to be a very old brown-back scorpion and therefore had little venom in it to cause a fatality. The doctor decided not to give any antidotes to Henry as apparently the antidote usually given could render a child to permanently loose their immune system to many things and that he would only administer it if the eyes dilated. We were told we had to remain in the hospital for 8 hours to ensure there would be no complications, during which time we cancelled their flight back to London that evening.

Brandon, who was out at the time, came back to find out what had happened and we stayed with Henry at the hospital, mostly on the floor and walking the wards. Eventually the doctors agreed it was safe to return home and we returned to England a few days later. As a result of the poisoning, Henry lost all sense of taste for some time but in the end made a full recovery.

The strange thing was that all this happened while our friend Peter Ives and his wife Ingrid along with daughter Isobel were with us. The previous day we had experienced another mishap. We all went out on a boat on Lake Mead with little knowledge of how to control it and we just ended floating around for ages in the cold weather!

IDS

With William Hague standing down the party had to elect a new leader and, bolstered by the support of Margaret Thatcher, it was Ian Duncan Smith (IDS) who was elected. As things would turn out he would be forced to resign two years later, but like William, still serves the party as a Cabinet minister in the Cameron government, specialising in social justice.

More of IDS later, but he was leading the party when Brandon and I went to the party conference in Blackpool. Lynn, Chel and I had a few weeks in Scottsdale, arriving back in time to see the final of the Baseball World Series on TV because the Diamond Backs were playing the Yankees. I suspect I now need to explain my interest in this sport.

The Diamondbacks had only been set up a year or so earlier, a brand new team in a brand new stadium in downtown Phoenix. It was in fact not far from our Scottsdale home and, along with Lee Wilson we'd got quite wound up on baseball and the new team. They had brought in some of the best players in America and I'd been fortunate to be at all their home games right up to the final. It was at that time that I had to fly home to the UK, but then found it was being shown on TV in the early hours. I still have my World Series hat.

Lee Wilson, my best friend across the Atlantic in Scottsdale sharing a beer.

Mum had not been too well around that time either so we moved her to a nursing home quite near Hutton Poplars for a few weeks. Didn't really appreciate it at the time but, as I remembered earlier in this book, she'd actually spent time in Hutton Poplars as a child.

Nowadays, the old school is still there and serves the community but the land contains new housing developments. In fact Brandon's first home, after leaving ours, was on that Poplars redevelopment.

Lynn and I went to the Dorchester for the Conservative Millennium Dinner, all dressed up but, just to show that I know how to treat a girl, we went to a Grant Thornton Inheritance Tax seminar first. Then, as the year ended in our usual flurry of dinners, lunches and other events, on Boxing Day we flew out, with Chel, Bradley and Lisette, to welcome the New Year, in Tobago.

Speaking of Cheralyn, who had just passed the theory part of her driving test at the time, she was having a few problems with a boyfriend. I won't go into them, but they did lead me to having a chat with Peter French, then a senior police officer, who gave us some good advice. He and his wife Linda have long since been part of the long list of friends we've made over the years.

I mentioned IDS earlier in this chapter and, as leader, he was invited to be guest of honour at a local Conservative dinner at the Heybridge. It turned out to be an interesting evening because, when Brandon was with Eric and Irene Pickles, a message about a man with a gun arrived. Not wanting to spread panic among the few hundred people there I was quietly asked to man one of the doors while Eric and Brandon got IDS to safety.

Normally of course IDS, as party leader, would have his own security people around him, but this was purely a local event and as a good friend of Eric's he'd just come down for dinner. Anyway the call went out to local police and suddenly we were surrounded by cars and armed coppers. Brandon and Eric had got IDS safely to one of the bedrooms and by then the hotel was locked up tight. Peter Ives and I managed to keep everyone in the ballroom relaxed and calm without telling them why.

It turned out that a gentleman, who had been recently released from prison, had turned up with a gun (that in the end proved not to be loaded) which he intended to use to threaten his girlfriend. She was a waitress in the hotel and it seemed she'd been seeing someone else. I've

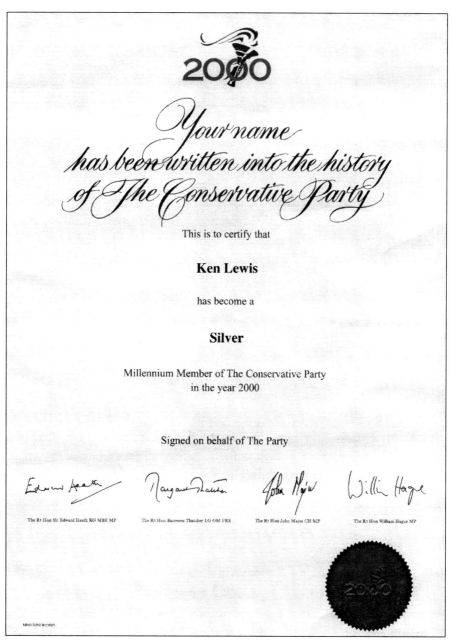

2000

Your name has been written into the history of The Conservative Party

This is to certify that

Ken Lewis

has become a

Silver

Millennium Member of The Conservative Party
in the year 2000

Signed on behalf of The Party

The Rt Hon Sir Edward Heath KG MBE MP   The Rt Hon Baroness Thatcher LG OM FRS   The Rt Hon John Major CH MP   The Rt Hon William Hague MP

never seen so much action taken for something that turned out to be so small, but it was all handled very professionally and the rest of the evening went off fine.

I mention this particular episode because it does tend to highlight how much deeper into active Conservative Party politics I was getting but I was still just as busy business-wise. I was still doing work for Cornpoppers and others, while of course Woodlands and Hutton Manor were taking up an increasing amount of time but, as ever, the family always took precedence.

In February that year Bradley and Lisette decided to take a sabbatical in the shape of a world tour. They were both working and had been planning the trip for a long time. They were young, had no children to worry about and could afford it, but I felt a little sad when I took them to the airport so they could catch a plane to Bangkok.

I think it was probably the longest period of time we had been separated from any of our children and while we were thrilled to see them off, we knew we would miss them. Then a few months later, on May 12th, Brandon and Justine took little Henry off for a few weeks on his first trip to the USA and, to make matters worse I got back from the airport to Upton Park in time to see the Hammers lose 3-5 to Manchester United.

I should also mention another moment of genuine sadness at this time. You will remember in an early chapter that after I left home a family, Frank and Doll Gilland, took me in. Frank had passed away long before but I had always remained in touch with Doll, who lived in Greenford, but now she died and I had another funeral to attend. It was the loss of another person very close to me, who had given so much help and support to a young man and for which I will always be grateful. I remain in touch with the Gilland family to this day.

The day the M25 caught fire

We were having regular stays in Scottsdale by now (and still do) but the three-week stay we had there in 2002 sticks in my mind, not so much for the break itself but the homecoming. It was almost biblical in the Charlton Heston sense, because it was the day the road caught fire, and not just any old road but the M25. We got back at Heathrow around noon, but never arrived home until 7pm following a dreadful journey that had taken as long as the one from Phoenix to London.

It was that year that our local efforts began to pay off with the Liberal Democrats, who had run the borough for over a decade, who began to lose control with a 5.5 swing from them to the Conservatives. They actually lost overall control a year later. Even better from my point of view in 2002 Brandon, still a councillor of course, was elected group leader, leading the party back into power in Brentwood two years later. As I write, ten years on, it still holds control with the Liberal Democrats looking like a spent force.

As I said before, the schools were also taking up more and more of my time and one weekend Woodlands had stands at two different exhibitions. One, a Homes Exhibition, was held in the historic setting of Ingatestone Hall (the ancestral home of Lord Petre) and the other in the Bluewater shopping mall. I was doing a lot of travelling back and forth over the Thames that weekend, helping to man both stands, then a month after that we had another stand, this time at Lakeside. We celebrated the Queen's Golden Jubilee at both schools that year and with a street party in Warley.

I should mention that at this time my Mum reached her 90th birthday and now living back in her own house in Westcliff. She was still resisting the idea of moving into a nursing home permanently so we went to see her at home, taking her great grandson Henry with us. He was two in August that year, while Chel was celebrating both her A-levels and her 18th birthday.

I also remember giving a couple of our American neighbours a 'cockney' experience that year. Lee and Rita Wilson visited from Scottsdale with their twins Adam and Jenna and we took them to Southend. They'd never been on a train on a pier before of course and nor had they experienced fish and chips under the Arches. Then we took them to the Gables, Leeds Castle and Bennihanas in London before they flew back to Arizona. It's always nice to return the kind of hospitality we received every time over there.

Eric Pickles came to Warley to open our new facilities there and also visited Hutton Manor, while swimming champion, and World Gold Medallist, Mark Foster, came to open the new pool at Brentwood School that we'd worked so hard to achieve.

Lynn and I had another 'sad' occasion that year when on October 1st our 'little girl' left home for the first time – the last of our children to do so. Not that Cheralyn was going far of course, because she was about to start reading Psychology at the University of Essex. We took her off to

Cheralyn's 18th birthday with the family

Colchester, stopping off at Tesco to pick up supplies and saw her safely into her new dormitory. If the journey there had been uncomfortable the one home was even worse, very quiet and solemn.

Still, the next day, after having dinner with Brandon and Justine, we had Henry for the day and that helped bridge the sudden gap in our lives. Colchester being so close of course Chel was often home again for weekends etc.

In fact picking her up and bringing her home for weekends became a regular feature of my life then. I would pick her up on a Friday or Saturday and she would be at home, getting her washing done and stocking up with food of course, before I took her back to Colchester again on Sunday.

Politically Brandon, now Brentwood's leading Tory councillor, was still looking around for a parliamentary seat and was considered for the Harwich one. I remember Brandon working hard to get it but was pipped at the post by one of the party's 'big guns', Bernard Jenkin, who still holds the seat.

Both of us were very active by then, attending such events as the BOCA (Brentwood and Ongar Conservative Association) Gala Dinner at the Heybridge, a Front Bench Club lunch in the House of Commons and the following night back to it for the Nottingham Conservative Lunch. Brandon was still retaining links there.

In fact with Christmas approaching there was a children's party, which Brandon and Justine took Henry to, in the Carlton Club, with Father Christmas present of course. Then we attended a reception followed by dinner there with Eric Pickles.

Our Christmas present from the family was of the kind Lynn and I always like – they took us to lunch at Rules, London's oldest restaurant. I say that because it was first opened by a Thomas Rules in, would you believe, 1798. This restaurant in Covent Garden specialises in traditional British food, game, oysters, pies and puddings etc. It's a real experience of course but the point that time was that it meant we could be with all the family and the reader will have gathered by now that that is what is all important to us.

Friends are too of course and I remember January 11th 2003 when I rushed back from taking Chel to Colchester to go to Upton Park to meet up with Peter Wayte and his son John Henry, my godson. John Henry was a Newcastle supporter and they joined Bradley and me to see the two clubs battle out a 2-2 draw. Then we went home where Peter's wife Liz had already arrived for the weekend. I remember it well because we had lunch at Masons in Brentwood following which there was a heavy downfall of snow, giving me the opportunity to teach my grandson how to throw snowballs.

My godson, John Henry Wayte, in Rio de Janerio

As Jack Benny said...

By this time I was banging the drum for the Tories more energetically than ever, and particularly so since Brandon's election campaigns. Locally I was doing a lot of leafleting for BOCA and attending meetings in the Secret Nuclear Bunker in Kelvedon Hatch. I'd been first Deputy Chairman and then Chairman of the Hutton South party for some years and I was nominated to take over as the BOCA treasurer and was elected.

More of that to come, but first I must mention the 11-week 'world circumnavigation tour' that Lynn and I took before the local elections in May that year. We'd been to many places and countries since getting together but this was a bit special. We flew out to Dubai for a week before going on to Sydney (via Singapore) and then on to Auckland in New Zealand. There we caught the 'Legend of the Seas' for a 19-day cruise calling at Boro Boro, Morea, Tahiti, crossing the International Date Line to the Hawaiian Islands for a few days in Honolulu.

Swimming with Dolphins in Hawaii

Then we went off to Scottsdale for a month before going to Los Cabos in Mexico where we boarded another ship, the Infinity, for a two-week cruise finishing up in Fort Lauderdale. We went on to Miami to catch a flight to Barbados before leaving for home, arriving back on Election Day, May 1st. Whew!

This was the election where the Lib Dems lost overall control of Brentwood and suffered a 5.5 swing to us. Brandon, who was Conservative Group Leader by then, went on to lead them to outright control the following year.

Mum, 91 that year, had finally agreed to go into Chadwell Lodge, a nursing care home in Chalkwell. Talking of birthdays, that year I was about to become a sixty-year old but, as Jack Benny once said: *'Age is strictly a case of mind over matter. If you don't mind, it doesn't matter.'*

He of course was a great entertainer, but I remember in my own younger days being a bit stage struck myself, though not as a comedian. I was a member of the St Luke's Church group in Shepherds Bush and, through that, part of the Worried Men's Skiffle Group – shades of Lonnie Donegan, and all that. I couldn't sing or play a guitar, but I did have a snare drum, a high hat and a set of drumsticks, so that all helped get me into the stage early on,

My reasons for mentioning this will become clear soon but, as with so many of my friendships, this was a group of local children who stayed in touch for many years and a couple of them felt it was time for a reunion. So I went off to Beaconsfield for that and enjoyed it all but on my actual birthday, Lynn had a few surprises for me.

She packed a bag and I was ordered to get into the car to be driven to London where we had tea at the St James Club and then dinner at the Savoy. We went to the theatre before going back to the club for the dinner and the night. The following day she had another treat in mind – a visit to the Churchill War Rooms which, being a wartime baby means a lot to me.

I thought we were then going to lunch back at the club but suddenly the whole family turned up and it seemed that we were booked into Fortnum & Masons for lunch. Then, as we crossed over to the South Bank, I could see the London Eye and made some comment about no one being able to get me onto that. Then I twigged that in fact that was my next surprise, that the tickets had been booked up and I had no option. It resulted in one of the best half-hour trips I'd ever had. It was absolutely marvellous.

Not that my day of surprises was over yet because after more drinks at the Savoy we headed for Rules for dinner, where I found Gareth, who had flown in from Australia, along with Roy and Reggie Hall. After that, surprises over (?) we had Gareth, Roy and Reggie the next day sitting and chatting in our garden when Gareth and I were whisked off by Linda Tingle and Barbara Young to lunch at Smiths in Ongar.

It did seem a bit odd at the time but while I was being decoyed out of the way my real and most magnificent birthday present was arriving and being set up in Roundwood Lake. It was in fact a full set of one of biggest drum kits, as beaten by Ringo Starr. The children had heard many stories of my early church group days and standing in at other gigs and had decided that at the age of 60 it was time I had my own kit. Recalling my early working life my American friends would say I'd been a 'drummer' selling Butterkist etc. – I guess even that description would fit. I still enjoy it today, but that wasn't all.

No sooner had I seen the kit and beaten out a couple of experimental rolls, than I was blindfolded and put into another car. I thought I was being driven miles up to London but in fact we were going round and round Brentwood. In the end we finished up at Hutton Manor where people had spent the whole day setting up my birthday party – a Western evening. I'd been a bit puzzled after being told to wear jeans, checked shirt and my cowboy boots, but now I understood.

There were lots of people dressed up as cowboys and cowgirls there and as I got out of the car a cowboy hat was plonked on my head and I saw my grandson Henry racing towards me. What a wonderful day all round.

Enjoying myself immensely playing with my birthday present!

They'd brought a Country and Western band down from the Midlands and a casino. There was a 'gun slinging' competition that detective Peter French was sure he would win; but now I can reveal that the UK's current Communities Secretary, Eric Pickles, showed he has a fast draw and beat the copper. Actually Peter has never lived that down, but what a wonderful event and what a wonderful and unforgettable sixtieth birthday I had.

Cowboy and Cowgirl at my 60th birthday party

Here I am cutting the cake at my 60th Birthday party.

Chapter 27

Winning Brentwood back

Yolanda makes it... just

I guess one of the several events that stood out for me that year (2003) was how our first grandaughter made Bradley and Lisette's wedding just a little bit more special for us, but before that the bridegroom's stag was one to remember as well. We'd decided that a couple of days in Euro Disney could be a good idea so around fourteen of us, including Brentwood MP Eric Pickles, caught the EuroStar to Paris for a two-night stay.

Actually it turned into a three night one because EuroStar broke down and they put us up for another night. The 'Two Ronnies' used to say – 'in a packed programme tonight...' – well, we had a packed one for a couple of days that began with our MP being stopped at Customs in Ashford on the way out. He was the only one of us to be stopped, questioned and searched. I am sure it must have been due to the hat he was wearing that made him look like he was going on safari. Believe me, he will never live that down.

Then we had Ron Warmington thinking that all the bikes in the hotel were for anyone to use, so he took one to cycle down to meet us in a bar. When he got back it was to find a very angry and vociferous family with a couple of hotel staff, wondering who had 'stolen' their bike.

My Mum had moved into Chadwick Lodge in Chalkwell on a permanent basis. She'd sold her home and everything in it, but had forgotten to mention that to me, so it had all happened before I had a chance to get involved.

Remember my birthday celebrations, and the drum kit? Well my friend and trainer Tony Betts had bought me an unusual sort of present

– twelve lessons with a drum instructor called Martin Clapson. Having not sat down at a set for over forty years I needed some improvement. Martin, who had played with some major bands, was brilliant and stayed with me long after the lessons had run their course. He'd still be with me if he wasn't playing in groups around the world.

We moved Chel's horse Joey to stables near Colchester so she could visit him more often. She had also moved out of the Uni dorm to a house in Greenstead that she was sharing with a friend whose parents had bought it for her. Lynn celebrated her 55th birthday (with a big bouquet from Eric and Irene Pickles), but for obvious reasons it was 'the wedding' that was taking up all our attention. Well perhaps not all our attention.

On September 12th a group of us went to London to check into the Four Seasons hotel, a group that did not include Brandon, Justine or Henry. That was because I have forgotten to mention that Justine was not only pregnant again but close to her time and she and Brandon had decided to stay at home that night.

At 1.30am the following morning Brandon phoned me from his car to say he was rushing Justine to hospital. Needless to say Lynn and I didn't get much sleep that night and at 4.10am Brandon phoned again to tell us we had a grandaughter. Wow!

This did present something of a family problem however because, apart from Brandon being lined up as best man, Henry was going to be a page boy. Justine of course would be kept in hospital to recover.

Unbeknown to us however Justine checked herself and her new baby out of hospital at 2pm and Brandon took her home where they collected Henry. Having made allowances for the missing part of the family, we were all getting ready for the wedding when to our surprise all four of them walked into the hotel. It was probably one of the great emotional family moments of our lives.

Not only did we see Brandon and Henry arriving to take up their duties but Justine with her baby, Yolanda, in her arms with them. It was a magnificent feat on Justine's part and Yolanda, at less than a day old, was clearly the youngest wedding guest ever. The wedding itself was a wonderful affair too, with the families getting to know each other and friends coming in from Australia and Arizona to help the young couple celebrate.

I guess Yolanda (who I call Yomay because her name is Yolanda May) was the icing on the wedding cake at the service, as well as the reception which also took place at the Four Seasons Hotel. After it Bradley and Lisette flew off to honeymoon for a week in Mauritius and then another one in Dubai.

Bradley and Lisette's wedding

I think, given our relationship with the Hagons I should mention another celebration. Earlier in the book I described how George Hagon and I were both passionate QPR supporters, while his son Paul had 'gone off the rails' somewhat to support Chelsea. He was celebrating his 40th birthday in October and his wife Jane had asked me to make a speech at his birthday dinner.

Unfortunately this dinner was to take place at the Chelsea Village Hotel which is part of the ground, but I had known the 'lad' since he was a kid so I agreed. We, including Chel who had a touch of tonsillitis at the time, were booked into the hotel overnight. We were given a tour of the ground and of the players' changing rooms which of course was a treat for us footie fans and it was a great event all round.

Before the year ended I organised a lunch at the House of Commons for the Brentwood and Ongar Conservative Association (BOCA) where I was serving on its Standing Select Committee. One group was given a tour of the House by Eric and the rest were taken around by Brandon who still had an eye on things electoral.

In fact the very next day we went with Eric and Irene on a fact finding mission to Great Yarmouth where Brandon was hoping to get selected as its prospective Conservative candidate. Since I once had many business interests there myself I was more than interested, but on that occasion he was not selected. Perhaps that could have been a blessing in disguise because locally by then he was leading the Conservative Group back to power in Brentwood, after many years in the wilderness.

In fact Great Yarmouth Conservatives selected Mark Fox to stand for them in 2005, but he barely dented the Labour majority. In 2010, as we will see, it would be a very different result there.

Brandon's big day

After all the excitement of Bradley and Lisette's wedding and Yolanda's arrival the rest of 2003 was a bit of an anti-climax in a sense, with all the regular events, dinners and celebrations taking place as usual. Lynn and I were also getting used to the idea of having a grandaughter as well as a grandson and that was all very wonderful.

We had all the family to lunch before Christmas and then we flew out to Scottsdale for both Christmas and the New Year where, bit by bit, the whole family arrived. Chel and her friend came with us, Bradley and Lisette arrived on Christmas Day with Brandon, Justine and their children turning up on Boxing Day. We spent New Year's Eve that year in a little 'Western' town in Scottsdale called Rawhide. It all sort of ended a memorable year, in memorable style.

We all got back to the UK in time for my local political activities to kick in again with BOCA meetings. As Treasurer and on the Standing Committee as an Executive Member I had plenty to do. Some of that was alleviated when Bruce Picking, a new BOCA member, agreed to take the Treasurer's role off me. Eric and I had hoped to persuade him to become Chairman but he did not feel ready but he did become an excellent treasurer.

Outside local politics I also still had plenty to do at Hutton Manor. One of the things I helped organise there was a Burns Night – an event which, because of the part it played in the early part of my Butterkist career, is always very dear to me.

But as far as local politics was concerned 2004 was always going to be a significant one. With Brandon now leading the Tory group in the council chamber there was a feeling that things were definitely on the up. The Liberal Democrats had been in power for twelve years but what happens to every majority party in government, local as well as national, internal divisions were starting to show.

Outside the group itself, BOCA was uniting behind Brandon and a lot of meetings were going on for the first half of that year in both Brentwood and Ongar. While Ongar was not part of the Brentwood Council scene, it was of course part of the Brentwood and Ongar Conservative Party who helped it fight for seats on Epping Council.

Just as importantly however, before all that kicked in, Lynn and I had another wedding anniversary to celebrate. Lunch at the 'Blue Strawberry' in Hatfield Peverel but then we flew off on a 10-week trip. First we flew to Buenos Aires where we spent a few days before joining a cruise ship, ending up in Valpareso. From there we flew to Lima in Peru, going on from there to Phoenix and to our Scottsdale home.

We arrived back home to be brought back down to earth again with some leafleting for the Tories and a fish and chip supper at Brandon's. We went to see Mum on the day before her 92nd birthday – had to be then because we had another big family event the following day. That was Yolanda May's christening in the Inner Temple where her parents had married, followed by a party at Hutton Manor.

On the subject of the schools around this time, following a disagreement with me our head teacher in Warley resigned. I mention it now because there was a legal ramification later, but before that we had another memorable birthday celebration I like to look back on. Roy Hall had decided to give his wife Reggie another surprise birthday present and to invite three of his closest friends and their partners along too.

We were asked to be in the Virgin lounge at Gatwick before their arrival so she was very surprised to see us there too. We were all booked to fly to Barbados but what Reggie didn't know and the rest of us did, was that Roy had booked a private jet to take off from there, to Mustique. There we stayed at Princess Margaret's favourite retreat, having a marvellous week on that stunning little island.

Then, once again, it was back to political reality and Brandon's big campaign in Brentwood. The election took place on June 10th, Cheralyn's 20th birthday and that must have been a good omen because it was an amazing result.

The Liberal Democrats had been in control of Brentwood Borough Council for twelve years by then, although the previous year they'd lost overall control. In 2004 they were humiliated as that year Brandon took the number of Tory seats from eight to twenty-one with a 4.9percent swing to the Conservatives. Among the lost seats were some of the LibDem's biggest guns and their senior councillors.

For Brandon of course, as well as the result making him the Leader of Brentwood's council, the swing to the Tories was much in line with the one he'd achieved in Sherwood in the General Election. It was certainly the kind of performance bound to be noticed by future selection committees and one he could (and did) build a political future on.

We attended the first AGM of the new council and Mayor's Reception that year with an element of special pride in our son as we watched him take charge of our borough in his first meeting as the Leader of the Council.

'Ted' and Colin

'....if we stayed true to the beliefs of the school,
we would all still be friends fifty years later'.

I make no apology at this point for another spot of reminiscence, and not simply because that is what this kind of book is all about – a selection of memories that collectively amount to a life story. No, this time it's because of something very specific that happened during my schooldays and had a very pleasant sequel in my sixties.

Back in the first chapter of the book I outlined some of my experiences at the St Marylebone Grammar School that actually began with a lecture by a couple of teachers who made certain predictions. I can even point to the exact day – September 13th 1954 – when with 92 other new boys I was in the school hall at 1.45pm to be given a kind of introductory talk.

That was given by two masters – Mr. Edward (Ted) McNeil and Mr. Colin Bosley – who made a speech about the history of the school we were about to join. They emphasised how lucky we were to be accepted into the school and spoke enthusiastically at length about its traditions.

I remember how the two of them made a deep impression on us because of their obvious affection for the school, but they also made a prediction. They told us that if we stayed true to the beliefs of the school, we would all still be friends fifty years later. To boys of that age of course half a century seems an impossible way off but, in fact as things turned out, many of us really had actually kept in touch over the years.

In August 2004 a couple of my closest school friends – Len Lewis (no relation) and Peter Bender, decided it would be a good idea to have what they called an OP's (Old People's) 1954 Golden Anniversary Lunch. I agreed and we invited as many people as we could find, to meet us in Kettner's Restaurant in Soho on Monday 13th September.

We were instructed to be there at 12 noon for drinks, lunch and, in the words of Len's letter *'The magic moment to commiserate or celebrate at exactly 1.45pm'*

There were forty of us and we were told that both Mr. McNeil and Mr. Bosley would also be in attendance. Of course the very thought of seeing them again was a cause for excitement in itself and it was so nice to meet them and shake their hands. We all met in the bar, had a few drinks and sat down to lunch but then, exactly at1.45pm – fifty years to the day, even to the minute – Colin Bosley stood up and banged the table to get our attention. What he said was this:

'Fifty years ago to the day I told you that you would retain a friendship with those around you and today there are forty of you here. Many of course were lost in the service to their country and some have simply passed away, while others were uncontactable, but here we are. For those of you who are here, I will call the roll,' he said, doing precisely that.

He had the names of every one of us written on his pad and as he called our names all of us 60-year olds had to stand up, put up our hands and say, 'Here sir!' It was a very special, almost emotional, moment in time and a wonderful reminder of that day back in 1954 when we'd all first met. A lot of photos were taken and it is still easy to recognise some of those friends from way back.

Since then we have continued having re-unions every few years but what a memorable day that first one was. While I was enjoying that, Lynn went shopping in the West End but joined us later for drinks. A joyful day followed by a more sombre one when we went to Anne Harding's (Tony's wife) funeral in Chelmsford. On a brighter note, a few days later we attended Abigail Ives' christening at Orsett Hall.

Rather a lot of lunches, dinners, celebrations and fundraising events around that time, including a BOCA dinner – well we called it the President's Ball – I organised in the Hutton Banqueting suite where senior Tory Dr Liam Fox came to speak to us.

Vic Young had taken me as his guest to the Brentwood Rugby Club lunch where, surprise surprise, I had far too much to drink, beer and wine etc. I suddenly realised that all the catering for this had been done by one lady and her daughter. I got up from the table, walked into the kitchen and was just saying what a great job they'd done when the door burst open and a couple of big guys rushed in. They were demanding to know why I had entered the ladies' domain because, apparently, that was not the done thing

I had not appreciated that but the ladies explained that I'd simply been thanking them and things calmed down. I went back to my table and a few minutes later the Secretary of the Club came over and said that what I'd done was extremely nice and a lovely thought. Then he asked if I would like to be a member of the club. Membership was in fact not easy at the time but my host Vic Young, proposed me and suddenly, all because of a misunderstanding, I became a social member. In fact I still am and enjoy every occasion I'm at.

Brandon, by now well settled in as the Leader of the Council, organised a business conference for all local businessmen at the BT offices in London Road where they looked after us very well. That night we were at the Town Hall again where West Ham and England legend Sir Trevor Brooking, who lives in Brentwood, was given the Freedom of the Borough.

London Bridge (U.S.)

The New Year, 2005, began and continued almost as 2004 had been – full of political activity, events and meetings of BOCA, and a lot of drinking, eating, training and travel. The schools were also taking up a lot of my time and early in the year the mayor visited Hutton Manor.

The guest at the football writer's dinner in the Savoy that year was Arsenal manager, Arsene Wenger. Lynn organised another Burns Night dinner at home that year as Burns Nights, of course, have been very important in my career, so my lack of Scottish ancestry is unimportant.

I mentioned the training because Tony Betts was still doing his stuff, either at my home or at his gym and I had now reached a regular 10-mile distance run. On the other hand I do remember having a Carlton Club lunch but, because John Kelsall and Kevin Springham were with us, we drank all afternoon and stayed for dinner too.

Actually it was due to Kevin that Lynn and I had to fish out our passports again. He and his fiancée Sam wanted to get married on St Valentine's Day... in the West Indies. His boss Robert Bartella had offered the couple his beach villa in Tobago but our problem was that we could not get a flight there in time, so they delayed it for a day. The wedding took place in a garden on the beach – a beautiful setting on a beautiful day and we all had dinner on the terrace in the sunshine.

Lynn and I were booked into a local hotel and the following night the happy couple came to dinner with us there and we had an enjoyable evening together. Lynn and I took the opportunity to spend a couple of days in Antigua on the way back.

We spent some weeks back in the UK, often visiting my mum in the nursing home or Lynn's mum Ivy, also planning Cheralyn's 21st birthday party, before jetting off again.

We flew to Boston to find ourselves landing in 10ft of snow. We were planning to drive to Cape Cod but the only way we could do that was to follow in the tracks of the snowploughs. In fact I heard later that we were among the last of the rental cars that the firm allowed on the road.

It proved to be a very long, tedious and scary drive but eventually we made it to Cape Cod. We spent a couple of days there before driving back through Boston to Salem, the home of the 'witches'. We wanted to see the history of so many people who were executed simply because they were believed to have had special powers.

From there we went home to Scottsdale where Brandon and Justine brought Henry and Yolanda out for a few weeks. They left for home from Phoenix on the same flight that Tony and Shelagh Betts arrived on, so we saw them off as we welcomed the Bett's, who stayed for ten days. We took them to the OK Corral in Tombstone and on to Lake Havasu, where we spent the night in a hotel on London Bridge.

Yes, I did say London Bridge and I do mean the same one I must have crossed many times in my young days. Lake Havasu City is in Mohave County Arizona and is a great tourist attraction for many reasons. One of the biggest, and most visited, is the original London Bridge that now crosses a 930ft man-made canal leading to the Colorado River. In 1968 when the bridge was replaced with a new one across the Thames the Americans bought it for $2.5 million.

It was disassembled, with all its stones etc. marked and shipped across the Atlantic where it was rebuilt at a cost of $7 million. It was quite an odd feeling to walk it again so many thousands of miles away.

After Tony and Shelagh had left Lynn and I went on another trip to see Middle America, initially to Oklahoma to Tulsa and Muskogee. Now that was a place I had to see because of my love for Country and Western music. It was made famous by the great Merle Haggard whose song, the Okie from Muskogee, is seen almost as an American anthem and is a great favourite with all fans of C&W.

We criss-crossed the States, staying in the same hotel as Elton John in

Kansas City, after which we went on to Witchita before going home to Scottsdale, to rest up before coming back to the UK.

That was on May 4th, the day before Election Day and the following morning, despite being a touch jet-lagged, I was up and about leafleting and 'telling' outside the polling stations. In fact after all that, followed by the count itself, I only got home around 5am. It was all worth it however, because Brandon had won a few more seats to consolidate the Tory majority in the council chamber.

We were getting ready for Chel's 21st birthday party but before that my mum had her 93rd and we went to see her. Despite her age her mind was clear, she knew it was her birthday and even how old she was. Despite my own birthday, and bear in mind I had been training and doing a lot of jogging, I went to Hyde Park for the Capital Help a Child 10k run and did it in 1 hour 8 minutes. Not bad for an old grandad, eh?

With the party coming up Gareth arrived from Australia to help celebrate it and on June 10th our girl reached, what used to be, adulthood. We all went off to London to the Four Seasons Hotel where I'd been working on arranging the party for months, and I got a real personal boost.

We had booked The Searchers for the evening and I went to watch them rehearse in the afternoon. They, very kindly, gave me the opportunity to sit in and play the drums for a short while as they rehearsed. (Just call me Ringo Lewis). When Chel was 13 they had promised to come and play, if we reminded them, at her 21st and they honoured that promise. It was one of Cheralyn's big surprises that day and the next day I drove home another one, the new Mercedes we'd given her.

The party itself had started at 5pm and had lasted till 2am Apart from Gareth we also had Lee and Rita Wilson with Adam, Jenna and a friend called Martha who had all travelled over from Scottsdale. They'd been staying in a hotel but they came home to stay with us for a few days after the party.

A few weeks later Chel put the icing on her own cake when, on July 21st, she graduated from the University of Essex with a Psychology Degree and received her BA with Honours. We took her to dinner to celebrate at Le Talbooth in Dedham and then, with a friend, on an Orient Express trip to the Beaulieu car museum.

Cheralyn's Graduation Day - Now a Bachelor of Science with Honours.

The Apache Trail

Chel had a very different trip a few weeks later when we took her and Brandon to Stapleford Abbots Flying Club for their first flying lessons and found it a dreadful experience. Not for her and her brother who loved it all but from a parent's point of view to see them vanish into the sky with an instructor it was pretty horrific. We didn't enjoy it at all until we saw them landing safely but we felt we had to be there.

I feel it's time to explain a little more about a couple of our friends, or should I say a 'couple of couples' because in both cases they're husband and wife. Take Peter and Linda French, who I have mentioned before, particularly in terms of some practical joking when we nicked his shorts while we were on holiday together.

Well a couple of weeks after Chel's birthday bash we went to Warley Park Golf Club for Peter's retirement party. He'd served over thirty years in the Met and the Essex police – in fact Linda had served in the Met police as well. Years earlier, with the Met, he'd sustained quite a serious injury when trying to detain suspects by hanging onto a speeding car. Now it was time to retire and it was a great party, with most of the guests of course being coppers.

The other couple I should mention at this stage is John and Deanne Kelsall who had retired to Fressingham in Suffolk. John had been a top headmaster of many schools in the UK but had spent the last eleven of them as head of Brentwood School, during which time he and Deanne had become personal family friends.

We also knew he was a good headmaster because of course Chel had spent seven happy and successful years at Brentwood. I felt we could use John's expertise and experience in Woodlands and he agreed to join us as a consultant. He is still with Woodlands Schools today but now as a main Board Director in charge of education.

Meanwhile Lynn and I were still 'globetrotting' that year and I remember we had a three-day trip to Iceland. For some reason or another Iceland had fascinated both of us and we found a very different country to the one we were expecting, but before then we took another Orient Express ride to Chartwell, in Westerham Kent.

I guess the name means more to people of our generation than today's, because of it being the home of Sir Winston Churchill. Today it is visited by thousands of tourists who tour the house and grounds that stand as a permanent reminder of our great war leader.

We were amazed by the rows and rows of his own paintings on the walls. When you remember that, even after the war when he was out of Downing Street for a while, apart from leading the opposition in the House of Commons he was writing great books and speeches as well as painting, you have to wonder how he found the time for it all.

Still travelling, we celebrated Bradley's 30th birthday in Portugal where Lisette had put in a lot of work for the event. She'd organised a dinner party in Xenia, a restaurant on a complex called Dunas Douradas where, if you recall, we'd once had a home ourselves. A couple of weeks later it was Yomay's (Yolanda's), Brandon and Justine's daughter, who was celebrating her 2nd birthday. A few days later, Lynn and I had the absolute pleasure of taking her and Henry out for a whole day to Colchester Zoo.

In October Lynn and I flew to New York for a couple of days before joining the Queen Mary 2, for a two-week cruise of the Caribbean. After that we were off to Phoenix to spend six weeks in Scottsdale, where Chel and her friend joined us for a while.

While we were there that time we went on a trip to a place that conjured up all kinds of 'John Wayne and Randolph Scott' cowboy memories. It is called the Apache Trail and is described in the tourist books as one of the most scenic drives near the Phoenix area. *'This well-travelled road affords visitors an incredible view of canyons, geologic formations, desert plants and trees, desert and lake views, and wildflowers in season'*, they say.

The trail, apparently once a stage coach one, is cut through the Superstition Mountains and Tonto Forest, where the Apache once lived (and fought). It ends up at a lake and a bridge called the Roosevelt Lake and Bridge. It is a great experience for anyone who ever gets to the town called Apache Junction – a name that even sounds like the title of an exciting western movie.

All good things come to an end however and we got back home to Brentwood in time for the Brentwood Business Community Conference and our flu jabs. With the run up to Christmas now underway it was once again a time of parties, lunches, dinners, meetings and other events, many of them connected with BOCA. We even went to a Christmas party thrown by Joey's stables.

Lots of them and dinners with the children of course, and after visiting mum and taking a wreath to dad's grave Lynn and I ended the year the way it had largely been spent – we flew out, this time to Dubai, for Christmas and the New Year.

Chapter 28

'Dad, we're on our way to Westminster...'

Lily the Cat

When I was running Butterkist my year used to start with my tour of the UK but now it's usually marked by the annual Football Writers Dinner and in 2006 it was for Bryan Robson. 'Captain Marvel', in his playing days for England and Man United Robson became Man United's longest serving captain and was the sixth most capped player for England for whom he scored 26 goals. He also captained his country on 65 occasions, so this was an award well deserved. He was a little unlucky in both the 1986 and 1990 World Cup finals being injured early on in both competitions but Bradley does have his shirt from them.

Lynn and I had actually arrived home from Dubai on January 6th when Brandon and Justine entertained us to dinner. Another visitor we had around that time was Bert Green from the Warley Park Golf Club who had become a great friend. Sadly he had just lost his wife Pat and Bert, a great conversationalist (particularly on the 'great game of golf'), was clearly missing her and needed someone to talk to.

Lynn, as it happens, is particularly good in that kind of situation and he clearly enjoyed talking with her but on this occasion I got a bonus too because he brought his grandson David. He was only fifteen but he showed me how drums really should be played. He was brilliant and I understand that he now teaches drumming.

Other than that it was a fairly normal start to the year with a Brentwood Rugby Club Lunch, a Burns Night dinner at the Gables and preparations to celebrate five years at Hutton Manor.

We were also visiting Mum who was getting more forgetful and a bit weaker while at the other end of the family age scale we were seeing more of Henry and Yomay. They often stayed the night and had meals, mostly pancakes, with us. Oh yes, we had another addition to the family – Cheralyn decided she needed a cat and 'Lily the cat' arrived.

Lynn and I had an anniversary coming up so we went away for ten weeks, flying first to Singapore to celebrate it. That caused me a little embarrassment because when we checked in at the Fullerton Hotel they gave me a form to sign and for the life of me I couldn't remember the date. I should have done because it was February 21st and when the hotel receptionist reminded me of the date I said: 'Oh God of course it is, it's our wedding anniversary.'

The girl obviously took the remark on board even though I didn't realise it at the time. But, while it took only a moment or two to sign in, by the time we reached our room a bouquet of flowers, a couple of cakes and a bottle of champagne with 'Happy Anniversary' on it was waiting on the table.

After a few days there we flew to my favourite city in Australia – Perth – where we started with a 3-day trip to Monkey Mia. This is a spot on the West coast north of the city where every morning a pod of bottlenose dolphins comes in and people can just go into the sea and swim around with them.

This is a wonderful experience my old friend and colleague John Walker had told me about many years earlier. It's a long trip with not much in the way of comfortable places to stop on the way and that is putting it as politely as I can. I'd been to Perth before this with Bradley and we'd tried to hire a taxi only to be told it was 500-600 miles north. This time however Lynn and I made it, coming back to Perth in time to catch a flight to Darwin where we spent a few nights before flying on to Sydney.

We met up there with an old school friend, Peter Atkins and his wife Gary. They turned the trip into a fantastic experience, taking us everywhere to show us the sights of Sydney, after we'd done Northern Australia on our own. What was even more fantastic was that Bradley and Lisette were also in Sydney at the time and we stayed in the same hotel. In fact we were in Australia when Lisette was six months pregnant.

It's always nice spending time with your children and we've been lucky with all of ours. Both Bradley and Brandon are self-made men and very successful in their own spheres of activity and in their family lives.

*Enjoying a beer with Peter Atkins in the garden of his Sydney home.
We've been friends since we were seven!*

Brandon, of course, is the more publicly known son because of his politics but Bradley has been equally successful in his own business life. Chel, who is largely responsible for pushing me to write this book, works successfully in an entirely different area but more of that later.

Not much for universities Bradley joined Crestco, an electronics settlement system, in 96 as trialling assistant testing the new system being built for UK equities settlement. He became team supervisor around 2000, becoming relationship manager in 2001 looking after UK wealth managers, stockbrokers, third party settlement agents that were members of CrestCo. A year later Euroclear bought Crestco and he began working for Euroclear.

Euroclear UK & Ireland is now the Central Securities Depository (CSD) of the United Kingdom, Ireland, Jersey, Guernsey and the Isle of Man. It provides advanced, low-cost settlement facilities for a wide range of corporate and government securities, including those traded on the London and Irish Stock Exchanges, and Bradley is now its Business Development Manager of Cofunds, as well of course as being a non-executive director at Woodlands Schools.

Anyway back to Australia where all four of us flew off to Brisbane, to spend a week on the Gold Coast before carrying on to Melbourne for the opening of the Commonwealth Games by the Queen. We spent some time there before we all went to Adelaide for the real reason for the entire trip. That was to go to the wedding of Gareth Thompson and Simone which was a wonderful experience but I did have one small, well shall we say, 'surprise'.

We were all staying in a lovely hotel where the function was being held but as we were sitting down to dinner I was suddenly informed that I was to be the main speaker and propose the toast. Now you will have realised by now that, when it comes to public speaking, I can usually hold my own and in this case I had half an hour or so to think about what I was going to say.

Actually it was quite easy because Malcolm Vaughan's England had won the Ashes the previous September, when a new cricketing star called Freddie Flintoff had been the main reason. So now I had to speak to an Aussie audience and since I had no intention of ignoring that, I got heckled quite a bit of course. But it was a good laugh and they were a lovely lot of people.

It was a great day and Gareth and Simone, who by the way is expecting as I write this, have stayed in touch and often come to the UK to visit us.

Sad times and great moments

Looking back on life as a whole I suppose we all go through various phases and for a while, after Lynn and I came back from the American 'last leg' of our trip to Australia, we did seem to have a lot of sad times. I suppose in a sense it goes with the age, both of ourselves and our friends, but to balance against that we did have one very bright spot amid the sadness.

After leaving Adelaide we'd flown to Los Angeles and then on to Phoenix to spend some weeks in Scottsdale. Well I say Scottsdale but during that time we also 'motored down to Minneapolis' and drove across North Dakota (staying in Fargo and Bismark), from where we flew down to Las Vegas before going back to Scottsdale. The name Phoenix, and I do not just mean the city, may have more significance shortly.

We got home just in time to do some leafleting for the local elections, including on election morning in Kelvedon Hall which I remember well. In fact until the January of that year (2006) it had been the home of former Conservative minister and Southend MP Paul Channon who died there. The son of Henry 'Chips' Channon, the diarist who'd worked in Churchill's wartime government, he was also part of the Guinness family and in 1997 had become Baron (Lord) Kelvedon.

A very successful minister Paul had served in many governments and in many capacities. Kelvedon Hall lies back at the end of a long driveway behind great iron gates that open up to let you in. Unfortunately they do not open up to let you out and after we'd delivered our leaflet we found we couldn't get out. That morning we'd got up early and by this time it was only 5.45am and we needed to wake the gatekeeper up to let us out. He was not best pleased believe me, but that night we were at the Brentwood Centre for the count where we saw Brandon take more council seats.

That was good news but then we had another sad moment. We did visit Dad's grave and went to see Mum whose health was not too good but then I had to go, with Cheralyn, to the funeral of Mrs. Fane. Now I have not mentioned her in this book so far but she was a special kind of lady and she had had an effect on the family, when she lived round the corner from us in our Emerson Park days.

In her younger days, known as Leonora, she had been a very talented opera singer who had performed in the great opera houses around the world. She went on to write books and becoming a lady who would give children some extra help in a variety of subjects. Indeed both Bradley and Cheralyn had benefitted from her help and we'd all become great friends with her and her husband. Her husband had been a talented artist and after he died she kindly gave me several of his paintings which I still have.

So close in fact that as a Christmas present one year we had them taken by a chauffeur driven car to the London Opera House for an evening out. Having already lost her husband she was getting old herself and died in May. Because she was well into her eighties we had expected only a few people at the funeral but it was packed, mostly with children from around the borough all wearing different school uniforms. It was quite a sight and a great tribute to Mrs. Fane, as we, they and their parents, paid our respects.

Not long after that I had another funeral to go to and speak at – this time that of Christine, the wife of John Walker my old friend and colleague from the popcorn days. Christine had suffered with cancer for over twenty years but was a real fighter and had done so for a long time until finally, the inevitable happened and she lost the battle and died.

I got the call from John telling me the sad news. We'd known it was coming once the MacMillan nurses had moved in to take care of her. John, who knew he could not do the job, asked me if I would kindly do the eulogy. I said yes straight away because I knew it would help the family and I might be a little less emotional than the rest of the family, though that proved not to be the case.

We'd had so many good times with our sales force and John, as they say, had been the last man standing. Even after I left the firm he was still in position, but then chose to leave of his own accord.

Lynn and I drove to Harrogate where, on John's recommendation we stayed at Nidd Hall on the outskirts of the town. He had remembered it as a very nice old country home but by the time we booked in it had become a Warner's Holiday Camp. To make things more awkward we'd invited John to come to dinner with us so we could talk through the next day of the funeral.

In a sense he was obviously in a pretty sombre mood and I guess he really needed what turned out to be a slightly humorous 'holiday camp' style evening. There were rock'n roll bands, people doing karaoke and wandering around in holiday mood. It did lighten the mood of the evening for all of us and John always did have a brilliant sense of humour.

Next morning Lynn and I took a ride to Ripley Castle and then on to the church where I gave the eulogy at Christine's funeral.

By now Mum was in Thurrock hospital while Brenda Warmington was in the Nuffield in Brentwood, but there was at least one bright spot around this time. Well two really because on July 7th we went to see Chel graduate and qualify as a teacher (she has two degrees). The other bright spot depended on Lisette and she came through as well.

She had gone into St John's Hospital in Chelmsford as by then she was due to give birth. Around midnight Bradley, who was with her there of course, thought it might be a good idea to take a walk round Tesco's who have a big store almost opposite. They obviously got back to the hospital because at 2.50am the baby, Phoenix Jack Lewis, turned up.

We got a call at 4.30am and, while my instinct was to react by saying 'Fantastic, well done', my actual words were: 'How good is that – a grandson born on World Cup Final Day'. So, on Sunday July 9th 2006, I was able to sit in hospital cuddling our new grandson and watch the cup final on TV at the same time. That was the game where the great French player Zidane got red carded for head butting and Italy won 5-3 on penalties. It was the day that Italy and the Lewis family both got a result.

Brenda

The arrival of Phoenix in the family did not, however, signal the end of that rather bleak period for there was still much sadness to come and that began with the loss of another dear friend. Although this time she was more one of Lynn's friends we were both close to Ron and Brenda Warmington.

Ron, you may remember from the previous chapter when he mistook someone's bike for a hotel one when we were in Paris on Bradley's 'stag do', but Lynn met Brenda in 1992 when Chel was twelve and hanging around some stables. Ron and Brenda's daughter Julie had a horse there and the two became friends. Then I bought Chel her horse for her 13th birthday and that meant the two mums were meeting each other more frequently.

They joined a badminton club together and became partners, playing a couple of times a week becoming best friends. Because of their relationship Ron and I came together and we all went out together, often with Mike and Pat Large who had been friends of theirs long before we knew them. We'd all spent some very pleasant times together but now

Brenda was in hospital – first in the Rivers Hospital in Sawbridgeworth before being transferred nearer home to the Nuffield, but she was clearly very poorly and we visited her frequently.

We went off to Scottsdale that year for a couple of weeks, mainly to see Brandon and his family who were out there. We surprised them by being there when they walked back in having gone out for dinner.

Lynn had always been a little concerned about being away while Brenda was so ill and, as we knew, was slipping slowly away. She had been extremely brave and had held on for many months but it was clear that there was no real hope. On August 11th we were sitting in a movie theatre when I got an e-mail on my Blackberry from Ron to say Brenda had passed away.

We were going home the following day so there was no real point in causing Lynn any more distress by telling her. She, however, has always had a kind of second sense and there were certain people – and Brenda was one – who she had a sort of telepathic link with. Without my saying anything she had already had a bad feeling about Brenda by the time we got home.

Coming back from the airport we drove through Brentwood, having to stop at the traffic lights at the end of the High Street, right next to Bennett's the funeral director. We did not know it but Brenda was actually in there and Lynn said she had a bad feeling and wondered how Brenda was. Trying to sound casual, I remarked that we would be home soon and would find out.

In fact I had pre-warned the children not to rush out to greet us, as was their custom, but when we arrived I sat Lynn down and told her the sad news I'd kept from her. She did not seem surprised and asked if Brenda was in Bennett's as we drove past but of course at that stage I didn't know but as it turned out her 'strange feeling' had been correct. I left her at home and went straight round to see Ron – in fact for some days after that we saw him every day.

I see from my diary that I was with him every day up to the funeral, and what a funeral that was. Ron and Julie had worked hard on it and it was held in his back garden – but what a garden. It held a magnificent marquee set up for lunch and a few hundred people arrived to honour Brenda. The coffin was in the garden and the service took place there, following which Lynn made one hell of a speech. Talking about her special friend she was brilliant with the words she chose in the kind of tribute that is always difficult to do when it's about someone that close.

Brenda had always made it clear that when she passed away she wanted, in her words, to go out with a big bang and we certainly saw to that. Sometimes in the past Brenda had often played practical jokes on me and I took her wishes literally and organised a pyrotechnic company to come and put on a firework display.

So at the end of her eulogy, Lynn said Brenda had always wanted to go out with a bang and she invited the guests to step outside. As they did, off went the fireworks. Thus, in every sense of the word, Brenda did indeed 'go out with a bang'. It had been a long day, but I was back there the next day to help clear up.

If course, while this chapter has been full of a lot of ups and downs it is important to remember that three of the most important people in our lives were growing up well and healthy. We were regularly visiting and/or babysitting, Phoenix, taking Yomay to Toys R Us for her 3rd birthday while Henry was already 6 years old and all of them giving us such pleasure. Still do, actually.

We were also regularly visiting Mum in hospital and looking for a nursing home for her when she came out, visiting one called Godden Lodge in Thundersley (Essex). Lynn and I were also still using the passports and flew out to Dubai for a week before, after visiting Mum again, flying out to Scottsdale for five weeks. This time we came home via (driving through) Nebraska, Iowa and Wisconsin before arriving in Chicago (Illinois) to fly home.

We got home on November 9th to hear some great news the following day. At 10.30pm, having just left the final selection meeting with Justine Brandon phoned us and I can remember his words very clearly.

'Dad, I'm on my way to Westminster. I have just been selected to stand for the Conservatives in Great Yarmouth at the next General Election.'

Mum

Great Yarmouth – the Norfolk seaside town where during my Butterkist days I had done so much business and where we had employed so many local people in the Docwra factory. The coincidence that I would be

441

going back there to help get our son elected to parliament almost seemed like a good omen, and I could hardly wait.

Thus on November 25th we had a meeting in Brandon's house with some friends to discuss how we were going to win the seat. We all took on separate responsibilities with mine being fairly open ended but in particular raising the funds to fight the General Election, expected in 2010.

That would not be easy for the constituency, which sent its first MP to parliament in 1386, had been held by Labour since 1997 when the sitting MP (Tony Wright) took it from the Conservatives. Now Brandon had a 3,055 majority to overturn so clearly it would not come without a hard fight and there was no time to lose.

In fact on the first Saturday after that meeting in Brandon's house we took a group in a minibus to a particular spot just outside Caister where we thought we were going to meet up with a group of local activists. There was just one young lad waiting there for us with some leaflets and no one else. Not the greatest of starts because even he had to leave, so there we were with some leaflets and a map, having to find our way around Great Yarmouth on a cold winter's morning. Now we knew just how tough this was going to be.

The one bit of good news I can remember after that was hearing from a Professor Roger Kirby, who I'd gone to see in Harley Street about a small medical problem, that I was alright. That was almost counter balanced by the news that Brandon had had a serious accident in his BMW, having lost control on a wet icy road and hit a tree. Fortunately he had not been seriously hurt although he was very shaken. I went back to the scene and had to climb up a tree to reclaim his number plate.

Before I leave the subject of elections it was about this time that Chel had decided to stand for the council, still led by Brandon. She'd been selected to stand for the Brentwood North ward so as the year began to end, apart from Great Yarmouth for one of our children, we were leafleting there for another one. So, 2006 had been a year with its fair share of high and low points in which we'd lost some friends but gained a new grandchild and with Brandon's political career taking a very positive turn.

As with most New Year's we went into 2007 in a spirit of optimism, electioneering in Norfolk and Brentwood, visiting Mum in Godden

Lodge and watching Mike Large celebrate his 60th birthday by showing us how to take the cork out of a champagne bottle with a sword. We had a bit more success in Great Yarmouth when a few more local people came out to help us with the leafleting etc. and I took Lynn away to Marrakech for a few days.

I should also mention that back in 2004, having served in various capacities in the Brentwood and Ongar Conservative Association (BOCA) I had been elected President. This was something I had taken very seriously indeed and although I stood down later that year I was still actively involved in local politics as well as, let's not forget, Woodland Schools where I seemed to be as busy as ever.

After our wedding anniversary Lynn and I flew out to Phoenix (the one in Arizona) planning to spend seven weeks or so in Scottsdale, where I continued training and even ran a half marathon in 2 hours 33minutes. Our return journey took us to Dallas, Jackson (the State Capital of Mississippi, Alabama where we stopped off in Montgomery and then to Birmingham.

We had intended spending a few days there before going on to Georgia but I suddenly got a call from home telling me that Mum had been taken ill and was in Southend Hospital. Apparently it was a matter of time so it was imperative that we got back home quickly. We checked out of the hotel and, because there is no airport in Alabama from where we could fly to the UK, we had to get ourselves to Atlanta.

While we were making arrangements to do that back home Bradley had been able to get us on a flight to Gatwick and we got to Atlanta with just an hour to spare. While we were waiting for the flight I phoned Southend Hospital to try to see how serious the position was. I got through to the ward only to be told that Mum was no longer there. Then, just as we heard the final call to board the plane a voice from Southend came back to me to say: 'We are sorry Mr. Lewis, You are too late – your mother is dead.'

The gate was about to close so I had no option but to get onto the plane and quickly e-mail the boys to say we were on it but that Mum was dead. This was the most dreadful eight hours I think I have ever experienced, knowing, or at least thinking, that we had not missed her by very much. I have crossed the Atlantic many times before and since of course but perhaps never in such an emotional state. I didn't sleep much but I did drink a lot and then we landed at Gatwick to be met by Brandon who, unbelievably, told us that the hospital had got it all wrong and that she was still alive.

It seemed that Mum was no longer in that particular ward and whoever it was I'd spoken to had assumed she'd died and had been taken to the mortuary. Now my emotions were really mixed – angry because of what I'd been put through and gratitude that I still had the chance to see her. Brandon rushed us home and then straight to the hospital where we were able to spend some time with Mum.

The next day Lynn and I spent most of the time with her. Chel and Bradley also came along but it was obvious that she was slipping away and we knew instinctively that this would be our last opportunity to say goodbye. We stayed with her until around 9pm and at 5am on April 20th I got a call to say Mum was passing away and I got there at 6am when she was pronounced dead.

I have made no secret that in the early days she and I didn't always hit it off and how at the age of sixteen she'd packed my bags and I'd left home. She was very much a lady who knew her own mind and stood no nonsense but over the years many fences had been mended. She had, after all, brought me up to have good manners, to be polite, honest and to respect others so in a way she had laid the foundations for what had been a successful future.

Both she and Dad had encouraged me to work hard at the studies that got me into the St Marylebone Grammar School. Ok, the school was probably a bit above me and I didn't do all that well there academically, but it did help me build on the strong character that I guess originally came from her. She was always very kind and caring to others and she was a marvellous grandmother, always pleased to be asked to babysit and had a lot of time to give Brandon, Bradley and Chel whenever needed.

During the early years of their marriage she was a waitress in Ealing but gave all that up as soon as I was born. From my parents I grew up to understand that looking smart helps, especially in my profession as a salesman, and I got most of that from Mum. She herself, whatever she was doing or wherever she was going, was always well-dressed.

All these things went through my mind, as of course they do for everybody who loses someone close to them, in those first few days. That day, after some formalities, on leaving the hospital I made a few calls to relatives to break the news before joining Lynn, Brandon and Justine, for Eric Pickles' birthday party. Eric had already got the news of course and, as ever, was ready with a kind word or two of comfort and being surrounded by friends at such times always helps.

Later that day Bradley came with me when Martin drove me to the hospital in an attempt to get the death certificate and it was just as well he did. We were told that no doctors were on hand and that we would have to come back another time but I knew that the department in Southend that registers death certificates closed at 4pm. Quite honestly I was shaken and upset so Bradley took charge and decided to throw what we call 'a wobbly'.

He sent me and Martin back to sit in the car but, from what I could hear when I came back half an hour later he was really in full swing. He was shouting, screaming and refusing to leave until someone found a doctor to sign, saying it was upsetting enough to lose a parent without all this hassle. Sure enough a doctor was found and the certificate was signed in time for us to deposit it.

I had to go back to Godden Lodge the next day to clear up Mum's belongings and of course to make funeral arrangements. All of this while we were leafleting in Great Yarmouth and Brentwood but on April 30th we held Mum's funeral in Southend, the service carried out by our local priest from Hutton. Obviously because Mum was a few weeks away from her 95th birthday there were not too many people there but all the family, including cousins I hadn't seen in years, attended.

The funeral itself was a bit delayed because a road accident resulted in the coffin turning up late and later on everyone came back to our garden for drinks. As it happened it was then, while talking to some of my cousins, that I learned more about Mum's early days than I'd ever known. In fact that was when I learned how she'd once been in Hutton Poplars, the children's home on the site where later both Brandon and Bradley had had a home while a mile further up the road I was running a school.

Chapter 29

Marathon man

Delaware completed the set

A week or so after the funeral service Martin and I were back out on the streets again, this time drumming up support for Chel who was standing for the Brentwood North council seat. She was up against a Liberal Democrat who had been in office for almost twenty years, yet she lost by only 102 votes. Next time would be very different but it also showed that Brandon's leadership of the council was having a very positive effect on the local Tory vote.

We said our final goodbyes to Mum when we had the internment at Southend Cemetery, just a couple of days before she would have been 95. Bradley and Cheralyn both came along and I made a note in my diary that at long last Mum and Dad were together again.

Shortly after that Lynn and I went on a cruise around the Med with Chris and Bob, Tony and Shelagh Betts and as a result I missed the first Cup Final at the new Wembley Stadium. (That was between Portsmouth and Cardiff and was won by a single goal by Harry Redknapp's Portsmouth). What made the trip really memorable was not so much that we 'did' Gibraltar, Nice and Monaco, Pisa and Rome and Cadiz etc., but because on the day we got back to Southampton, I went down with a touch of food poisoning.

Life goes on of course and, as well as doing a lot of running, I am now constantly travelling up the A12 again, on my way to Great Yarmouth to help Brandon start his campaign. Quite like old times in some ways, except that now I was helping to sell my son, rather than popcorn. As for my own running I managed to complete a 20-mile run. As you have probably guessed, I was in training for the 2008 London Marathon by this time. (A few weeks later I did the full 26 miles).

Three grandchildren mean three birthdays a year for the grandparents of course and in July Phoenix kicks them off with his first one. We went with Bradley and Lisette to Colchester Zoo with him to mark the occasion, then we helped Brandon and Justine celebrate Henry's 7th after which, almost before we knew it, we were celebrating Yomay's 4th as well.

I've never mentioned Elsie Morgan before but I think I should do now as around this time we were visiting her in hospital. She was in fact Linda Tingle's and Barbara Young's (the original head and deputy head of Woodlands Warley) Mum, but she was a remarkable lady in her own right. Even in her 80s she was giving help and advice to the young children at the Warley school on a one-to-one basis.

Any of the youngsters who needed a little extra special help would be sent to spend an hour with 'Mrs. Morgan'. She was hard and strict but also bright and loving – all in all a really lovely person to be with. I suspect that in many cases the children, as Chel did, just loved their time with her.

Well into her 80s she had managed to look after herself at home, but when Linda had moved abroad (France and Croatia) and Barbara was busy with the school and her own daughter Helen who lived on the South Coast, she'd moved into a home. She died later that year, shortly after I'd called in to see her, by which time she was blind and having difficulty moving around. I took her some flowers that she enjoyed smelling, but she had not lost her wicked sense of humour.

I asked her if everything was ok and she told me that the people in the home were stupid because they had just installed a new TV – which was not much use to people who couldn't see. She laughed as she said it and I asked her if there was anything I could do for her. 'Yes Ken, get me out of here – can you do that?'

An intelligent lady she was always laughing and we still miss her. The funeral was held in Chelmsford and was attended by an enormous number of people, many of them former students who she'd helped.

But I digress a little, because before that Lynn and I had flown out to the USA, where we achieved a personal ambition. I'd been crossing the Atlantic ever since my popcorn days of course and, apart from owning our own place in Scottsdale, over the years Lynn and I had also done a fair bit of travelling up and down the States as well. This time though, would be a bit special.

We flew out to Boston with Mike and Pat Large, with whom we toured New Hampshire, Vermont, New York State and Connecticut before going back to Boston, where Mike and Pat flew home. We went on to Phoenix to spend five weeks in Scottsdale where Brian and Jan Dudley came out to spend a few weeks with us. Brandon, Justine and the children were in Florida around that time and Cheralyn managed to come out to stay with us for a week.

Then Lynn and I went on a road trip to Utah before spending another week in Scottsdale until November 3rd when we caught a flight to Charlotte in South Carolina. We drove through the state and through North Carolina to Virginia. Then it was on to West Virginia, through Maryland, to Delaware and that was important to us.

In fact the whole trip was important on a personal level because it had been my dream for a long time to visit the entire 'United States' – all fifty of them. This time we'd been visiting some States we'd never previously visited and Delaware completed the set, so to speak.

In a way it seemed appropriate that we, a couple of Britons, ended up in Delaware because it had been one of the first states to sign up to fight the War of Independence. Its state capital Dover was named after our own one in Kent by its founder William Penn in 1683. We went to their Visitor's Centre (Center in America of course) and spoke to people, proud of their revolutionary history. They were surprised that we'd left their state to be the last in our personal pilgrimage, but thrilled for us that we'd finally made it.

We were shown the house from where Caesar Rodney, a local leader and revolutionary, made an historic ride to Philadelphia – getting there in time to throw Delaware's weight (with eleven other states), into signing up to what ultimately became the Declaration of Independence. They made us very welcome in Delaware and we enjoyed our time in it before driving back to catch the plane to Heathrow, home and, oh yes, toothache. Well at least it wasn't food poisoning.

The marathon Imodium precautions

We were back in time for the usual Christmas preparations though the toothache did threaten to cast a dark cloud over that because it turned out to be an impacted wisdom tooth that needed a visit to hospital. That meant a day in Hartswood Hospital in Brentwood but, what with campaign organising and fund raising for the Great Yarmouth campaign already under way, along with all the other regular pre-Christmas festivities etc. I was too busy to let that stop me for long.

I should mention one unusual aspect of that particular Christmas however because it involved me getting out my old Father Christmas outfit again. Older readers might remember the old BBC radio show 'Educating Archie' which featured a ventriloquist on radio. Well my old 'Santa Clause' gear was dusted down and used again for a radio show. I was asked to wear it again for a Questions and Answers programme with Eric Pickles on local radio Phoenix FM, and it was all great fun.

Then Lynn and I flew out to Dubai for Christmas and the New Year, getting back again on January 2nd (2008) in time for lunch at Rules with the boys and the Football Writer's Dinner. The Savoy was closed for refurbishment so that year it was held at the Royal Lancaster Hotel, with the guest of honour being David Beckham. He proved to be easy to talk to and a real gentleman who took having his photo taken with several hundred people in his stride.

Shortly afterwards I took Lynn to New York on one of the best airlines I have ever used – Eos. This was an American based all-business airline, founded in 2004, that flew out of Stansted to New York (JFK) and had originally been called Atlantic Express. It was very comfortable and we enjoyed the flight but sadly a few months later, in April, it had to file for bankruptcy in America which was a pity.

Not that our trip had been without incident. We got to the lounge for a glass of champagne when I realised I'd left my Blackberry in the car.. I made what turned out to be a stupid comment to Lynn – 'Oh my God this will ruin my holiday. (Oh, how dependent we are on technology these days).

I made a quick phone call to Chris who managed to get onto Martin who was driving my car home after dropping us off at the airport.

Fortunately he was already on his way back to the airport, having spotted the Blackberry and done a U-turn. He managed to get to the Eos desk and they got my beloved piece of technology to me prior to our boarding the flight. I always find it difficult to be away from the children without direct communication and in that sense nothing has changed.

After a couple of days in New York we boarded the Queen Mary 2 for a two-week cruise along the Eastern seaboard – Newfoundland, Nova Scotia and down the St Lawrence Seaway to Quebec. Then we sailed to Halifax, Boston, Maine and Rhode Island (the smallest state in the Union) before arriving back in New York, and on from there back to Stansted.

Got back to resume training for the London Marathon, with a number of half marathons thrown in for good measure. In fact by the middle of February I'd managed a 22-mile run which is as much as you are expected to do before a full marathon. That included the Brentwood half-marathon on May 9th where I ran to support and raise funds for the Mayor's Charity.

Before all that however something else happened that in retrospect seems a little ironic bearing in mind our troubles over the tree felling when we'd moved into Hutton. On March 29th Ron Warmington came to see me with a colleague called Ian Marshall, to attempt to persuade me to join the Hutton Mount Association – one of the objectors when we knocked all those trees down.

This particular association represents over 550 homes and 2,000 residents, on the Hutton Mount estate. Ron had been a member and was considering rejoining, but only on the proviso that I went along as well. His idea was that it would help bring about a different relationship with Hutton Mount Ltd and it was one that Lynn too felt was right. She said I should join because we not only live on the Estate but love it, take pride in it and that it would be a chance to help in some way or another.

I had no idea how and had no experience, but I was being almost blackmailed into joining because if I didn't Ron, who did have all the experience and knowledge they needed, wouldn't join either. So I agreed and although I had intended being a member for just a year or so, four years later I am still a member.

Brandon, who was also running in the London Marathon, and I went to the Excel Centre on the Wednesday before the event to get all the information, including our numbers that we needed. While we were there we happened to bump into my own GP Dr Kannan Athreya, who gave us some advice he thought we would need.

Looking at Brandon he said: 'You will not need my advice because at your age you will be fine.' In my case however he said I would need some serious painkillers for my knees. Fair enough because, having run 1,000 miles in ten months of training, they had pretty well gone and clearly I would be needing some help getting round the course in that sense; but then he added something else. A very experienced marathon runner himself, he told me to take some Imodium as well.

Well it's obvious what that does of course, but I couldn't understand why he felt it was necessary to take a medication usually associated with keeping the bowels under control so he explained. It seems that after around 18 to 20 miles the body starts to relax in all areas, so his suggestion was to take the stuff before and during the marathon. It did seem to be a strange thing to take at the same time as painkillers, but he grinned and pointed out that 'It is for one day only'.

On Sunday April 13th we were up at 5.30am, having not slept much anyway and we left at 7am to get to Greenwich Park at 8am. Then the competitors have to stand around, getting cold for a couple of hours, waiting until it all starts off at 10am. What a wonderful experience it all turned out to be!

I managed to see some of the family and some friends in various places around the route but on the day of the Marathon you have a million friends. As you run towards them everyone is calling out your name which along with your number is pinned to your chest. It seems like everyone there is there for you, and that gives you a marvellous lift.

I was seeing family at about nine miles and fifteen miles as well as friends along the route. What I do remember is finishing wishing I'd gone faster because I felt pretty good at the end of the run but, of course, the main thing is to finish. I had started the race with Brandon, who finished well ahead of me of course, but I was glad to have even completed it, getting my medal for the 5 hours 52 minutes it took me.

In fact I was on such a high that when we got back to Shenfield Station, although our cars were in the station car park, I refused the lift home. With my medal hanging around my neck (I never took it off for two days and nights) I jogged back up the hill to home where Bradley got

quite emotional, hugging me to say 'Well done'. I think that was also due to the amount of money (£9k) we raised for the Variety Club, which he also works very hard for.

Mind you, it did nearly get me thrown out of the rugby club. The day before the Marathon had been the occasion of the Rugby Club Lunch and, alcohol being taboo the day before the race, I was not pouring beer and wine down my throat as usual. I found that very difficult to live down.

Sardinia surprise

Back in the real world again I did take the medal off to go leafleting in Brentwood and Great Yarmouth, where we launched what we called the 'Dawn Raids'. That involved us getting up and meeting at 5am to do the leafleting and helping the campaign generally.

As things turned out Brandon had some real good results that day both in Norfolk and Essex. As the town's prospective parliamentary candidate he helped increase the number of Tory seats on the local council in Great Yarmouth, while doing the same again in Brentwood, where he was still

Leader of the Council at the time. (He stood down from Brentwood the following year to concentrate on Great Yarmouth)

Not long after the elections I was invited to a dinner at the Ivy Hill House in Mountnessing for a Chelmsford Conservatives evening, where the guest of honour was the Tory Leader, David Cameron. He made a point of coming over to our table for a chat and to tell me how well he thought Brandon was doing, so clearly he had his finger on the way things were going. It was an interesting comment because I said to him:

'If you held an election right now, I think Brandon would win by anything from five to ten thousand votes.' That was how confident I felt, even though we were fighting a seat with a comfortable Labour majority.

Cameron smiled and replied: 'Yes, he is doing well and I do expect him to win, but one vote will do.'

I was still keeping fit and about this time a local fitness trainer came to see me with an idea to encourage young runners. I knew Keith Morton because his parents also used to run a school (Bell House) in Brentwood but he'd also been a successful trainer who had been credited with helping Frank Bruno win his World Heavyweight Championship title in 1995. (Bruno at the time lived in Brentwood and was a Tory supporter)

Keith was approaching local schools with the concept of a mile run for primary and junior schoolchildren, before they went up to 'big school' so to speak. The Morton's Mile, as it was called, was basically a race against the clock with all youngsters doing the mile within a set time, getting a medal while those who didn't do it in the set time, at least got a certificate to say they had run the race. Everyone was a winner.

We had the finals (between individual schools' winners) at Hutton Manor and it went very well. Keith also got a result because he sold me a walking machine and signed me up as a member of his Hutton based personal fitness club. I have trained there ever since and because of the superb system he has in his club, I attained a level of fitness that probably saved my life, as you will read later in the book.

On the subject of health little Phoenix was having a few ear problems and it was decided he needed to have gromits, so he went into the Portland Hospital in London. I went there with Bradley and Lisette to be with him, managing to find a soft toy in Liverpool Street station to take to him. Shortly after he had his naming day and we all celebrated at Hutton Manor.

I was also still spending a lot of time going up and down the A12, to help Brandon's campaign in Great Yarmouth but at this stage, events closer to home were demanding attention too. By now both our schools were doing well and attracting attention from within the industry. Barbara Young had asked me to buy her shares and her sister Linda (Tingle) and husband Alan sold me theirs too.

Now we were getting offers to buy the schools but from people who, in my view, didn't understand that for me it was not just a business. It had become a passion that other members of the family share, and we work very hard to keep them going. How long it remains in the family is to be seen but we will do our best to keep it that way for the foreseeable future and hopefully for future generations.

As I have written it had been a very busy couple of years but what I haven't mentioned until now is that I'd spent a lot of time during them, planning a very special birthday celebration.

Lynn was heading for her 60th birthday and while we have travelled a lot of course, one place we always wanted to visit was in Sardinia. That was where I wanted to take, not just Lynn and the family, but as many friends of our very wide circle as I could. That was why organising an all-inclusive trip like the one I had in mind was difficult and time consuming. The people invited had to be sworn to secrecy and well in advance so they could arrange their own calendars.

I found the Hotel Romazzino and, without Lynn knowing anything about it, I'd written to the special friends and the family warning them of the plan. Then I started making plans to hire out the entire Club Class area of a BA flight, dealing with the hotel and planning a few extra surprises like flying Lee and Rita out from Scottsdale to join us and get them into the Gatwick Lounge without Lynn spotting them.

It had been quite a job actually making sure that for two years no one made any contact with Lynn about her birthday. I just told her that we were going to Sardinia to celebrate her birthday and that Chel would be joining us with a friend. I said we'd have a proper celebration with the rest of the family when we got back.

Come the day and Martin, who was driving us, had already stowed his own case in the minibus. Brandon and his family popped over to say goodbye and then went back home across the road. Bradley and his family also arrived to see us off and Lynn, a touch tearful now at leaving her family behind went back into the house to collect her handbag.

When she came out she was surprised to find that Bradley, Lisette and Phoenix had sneaked onto the bus and were sitting on it waiting to go. Then a few more friends – her long term friend Joan Munroe, Chris and Bob (Howes) and Peter and Linda French – all turned up and got onto the bus. We arrived at Gatwick and Martin surprised her by parking the bus and coming back to join us as well.

We all made our way to the lounge where, sitting waiting, was Roy and Reggie and – the biggest shock of all – was to see Lee and Rita from Arizona, who had flown in the previous evening and had stayed at a nearby hotel. Then, just when she thought she'd had the last of her surprises she spotted Brandon, Justine, Henry and Yomay, sitting quietly grinning in the corner.

That was when the penny dropped that all our family and friends were together then, when we got on the plane, she found Geoff and Val Purdy there as well. We had a good flight to Sardinia where we were collected by coach and taken to the hotel where the 'icing' was really put on her birthday cake to find the Hagons – Paul, Jane, Sally and Michael – who'd flown out a few days earlier and were waiting to greet us.

My godsom Michael Hagon with his sister Sally

The weather was kind, we had great fun with the kids in the pool, some excellent meals and good company. It was one of those occasions that will stay with us forever and if I had the time and space I could write a book on that trip alone. We had a wonderful five days, all of us getting up to all kinds of pranks – one of which actually ended up on a website called Pete's Pants. That involved former 'top cop' Peter French, and no one has ever actually confessed to stealing his room key. The story of his pants (and a pair of sunglasses that were returned to him) went global, turning up on the internet as 'Who has seen Pete's Pants?'

Paul Hagon with his daughter Sally

Pictures were taken and they turned up at mosques, castles and a volcano, just about anywhere in the world. There is no doubt that Pete eventually accused the right person of the 'crime' because he accused everyone, even poor Joan Munroe who would not have said boo to a goose. Now, but on the basis that he accused everyone, I have to say to Peter that you had it spot on. Geoff Purdy was heard to say that if Peter French was Brentwood's top cop, he was glad he lived in Lichfield.

They eventually turned up, nicely framed, to be auctioned off at one of our Christmas fundraising parties.

I must add that we realised that Peter had lost his detective skills when he told me that someone had stolen his sunglasses and he was going to search everyone's rooms to see if he could find them. He had not quite worked out that even as he told me this I was actually wearing them.

Peter has now retired from the police but had his house broken into while he was asleep on the premises. Now he is a security adviser to various airlines around the world.

And that was 2008

I guess that after the 'celebration in Sardinia', the rest of that year could easily have paled in comparison but in fact it was as busy a time as ever. We had all the grandchildren's (as well as our own children's) birthdays of course, a lot of pavement bashing in Great Yarmouth, and with me doing 10k jogs around Brentwood, sometimes with Chel.

Nor had Lynn and I done all our globe-trotting for the year because, after flying to Venice for a few days, we then boarded Cunard's MS Queen Victoria for a cruise that took us through Greece, the Ukraine and Turkey before finishing in Rome. Then, after we'd seen England beat Kazakhstan 5-1 at Wembley and organising a Race Night to raise funds for BOCA, we were packing our bags and sorting out our passports again.

This time it was to fly out for our now customary break in Scottsdale so we flew out to Phoenix to spend five weeks at our other home in Arizona. Chel, who was visiting a friend in Toronto at the time, flew down to Phoenix to spend ten days with us before she went home. Did I say five weeks in Arizona? Well, not exactly all the time.

After Chel left, Mike and Pat Large arrived to stay with us for a week and after they'd gone I took Lynn off to Las Vegas for three days and

On board ship and ready for dinner

nights, this time driving there by road. A brief week's rest back in Scottsdale and we set out on the road again. This time we wanted to see New Mexico, staying in the state capital (Santa Fe) and going on to Albuquerque before going 'home' to spend Thanksgiving with Lee and Rita. We got back to Brentwood just in time to see the Christmas lights switched on.

That year Lynn and I were invited to a Variety Club lunch at the London Hilton during which they had a thank you to the runners of the London Marathon

458

who had raised cash for the charity plodding round the capital. As the old boy in the team I was asked to stand while a couple of thousand people applauded me. Quite a humbling experience, but the following day we were in London again celebrating another one.

In recent chapters I have been mentioning Michael and Pat Large quite a lot so it is clear that by this time they were firm friends. We'd all met through mutual friends – Ron and (the late) Brenda Warmington – and had spent holidays (and lunches) together, but this was a very different celebration. We met them in the London Hilton after they and members of their family had been to Buckingham Palace, to see Mike get his OBE from Prince Charles.

A very successful businessman in his own right Mike had (and still is) also been very active in organisations like the Institute of Directors and the East of England IDB which works to bring European business to East Anglia. Always a generous person in so many ways, he is particularly so with his time for causes he believes in and that of business in East Anglia is one. Mike has been responsible for helping many people, associations and businesses in so many different ways over many years and thoroughly deserved to be part of the Honours List that year.

I have to say that when I heard the news early on a Saturday morning I had to phone him because I was so excited for him. In fact I think I was more excited and got a bigger kick out of the news than he did at the time, though he is by nature a very calm and collected man. Mind you he had probably got used to the idea, having had a little knowledge about it earlier and keeping it from everyone, except Pat of course and even from her until the day it was announced.

However for most of us who knew him it came as a total and very welcome surprise as well as a great thrill that someone got the OBE for so many good reasons and not just for their musical or football abilities. Congratulations again, Mike!

We had lunch at the Hilton before going on to the Institute of Directors where Mike had been President, for even more drinks and celebrations. It proved to be a wonderful day and a wonderful evening, tempered however when we got a phone call from Bradley to say that Bill, Lynn's father, had been taken into hospital.

So, as we approached Christmas it was a very hectic time with all the school events, Rugby Club lunch and of course the official OBE celebration party at Mike and Pat's home. Ivy (Lynn's mum) was in a BUPA home while Bill was in the Queens Hospital in Romford, so both were being looked after well and in fact a lot better than if they were at home.

We had a Christmas lunch with the Hagons, visited Mum and Dad's grave with a wreath and, after a family Christmas lunch at home we flew out with Cheralyn and her friend to spend Christmas and the New Year in Dubai. Well after all that's where we had started the year, so what better place to end it and start the new one?

Chapter 30

The Battle for Great Yarmouth

Ecolution and Bill

Back in the autumn of 2007, with Gordon Brown only just installed in No.10 Downing Street as Prime Minister having taken over from Tony Blair, there had been a lot of speculation over whether or not he would call a snap General Election. It is usually the practice for new prime ministers to call one as a kind of vote of confidence and a renewed mandate from the people. Many believe that at that stage he might even have won it but, in the words of some political journalists at the time, he 'bottled it'. He'd clearly waited so long for the job that he was reluctant to risk losing it.

As a result, as things for the government got worse, there had been constant speculation about when he would call one, but he'd not done so and, as 2009 began, that was rife. He had until 2010 before he had to call one, but for months refused to do so. For Brandon, preparing to fight for Great Yarmouth, it was a mixed blessing.

On the one hand he had to be patient, while on the other the increasing delays caused by Brown's reluctance to go to the country gave us more time to fight the campaign in Norfolk in an increasingly favourable (for the Tories) light. For many reasons, often outside of politics, the nation's economy was becoming more and more critical. Labour, showing its inability to deal with it, was losing ground in all the polls and putting the election off all the time.

So by the time 2009 opened, we were fairly used to the idea that our real test would come the following year – as it proved to be. Nonetheless we'd had the bit between our teeth ever since Brandon had been selected, and we were already spending a lot of time in Norfolk beefing up our campaign. Having said that we still had time for family and other things, even business and in that sense a new name came into the Lewis equation – Ecolution, a growing one in the green energy industry.

This was no sudden introduction though, because we'd known the firm (albeit under a different name) since we had the house built in Hutton in 1997. In those days they were into plumbing and had done a lot of it for us in the new house, which was where and when we met Andrew Knapp. He'd always been on site and had actually carried out a lot of the work himself but then his company, now called Ecolution, had moved into renewable energy systems, mainly solar power.

By this time the company was pretty well developed in terms of solar panels, heat pumps of all kinds and, to a lesser extent, wind turbines. Whether it is being contracted to design and install solar hot water systems in a residential scheme in Purfleet or providing the University of Brighton with a solar heated swimming pool, Ecolution is proving that the, relatively new, industry has a bright future.

Having got to know me pretty well Andrew now came to see me to discuss the company. He felt it needed some help and asked if I would think about someone who could join it in a non-Executive Director capacity to bring some business expertise. Clearly he had me in mind but I had to explain that I was actually quite busy with the schools and also that we anticipated a General Election could be called at any moment and, if that happened I would be even busier. As I explained at the start of this chapter Prime Minister Gordon Brown had been keeping everyone, even his own party, guessing as to whether and when he would call one.

I promised I'd give it some thought and that would be the end of the matter, though I did agree that Andrew could bring his brother Kevin, who was the company Chairman over for a chat on a future occasion. When he did we all 'gelled' immediately, despite the Knapp brothers being Chelsea supporters and their MD Richard Jenkins being a WBA fan. However I still thought that would be the end of the matter, even though what I was really thinking about was who (rather than me) could help them. As time will show I did eventually get involved.

Anyway, back to the start of 2009 the guest at the Football Writer's dinner (held that year at the Royal Lancaster Hotel) was Harry Redknapp, currently the Spurs manager but a hot tip to become the England coach. As I write this whether he does or not seems to depend on him and whether he wants to build Spurs up into a major club rather than the 'poisoned chalice' of the England job.

Bill, Lynn's father was still in hospital, in King Georges Hospital in Ilford, having been moved from the Queens in Romford. It made it easier for us to visit him and then go on to see Ivy in the home she was living in, before going over to their home in Rainham to check all was well in their absence. Then, after spending a day leafleting in Caister, we got the message to say he'd taken a turn for the worse and rushed back to Ilford.

We got there to find he was in a bad way and it was pretty clear that he was coming to the end of his time. All we could do was to be there for him and while we had a lot of activity at the schools, with Nature Trails in each, we spent a lot of time visiting him and Ivy. Lynn was also having problems with her back and was having tests and scans, with me having to drive her to the Medical Centre three times a week despite the heavy snow we were experiencing at the time.

Sadly on Wednesday February 18th that year Bill died and for Lynn it could not have come at a worse time. There's never a good time to lose a parent of course but she was still visiting the Medical Centre and the Nuffield Hospital and it was becoming obvious she would need an operation. On hearing that Chel, Brandon and Bradley all came to see her and that gave her a boost, especially since it was just a few days before our wedding anniversary.

On February 25th the whole family gathered, for the first time in many years, to lay Bill to rest. On such occasions families do come together and he really did get a good send off. Lynn and Tony, her brother, spent time considering what sort of music would suit the occasion and had come to the conclusion that two songs in particular would be right.

To start the service they had Frank Sinatra singing 'I did it my way' – what could be more fitting for a man who always had done things his way? Then he was played out with 'I'm forever blowing bubbles' – the signature anthem of his beloved West Ham United. It couldn't have signalled a better send off and he would have loved it.

Kaden

One of the few things that could cheer Lynn up at this time, especially with me spending so much time in Norfolk, was the grandchildren. So we were having Henry and Yomay over for deliberately organised sleepovers, and spending time with Bradley and Lisette which, of course, meant Phoenix too. Later that year things in that part of the family would get even better.

Meanwhile on March 2nd I took Lynn away to Scottsdale for seven weeks where Bradley, Lisette and Phoenix arrived for a holiday while Brandon and Justine took Henry and Yomay off to Italy. Chel turned up in Arizona with a friend as well, before we all came back home again in time for the end of the football season, and to resume the battle for Great Yarmouth. Speaking of football, even Lynn came to see Everton beat Manchester United (4-2) and she's not even interested in football – but Brandon brought Henry and that always makes her day.

With County Council elections definitely on and the persistent rumours of a General Election I found myself spending a lot of time plodding round the streets in both Brentwood and Great Yarmouth where of course they had local elections too. Even more, in June the European Elections took place as well and all this meant of course that Brandon and his team had to be out there showing they were working for the local Tory campaign. I was doing some travelling, almost commuting, up and down the A12 at that time.

On polling day itself we were up at 4am in Great Yarmouth for the 'Dawn Raid' and spent a hectic day there canvassing and telling etc. But we did get away by 7pm so managed to be back in Brentwood in time to vote ten minutes before the polls closed that night.

I should mention that just before this election Brandon had stood down both as Leader of the Council and as a Brentwood councillor, in order to concentrate on Great Yarmouth. However by then he had done his job and the Conservatives were not just back in control in Brentwood but were increasing their majority too. In June, coinciding with the Euro elections that year, a candidate to replace Brandon, held the seat in a bye election for the Tories.

We also had our fair share of invites to weddings and other celebrations but on July 15th we had a day out at the American Embassy in Grosvenor square. Well it wasn't intended to be a day out because all we wanted to do was to renew our Visas but we arrived on time at 10am and finally emerged at 4pm. I won't go into too much detail but what a day! We spent it sitting, waiting and being interviewed before finally emerging without the passports or visas, that all turned up a week later.

Fortunately, as things turned out I was lucky to get a visa that allowed us to spend six months in any twelve in America – fortunate because of something that happened to me in 2011 that we will come to later. Actually I had been having trouble with my knees ever since the marathon and was seeing physiotherapist Mike Conyer on a regular basis but that was unrelated to what happened to me then.

Lynn and I did go to see a country singer, Martina McBride, thanks to Chel who had booked the tickets a year in advance for herself, forgetting she would be on holiday with friend. We had a great night but of course it also meant that a bit later I had to go to Gatwick to pick her up. In fact during her 'growing up' years she always used two of her favourite words whenever she picked up a phone to ask if she was through to 'Daddy's Cabs'.

Mike Conyer and I had reached the conclusion that although there had been a slight improvement with the knees, there was little else that could be done and I would have to live with them. Still plodding around the streets of Great Yarmouth helped a little.

Then Lynn got a great 61st birthday present when, just a day before it on the 29th August, Bradley phoned us at 2am to ask if we would go over to their house. He wanted us to stay the night and look after Phoenix so he could take Lisette, who had gone into labour, to hospital. Of course we could.

Later that morning the call comes from him that our new grandson Kaden, for that is what they called him, had been born just after 8am. He weighed in at 7lb 7ozs and what a birthday present for Lynn. Pretty good for me too, becoming a grandfather for the fourth time on the day I was off to Wembley for the Carnegie Challenge Cup final.

Then we rushed off to St John's Hospital in Chelmsford again (where Phoenix had also been born, but this time without a walk round Tesco's) to meet Kaden Lewis. Bradley and Phoenix came home to have breakfast with us – they also joined us later at the London Chop House for Lynn's birthday dinner, a kind of double celebration. A few days later Lisette and Kaden came home and we all trooped round there to see him again, before going to dinner at the George and Dragon in Mountnessing.

Still deeply involved in the Conservative Party I was suddenly invited to a Renaissance Club dinner with Lord Basil Feldman. Although I was his guest I had no idea that I would have to 'sing for my supper' because, unbeknown to me during the meal I was put on the spot. They asked me to make a speech about Brandon – his progress since Sherwood and how he was doing in Great Yarmouth. Fancy asking me to talk about Brandon!

Of course I assured everyone in the room, both political and business people that he would win Great Yarmouth, still then a Labour held seat of course. I was supremely confident but of course busy making a rod for my own back because after making such claims in such company, we had no alternative but to win. So dodgy knees or no dodgy knees the next day I was out leafleting in Norfolk.

'Drum sight' at the OK Corral?

Still working hard with the schools of course and I would like take this opportunity to highlight a rather special teacher for whom we held a special party. Pam Tee had been a member of the Warley staff for twenty-five years, an unusual amount of time for a teacher to spend at one school.

On a personal level she had also helped Cheralyn get through her exams for Brentwood School and we're all grateful to her for that too. Both Pam and her husband David (who became mayor of Brentwood) have always been special friends. Very supportive of Chel and despite being retired she still helps us out at the school when she can.

Another point about that day is that that night Lynn and I went to the Carlton Club where I'd organised a fundraising evening for Brandon's campaign and we were lucky to have a super guy there called Jeremy Hunt. Very friendly and a brilliant guest who spoke well and we were grateful to him for turning out. He was clearly an up and coming MP on the parliamentary scene and as I write this he is responsible for Sports in this country and that includes the coming Olympic Games. Like any government minister, of whatever party, he will always be susceptible to criticism at times, but for us he was brilliant and I remain grateful for his support.

After a busy round of social activities allied to the political ones that involved an increasing amount of time in Norfolk, Lynn and I flew out to Scottsdale on October 15th for a six week break. While there, we went to the Gainey Ranch Golf Club BBQ with Tony Gillett, an English friend who now lives in Scottsdale. He is very keen on lamb which (come on, this is cowboy country), is very hard to get in Arizona, so Lynn made a special effort to get some and invited him round for lunch.

Then Mike and Pat Large, along with Ron Warmington and his friend Monica arrived to stay with us for a week, so we took them on a tour starting at Fountain Hills. This is a town in Arizona, nestling in the foothills of the McDowell Mountains which describes itself as a 'piece of desert paradise' and which is noted for the world's fourth largest fountain, installed in 1970. The fountain sprays water up to 560 feet for about 15 minutes every hour at the top of the hour. The plume rises from a concrete water lily sculpture in the centre of a large man-made lake and is something to witness.

Mike and Pat Large enjoying dinner on one of our many holidays together

467

Then we took a long drive to Tucson, where we visited the Sonara Desert Museum but I think for them, more importantly, we went on to Tombstone – the town associated so much with the history of the 'Old West'. Here they still enact the legendary Gunfight at the OK Corral for the tourists and we went on from there to visit the equally legendary Boothill Cemetery and the Birdcage Saloon (now Theater). It was there that something extraordinary happened to me that might help to explain the rather odd and contrived sub-heading to this chapter. Just put it down to my sense of humour.

In the Saloon the manager came up to me and introduced himself to me as someone he recognised. Remember this is in deepest Arizona and he knew me from Shepherds Bush, a place in London I'd left years before. I'd never seen him in my life but he not only remembered me, but knew I played the drums. Mike, Pat, Ron, Monica and even Lynn looked on in amazement as we went down memory lane.

It turned out that he himself had been a drummer, working with bands backing the likes of Tommy Steele, Cliff Richard and many others during those 'swinging sixties' days. I still don't know how he remembered me in the first place but especially my association with the drums, but it resulted in a couple of hours drinking with him in the bar. Time seemed to fly by as we chatted about our mutual musical love, in an old Western 'saloon' not far from the OK Corral in Tucson.

Eventually we dragged ourselves away again and went on to the Gosfield Ghost Town and Apache Trail – an old stagecoach route through the Apache Mountains and presumably a lot less dangerous than it was when Cochise and Geronimo rode it. Actually there is a five mile an hour limit on the trail that winds steeply through 40 miles of rugged desert mountains, past deep reservoir lakes like *Canyon Lake* and *Apache Lake*. The narrow, winding road is unpaved from just east of the town of *Tortilla Flat* to *Roosevelt Dam*; there are steep cliff drops and little in the way of safety barriers, so it is not for the faint-hearted.

The next day we had a much needed rest for shopping and relaxation. I had also reserved a private room in a local restaurant where we had all our Arizona friends sitting down together with our English guests.

After our guests had gone Lynn and I had a couple of quiet days before setting out on another road trip to Portland, when we drove down the Oregon coastline to Mckinlyville. We stayed there overnight before driving down to California, staying in Nappa where we could visit the Nappa Valley wine area. Then we went on to Sacramento, California's state capital, before going home to Scottsville to rest up for another week before coming back to Brentwood.

I think, before I leave the subject of Scottsdale, I would like to mention again our very good friends Lee and Rita Wilson, with whom we have had so many wonderful times. I think I have mentioned them before, but for over twenty years now they have looked after our Scottsdale home in our absence and have become very good friends. They often come to the UK to visit us and they never miss a special family event and I would like to take this opportunity to thank them for their friendship and all they have done for us over the years.

We arrived back in the UK in December, where it seemed to be particularly cold (after Arizona) and more so pounding the streets in Great Yarmouth where Brandon was still campaigning vigorously. The following year (2010) time would be running out for Prime Minister Gordon Brown, who by law would have to go to the country and we were prepared for it.

Guess who came to dinner

Having 'survived' Christmases with our own children when they were kids, grandparents always get a second crack at it when their children turn up. Of course in 2009 we had an extra boost with Kaden's first one, though at his age he wouldn't have appreciated it as much as we did. We'd been having him at home more and more, getting to know him better and getting used to having four wonderful grandchildren instead of three.

With Henry being nine and Yomay six by then, the younger element of Phoenix and Kaden as well meant we were enjoying the excitement of Christmas for all ages. From their point of view there was added excitement because before Christmas that year we had a lot of snow. Not that Kaden was much into throwing snowballs and building snowmen but his cousins certainly were.

Great for the kids of course, but not so good when you're an adult, not long returned from the warmth of Arizona, pounding the streets of Great Yarmouth with leaflets. In fact one day it was pretty icy and it was only

Kaden and grandad looking good in their caps

Martin's quick actions in catching me as I slipped that might have saved me from a difficult and painful Christmas.

We had our Christmas Day lunch at Brandon's that year and that evening I took Henry and Yomay to Ron's house where he had a fireworks party, while Lynn took her mother home. We enjoyed our New Year's Eve dinner party at Bartellas to celebrate the arrival of 2010 – a year that would have great significance for the family, especially for Chel. Now that Brandon had gone she was actually standing for Brentwood South in the local elections that year so we were helping her as well as her brother in Norfolk, but as things turned out there was more to it than that.

Lynn and I did make it through the snow to Burnham on Crouch where we'd been planning to meet Ian Yates and Ron Warmington and where Ron was planning to do a skipper's course. He'd had a boat made in Holland but needed to know how to sail it. Unfortunately, due to the snow, Ian had been unable to get out of Cheshire but we met up with Ron and I did have a problem he will not know about until now.

During dinner I bit into a piece of crackling and a tooth fell apart. I was very conscious of this and pretty concerned about it too of course, so we left early. That made sense anyway, since the snow was coming down again and the road from Burnham is pretty horrible at the best of times. I did however manage to save the broken pieces of tooth which I took to an emergency dentist the next day, though it did take a few more visits to sort out properly.

Finally the snow stopped and gradually thawed out so campaigning, for this was of course definitely going to be election year, was going well. Eric Pickles was pretty secure in Brentwood, but we still did some work for him as well as for Chel of course but clearly Great Yarmouth was uppermost in our minds. We got back one night in time for Emma's party.

Emma? Well, a nurse before going to Morton's and also a London Marathon runner, Emma Lynch is one of the personal trainers who had been looking after me at the gym and we had a great rapport. She'd spent weeks in the gym telling all and sundry that I was going to buy her a car for her 40th birthday, so I could hardly miss that.

Lynn and I turned up at the Eagle and Child for her party and gave her a radio-controlled toy car. She loved it, but I understand it has driven her cats mad. Emma is also one of the daughters of the editor of this book and they too have a great relationship – though he consistently tries to get her adopted. Although I knew Brian briefly through Peter Pryke it was through Emma that we got together about him working on the book.

The next day we went to the Football Writers dinner at the Royal Lancaster where the player being honoured was Chelsea's (and former West Ham) Frank Lampard. Like Chel he'd gone to Brentwood School, which is possibly why she was there that night, with her boyfriend of the moment. Also sitting at our table that night was a friend (and client) of Bradley's called John Beeston – a Scouser and a Liverpool fanatic, but there you are. He'd been a client of Bradley's for around fifteen years and long become a friend who has come with us on many football occasions

Anyway, Chel's boyfriend seemed to spend a lot of his time that night talking to Liz Wayte, my lawyer's wife, rather than Chel and it did not help his cause. It was clearly irritating our daughter, but fortunately for all of us there was another attraction. John Beeston was on Chel's other side so she spent a lot of time at that dinner talking to him. In fact they were getting on so well that night that he invited her to go for a drink with him sometime and she, knowing her current relationship was about to end, (Hell hath no fury like a woman scorned, etc.) said she would. It took some weeks but they went out to dinner and on other 'dates' and the inevitable happened.

They fell in love, moved in together and the following Christmas they went to the Lake District where, on Christmas Day, he rang me to ask for my daughter's hand in marriage which I was more than happy to agree to. Without her knowing he'd taken the engagement ring on holiday with him and was on the point of asking her when he phoned me. She said yes, we had a big engagement party in London, and in a few months from now (in June 2012) they will be getting married.

Lynn and I will have a new son-in-law and Chel won't be phoning Daddy's Cabs so much anymore. She was also, as I will explain next, largely responsible for this book. I should add at this point that we are as proud of our wonderful daughters-in-law as we are of our own children, and will be equally so with John.

The pace hots up

While the whole country was waiting on him to name the date for the election Gordon Brown was still keeping everyone waiting, but his options were running out and it was clear that it would not be long. In any case there would be local council elections in May, and it was being generally assumed that he would call it for that day so things were hotting up all round.

In Brentwood, where Chel was standing for the council and where we would also be helping Eric Pickles retain the seat, but of course we had an interest in Great Yarmouth too. Eric's seat was a 'safe' one but Brandon's work in the Norfolk (Labour held) constituency would soon be put to the test.

From January onwards that year we were raising our game, particularly in Great Yarmouth, with a series of fund raising events and on the streets themselves. We were taking groups of friends and supporters from Brentwood up to Norfolk on a regular basis at least twice a week. Brandon himself had been part of the pretty experienced Brentwood

The then Prime Minister, John Major,
sharing a football joke with Lynn and myself at the Dorchester Hotel.

team for many years of course and now that was paying off in terms of volunteers.

I need to put on record that they were a Godsend and we have always appreciated the help they gave us, especially in the early days when Brandon was new to the town and needed a lot of help. Among the fundraising events we attended was one I organised in the Carlton Club where our guest speaker was former Prime Minister Sir John Major.

Now we had met Sir John back in 1991 a year after he took over from Margaret Thatcher. He'd invited Lynn and me to a special dinner in Downing Street following our meeting at a Lords Taverner event. I seem to remember offering to buy a new kitchen for No.10 but being told I couldn't because the house belonged to the state and not him (see chapter 18).

That night Lynn and I took some of the correspondence involved in that in case we needed to remind him, but what I remember most about

Lynn and myself with John Major, at a function at the Dorchester Hotel

the man was his charming attitude towards everyone. He turned up early and instead of rushing in for dinner wanted me to introduce him to Lynn and other guests who were milling around the bar. We went into dinner, sitting around one big table and Sir John gave a very interesting speech before answering questions. There was no hurry, no rush and he stayed for a very long evening, answering questions and giving people his time. A great evening with a perfect gentleman.

I feel that at this stage in the book I should explain how it came about, though I think Cheralyn, whose idea it was, will also add her thoughts about it later. I would remind the reader of the rather unusual and splendid time we had in Sardinia celebrating Lynn's 60th birthday. As I wrote we had so many friends and family there and inevitably on such occasions a lot of reminiscing took place. It turned out that Chel was wandering round different people's rooms, drinking champagne on their patios with them etc., and hearing lots of stories about 'her dad's' early days.

She recalled later that sometimes she was in hysterics learning about some of the things we'd got up to in business and on trips etc. – things she hadn't known before. This all made her think that she would like to know more about that and the background of her family in general.

Lynn and I took her to Bahrain for a week over Valentine's Day – a place we hadn't visited before and where we thought we would have a quiet time just reading etc. It was at that stage that Chel suggested I write the book – something Lynn had been saying for a while although she was thinking more of a novel. There was always the old saying about a book being in every man but I had always resisted the idea.

Chel's request however made more sense because she said, quite rightly that I knew very little about my own past and family. With my own parents gone she didn't think I should leave our children in the same position as both they, and their children to follow, might be interested in their family's background.

I took it to heart and decided I would write some form of background document about the family though I had little idea of where to start. I did however have one thing going in my favour – I have been an inveterate diary keeper since I was a kid and most of what happened to me is in those diaries. I came back to the UK and discussed the idea with my secretary Chris, saying I would have a crack at it.

Originally I felt that if we started working on in on March 1st (2010) we would aim to finish it by March 1st 2011 – a significant date because on that day Chris would have been with me for 40 years and the book would be a kind of celebration.

I had no idea what would be involved and since at the time I was also heavily involved in Brandon's (and Chel's local) campaign, I could do virtually nothing on the project. Now, in 2012 and with some help, particularly including that of Chris, the book is finally nearing completion having been closer to three years than one.

It actually begins in the 1880s when a poor Jewish immigrant came here from Poland and goes on to 2012. As I said I had no idea or any conception how much time I would be spending on election duties in Great Yarmouth etc. when we started but I thank God for two people to have made the book happen.

Chris, who has had to type out every single word I have dictated, or handwritten, even though the majority of them have not been used by my editor, former journalist Brian Lynch. He has researched, where necessary, and edited those words so you, my reader, would not be as bored as perhaps you might have been. Without Brian's input, or should I say 'Output', this book would have gone to a thousand pages.

In fact the timing of the book is now being targeted to finish with Chel's wedding. Well, after all it was her idea.

Chapter 31

Brandon Kenneth Lewis MP

Brown bites the bullet

On April 6th 2010 Prime Minister Gordon Brown, having run out of options, finally announced the date of the General Election – May 6th, the same day as the local government elections. Saying he would seek a 'clear mandate' for his Labour Government, Brown said he was seeking a fourth term (three of them under Tony Blair), but the truth was that he had held out until the last possible legal moment under the constitution to hold one.

For me this meant choices, yes – but the best kind. With one of my children running for Westminster and another (Chel) running for Brentwood council, it was clear there was a lot of work ahead for 'Team Lewis' both in Essex and Norfolk. At last, after all the months of groundwork in Great Yarmouth especially, we had our chance.

However before Brown bit the bullet, we'd had a busy March in which I had another visit from Ecolution. This time Andrew Knapp brought his brother (and company chairman) Kevin to a meeting to discuss my potential involvement.

We did talk in more detail about the possibility of me taking a non-Executive position with the company, but again I pointed out that for the moment all my concentration had to be focussed on the forthcoming elections. I needed to know the election was over, before I could be sure I had a reasonable amount of time to be able to help them, if indeed I could.

That month we had school open days, as well as evening meetings with the Hutton Mount Association and Hutton Mount Ltd. Michael

O'Connell, who heads up HM Ltd, Ron and I got together for a chat that we thought might help and one day lead to fruition. I was now leafleting for the local elections as well as in Norfolk of course, but my biggest distraction at the time was Lynn. She was seeing a specialist about back pain that we thought might lead to an operation, and as part of that she went into the Nuffield for an overnight stay.

I was due back in Great Yarmouth, but had to leave early to collect Lynn from the hospital. It was Mother's Day but she was still unwell and unable to leave home, so I went with Cheralyn to see Lynn's mum Ivy at the nursing home. When we got back Lynn was no better and the next day was back in the Nuffield. Chel herself was so relaxed about her own election that she flew out on a girl's holiday to the USA, spending some of it at our Scottsdale home.

I had another long meeting with Ecolution, but this time Kevin brought his Managing Director Richard Jenkins for a chat as well. I had insisted that if I was to be brought onto their Board it was important that their MD was happy with me and the situation. Having been in such situations in the past myself, I did not want their MD to be unhappy about whoever the family was bringing in – I've seen it before and it never works. As it happens we hit it off immediately (despite his being a West Bromwich Albion supporter) and anyway the company's technology fascinates me. I enjoy being part of what they are doing.

Normally we would have spent some of our time then out in Scottsdale but for the first time in years, for obvious reasons, we decided to give it a miss to spend more time in Great Yarmouth and/or Brentwood. As the big day approached I was almost permanently based in Great Yarmouth and we booked a private room at the Star Hotel there for election night. The idea was that once the polls had closed our supporters could go there and watch the events of the night unfold on TV.

I should point out that, along with Martin Bevan (who with his wife Linda has worked for us for many years), I was putting in a lot of time backing Chel's campaign in Brentwood too. Then, at last, the big day, May 6th arrived and Britain went to the polls. What a day!

We were due to start work at 5am though, being unable to sleep, I was sitting in the lobby of the Imperial Hotel at 3.30am. I was so worried about oversleeping I just got up early and went downstairs ready to meet the others at 4.30am. It was a long and hard day with even Lynn spending some time on 'telling' duties at several locations. Normally she would have been on catering duties but this time she was in the front line with 'Team Lewis' in full cry.

At the end of the day it was back to the hotel for a brief rest and change before going off to the count at the Town Hall. Entry to the count is quite strictly limited so most of us were at the Star Hotel next door where we'd booked the room. I was actually involved in the count and explained that we had forty or fifty people next door who had been very helpful and asked local officials if they could join us.

They found a very helpful lady who said 'no problem, here are some extra badges, but no more than three at a time. I spent most of the evening going backwards and forwards to the Star to bring small groups back into the hall to see what was happening and to give Brandon some moral support. Among them was Bradley who, with his friend Tony Lawler had worked hard for us during the campaign.

For anyone who has never been to an election count let me explain what goes on. Each vote is counted and put into packs marked with red, blue or yellow (denoting Labour Conservative and Liberal Democrat parties of course) flashes. Each pack is then lined up with its relevant colour showing, so that throughout the evening, as the votes are counted and stacked, you can see which candidate is leading the race. Sometimes there is a clear leader and sometimes it is much closer, but it all adds to the general excitement (or gloom if you are lagging behind) of the occasion.

We'd been on the wrong end of such a vote back in Sherwood but this time it became very clear early on that Brandon was doing very well. He was getting far more votes than the other candidates and was a clear leader. The excitement mounted and the confidence grew with every hour, as the blue labelled pile got longer and longer, stretching out beyond the other piles towards the winning post.

We were getting more confident in Great Yarmouth, but of course we also had an interest back in Brentwood, where we didn't know what was happening. However Cllr William Lloyd, a friend of Chel's who was hoping she would be joining him on the council, was in direct contact with the count back in Brentwood via his mobile phone.

He was on the other side of the room but suddenly his face broke into a broad smile and he looked over to give me the thumbs up sign.

Cheralyn had done it, and by that time it was pretty certain that her big brother had done it too.

It was a good night for the Conservatives around the country anyway, but in Great Yarmouth Brandon had achieved a massive 8.7% swing from Labour. That night he got 18,571 votes compared to the sitting MP's score of 14,295 to take the seat. It justified all the hard work we'd all, including himself of course, done to help him achieve his ambition. You can imagine just how proud Lynn and I were that night too, hearing our son's name being read out by the Returning Officer as the winner in a General Election that we'd all fought so hard to win. Bradley was also present to hear the announcement so it became a real family occasion with only one member, Chel who was otherwise engaged in Brentwood, not on hand to enjoy it.

Team Lewis now had a local councillor, Cllr Cheralyn Lewis, and an MP, Brandon Lewis, in the family. After an exhausting celebration in Great Yarmouth that night, we had a champagne one for the family, including John Beeston, in Brandon's house in Brentwood the next day.

'You're Dad's best mate. Who else?"

The rest of May was a little easier on the feet in terms of canvassing etc., but plenty was still happening. I was now very involved in meetings with Ecolution, Hutton South Conservatives, the Hutton Mount Association, Police Neighbourhood Watch and the Brentwood Council AGM, where the mayor is formally elected and when Councillor Cheralyn Lewis was making her first appearance.

Even nicer perhaps was the invitation Lynn and I received from Brandon and Justine to have lunch with them in the House of Commons, to see his new place of work. On the down side I had to take Lynn to hospital for an operation on her back. She was there for four days with me getting her home just in time for me to nip off to Wembley to see England beat Mexico 3-1.

Almost a month later, on Thursday June 3rd 2010, Brandon made his maiden speech in the House of Commons and I make no apologies for including some of it here. I do so partly because of course it was his first speech in the House of Commons, but also because, coincidentally in view of my growing involvement with Ecolution, part of it was on renewable energies. He told the House:

'*Earlier, I was pleased to hear my right hon. Friend the Foreign Secretary mention the green agenda, climate change and the need for new energy sources in the future, because all that represents an opportunity for Great Yarmouth… Great Yarmouth can benefit from renewable energy. I believe that I can work with my hon. Friend the Member for Waveney (Peter Aldous) to make Lowestoft and Great Yarmouth an epicentre for renewable energy in our region, as well as in our country and in Europe.*

'*We in Great Yarmouth already have the experience of working with the offshore oil and gas industries, and the offshore wind farm at Scroby Sands used to be the largest in Europe. A new wind farm is coming, and there is the local potential to exploit marine energy and other renewables, because we have the necessary experience and expertise.*

'*Most importantly, our phenomenal new outer harbour has created a deep-water port that will allow us to service the industry, not just through facilitating its supply chain when it is built, but by acting as its construction base. I intend to play my part, loudly, in bringing that about. I have already talked to Ministers to ensure that Great Yarmouth gets a really good shot at delivering on some of the opportunities arising from the new energy industry.*

'*I want to protect and grow our economy, and to protect and grow energy for our country in the future*' he declared.

For any new MP, making his or her maiden speech must be a bit of an ordeal but having made it, Brandon could now jump up and speak in debates in the House whenever he gets the chance or inclination to do so.

A month after he'd emphasised his interest in renewable energies in the House of Commons on July 2nd his father showed his interest as well by attending his first Ecolution Board Meeting in Kempsing (Kent). That was followed by what the Americans call a 'town hall' meeting which is not (as I thought at the time) one in an actual Town Hall, but one of all staff of which I was now the 26th member. I suppose it's a measure of the company's success that as I write this book I think in terms of staff numbers we are in the eighties.

Lynn and I attended another important function around this time when we were invited to Cheshire to celebrate Ian and Pat Yates's Diamond (60 years) Wedding. Readers will know that Ian is one of my most long standing friends – the man who I'd once sold a few tons of wrapped soft caramels that I suggested he sold on as fudge. We were booked into Mottram Hall, an 18th century Georgian country house set in 270 acres of stunning Cheshire parkland, that now serves as a top De Vere hotel. The celebration however, also to mark Pat's 80th birthday as well as their wedding anniversary, was held in their son's garden.

In fact Jeff Yates asked me to make a speech that evening which I was initially reluctant to do, saying I was sure someone else could make a better one. His reply, plain simple and direct, lives with me to this day: 'You're Dad's best mate. Who else?'

So that was that, question answered; but my main problem was balancing the speech between two different occasions, the wedding anniversary or Pat's birthday. I decided that I would slant it towards Pat, not just because she is the better looking between her and Ian, but because she has always been the mainstay and strength of the family. Anyway Ian had already had his 80th birthday, where I had also made a speech.

A week or so later he rang me sounding a little upset. It appeared that, because Pat is a bit hard of hearing and can't always hear everything said, she'd asked him to contact me to see if I had a copy of the speech I could let them have. Since I have a copy of every speech I ever made that was no problem, but he was upset because she hadn't asked him for a copy of his speech.

Anyway it had been another great party in the typical Yates' style and very classy, well perhaps except for the oil-drum band, but Ian loves them and Pat couldn't hear them too well. The marquee in Jeff's garden was set up to look permanent with flowers and even chandeliers. It was also full of so many wonderful friends that we'd met over the years ourselves.

We had to get up early the next day and get home for another party – this time at Brandon's house. He wanted to thank everyone who had helped get him elected as an MP. I think it was only then, at the end of it all, that everyone had that 'phew' feeling that it was all over and we'd done it. It was nice to relax and it's always nice to say thank you to people who have helped so much.

Roots

I suppose that, given the kind of hectic life I'd been living in the early part of 2010, the second half of it would be almost an anti-climax, and it was certainly more relaxing. There was always business of course, with both the schools and Ecolution now taking up a lot of my time, but all the pressure of active politics had gone, so Lynn and I could settle down to a few months of family events, socialising and travelling both on land and sea.

One of the trips we took was a rather unusual ten-day cruise on the Cunard liner Queen Victoria. It began in France where we took a tour of the D-day landing beaches in Normandy, places I had always wanted to see. Then we did a circumnavigation around the British Isles going to Cork and Belfast, then over the Irish Sea to Liverpool before going around the top of Scotland via Glashow and Edinburgh before returning to Southampton. A very interesting tour – especially for Lynn, who had never been to some of these British cities.

Then we took Henry and Yomay on a little tour of their own to London – lunch at Langans before boarding an open top bus to tour the city, ending up at the Tower. From there we took a river cruise down the Thames to Westminster Pier where we got a taxi to Hamley's toy shop (where else?). By the time we got home I'm not sure who was the most knackered them or us. The next day we were up at 6.30am to see them all off when they went with their parents, Brandon and Justine, on holiday to the USA.

Following on from the Queen Victoria and Thames cruises, we joined Ron Warmington in Wargrave (Berkshire) which lies on the Thames. He'd commissioned a boat to be built in Holland and, having been completed and done its sea trials, it had been delivered there. We went, along with Mike and Pat, Ron and Helen (who was now his partner), to enjoy the day on the boat, stopping off at Sonning. Now there is a place worth mentioning in this book, if only because of its 'fame' in another one.

Situated on the river and sometimes called Sonning-on-Thames it is a village in Berkshire a few miles east of Reading. It was described by novelist Jerome K Jerome in his famous 'semi biographical' humorous travel book 'Three Men in a Boat', as *the most fairy-like little nook on the whole river'*. Even today it's hard to disagree with that description of such a beautiful little village. Coincidentally, in view of the trip Lynn and I had previously taken to the Normandy beaches, the man in charge of those landings, General Dwight D Eisenhower, had lived there while planning D-day. In a sense within a short time, Lynn and I had seen where they started and where they'd happened.

Bradley had decided, and obviously I went along with it, that it was time four year old, Phoenix was introduced to football. It was Saturday 14th August and the Hammers were entertaining Bolton on their first home game of the season so we took him to Upton Park. In retrospect I'm not sure it was the best kind of introduction because it's quite a daunting place to take such a young boy, especially on a day when the home team was beaten 1-3 and West Ham fans do not take that sort of thing lightly.

The bubbles had been burst that day and on leaving we found Green Street packed with demoralised, bitter and pretty vociferous fans. It was made worse because for some reason Upton Park Station was closed and we couldn't get a taxi for love nor money. Buses had been laid on but they were full and barely moving. In fact the whole of Green Street was packed solid, with no traffic whatsoever moving and there we were with a four-year old boy. We had to walk him half way to Stratford before we were successful in getting a cab to stop for us.

After that however, we had a week or so of celebration with birthdays like Kaden's (1st) Lynn's 62nd and Bradley's 35th – all in the Algarve. We did have a bit of a scare however, when Phoenix had to be rushed into hospital – first Basildon and then to the Children's Hospital in Whitechapel. It was nothing to do with having watched West Ham though and fortunately he was out and about in a few days and home in time for his cousin Yomay's seventh birthday party.

Lynn and I, still making the best use of our passports and visas, flew out to Atlanta where we stayed the night before embarking on another road trip. This time we drove through Georgia into Florida to Pensacola. Then, the next day, we drove through Florida, Alabama, Mississippi and into Louisiana, where we stayed in the State Capital, Baton Rouge. Then we drove into Texas, staying in Houston before flying on to Phoenix and then 'home' to Scottsdale for six weeks where for a week we entertained Mike and Pat Large before coming home to Brentwood.

Speaking of Mike and Pat we also went on a quick pre-Christmas trip to Europe with them. We travelled on the Eurostar to Brussels, then going on to Luxembourg, visiting Trier in Germany and the Christmas markets there. I mention it because when we started to go home it was to find that snow had disrupted the Eurostar and our train had been cancelled. The one we did finally get on stopped at Ebbsfleet, which was a bit of luck because that was where Mike had left his Jeep. It was snowed in along with all the other cars in the car park but we managed to get it out and up a slip road onto the A20.

Unfortunately the police had closed that but after a chat and since Mike was driving a Jeep, they decided to let us go but when we got to the motorway that was closed too. We had to find our way home through all sorts of back roads into London and then back out again to head for Essex. Mike did a brilliant job and eventually we all got home.

That December the snow came down more heavily again, bringing disruption so I'm having to collect Chris and take her home again because she hates to drive in snow. With the schools closed all the kids are out in the road playing snowballs and generally enjoying themselves but when the weather cleared on a Saturday morning Ron and Helen turned up with a Waitrose bag.

Knowing Ron as I do I'd imagined it would have some bottles of wine in it, but it turned out to be Harry. He was a three-month old British Bulldog that they had just bought and wanted to introduce us to. Needless to say, within a very short time, word had got out and Brandon and family arrived swiftly followed by Bradley and his, to see the new puppy. What a combination – excited kids and a new puppy.

After a pre-Christmas lunch in London and seeing as how we were in the capital, I suddenly decided it was time for a trip down memory lane with Lynn to show her my roots. We caught a train to Shepherds Bush station which had now been renamed Shepherds Bush Market Station. I'd spent a lot of my youth in that market – indeed from memory I think it could well be where I learned the art of salesmanship which became so important in my career. In fact my first job in selling was in that market, and then Petticoat Lane and Club Row in the East End.

We came out of the market and walked down the Uxbridge Road, passing the St Stephens' Church where I'd once been a choir boy and server. It appeared to be smaller than what I remembered but apart from that seemed to have changed little. From there we walked down past Loftus Road, where you can see the QPR floodlights, and into Arminger Road, the street I'd actually grown up in. I remembered it as a kid as being a very long road, but in December 2010 it looked a very short one.

We stood at the gate to Number 24, our old house where nothing appeared to be different, except that the front garden seemed to be smaller. The coal cellar was still there, a round black lid that used to come off every few weeks for the coalman to shoot the coal down into it. I always used to wait for them to get a cuddle and ending up with what Mum used to tell me was a very black face. The coalman, like the knife grinder who used to tour the streets sharpening knives and the chimney sweep, is one of those long vanished pieces of history.

Outside the house where I used to park my Hillman Minx there was now a line of parking meters. As I looked at them, a man came out of No.22 next door to ask what I was doing. I explained I'd been born in that house and had lived there until I was a teenager, but had not been back for over fifty years and I'd just been curious about where I'd grown up.

I told him that in the house where he was living, in my day there had been a couple of ladies who I used to call auntie. He said our old house was now owned by a Spanish lady, but she was away so there was no point in knocking there. I'm not sure I was going to do that anyway but it was a very strange feeling seeing how much the street and so many other things like the church had 'shrunk' as I'd got older.

We walked to the end where there was a big house, but that didn't look so big now either. I suppose one day I might go back and take another look, but by that time it was getting dark and Lynn wanted to get on to see the Westfield Centre – a whole new shopping complex – which is not far away.

I want to finish this trip down memory lane with a quote from a former American journalist and author, the late William Hodding Carter who wrote: *'There are two lasting bequests we can give our children: one is roots, the other is wings.'*

When it comes down to it, I suppose that is the philosophy and the reason this book is all about.

A happy Christmas

I have just finished the last sub-chapter mentioning our children who, as anyone reading this book will have realised by now are, with their children, all important to Lynn and me. In that context of course, Christmas is always a bit special too. In many ways it's a season created for children as, having performed the 'Santa Claus' role in costume on many occasions, I can verify. Christmas 2010 however will probably always be a bit more special, especially in terms of one of our children in particular.

Chel had gone away for the season with John and asked me to supervise a guy who was fitting shutters in her apartment. Fine, except that this was Christmas Eve – a day we usually spend preparing for the big day to come. 'It won't take long', she reassured me. Huh!

To start with he didn't want to bring his van all the way because of the ice and snow, so I had to help him actually carry the shutters into the apartment. Then Lynn and I had to sit there from 11am to 4pm with nothing to do except look at our watches while he, somewhat reluctantly, worked on the shutters. While everyone else was getting ready for the event we had to sit, away from our own house, watching and waiting.

Eventually he did finish and we got home with just enough time to get changed for drinks at home with Mike and Pat, Ron and Helen, before going off to meet Peter and Linda French for a Christmas Eve dinner, and then back home again for a few drinks. Even that did not prepare me for what happened the following morning.

I have actually mentioned it before, but because it made that Christmas even more special, I will do so again. First thing in the morning I got a phone call from John Beeston in the Lake District. A 'scouser' from Liverpool he had been a friend and client of Bradley's for many years who was also (surprise surprise for someone from his part of the world) a keen football fan who, when Lisette didn't want to come to the Football Writers Dinner, was invited by Bradley to take her place.

That was where, at a previous dinner, he'd originally met Cheralyn, had invited her out and their relationship had progressed from there. They were in the Lake District that Christmas when he called me to ask me for the hand of my daughter in marriage. To be fair this did not come as a complete surprise, while the timing did and I had not expected it so early.

In fact, knowing John to be a bit of a romantic Lynn and I had quietly decided that they would get married and that he would actually propose to her on the coming Valentine's Day. So he caught us out with what was good news and from memory my reply to him that morning was: 'John, most certainly yes but you had better take good care of her.'

He promised to do so and so far he has, but from what I can gather Chel was even more shocked, in the nicest possible way of course, at the proposal than we were. He'd secretly ordered the ring and presented it to her that day, and I think she spent most of Christmas Day 2010 between telephone calls and Facebook. I know that within minutes we had pictures on our screen of a stunning engagement ring, so it looked like the last of our children was heading towards marriage.

Following all the excitement we walked up the road to Brandon's for drinks and to break the news and then on to Bradley's for Christmas Day lunch where you can guess what the main topic of conversation was. Bradley's pal was marrying his sister and that made it all a pretty special day. We went home and then back to Brandon's to continue the celebration.

On Boxing Day everyone came to us for a big breakfast and round to Ron's in the evening for a BBQ and firework party. The following week, on New Year's Eve we had Mike and Pat, Ron and Helen call in for drinks and then Cheralyn and her fiancé John arrived with some of their friends to take us all off to Bartellas for the New Year's Eve party. There Peter and Linda French, with Andrew and Sam, joined us and we all had a good evening that never ended until 1am on the first day of 2011.

But what a year it had been. Political success for two of our children, with an engagement for one of them. Both of the schools were doing well and my relationship with Ecolution had grown significantly while Lynn and I had cruised to Normandy and then around the UK, up the Thames, travelled through America's Deep South and I'd gone back to my 'roots'.

Chapter 32

I did it my way

I've lived a life that's full.
I've travelled each and ev'ry highway;
But more, much more than this,
I did it my way.

The City at night

I guess everyone looking back on their lives likes to think that, in the words of the old Sinatra classic, they did it their way. I'm no exception, except that I am still living it, still doing it and fully intend to carry on doing it my way. Having said that of course I am acutely aware of my age (I'm reminded of it whenever Brandon has a birthday) and however fit and active we are, we all get the occasional aches and pains and I will come back to that later.

That applies to horses too and our first 'trip' of 2011 was to the stable to visit Joey who we'd been told hadn't been well, but I seem to remember doing a lot of other trips around that time – to the local refuse tip. Cheralyn and John had moved into their new home (now complete with its shuttered windows) and helping them move involved clearing up and dumping a lot of rubbish.

Oh yes, at the same time I was teaching Henry to play snooker, but he'd also joined the Brentwood Rugby Club in an effort to learn the game before he moved on to senior school. I'd pop down to see him on Sunday mornings and he was getting better all the time. I will always remember seeing him in some remote part of the field waiting for the ball to end up in his arms and in no time he was in the thick of it. He vanished beneath a crowd of boys and the only way I could spot him was because his multi-coloured socks were sticking up out of the scrum.

The following week I went on to attend my first Ecolution AGM but around the same time Bradley had to go into hospital in London for a small operation – a day and an overnight stay. I went to see him and after I was thrown out around 9pm, I decided it was time for another trip down memory lane and walked to Liverpool Street through the 'City'.

A hectic part of London during the day of course at that time of night, apart from cleaners going to work in its various buildings, the City is virtually deserted – yet it remains an interesting place to walk through. You are walking through history. The Bank of England and the Royal Exchange are there of course, but also Pudding Lane where in 1666 the Great Fire of London had started in a bakery. For three days, from September 2nd to Wednesday the 5th the fire raged, destroying everything (mainly wooden buildings) around it until it was quelled, ironically it is said at Pie Corner.

It had even damaged St Pauls Cathedral so perhaps it was fitting that its architect, Sir Christopher Wren, was commissioned to design and build the Monument, another structure I passed that night, to commemorate the disaster. With over 300 steps to reach the top its height is said to mark the distance to the Pudding Lane bakery where the fire had started.

It's probably safe to say that it wasn't until the London blitz in 1940 wreaked havoc, that a similar disaster took place. Perhaps one good thing that did come out of it was that it's often claimed that the fire finally cleansed and cauterised that part of London of the plague that had decimated it the previous year.

Yes I did say 'memory lane', but of course that didn't apply to me personally as far as those days were concerned other than in an historical sense. However in my own early working days I had worked long and hard in the City selling biscuits and Butterkist. I'd also made many friends there, George Hagon for example, and walking through those historic streets that night did jog a few personal memories in so many ways.

On the subject of business, my involvement with Ecolution was getting stronger by now and I had taken my lawyer Peter Wayte to meet them to see if he could help, but we also had another sad occasion around this time.

I've not mentioned his name before, but George Millett was Brenda Warmington's dad, Ron's father-in-law of course, and a really nice guy who'd become a family friend. I was working in Great Yarmouth, with the coming council elections in mind, when we heard he'd been taken into the Queens hospital in Romford so I went off to visit him.

Over the next week or so I was having Ecolution (who had an impressive stand at the Excel Exhibition) meetings, visiting George and oh yes, Lynn came to see a Cup Final. It was the Carling cup when Birmingham beat Arsenal 2-1 and Lynn, who is not a great football fan, heard that I was going with Brandon and Henry and if Henry was going then so would she. Added to that was the fact that Mike was bringing Pat, so that settled it. I don't think it matters to Lynn who is playing so much as who we're having lunch with.

We visited George who was looking pretty weak and frail by now. It was clear that it would not be long and the next day he passed away. I went round to see Ron to spend a little time with him. A week later we attended George's funeral in Upminster, followed by a reception at Marygreen Manor in Brentwood.

There was one happy landmark at that time though – Hutton Manor was celebrating its tenth year and we had a 'birthday party' there. We were also discussing launching a new venture, Little Acorns, to cater for children from three months to five years, when of course we would hope to sign them up for Hutton Manor or Warley.

It was Graham Green who wrote that *'There is always one moment in childhood when the door opens and lets the future in'* and it was our thought that we could provide that early door. We actually launched it later that year, in December, and so far things are looking good for its success, full up with more than 70 children attending. We are working on another Little Acorns for Warley too.

We had another party round that time – Chel and John's engagement party in Boisdales, the London 'Scottish' restaurant. That was a special evening for all the family and also gave us the chance to meet John's Mum, Jean. Like her son she is a typical Liverpuddlian, with a wonderful accent and a sense of humour that fitted in well with the occasion, so we had a great night.

Elmo, vertigo and mischief under the gazebo

I have often mentioned Lee and Rita Wilson, our neighbours and great friends in Scottsdale and on Election Day I was busy leafleting in Bradwell (Great Yarmouth) when they arrived to stay with us for a week. I got home in time to take them to dinner and then, when everyone had gone to bed I went to the Brentwood count.

While they were here I took them on a visit to our schools and then on a trip to the seaside – to Great Yarmouth. Where else? They'd watched Brandon grow up over the years and wanted to see the area we'd so often talked to them about as 'Brandon's Patch'. We had a lovely day there, giving them a complete tour of his constituency, before coming back home in time for dinner in Writtle.

We took them to the Carlton Club for a fundraising dinner (for Brandon) where our guest speaker was Eric Pickles, who they'd met years earlier when he'd given them a tour of the House of Commons. Then they went off on a cruise to Barcelona for a couple of weeks, before coming back to stay with us for a day before flying home to Scottsdale.

In early June I was out leafleting with flyers about Little Acorns, our new venture. It had looked promising but we decided to do some marketing by putting some leaflets out locally. Normally, being fit and everything, I am usually at the front of the group, sometimes even jogging, but on this day something went wrong.

Suddenly I was finding it hard to even walk, getting badly out of breath and falling behind the others. One of our group, Jonathan Tee, suggested that because I was looking very grey I should pay a visit to the doctor.

He was very right of course and when I did so it was to be told I had picked up a virus which had caused vertigo. So I was given some tablets, but unfortunately they made me feel worse. I just seemed to sleep, completely missing a couple of days – something that had never happened to me before.

In fact I was still feeling pretty rotten when I had to drag myself to Hutton Manor for a final meeting with the Inspectors to hear nothing but good news from them. They were very complimentary and also very encouraging about both our schools and our nursery venture. That, along with the fact that it was also Chel's birthday, did give me a lift. The following day I felt well enough, well just about well enough, to go to the Warley Summer Fayre, where I managed to last the day before going home and back to bed.

On June 18th Lynn and I took Henry and Yomay to London to see Schrek the Musical at Drury Lane. I know it was the date because the idea was for us to get them out of the way while Justine got Brandon's 40th birthday party – a barbeque in their garden – ready. She had been planning this for months, organising a marquee, caterers, the whole works and she is pretty good at it.

Sadly the one thing even she can't organise is the weather but, even though it never seemed to stop raining, it turned out to be a great evening and we all had a wonderful time. Celebrating your child's 40th birthday does give you a feeling of age – especially when it's also your birthday – but I guess that by then that was true for both of us.

A week later Ivy came over so we could celebrate her 87th birthday and that day we were also invited to pop over to Brandon and Justine's. We were a bit curious about that to be honest, but it turned out that Justine had decided it was time to celebrate my birthday too. Brandon had already had his party of course, so when we got there it was to find the champagne had been laid on for me, along with a birthday cake. A lovely touch and thanks Justine.

On July 2nd we had a new member of the family arrive. Chel had decided it was time she had a dog, and bought a black miniature Schnauzer which she named Elmo. He settled in well, but as I write this it does appear that no one appears to have told him that he is supposed to be a miniature because he has grown more than a little. Actually he is a beautiful little animal who has become part of her, ours and everyone else's home as he seems to travel to most places with Chel and John.

Now I know this book is about me and my family but it should also be apparent that we have a pretty wide circle of friends so get involved in a lot of events with them. Too many for them all to be included here but I think I should include one of them in particular – the wedding of Mike and Pat's daughter Claire – because it was pretty spectacular.

It all started off with a pretty soggy barbeque with a lot of Gerry's family from America who, because it was July, were expecting some pretty good weather but we all got wet. Claire more than most in fact because, trying to be helpful, I prodded the canopy of the gazebo and she copped most of the water that spilled out of it. Everything went quiet as we waited for the explosion but, typically, Claire laughed it off and went off to change.

Then there was the wedding day itself, which happened to be on Phoenix's birthday so after the wedding in All Saints in Hutton we popped round to see the birthday boy, before leaving for Le Talbooth in Dedham for the reception. The church there is a very old one steeped in history (and Constable Country charm) and the Americans of course fell in love with it. Claire had arrived for her wedding in a horse-drawn carriage and she and Gerry left in it for the reception.

Despite being an old fashioned hotel Le Talbooth has a very modern feel about it, as does the nearby Milsoms Hotel where we were booked in. On the banks of the River Stour we were all out on the green drinking champagne and listening to a steel band. Now Claire is very attached to her horse, well the one she shares with Pat, and had decided that while he couldn't be at the wedding he could certainly come to the reception.

In fact he was probably the smartest dressed of all of us that day, all made up in the colours to suit the bride's own colour scheme. He had a quick look around and was then on his way home while the rest of us enjoyed the reception itself. I am told there was quite a lot of alcohol at this party, both on the tables and provided at the bar. All the tables were named after well-known places in both England and the USA, and we had a wonderful evening. It seems that at the end of it all I was on the dance floor waving the Stars and Stripes flags singing 'New York New York.' It was certainly a very generous event.

I do know, well at least I do now, that while some Range Rovers had been provided to take us back to the hotel, I had either not been told or had forgotten. So I dragged poor Lynn off to walk back instead. Pitch black unlit village streets, with virtually no pavements and her complaining bitterly all the way until we reached the hotel. The next morning we had breakfast with the family who told her about the Range Rovers and that they'd been surprised they couldn't find us to give us a lift back. Yes, they can be very helpful... sometimes.

A great picture of our four (at the time of going to press!) grandchildren all wearing their Woodlands School or Little Acorn uniforms

Well said, Henry

Not long after that it was end of term, so all the Speech Days, prize givings and leavers ceremonies at both schools were taking up our days but one of them was special. The Head Boy at Woodlands Schools had spent eight years with us before moving on to Felstead and he made a most special speech in a moving ceremony. It was also a bit sad too because for all those years I had not been able to walk into Hutton Manor without him jumping up and cuddling me and I knew I would miss that and do.

The Head Boy was of course Henry our first grandchild, and if anything gives us personal satisfaction about being involved with the schools, it was his success there. Actually as grandparents it still gives us a buzz to know we have helped in the education of all of our grandchildren. Henry had done extremely well and had gained a place in the highly regarded Felsted School where he has settled in just as happily and appears to be doing just as well.

Sadly, about that time Lynn wasn't doing so well, suffering with her back and hip. We were visiting various specialists who all seemed to have different opinions and in the end she had pain-killing injections that did give her relief, for a while. Further decisions will have to be made on dealing with this problem sooner or later with a hip replacement.

In keeping with my promise to Chel I had been making inroads into this book, largely drawn from the diaries I have always kept. Believe me when it comes to diaries, Samuel Pepys has nothing on me because I've been keeping them both at work and at home, so there was a lot of material to put together.

In fact I realised that if I used every word, the book would finish up longer than War and Peace, more boring than an old Hollywood 'B' movie or counting sheep. What I needed was a professional touch – someone to re-write and/or edit my notes and to research any corroborative or supplementary material needed.

Some years earlier at Hutton Manor Peter Pryke, who was head there at the time, introduced me to retired local journalist Brian Lynch, who also happens to be the father of Emma – one of my personal trainers. He is also the author of several books, including some biographies, so I made contact and he came over to Lake View to talk about it. That was when I realised that we also had several things in common, including a shared sense of humour.

Yes he is a lifelong West Ham supporter, but that's fine because these days – Upton Park being closer than Loftus Road – I am too. Furthermore he had an uncle called Bill Heath who, would you believe, used to play for Queens Park Rangers around the time they were starting to interest me as a kid. Anyway we did a deal and ever since he's been steadily fighting his way through all my lengthy notes, striving to draw out and create a credible and hopefully interesting story that won't send insomniacs into a coma. *(Let's hope so! B.L.)*

One of the subjects Brian has written for before is John Bairstow who, apart from founding the famous Bairstow Eves estate agency had also created the once huge Queens Moat Houses Hotel group. John had also fought in one of the most famous battles of the Korean War (on the Imjin River with the 'Glorious Glosters) and with Brian I had lunch with him in Marygreen Manor, which had in fact been his first hotel. A nice guy and it was good to meet and chat with him.

I spent the next few months on my regular routine of family and business events and celebrations, but before I go further there was one other sad duty to perform. I have mentioned an old friend, Gerry Robinson, before and when he died I was asked to help spread his ashes.

As it happened Gerry had been a well-known local cricketer in Market Harborough, before turning umpire and his local club had agreed with his wishes to be buried on the very spot where for decades he'd stood so many times. So I drove to the cricket club in a Northampton village where, on a blustery and rainy day, a group of us walked out to the pitch where, on the umpire's spot, a small hole had already been prepared. It was there that we laid Gerry to rest that day.

The schools were closed for the summer of course, but Ecolution was taking up more of my time and grandchildren always have birthdays. Henry for example had his 11th, Yomay her 8th, Phoenix's fifth was coming up, not forgetting young Kaden's second birthday. Actually Henry was with his parents on holiday in San Diego but we managed to have a phone conversation with him. Then Lynn's birthday was looming on the horizon so I took her, our family and friends to the races where, at Lingfield, we had nice little box and a great day out.

I also have sons and a daughter of course and around that time I had things to discuss with Bradley. They may all be grown up and that, but it is still nice to be consulted as a dad and I'm no different. In this case it was Bradley who wanted not so much advice as reassurance, or at least someone to bounce his thoughts regarding a career change.

He'd been in the same job at the same company for over sixteen years and, while he'd often thought about a career change, he'd never felt the time was right. I knew he'd been headhunted, which always makes things easier, and now he was thinking that, at the age of 36, the time was right. In fact he'd been head-hunted for several positions in the City and had been flattered and excited that other City organisations wanted him to work for them.

We would sit and talk over the pros and cons and I tried to advise without actually recommending one way or the other. That, I have always believed, is the individual's own choice. You can always give people seeking advice your point of view but you can also give them inaccurate information without meaning to. I did agree with him however that it was probably the right time to be thinking of moving on. He was still on the right side of 40 and was being offered a substantial improvement in every way with the new job.

A better income and the opportunity to work closer to home was a clear inducement of course. I am proud to say however that what seemed to him to be the most important factor was that he would be able to see more of his family. I hope I've made it clear in this book that 'family' means a lot to us Lewis's. What kept coming back to him time and again as he turned it over in his mind, was that he would be able to have his tea some, if not all, of the evenings with Lisette, Phoenix and Kaden.

So he 'bit the bullet' and took the new job. Now, a year or so further on, it is easy for us all to see that he made the right decision and how successful he's been with his new company. I remember how, on his 36th birthday Lynn and I went with him Lisette, Phoenix and Kaden on a day out to London. That included a walk about through Harrods toy department (of course) and a trip on the London Eye after which they went home while Lynn and I booked into a hotel in Waterloo and went for an Italian restaurant for dinner.

That was so that the next day we could meet up with Mike and Pat to take a steam railway trip to Padstow, staying in Rick Stein's hotel for a few nights while we visited Lands End and St Ives.

Lynn and I prepared to fly out to Arizona for what had been planned as our usual two-month break, but for some reason I had already broken my usual habit by signing and getting my Christmas cards ready for posting. Normally when we go to Scottsdale we're back in November, when I get round to sitting down to sign the many Christmas cards I have to send.

This time I had some free time in September and for some reason sat down to the job then. It may also be because I needed an excuse to have a break from writing up the notes for this book. The reasons why it all seemed so prophetic will become apparent in the next few pages.

Scarey times in Scottsdale

'I had flatlined, and was clinically dead...'

Chel and John, who had been holidaying in Florida, came to Scottsdale to stay with us for a week before going on to Las Vegas and then going home but I had business of a sort to do there as well as relaxing. Back in Brentwood Woodlands Schools had been in contact with a school very similar to ours in Arizona. Called the Camelback Desert School it is actually sited in Scottsdale and I'd agreed to spend a day with them, learning from each other how we do things.

It was a very informative and useful day. Woodlands Schools has remained in touch ever since, but about the same time both Lynn and I were feeling a little poorly. We went to see a local doctor who gave Lynn some pills to counter some allergies she was suffering with.

His diagnosis for me however was very different – a low pulse, high blood pressure and a heart problem which, to be honest I did not believe. I have always felt fit and active. However, after three ECGs (electrocardiograph tests), he convinced me to see a cardiologist, so the following day I did just that. He proved to be reasonably relaxed about it, saying that I was definitely not right but he agreed that I could go on our planned trip the following week, providing I went back to see him on our return to be fitted with a heart monitor.

So Lynn and I flew to Denver and had a very pleasant trip driving thousands of miles through Colorado and into 'cowboy country' I'd always wanted to see. Cheyenne, the state capital and onto Laramie, driving through Wyoming, Evanston and through Utah to Salt Lake City, before flying back to Phoenix and home to Scottsdale.

As promised I went to get fitted with the heart monitor which I wore for 24 hours. Two days later I got an urgent call from the trauma centre asking me to get there immediately – in fact within thirty minutes. They told me I'd been booked in for an operation there the following day and I don't mind saying it put a bit of a crimp in the day – all very scary. It was just as difficult for Lynn of course who was also mentally exhausted and since all the family was back in the UK it was just us.

As I have always said however we were fortunate in having such good

499

friends and neighbours in Scottsdale. Lee and Rita Wilson dropped everything, stopped work and rushed to see us to lend us their support. They stayed with Lynn throughout the time I was having the operation and were there when I got back to the room, complete with my new pacemaker, a few hours later.

Rita took Lynn home for a shower because she'd slept the night in a chair beside my bed, where she was planning to stay the following night until they got her a room next to mine. It turned out that I'd been pretty lucky because, according to the results, I had flat lined and was clinically dead, though I never felt a thing.

I was also lucky in another respect too and that was the fact that I had a superb medical team looking after me. In fact I could not have been in better hands and it wasn't long before I was able to return home to the Gainey Ranch complex and our house. I rested for a while and then we were able to celebrate Halloween with Lee and Rita who, like all our neighbours there, had been fantastic.

At this stage, apart from Chris and the family, nobody back in the UK knew what had happened. I had phoned Brandon as I was being rushed to the hospital (at 2am UK time) but made it clear that no one was to know until at least after the operation. Even then we'd let very few people know, and certainly not Mike and Pat Large who were due to arrive to be with us in a few days.

When they did arrive we went out to dinner with them and told them what had happened. Mike's response was to say: *We would never have come out had we known*, but to be honest more than anything Lynn needed and appreciated the company and we had a great time. In fact the following week we all went to Las Vegas where we had some wonderful days dining out and visiting shows. They flew back to the UK from there, but Lynn and I stayed another night.

I was still convalescing of course but I had been booked to attend an educational conference in Tucson and since it was only a few hours away we decided to go. It proved to be very interesting, dealing mostly with health and safety issues relating to children and it's always good to see how other countries handle such situations with young children.

Then, on Thursday November 24th we celebrated Thanksgiving, one of America's great feast days of course, in Lee and Rita's home with their family. Had things gone to plan of course we would have been back home in the UK, writing up my Christmas cards by then, so it had been fortuitous that that had been done before we'd left for Scottsdale.

While Brandon had put a complete block on anyone from Woodland Schools contacting me Ecolution, apart from its Chairman Kevin Knapp, knew nothing about my situation. He'd kept it confidential anyway so I was able to take part in Board meetings, and even the AGM, by conference calls.

I had more appointments with my cardiologist Alan Tenaglia and my surgeon David Riggio, who I mention here now because they are such special people who helped me in so many ways. Perhaps I even owe my life to them but certainly owe them so much and I thank them for what they and their teams did.

Roy and Reggie arrived to spend some time with us while on their way to Vegas and Cheralyn arrived with John to spend Christmas with us. Brandon took his family to the Canadian ski resort Whistler (British Columbia) for Christmas. By then the family had more or less decided that Lynn and I would remain in Arizona and enjoy a Christmas in the sun. On Christmas Day, after having Lee, Rita and their children over for drinks, Lynn did a typical British Christmas lunch for the four of us.

We all arrived home on New Year's Eve, at exactly the time Brandon and his family got back to Heathrow. We all got back in time to see the family before going out with Cheralyn, John, Mike, Pat and other friends to dinner at Masons in Brentwood.

Chel with her horse Joey

Chapter 33

Happy is the bride that the sun shines on
(Proverb)

In good hands

Still taking things a bit easy I started the New Year working on this book, but then the family started to arrive – Bradley's in the morning and Chel came with John in the afternoon. Then we all went over to Brandon's for drinks in the evening, to complete a nice quiet family gathering to celebrate the arrival of 2012.

The next day Chris came over, despite it being a bank holiday, to help catch up with the post and the book etc. I should explain how the book is being put together. While we were in America I had plenty of time to write up my notes which are all handwritten from my diaries. Chris types them up and they are then sent on to Brian Lynch who works on the book from there. He edits/researches and writes the chapters before returning them to me for corrections and alterations.

Then Lynn and I had to have the flu jabs we would have had if we'd been back home when we should have been. Still, better late than never I guess. As we had been out of the country at Christmas we paid a visit to Mum and Dad's grave, where we found that Chel and Bradley had left a very nice wreath. Then it was off to meet Paul Kelly.

He is a cardiologist who, now I am back from Arizona, will be keeping an eye on me. While in Arizona Mike Large had been shocked at the news of my problem and had started to organise who I should see when I got back. Mike had been Chairman of the Board of Governors of Basildon Hospital for four years and in that role had helped to make some very senior appointments. Paul had been one of those appointments and Mike had got in touch with him, so all I had to do when I got back was make the appointment.

I did so and it didn't take me very long to see that I was in good hands and subsequently I made other visits to him at the Wellesley Hospital in Southend. I also went to see my friend and local GP Kannan Athreya, for a check-up and to update him on what had happened in America.

Not long after that I went to my 29th FWA dinner which in 2012 honoured two Manchester United legends. One said to have retired at the time, but came back during the season to prove his worth once again, while the other is now helping to coach the England team. They were Paul Scholes and Gary Neville who, with the likes of David Beckham, Ryan Giggs and Gary's brother Phil (now with Everton) were the 'Busby Babes' (or at least the Ferguson versions), of their generation.

We spent a lot of time after that wining and dining with our friends and family, while I also worked hard on this book which I need to almost complete before Chel's wedding in June. Since all this was her idea I think that would be an appropriate stage to take it to and we had a lot of heavy snow that made it easier to stay at home and write, write and write again.

By the time February dawned, apart from regular training, I was spending a lot of time in the dentist's chair. Lynn was still having problems too, so I took her back to hospital to see a pain specialist. My prospective son-in-law John, a Scouser to his fingertips, I took to Wembley to see his team Liverpool play Cardiff in the Carling Cup Final. He went home a happy man after seeing them beat Cardiff (admittedly on penalties) 3-2.

As I said before we were doing a lot of wining and dining with friends and one day Peter and Liz Wayte took us out for lunch to an Essex pub in Clavering called The Cricketers. I mention it because, apart from providing us with an excellent lunch, it has its own claim to fame.

It's run by Trevor and Sally Oliver and if their name is familiar it is probably thanks to their son. Having started to learn to cook at the pub their son Jamie went on to find fame and fortune as one of the country's top celebrity chefs. He started on TV as the 'naked chef', not because of his tendency to cook without his clothes on but because of the simplicity of his recipes. Of all the celebrity TV chefs he is probably the most down to earth, so to speak.

He went on to run national and international campaigns (here and in America) to improve the quality of school meals and launch his own chain of restaurants called Fifteen, where he aimed to give young people the chance to become chefs in their own right. He was also, for some eleven or so years, the 'face of Sainsburys'. His dad provides a good lunch too.

One or two sad moments for Bradley around that time though because In February I took him to Wembley to see England play Holland and the Dutch beat us 2-3. As I have mentioned before, even as a youngster Bradley was never happy to see his side lose and, patriotic to his fingertips, that applies particularly to England. On a happier note Lynn and I went to the Cliffs Pavilion in Southend for lunch and to see the 'Rock and Roll Sixties Show' which starred many of the 'old time' rockers like Peter Noon (lead singer of Herman and the Hermits).

It also featured Brian Hyland, the American rock star whose name was made with his 'Itsy, Bitsy Teenie Weenie Yellow Polka-dot Bikini', so I suppose appearing in a seaside show was very appropriate. Not that you see many of them on the beach in Southend, but it was a great show and really took us back in time – still back to the present.

A lot of schools activity was taking place around now with Open days both at Hutton Manor and Warley, while we were also out leafleting for Little Acorns. I think the Hutton Manor open day was the most successful we ever had, followed by a similar success at Warley. We were also starting to make early preparations for Chel's marriage to John.

That was fixed for June 8th in Arizona but, since it was unlikely that many of her friends would be able to travel to that, we decided it would be a family and close friends affair, with a garden party at home in August for everyone else who want to share in their celebration. It was for that part that we began to make plans and bookings etc. for marquee, music and catering.

It was a busy time because apart from the school's board meetings, the Hutton Mount Association and an Ecolution board meeting I also had to go to Weald Park. The Brentwood District County Sports day was taking place there and I had been asked to present the medals and prizes – a very nice task I really enjoyed undertaking.

I should have gone to Specsavers

In March 2012 our friends Mike and Pat Large treated us to a couple of days away, a really nice present that we were looking forward to immensely. They collected us at home and drove us to Ebbsfleet where we caught the Eurostar to Paris. It proved to be a lovely two days, spent drinking wine on the Champs Elysees followed by liqueur coffees and a visit to the Lido de Paris, which is where I began to realise I was getting older.

It happened as we were watching the dancing when after about half an hour, I whispered to Mike that one of the dancers was topless. Then I spotted another and another, before finally realising that in fact they all were. Mike, Pat and Lynn were all highly amused, telling me that I was simply getting older, especially when I pointed out that I had been distracted by the feathers the girls were using.

Perhaps, in keeping with the spirit of the TV advert, I should have gone to Specsavers before we left, but next time I will take my glasses or even binoculars. It was a great show nonetheless. The following day, after a visit to the Eiffel Tower, we boarded a boat for a lovely trip along the Seine with lunch and some really fine wines.

The sad part was that we had to catch the Eurostar to go home, but we'd had some good weather and it had been a very pleasant break with some very special friends.

The next few months were taken up with our usual social calendar and my working agenda, with the schools and Ecolution. That included a 70th birthday party in Hutton Manor for Alan Spencer. Alan had been with us in Hutton Manor ever since we opened the school in 2001 and had always been a special member of the company. While on the subject I should also use this opportunity to thank Rachael Holmes, who has been looking after the catering side for both children and staff ever since we opened.

Lynn had a deep silicone injection in the Nuffield Hospital, which we hoped would get her through the next few months leading up to Chel's wedding. We know now that a hip replacement is on the horizon but for the moment that has to do.

Like any grandparents we held our breath when Henry went ski-ing in France with Felsted School, eagerly awaiting his safe return which of course he did. It's always nice to know they are back safely, though he did tell us he got lost a few times, off piste of course. In the meantime his father was appearing more and more on the television talking politics, though we often only heard about it from friends.

Still busy with the schools and Ecolution, I was also having a few problems with my teeth so started visiting the dentist regularly. That never stopped us enjoying meals at home with Eric and Irene Pickles, who came with Brandon and Justine, so one Friday we had two MPs at our dinner table. The next day we had a fish and chip supper with Mike and Pat Large and then the family came for Sunday lunch.

I took Bradley to Wembley again for a cup semi-final match and since it was a Merseyside game featuring both Liverpool and Everton our future son-in-law John, (a 'Scouser' of course) came with us. He was pretty happy when Liverpool beat their local rivals 2-1. He came with me and Mike Large, who was in a lot of pain at the time, to see the other semi when Chelsea beat Spurs 5-1, going on to beat Liverpool 2-1 in the final as we shall see shortly.

Speaking of football as we were still working on preparations for Chel's wedding and other things I went to Stamford Bridge to see Chelsea play QPR. The point was that I was the guest of Chelsea supporter Paul Hagon – yes the same Paul Hagon I took as a six-year old to see QPR play Chelsea at Loftus Road. That may have been the Easter game where we beat them 6-0 but this time they beat us 6-1 and at least that made Paul very happy.

There was a lot of electioneering, both in Norfolk and Brentwood, going on at the time but we also had another moment of sadness when we lost another old friend. We have over the years done a great deal of travelling and for much of that time the arrangements were made by Maurice and Lesley Buxton who ran a local travel agency. They had become great friends and thanks to them Lynn and I, along with many of our other friends and family, had a lot of wonderful memories and experiences as well as seeing some spectacular sights around the world. Sadly, in April 2012 Lesley passed away and of course I attended her funeral.

A lot of planning and preparations for Chel's wedding, only a month or so away now and one task was going to Southend General Hospital for a check up on the pacemaker. The test went well, which was just as well because I was still visiting the gym most days. We were also making arrangements for the UK celebration of the wedding with caterers, marquee suppliers and wine merchants.

We had another Hutton Mount Association meeting followed by an Ecolution board meeting and interviewing for a new Financial Director for the company. Then it was local Election Day and I spent it in Gorleston, getting back in time to attend the Brentwood count.

I suppose leaving for Arizona a month before the wedding, was almost like taking a rest.

Snake in the glass

Before we did however there were one or two other traditions to follow, the first being Chel's bridal shower, which seems to be the modern female equivalent of the groom's stag night.

It seems that the shower, which was held in our garden, went well. I'm told it was all good fun and everyone there had a few drinks. The girls all got dressed up in 'hen night' gear and went out for a meal going on then to the Eclipse nightclub in Brentwood, courtesy of Kevin Springham who ran it.

We blokes of course did what you would expect seeing it was also cup final day. As it happens it turned out not to be a good start because the groom, John Beeston and his best man Barry Ellias, were both Scousers and since Chelsea beat Liverpool 2-1 that day the result did not sit well with them. Still we had a good day and finished up in the Victoria Arms pub with another dozen or so guys before going on to the Imperial Peking for a meal.

Then it seemed like a good idea to pop over to the Eclipse to see how things were going. I went round saying hello to everyone until I caught Chel staring at me in a kind of 'what are you doing here on my hen night' kind of glare, so I left. I didn't need to know what happened after that but I hear they all had a good time and some went back to Cheralyn's. I hear they even found the occasional guest sleeping in the hearth.

All the family came over to see us off as Lynn and I flew out to Arizona on May 8th to prepare for Chel and John's big day there on June 8th. During that month, apart from preparing for the wedding, we went out

Our godson Kye Springham with his sister Tierney

for a lot of meals with friends, as well as a Country and Western show featuring Kix Brooks, who used to be part of the Brooks and (Ronnie) Dunn duo, and who were very big in the States until they broke up in 2010.

Just over a week before the wedding I had a checkup with Alan Tenaglia, the guy who sorted me out originally and had planned my pacemaker operation, and he was happy. That day Cheralyn and John also arrived in Scottsdale and we met them at the airport. The next day they flew to Las Vegas to meet other friends who had come for the wedding and for the next few days 'Daddy's Cabs' was back on the road, going to and from the airport to pick up family and friends and take them back to the hotel.

That was the Hyatt Hotel on Gainey Ranch where all of the guests, other than local ones, were staying, but before I go further I need to explain how I got Cheralyn and John jailed.

On June 6th we took a group of guests to 'Pinnacle Peak' in Trail Dust Town in Scottsdale, where there is an old time 'Western Bar' and the staff are dressed as cowboys, even wearing holsters. They do not contain guns

Family photo the night before Cheralyn and John's big day.

however but scissors and if any man ventures into the place wearing a tie it gets cut off and hung from the rafters.

The steaks include 'cowboy and cowgirl steaks, the 'big cowboy' steak and filet mignons. Other choices include 'Bucket O Bones', which are racks of pork, barbequed chicken and 'wrangler' burgers – all served with...cowboy beans of course.

They also have other attractions, like rattlesnakes in glass cabinets. It all makes for a great night in which people started to really get to know each other, relax and generally have a good time. The real fun however started the next day.

By then everyone had arrived and it is an American tradition to have a 'Rehearsal Dinner' on the night before a wedding. It's not really a rehearsal so much as providing an opportunity for all the guests to get to know each other and we'd decided to make it an unforgettable experience for them as well as the happy, but nervous by then, couple.

There is an 'authentic' western frontier town called Rawhide, at Wild Horse Pass in the Sonoran Desert in the Gila River Indian Community – get the drift? It's a place with so many western legends attached to its history. It's even claimed that the likes of Wyatt Earp, Bat Masterson, Doc Holiday, Billy the Kid and even Annie Oakley have ridden into town in their day. There's a stage coach, an Old West train and farm with lots of animals for the kids to meet.

It can also take a joke against itself because, while a lot of panning for gold takes place, it has spread the story that the biggest gold nugget in the world is waiting to be discovered there. It also has a sheriff and a jailhouse and for ten bucks you can even have someone arrested and jailed. So of course we fixed it for Chel and John to be arrested and jailed, before we all headed over to the saloon for dinner.

We had a coach taking us everywhere so we could all have a drink without worrying, and we did. In fact, to get back at me for getting her and John jailed, Chel managed to get me on stage singing the old Garth Brooks hit 'Friends in Low Places' where the lyrics include: *'Cause I've got friends In low places Where the whiskey drowns, and the beer chases the blues away...'*

It was a great and memorable night all round, especially for the kids who were going on rides and panning for gold. By the end it was clear that everyone was very happy, friendly and looking forward to the main event the next day.

Dimps' big day

Brandon and Bradley, both by now established family men with wonderful wives and children, will forgive me when I say that their sister's wedding was very different than theirs had been, for several reasons. Yes, they had both plighted their troth in London while Chel's was under western skies in the sunshine of Arizona but, as the father of the bride, my own role this time was more tears than cheers.

It was of course the culmination of months of preparation and planning, most of it done by Cheralyn herself and there was a moment when it was only the pressure of her firm hand in mine that helped me control my emotions. Perhaps I should start at the beginning of that wonderful day, June 8th 2012, when we gathered in the garden of the Hyatt Hotel and Spa in Scottsdale where we've had a home for 23 years.

Like the rest of us Chel spent a lot of her life from a child there and we all have very happy memories and have made many friends there. So we weren't too surprised when she chose Scottsdale as the place where she

511

wanted to get married. We had many friends and family from the UK there, as well as those from Scottsdale itself and when we gathered in the garden at 5pm (where it was 103F in the shade), the atmosphere was as warm and happy as the day itself.

That perhaps for those of us who were in dark suits etc. was a bit of a downside but fine for the women, especially Lynn who looked stunning (as she always does anyway) in a lovely mauve outfit. Like the other girls she had spent the morning in the hotel's beauty salon and they all looked spectacular. She also had one other advantage over me – she'd seen Chel in her wedding dress, so was prepared for her entrance. I wasn't!

Suddenly Brandon had arrived to escort Lynn to her seat and I was left waiting for the bride to appear so I could do my duty. When she did it took my breath away, she looked so stunningly beautiful. Not for the last time that day I felt a lump in my throat – was this vision in white the same little girl I'd driven to school so many times, the same young woman who'd done so much for other young people back in Brentwood? Finally I knew how Justine's and Lisette's fathers must have felt on their day.

Traditionally of course it's the bride's mother who is supposed to shed a tear or two, but at that moment her father came close to it as well. Chel herself quickly realised what an emotional moment it was and it was her firm reassuring hand in mine that got me over it. The next one of course was when I had to give her away and hand her over to John – my last function in the actual ceremony before joining Lynn with the rest of the guests, who included John's 74-year old mother who had flown from Liverpool to be there, his best man Barry Ellias and some of his work colleagues. So the 'Scouse' brigade was well represented.

As for the ceremony itself it was of course very different from the usual and more formal UK church wedding. No less religious in its context but a lot more relaxed, with all the guests sitting at the edge of the lake and, would you believe, a clearly very modern preacher reading the service from his iPad, rather than a prayer book. Chel had three bridesmaids – a friend she'd known since she was three, a Brentwood School teacher she'd worked with and her niece 'Princess' Yomay who of course was revelling in the whole experience.

Part of this 'U.S. style' wedding was for the guests to hear the bride and groom, not just responding to the preacher's words but, through him, making their own personal vows and declarations of love for each other.

Cheralyn and John's wedding day

John and Chel had both sent the preacher their vows and he read them out to the couple and to the guests. I think that listening to those words from each of them was when it first hit me how right the wedding was and how much in love with each other they are.

It was a very moving part of the ceremony which finished of course with John being invited to kiss the bride – something he did, perhaps with relish and a feeling of relief that it was all over and he could relax. As indeed we all could and we moved into the reception where Cheralyn sprang another surprise.

We'd decided to have the speeches before the meal, so that those who were speaking could enjoy it rather than worry about their speeches through it. Obviously I would be one, with John and Barry the best man, but the event needed an MC which Chel had assured us she had organised, which she had. Swearing him to secrecy in advance she'd asked her nephew Henry, the son of a politician, to step in and he did so magnificently.

My own speech to begin the session was what would be expected from the father of the bride, tongue in cheek at times, emotional at others. I said we'd had Chel late in life but had always been determined to be around for this special day and that she'd said she wanted a small affair with just family and special friends there so everyone there was special.

I did my best to embarrass her, saying she had now married a Scouser and would have to live with that! Chel had organised the wedding herself, and brilliantly! I just stood back and let her get on with it – and where was John? Well he was right behind me!!

Then I moved onto him saying he had never gone out of his way to impress me but that he had. 'Chel at least you married a real man – one who to date has shown how much he cares, loves you and looks after you and that is all that matters to us in the Lewis family,' I said, before getting more serious and emotional about the bride.

'Wow! Just look at her today – stunning. I always knew it would be difficult to give my daughter away. After all I'm half Jewish and we never like giving anything away but it's been even harder than I thought it would be. Chel, you are a picture to remember forever.' I even managed to get in a joke about 'Daddy's cabs' before handing over to John.

Like any bridegroom he was very nervous but revealed another secret about his relationship with the new Mrs. Beeston. He spoke about how

Eleven Lewis's and one Beeston on the eve of Cheralyn and John's wedding

Ten Lewis's and two Beestons on their wedding day

lucky he felt to have found Cheralyn, how much he loved her and what a good friend she'd been to him.

Then he told us that he always called her Dimps.

...and now!

Most good books finish with a happy ending and it was always the intention to finish this one with Chel's (or should we now call her Dimps?) wedding, since it was her idea in the first place. It was largely meant as a family archive so that one day perhaps Henry, Yomay, Phoenix, Kaden and whoever else comes along to read it will have a proper idea of their roots and hopefully benefit from the lessons their grandparents learned and recognise the values we hold.

In fact the new Mr. and Mrs. Beeston had two wedding celebrations – the one in Arizona I have described above and a second one in Brentwood, so more of their friends could celebrate with them. We did, however, need time to get over the first one so everyone spent the next day literally relaxing before starting to leave for home the day after that.

That was June 10th when we had another party in the hotel to celebrate Chel's birthday and that threw up a number of curious coincidences. You see it was her 28th and, apart from some shrewd planning to ensure she got another set of presents for her birthday a few days after opening her wedding presents, it was a kind of family tradition too.

My dad had married my mum when he was 28 and I'd married Lynn when I was the same age. Both her brothers had married at 28 and that had been Chel's intention too. However the dates were complicated with people having to go home for school and work commitments, so she'd had to bring the wedding forward by a couple of days, but we had a lovely brunch for all those who had stayed on.

The day after that Chel and John were due to leave for their honeymoon to Hawaii, when all that careful planning fell apart. The preacher, you see, had gone home with the wedding certificate, but it needed to be signed off by the Courthouse in Phoenix within thirty days of the wedding to make it legal. Chel and John were due to fly out for their honeymoon at midday

The preacher lived about an hour out of town, while the Courthouse

On board ship during our Alaskan cruise

was another half hour into Phoenix, so it meant a crazy dash that morning to collect the certificate and race back to the Courthouse with it, so Chel could legally be Mrs. Beeston. We got it all done just in time for them to take off for Hawaii. Whew!

That meant that Lynn and I could relax a little at last, so we went off for a three week trip for a rest. Did I say a rest? We flew to Calgary in Canada from where we had coach trips to places like Banff and Lake Louise. In the British Columbian ice fields we actually walked on a glacier and ended up in Jasper. There we caught the Rocky Mountaineer train through the Rockies to Quesnel, before going on to Whistler and eventually Vancouver.

Then we flew on to Anchorage, caught another train to Seward and then had a cruise down the Alaskan coast back to Vancouver, where we spent another couple of days before coming home to the UK. When we did it was to find a new car in the garage and the grandchildren gone.

It seems Brandon had got fed up seeing me driving an old car and always talking about getting a new one so, without telling me, had gone out and bought a brand new Lexus. Now, being a politician, this might also have been his way of softening us up a little, because while we were away he and his family had moved.

For fifteen years he and Justine had lived and raised their family next door so we were very close to our grandchildren Henry and Yomay, but they'd moved to a village near Chelmsford. It was probably a good idea and very thoughtful of them to actually move while we were away, making it less stressful for us, but the day after we got back we went to their new place for breakfast. That night we had dinner with the newly returned from Hawaii, Mr. and Mrs. Beeston.

So it was 'back to normal' time with a management meeting at Hutton Manor and celebrating Phoenix's sixth birthday. It was end of term so both schools were involved with plays, concerts and leavers' assemblies and I even found time to go for a haircut. We are also preparing for Chel and John's UK 'do' at home so lots more arrangements to be made there, not forgetting to book a cruise for later in the year with Mike and Pat Large.

It wasn't all back to normal though because, thanks to Bradley, I did learn something new – how to drive a tank and learn that an FV432 armoured personnel carrier does not have a reverse gear. This was an experience provided by Brad as a birthday present and I think it's worth talking about.

Juniper Leisure is a corporate entertainment firm in Winchester and we started with a briefing on safety and warnings on how we could all kill each other – then we were split into teams of 6. I was in the blue team and we started with the FV432. We all went over to our instructor for a briefing who asked us who wanted to go first. Everyone went very quiet so, being the oldest by about 40 years I volunteered and got pushed down inside with my head out of the top.

They gave me some eye glasses and an explanation about six gears that meant nothing to me. They told me about the two sticks that turn the thing left and right, and then off we went into the battlefield.

I seemed to be doing ok until I reached a big bend to bring us back to base and our instructor told me to pull the left stick. I got mixed up, pulled the right stick, couldn't find the brake and ploughed into a corn field. That's where I found out there is no reverse gear, so was told to plough through it.

Finally I got back, where Lynn was laughing and the guys were telling me I should have carried on and taken a few trees down on the way back. The instructor did say he'd seen worse, but I think he was being polite. Still, I did get applauded by those watching as I clambered out.

Then all six of us due to go out on the Honda 250cc quad bikes, were given helmets, goggles, gloves and mufflers to cover noses and mouth. We were told to get our arms covered before having a few minutes to try them out, by going round in a circle. The instructor had to decide on the six positions and yes I was placed at the back before we went out into the wilderness.

Somehow the pack and instructor got away from me and I decided to turn back. Somehow I went through a pond and into a bit of forest, taking down a bush to find myself going towards the others who were coming towards me. I was told to wait while another instructor was sent out to keep an eye on me from behind so I didn't get lost again or end up in front of an incoming tank. I got back covered in mud I can still taste, to another round of laughter from the blue team who by then were back at base with a cuppa.

Then it was time for the Chieftain main battle tank and wow, that is some big piece of kit. One person goes downstairs with goggles and headphones connected to instructor with the rest of the team staying on top. This time I went second and when it was my turn, some of the guys from the mauve and red team came along for the laugh so I had 16 people on top. I got inside and found some pedals, so gave it some welly ...and got stuck in some mud.

I managed to get it to the top of the hill, but then I had to reverse it, just by following instructions, back down while I was still looking forward,. I got it back to base just before touching the wooden barrier, where I was told all the onlookers got out of the way in time.

Then, just when you think it's all over, you're told to gear up for your individual drive of the Abbot Mobile gun, so off I went again. First again, because I wanted to get home, but that drive was ok and by then I think I had the hang of it so I was first back to get my certificate.

Lynn apparently had a lovely day, a bacon roll and a cuppa while reading the Daily Express for five hours. For me it was time to change into a fresh set of clothes – in a field behind my car, so thanks Brad! Would I do it again? Yep, but perhaps blue is not always my colour.

The event really dominating our minds at this time of course was Chel's and John's 'UK Wedding'. We'd had a wonderful wedding for them in Arizona back in June, but it had always been agreed that we would hold a further celebration for them and all the friends who hadn't been able to

The whole family together for Chel's 'UK wedding'

make it, at home. So a marquee went up, a stage was built, a bar installed and on August 4th 140 people arrived for the big day.

It had not been the best of summers and while we'd had the most dreadful weather previously on the day the sun came through for us. It helped us have a beautiful afternoon and evening. David Tee, a fellow Brentwood councillor, a good friend who is married to Pam, the longest serving teacher Woodlands ever had, is also qualified to carry out weddings.

He arrived in his cassock and with his bible to carry out a confirmation of the wedding, along with a blessing which was absolutely beautiful and welcomed by all. The food was great, the alcohol flowed and the Tornados – a famous Sixties and Seventies band, took the stage and played until late. By the time it had all ended we felt that everyone had had the opportunity to enjoy the occasion.

Lynn and I felt that we were now at the stage where all our children were happily married so it was time we could relax. Well at least until the next day when it was time to clear everything up when Geoff and Val Purdy along with Ian Yates all pitched in to help out. Then, the next day I was back in the Great Yarmouth area of Bradwell, leafleting for Brandon. Life was back to normal.

That week ended with an Ecolution Board meeting and the final weekend of the London 2012 Olympics. I was very fortunate because Brandon had tickets for the Wembley final where Mexico surprised everyone by beating Brazil 2-1. I guess it's almost fitting as the book comes to an end a football match is mentioned and with the new season about to start.

On August 12th we were lucky to be able to join Mike and Pat Large at the Olympic stadium for the closing ceremony – a really special event and the last one of our lives to get a mention in this book.

Actually there was one more 'special event' and a much more personal one I should mention. After visiting a Cruise Show with Mike and Pat in Colchester, Lynn and I drove down to the Mercedes Benz World down in Weybridge to meet up with Brandon and his family because it was Henry's twelfth birthday. One of his presents from us was the chance to drive a Mercedes A Class on the famous old race track called Brooklands – the place where it is claimed British motor racing was born.

We arrived just in time for me to join him as a passenger and what an experience it was for me. There I was, driving around Brooklands with my grandson Henry behind the wheel, in a sense reminding me of what being a grandparent means.

We started with a Grandfather entering the country in the 1880s, without a name and a job of course. Just a struggling Polish Jewish immigrant, who came here looking for a better life. We finish it with a family that now consists of three children, their spouses, our grandchildren and not forgetting a Great Grandmother in Ivy Johnson who incidentally managed to come to Chel's wedding celebration in our garden.

From now on we expect our lives to be calmer but you don't always get what you hope for. If you have come this far in the book you will have realised it was not meant to be a great novel but a kind of family archive meant to be of value to the Lewis's and Beestons who follow in years to come.

It started with Lynn nagging me for years to write a book, though not necessarily an autobiography. Cheralyn then pushed me into the idea that while I have very little knowledge of my own background we should not leave our children and their children in the same position. The book is meant to show those who follow, just where we came from, how Lynn and I started our lives together and our journey to date.

It's been fun, arduous, full of tears and laughter, happiness and sadness but above all, if I had to judge, I would say reasonably successful. I cannot think of anything I would have changed or felt disappointed about. I just feel so happy and tremendously lucky to have come this far, with the help of Chris Howes and Brian Lynch, to have put it together.

I hope you find it interesting and if you have a copy you are probably in it but I do apologise if you are not. There have been so many people and events to mention that it was not always possible. I am sure that as I head towards my 70th birthday I may have left out a few memories, but I did the best I could in putting together a lifetime of memories, ambitions, stories and people. I hope I have succeeded.

Cheralyn with her hubby and brother
on the occasion of her graduation dinner in Westminster

For those of you who I have mentioned and who have helped us through our lives I say a simple thank you! I understand that the next chapter has been written by you – family and friends, who wished to send comments, their own memories and stories. At least I have something to look forward to myself when I eventually get my hands on – in the immortal words of Ernie Wise – is the Book Wot I Wrote.

. . . .

As I finish the book I have to say how proud I feel to have become a very small cog in a rather big wheel at Ecolution. As the non-executive Director on the Board and a very minority shareholder I have learned a lot from the Industry we are in and have found a company that has an extremely loyal team to work with.

Kevin and Andrew Knapp and Richard Jenkins, who are the Board, are extremely intelligent and very hard working Directors. They have formed a fantastic team around them and I was privileged to have been on their table on the 22nd November for the Kent and Sussex Business Excellence Awards for 2012.

We knew we had been nominated amongst 28 entries for the Best Growing Business and we actually won the Award. However, we did not know until the evening that we had also been nominated for Business of the Year which we won as well.

What I found particularly interesting during the night, looking at the faces of those attending for Ecolution, was not just the expectancy in their eyes, but the excitement of actually winning the Awards showed that they individually felt they had all won them. The following morning the whole company was thrilled. In fact, the last comment I received from Christine Daly, PA to the Directors, was "We are still smiling from ear to ear this morning and the staff are really pleased". However I was not entirely sure they had all made it home last night having left them in a real party mood!

. . . .

Now it really is time to call a halt to this story, but of course it is not the end of the journey. It's been a road that has given me so many experiences and opportunities, as well as so many great friends, of whom of course my greatest pal is Lynn.

As I said above there have been so many I have not even had the chance to mention in this book, but they know who they are and what they mean to us. So to them and especially to our children, to Justine, Lisette and John and our grandchildren, on behalf of Lynn and myself I say a heartfelt thanks for everything, with an extra big hug for Chel, who just as I come to the end of writing the book, revealed the most fantastic news that she is pregnant and the baby is due in May 2013. To become a grandparent for the fifth time will be great and of course a bit special when it is your own daughter. Strangely and rather coincidentally, this book started out because Cheralyn persuaded me I should write it and it finishes with her wonderful news.

As for me, well I've always been a 'glass half full', rather than 'half empty', kind of guy and who knows what is yet to come. Six months before I was born in 1943, the Prime Minister of the day described a rare wartime victory, using words I'd like to borrow to express how I feel at this moment. He said:

'This is not the end; it's not even the beginning of the end. But it is perhaps the end of the beginning....' Winston S Churchill Nov1942

I don't think I could put it better! *Kenneth Lewis October 2012*

I've got the morning sun
I've got the evening breeze.
I've got the woman that I love lying close to me.
I've got a few good friends & my kids are made.
I've got the moon & stars above yeah I've got it made.

Before tunring the page...

Brian Lynch, who helped with editing the book, suggested that the writing of the final chapter should be turned over to my friends and family. Brian contacted many of my friends and asked them to contribute a few words and recount any stories they may have.

From the start of this process I elected not to read any of the forthcoming pages, even before going to press! The first time I will get to read the last chapter is when I present copies to Lynn and the children.

Chapter 34

A final thought

'The only reward of virtue is virtue

The only way to have a friend is to be one'

Ralph Waldo Emerson

Writing about yourself is all well and good; but to give an all-round picture of your life you need to import not just the views that others have of you, but of forgotten memories you shared with them and that they might remember.

Over the course of my life and career I have made so many good and valued friends and, with Lynn, have brought up a remarkable family. It is with that in mind, that I have invited them to write down their own views/memories etc.

This also gives me the chance to thank them all for their friendship and, in the case of my family, for their love and support.

Ken Lewis

Brian Lynch, Editor
The man who stays in touch
As a biographer I am more used to including personal views on my subject, than I am able to as an editor. In the first case I would be actually writing the book myself, while in this one I am using words mostly

already written by Ken himself, so I cannot put personal views. My job is to interpret them in a readable way.

Hence I am delighted to be part of this chapter which is written by the family, friends, of which there are many, and acquaintances that Ken has accumulated over the years. Yes, it sometimes gives them an opportunity to have a sly dig at the man in a shared sense of fun; but their recollections also show a true love and deep respect for the guy.

Successful in business, Ken has also been very successful in building up a wealth of friends. We all do that over the years, but most of us lose touch with them as time passes. People who have worked for (or with), him or have socialised and celebrated with him and generally enjoyed being part of not just his, but Lynn's lives too for their friends are mutual. This is a man who stays in touch with his friends and where the word 'lifelong' means exactly that.

In the relatively short time I have known him I believe I've discovered why, and also why he engenders total loyalty from them. We do seem to have a similar sense of humour, but as an author and journalist I've found that working on this book from his notes very uplifting too because there are things we share.

We were brought up in different parts of London – me in the East End during the war, him in West London (where he supported a football team one of my own uncles played for) after it. It is perhaps those backgrounds that made us both family men – though I have significantly failed to get him to adopt Emma, my youngest daughter, a trainer who helps keep him in shape.

In both cases our roots are immigrant, his being Jewish and mine Irish – but we are both profoundly 'British' and we share a great sense of 'Queen and Country' patriotism.

I hardly knew Ken when I started this venture for him; now I seem to know a lot about him – and I like what I know.

Lynn Lewis
My eccentric, and not so quiet, man
The date was August 1968 and life for me at that time was quite normal for a 20 year old. Lots of friends, a great family life and a good job with

great prospects in an estate agency. But, having been in that job for 4 years, boredom was setting in so I decided it was time for a change.

Having worked so long in an estate agency in Rainham, I knew every property, builder, solicitor etc. in the area. But working on Saturdays had also become a problem, as my friends all seemed to be off on great weekends while I had to work.

One weekend I bought the Dagenham Post and looking through the job adverts, saw one saying: *'Secretary required to Sales Manager of Clarkes Cereal Products Ltd'*. I rang the number and made an appointment for an interview. It seemed like a new venture for me, in food products – a completely different field.

So I attended the interview and was offered the position by Mr. J. K. Lewis – Sales Manager, starting my new job 2 weeks later. Little did I realise at the time how much my life was to change as a result.

My new boss was very nice, kind and considerate. Also he was away a lot, which made life quite easy but, after 6/8 months of a good professional working relationship, things started to develop between us. We went from boss and secretary, to good friends and companions, being very comfortable in each other's company. Inevitably we were falling in love.

We worked well together and played well together, complimenting each other and supporting each other. That has continued throughout our lives, working together to build a happy and successful family unit, which is still in progress today.

Life has never been dull with Ken and if nothing else his eccentricity, bless him, has certainly made it interesting. I've travelled the world with him and our family, meeting and making so many wonderful friends along the way.

I will always be grateful to Ken for that alone, but the most wonderful gift I ever received was my three fabulous children Brandon, Bradley and (at last a daughter) Cheralyn. I am extremely proud of all of them, especially in having achieved great things in each of their chosen professions. They've been the light of my life, but now four more new and younger lights twinkle in our lives – our four wonderful grandchildren – Henry, Yolanda, Phoenix and Kaden.

Our kids have brought us so much worry, joy, love and devotion, such a mixed bunch of emotions at different times – but this is life and such a wonderful one. We never stop worrying about our kids, and now our grandchildren of course. That is how it is and I wouldn't have it any other way. Thank God, they are all so well grounded individuals with great personalities. They all have the Lewis gene, so hard work is not something any of them will shy away from.

Ken has worked his butt off over the years, to build and support the family, and I am proud to have been part of that. We've had lots of ups and downs along the way, but hey, we got there. I feel that time together now is important for us and we should try and grab it whenever and wherever we can.

Both Ken and I were also both very fortunate to have had such caring, loving parents. I was born in Barking, lived with my grandparents, who spoiled me rotten for 5 years, and I loved them to bits. Moved to South Hornchurch with my baby brother Tony in 1953 and had a wonderful, but very strict, childhood. We certainly learned right from wrong at a very early age.

My parents were also wonderful grandparents when their turn came and could not get enough of our children when they were young, taking them on lots of day trips to the coast, usually Southend. To this day Bradley has a love of the place and takes his own kids there whenever he can.

Babysitting was always available too, with them usually coming to sit one evening and staying 2/3days. My dad had the patience of a saint with the boys – while Cheralyn did not need it, since she was such an easy child to manage. Those were very happy times for me, sharing my children with my family.

We miss the grandparents enormously, although my mother is still with us, fighting the good fight and bright as a button at 88, bless her.

Good memories are everything in life, great to share with each other and there are some great ones in this book. We still have lots of memories still to create with our wonderful family and friends Ken, so let's go and do it.

A note to finish on and which I think wraps it up. ....

One luckier than I
I cannot comprehend,
For I'm actually in love
with my very best friend.

Ivy – Mother in law
Our lives changed when we met Ken
I have never suffered the old mother in law jokes from Ken, my son in law of 42 years. We always had a good relationship built on respect for each other and laughed a lot, though always pulling each other's legs about things going on.

He has a knack of winding me up and I did not always realise it, so the banter was sometimes quite heated. Now Bradley does the same to me – chip off the old block as they say.

Bill and I both had a lot of love in our hearts for our family, which we enjoyed to the full, babysitting a lot for the children and having lots of good times. We had many happy memories of our time with them.

Ken also introduced us to a world outside the UK, taking us on some fabulous holidays abroad, something we would never have attempted on our own. Sadly Bill was never very adventurous so most of our holidays were spent on the east coast.

Bill and I had a good relationship with Ken's parents and spent a lot of time with them in the latter years, listening to all of Henrys great stories of the early years of their life.

We also met some lovely friends of Lynn and Ken through the years and became great friends with them also. The grandchildren too have developed their lives wonderfully well. It has been great to watch the progress and now I am a great great grandmother, who would have thought it!

Ken has given us some wonderful memories, which I now share with my friends most days in my care home. Our lives changed when we met Ken, as I am sure he changed a lot of people's lives over the years. I had a front seat view of all the changes in the Lewis family life, but the best thing of all is that it has not changed the caring person I have always known.

At 88 years old I feel those years have been all the better for knowing Ken, my son in law.

Brandon
This is one of the hardest things I have been asked to write. It is difficult because it is hard to put into words what a father has done, it makes it clear just how much we take for granted what our families do. It is that

much harder to outline thoughts and experiences of someone who has been there from the very start, father or mother.

When I was very young I saw little of him, his work meant he was often travelling and when home he worked long hours. I never had any problem with that as mum had always made a great home for us and in that sense they were always a superb team. When he did have time off he was very focused on the family being together.

I recall, even when I was young, being fairly aware that Dad was working long hours to ensure we had a nice home and a good life. His effort and time put in back in those early days laid out a set of circumstances that allowed all 3 of us children to work towards our own goals. He created a financial security for the whole family that meant we could focus on achieving our goals without having to worry too much about finance.

That meant that we could progress to University, or go out to work, as we wanted to rather than circumstances forcing us, we were able to make our own decisions. That is a powerful position to be in and one that all three of us I suspect will want to emulate for our own children.

To outline the impact a father has is difficult as between he and my mother they are responsible for the foundation of my life. They created an environment that led to the establishment of the character I have today. So to outline all they did for my siblings and me in my early years within the confines of a few words, simply cannot be done. For that reason I will just outline a couple of contrasting memories that hopefully give some colour to my relationship and understanding of what I owe to my parents. I will stress again, I cannot really do justice to what I owe either of them in the space of these few words.

Dad was always very focused and precise, I still recall a manifestation of this whenever we went out and his obsession with things being correct meant he had to check every door and lock and window twice before we went out, or before bed checking every window more than once. Pleasingly for my mother this has subsided greatly in later years.

When it came to a choice of secondary school my parents did not want me to board, which was to my frustration. I had a fixed idea of where I wanted to go and it was not the school they chose, I did not enjoy their choice of school at all...but as life progressed I realised, as often was the case, they may have had a point. If it was not for their choice of school

I would not have met my wife and she and our children have been the greatest part of my life. They knew best even then.

As a second and final example of the impact my parents have had on my life and especially in this case focusing on my father, I will come much more up to current days. In 1997 I decided to get actively involved in politics. From the beginning Dad was fully behind me and supportive of what I wanted to do. Initially I just wanted to get involved in my local area and help to improve things, but as time moved on and I became more involved I started to look at the national picture. In 2001 I stood as a candidate in Nottinghamshire and in 2010 I became an MP. In both cases Dad was there full of support.

It is fundraising that can decide how good a campaign will be as it is fundraising that will decide what you can afford to do. However, the most vital role my father filled was the real hard work of walking the streets. He has walked every single street in my constituency with me and with other volunteers delivering leaflets. He has spent more hours than I can begin to count out on the streets in rain and snow as well as sun and wind, delivering leaflets and magazines and newsletters for my campaign.

Even since I was elected he has continued to help and continued to deliver leaflets and notices of surgery days, as well as still helping to organise fundraisers through the year. He has been an amazing support, not just emotionally by giving that moral support but with his direct on the ground hard work. I am sure that if I looked at all the work that was done leading up to the 2010 General Election in Great Yarmouth he has personally put in more miles in his legs walking the streets of my constituency than almost any other volunteer.

Without his support in those early days, by ensuring I went to the right school, that I had a good childhood with a structured family and without his support on the ground in these last few years (support that shows no signs of abating) I would not be where I am today.

I will finish as I started. It is almost impossible to list all the things my parents have done over the years that have made an impact or difference in my life, as everything they did through my childhood would need to be noted. That is why I not only love him, but also have huge respect for him and all he has done.

From the beginning, every little trip we had, every bit of advice (whether welcome at the time or not) has an impact on a child. That is why family is so important in our lives, whether we realise it or not. The exercise of putting these words together for this book has made it clear just how hard it is to outline what my father has meant to me and what he has done that has had an impact on me.

The simple answer is everything. The difficult and full answer would be a book in its own right.

Justine (daughter in law)
He is truly one of a kind

It surprises me to realise that I have known Ken for almost 28 years. Wow, how time flies! Back then in 1984, (I was 11 years old, had just started Forest School and would see him drop and collect Brandon from school or the school bus) it was hard not to notice him – swaggering around in his Bentley with private number plate, whilst puffing away on a huge cigar – how things have changed.

Now he is as fit as a fiddle and loves his "Woodlands Schools" logoed Smart car. I would never have believed back then, that this is how he would be, all these years later. I guess it shows how time and life changes us.

Due to his various business interests over the years, he has become a relatively well-known local figure. Many people who only know him by reputation (usually driven by their perceptions of wealth) often have misconceptions about him and are surprised at how down-to-earth he is when they meet him. The postman/refuse collectors etc. are treated the same as his longest standing friends.

Those of us who have known him well for many years, know there is one thing that forms the core of his constitution, has driven him to success and is his absolute priority. His FAMILY.

Whilst I am sure that at times, members of this inner circle (me included) have tested his patience and feelings, he has been, is and always will be, fiercely loyal and protective of it. Whilst us Lewis's are not averse to a disagreement here and there, we like to keep it 'in house'. Laundering ones dirty linen in public is simply not cricket…for ANY of us.

It surprises many people that despite his success in business and the wealth that accompanies that, it is not material possessions that drive Ken, but simply the security that the money provides. While he has been known to splash out on flash cars for himself and his family, it has always been to provide all that he never had himself.

He is known for his love of throwing a party with the invites spread far and wide – we like to call it The Ken Lewis Roadshow! I'm never sure where his pleasure in organising these events lies, as he never seems to enjoy them himself –always buzzing around making sure everyone else is having a good time and forgetting to enjoy it himself!

It would be fair to say that over the years, Ken and I have not always seen eye to eye. While I'm sure the reasons behind these rare occasions are long forgotten, we have always got over them. I would like to think that the deep fondness I have for him is reciprocated and any disagreement is due to us both having strong opinions and beliefs which we need to defend.

Not just out of respect for the fact that he is Brandon's father but for me personally. He has been very kind and thoughtful, including me in many events which I would have never otherwise been able to experience.

So, despite him being a pain in the backside at times, and as I often tell people, I really could not have wished for a better father in law (and Lynn as my mother in law). He is truly one of a kind……!!

And...
A Poem For My Grandad Ken
Roses are red
Violets are blue
Grandads are special
But none as cool as you

Now to the real story!
My grandad must like animals,
He calls me cheeky monkey
And tells me stories about ponkey the donkey
But I still think he's funky

I've seen pretty lights
And flown through the air
But to me, he's just like Superman

The three little pigs (Henry, Phoenix, Kaden are the little pigs)
And a naughty silly slob (Yolanda is the silly slob)
All that we get is raspberried on our bellies
But I'll always be his Princess Yomay!

Yolanda May Lewis

My Grandad Ken,
by Henry

My earliest memory of my grandad, is when he dropped me on my head, but it can't have done too much damage because I heard that he did the same to my dad! And look where he's ended up getting to.

When I was younger, my grandad and I used to like play fighting – we called it Duff Duff time. From then on, he became known as Grandad Duff Duff and he still signs of on all my birthday and Christmas cards 'Love From Nanny Sparkle & Grandad Duff Duff'.

For a while he was also Grandad Quack Quack because even though at that time we only lived two doors down the road, he still used to show the ducks on the lake outside our houses, and always used to say "quack, quack, quackedey quack quack!"

Now we have moved house what I will miss the most is being able to walk down the road to visit. Either to go and have a swim or have a game of snooker or even just seeing grandad, and there are many, many more reasons to choose from but the one I think I will miss the most is just seeing my Nanny and my Grandad.

Bradley
I owe them everything

Simply if it was not for my mother and father then I would not have the life I experience today of good health, comfort and happiness with my wife and kids.

I owe them everything, as they gave me the opportunities to be successful via the support, education and the manner in which they brought me up.

They are an example that I wish to follow and emulate with my own wife and children.

However, I do blame my dad for making me a QPR fan. I have tried everything including West Ham season tickets but I just can't get rid of my gut instinct to support QPR!

We used to have the best Saturdays any child could ever have growing up with our dad dropping us off at school in the mornings and then picking us up and driving to QPR in the afternoons. Great quality time spent with him sharing a passion of football.

Cheralyn (Chel)
I will always be my Daddy's little girl

Sitting on the veranda of my hotel room in Sardinia in August 2008, I looked at the people around me. We were celebrating my Mother's 60th Birthday and having a glass of champagne with friends and family. I took a moment to stop, watch and to listen.....there were tales being told.

Tales of the 'old days' – funny stories that people recalled from days working with my Dad in all sorts of different capacities, and the 'naughty' deals that may have taken place. I learned how Dad had sold some dodgy toffee to my Uncle Ian as a joke and heard talk of riding horseback in the desert with rattlesnakes.

I realized that my brothers may remember these events, but I wasn't around at the time or was too young to recall them. Everyone was in fits of laughter listening to these 'tales of old' and I could see such joy as they recalled more and more stories. I realized there was so much that I didn't already know, that I wanted to learn about Dad's life.

With this in mind I decided that he needed to write a book. He refused, said nobody would want to read it and anyway he was too busy to write it. I left the idea there and in February the following year revisited it while we were sitting around a pool in Bahrain. I think I applied enough pressure that time, because eventually he gave in and said he'd think about it.

I now look forward to reading and learning more about Dad because I don't want to see any of it until the book is finished, but I do want to thank him for doing it. I hope that it has brought him back some fond memories whilst writing it.

I cannot thank Dad enough for everything he has done and continues to do for me. He is full of support and encouragement to all of his children, at all times. We know we can always look to Dad when we lose faith in ourselves.....he never does.

I will always be my Daddy's little girl, even though he will walk me down the aisle this year to be married, and I will always love him with all of my heart……

Love Chel xxxx

In the words of our favourite Country singer George Strait:

'Let me tell you a secret, about a fathers love
A secret that my daddy said was just between us
Daddies don't just love their children every now and then
It's a love without end, amen.'

Son-in-law John Beeston
Ken, I feel both proud and privileged.

I have been a client of Bradley and a friend for over 10 years, meeting Ken through Bradley when I attended a few Football Writer's dinners. In all those years I hadn't met Cheralyn until January 2010 when we both met at the Football Writers Dinner honouring Frank Lampard. Little did either of us know that evening that we would fall in love and be getting married 2 years later.

I've got to know Ken over the years and in a lot of ways he reminds me of my own father who sadly passed away in 2010. A most generous family man who has achieved so much in his life, he is a man who I have the upmost respect for.

Ken, I feel both proud and privileged to be able to call you my father in law. As I promised you on Christmas Day, I will always take care of your daughter Cheralyn, who has my heart and is my world.

Paul Hagon
My dad's mate... my mate

'He always makes you happier for being in his presence...'

(Editor's note: It's pretty clear from this book that apart from any material wealth, Ken (and Lynn) are rich in friends and perhaps none more so than George and Rina Hagon along with their son Paul.

With his parents now passed on, the job of telling the story of their friendship – i.e. the family Lewis and the Hagons – fell to Paul, and what he writes shows very clearly how deep and meaningful that relationship was and remains to this day.

So much so that to be fair to everyone, I had to be very ruthless editing his contribution. I have however tried to retain the essential sense of memories that span generations in what does appear to have been a very special relationship. B. L.)

I cannot remember not knowing 'Uncle Ken' or the lovely Lynn, because they have always been in my life. You see, all the very best times have been shared between the Lewis and Hagon families – and at the worst times Ken has always been there right by our side, offering support.

I have 48 years of memories – some that make you smile or laugh until you cry, and others where you cry for other reasons. That is the measure of this remarkable man, my friend, Jack Kenneth Lewis.

When he was running Butterkist one of his biggest customers was Palmer & Huntley (P&H) where my dad George was Commercial Director. More importantly they were best mates, both with a passion for Queens Park Rangers. I think I let them both down by becoming a Chelsea supporter, but the relationship went beyond them to Lynn and my mum Rina – they might have been mates but the families were too.

In those days Ken and his Sales Manager Ron Gweneli used to visit their best customers, at their homes at Christmas. He used to get to our house around 10.30pm when the doorbell would ring and Dad would say 'Who the hell is that?' Then they would fling the doors open and stay for a few hours. Ken would be out on that run every night during the run up to Christmas, because he felt it was important to see the people he was doing business with to thank them.

I remember the 'Dogs Nights' at Romford Stadium where Ken sponsored one of the races, the Butterkist Cup, and when I was giving out free bags of Butterkist with Brandon and Bradley. Then everyone would go back to Ken and Lynn's for an evening garden party where sometimes even the sons of major suppliers were thrown into the swimming pool with their clothes on.

Cleverly, Ken always used holiday incentives to boost business with bestselling wholesalers and retailers being taken on trips to Spain, America and the Far East. They stayed in the best hotels or went on cruises and apart from being good for business they helped create long and deep friendships that exist to this day.

If it wasn't for Ken it's unlikely that we'd have ever gone on the QE2 or Concorde, gone to ranches in Texas or even visited the Alamo. In fact if it wasn't for Ken I wouldn't have needed stitches after cutting my foot playing football in Spain, got lost in total darkness after our car broke down on a Dude Range with snakes about, or ridden a horse that bolted. Ian Yates used to call them the Ken Lewis Do-it-Yourself Adventure Tours.

Ken really was the driving force at the House of Clarks – having been a van driver at Pantos, he'd then risen through the ranks to MD and then owner. He never let up and it was his enthusiasm, hard work and innate business sense that drove the business forward. Events like the Clarks Night that he ran every year, ensured that the House of Clarks always punched above its weight.

As for him and my dad they were soul brothers and real mates and as a result the ties that bind the Lewis and Hagon families together are strong to this day. There are so many Ken and George stories, legends even. On Ken and Lynn's wedding day when Dad was best man he was just about to make his speech when Ken urged him to hurry it up so they could see QPR in the second half... and they did.

I will never forget having to phone Ken and Lynn in Scottsdale to tell them about Dad's passing and how Ken had to pull all sorts of strings to get back in time for the funeral. In the end we put it back a few days to make sure that Ken and family would be there.

As the hearse pulled up I know Dad would have been delighted with the floral tribute that Ken and Lynn had organised to run alongside the coffin. It was just one single word – MATE – and that summed it all up. Dad would have been proud to know that his son and his best mate helped carry him to his final resting place. Since he died, Ken has always kept a fatherly eye on me.

I will always remember the pride that Dad, Mum and I took in being Godparents to Brandon, Bradley and Cheralyn, and the comfort that my own children, Sally and Michael, have the best Godparents we could wish for in Ken and Lynn (for Sally) and with Bradley and Cheralyn, (a beautiful bridesmaid on her tenth birthday at our wedding) for Michael.

I think to sum up, one of my best memories of Ken is one he probably won't even remember. We'd been to Euro Disney to celebrate Bradley's stag weekend and on the way back the train broke down. Having sat there for three hours we were all taken off the train and I remember being in a long queue just behind a family with two young children who were absolutely exhausted and out on their feet.

Ken, being Ken, started talking to the children and soon they were bright and alive again, reliving all the fun they'd had in Euro Disney. The parents were so grateful that he'd made this long queue bearable for their children and for me I think that sums the man up. He always makes you feel happier for being in his presence, and that's a precious gift to have.

The story of Ken Lewis is of course also that of Lynn Lewis. Without her being the steadfast rock of the family, I am sure they would not have been able to achieve all they have. As for Ken, well there will never be another because after they made him they broke the mould. Thanks Ken, thanks for everything.

Pete Atkins (childhood friend)
We would duck behind a bush for a Woodbine

I first met Ken when I was 11 and we both went to St Marylebone Grammar School.

We were in different classes and we only really teamed up when I moved from Camden Town to West Ealing when I was 14.

St Marylebone Grammar School was a very prestigious boys' school founded in 1792 and has produced many high profile people over the years. Ken and I had a great social time and, unfortunately, we were not what you could call ideal students.

Lunchtimes were a great time to go to Queen Mary's Rose Garden in Regents Park and chat up the girls from the local girls Grammar School. As well as them, on hot days in the summer the girls from businesses used to come and sit or lay on the grass during their lunch hour, an act that used to drive us crazy.

Talking of the young Grammar School girls, every year our school held a dance for the seniors and these girls had a formal invitation. Leading up to this terrifying event we used to practice waltzing and quick stepping in our school hall using a chair as a partner. *(Ken says: 'I loved those dances – my mum used to make me take dancing lessons as a boy and I still have my silver and bronze medals')*

On the afternoon of the great event, we lined up along one wall of the hall and the girls were daintily lined up opposite. We were terrified to cross that no man's land in case we got a knockback. It was a long afternoon.

Being in central London, the school had no adjoining sports ground and we all had to march in some sort of order to Marylebone Station and get the steam train to Sudbury. The trains had the individual carriages and of course only having three or four teachers with us, a lot of the carriages were unsupervised. A lot of Woodbines were smoked and many a memento was unscrewed from the carriages.

One of the activities that Ken and I were not too keen on was Cross Country running. We would take off and duck behind a bush on the way out that was handy for the way back having a drag on a Woodbine while we waited. *(Ken says: 'actually I was always a cigar smoker').*

When the front runners came back on return we would then join the pack, puffing our heads off in pretence of exhaustion. Our average times were pretty good. Our ball sports were cricket in summer and rugby union in the winter. I remember the great big communal bath that we all climbed into after a particularly muddy day. We were just as dirty when we got out as when we got in.

I guess Ken, that you would have covered School Camp. The long walks to Leith Hill when we used to get lost and met two chubby daughters from the village shop at Forest Green.

Ken lived at Arminger Road Shepherds Bush and this was fairly close to where I had moved to Ealing. Ken was a member of the St Luke's Church youth group sports club and asked me to come along and this was where I would meet people that would become lifetime friends and also my elder brother Bill met his wife to be, Janice. I am forever grateful to Ken for this. Not sure about Bill or Janice as they were to divorce later.

St Luke's Church had a hall that the Youth Sports club could meet on Sunday and Wednesday nights. You could not go on Sunday night unless you attended the Evensong Church service; this was a real pain as the Vicar was really long winded and boring. At the club we used to play badminton, darts, play a record player and dance. This was our real interaction with the opposite sex. School of course being all boys.

In my experience there was not the same openness about sex as there is today although the desire was very much the same. The girls were all lovely and we had our share of girlfriends. In the summer we organised train trips and walks in the country. These were great fun and photos do exist of these times.

In those days I spent lot of time at Ken's house in Arminger road. Being an only child he was a bit spoilt by his mum who absolutely doted on him. Unfortunately however she did not want him to grow up and was to cause him a lot of heartache. I remember he had a Grundig tape recorder and used to delight in pretending he was a horse race commentator so we used to listen to commentaries of imaginary races. These were happy days and we spent a lot of time together. A big upset was when Buddy Holly died. We were great fans of his and we did not play any of his records for three months.

Sometimes on a Saturday when QPR were not playing at home (we used to sneak in at half time), we used to go and play whist. The local pensioners club used to have a 'whist drive'. You paid your two bob to go in and Ken and I would team up, four at a table. At the end of a game the winners moved to the next table one way and the losers the other. By the end you'd played against every set of partners and the overall winning pair collected the cash prize. Of course we almost always won, because we could see the cards and hear what was going on.

At the end of Arminger road was a music rehearsals hall and we used to see a guy called Terry Nelhams from Acton. His stage name was Adam Faith – a very well-known pop star in those days. *(Ken says: 'We also had Marty Wilde and Joe Brown who, having once been his 'gofer' i.e. go for this, go for that, I have kept in touch with')*

When I was 17 I bought a brand new motor bike a 175cc BSA and one day I was parked outside Ken's house. The kerbside camber was a bit steep there so I parked the bike with the rear wheel to the kerb and the front sticking up and out towards the middle of the road. Ken came down and we just wanted to go somewhere quickly. He still had his slippers on.

He hopped on the back, but before he had settled properly I revved up and let out the clutch. The next thing I saw were a pair of slippers flying up into the air and Ken flat on his back on the pavement. Fortunately he was not hurt and after a few unkind words from him, we were able to laugh about it. Not long after Ken turned up at club with a set of car keys, a Hillman Minx, and he was in the big league with the girls, lucky bugger.

Then we drifted in different directions, Ken had his domestic difficulties and I was going out with a girl from work who lived at Southgate, the other side of London. He got married at an early age and I think lived out Hendon way, while I left home a week before my 20th birthday and lived at Holloway. It wasn't until 40 years or so later that we met again.

In that time I'd got married, had two daughters and had moved to Australia when I was 28. During that time the internet had come into being and I was contacted by Beryl Webb, nee Lee, an old member of the St Luke's Sports Club and old friendships were renewed. Beryl organised a re-union and I came back to England where Ken and Lynn made me and my Aussie wife Garrie (I'd divorced and remarried in Oz) very very welcome.

Chris Day (Friend and colleague)
I left that day feeling optimistic

I first met Ken Lewis when he interviewed me for a job at House of Clarks in the summer of 1981. I went to Blackborne Road very nervous and, waiting in reception, I wondered what Ken would be like. There was a Rolls Royce in the car park and the building I was in was old, dark and smelling of cigars.

I waited in a room and in walked Ken. A young man, fast talking, obsessed by the company and his plans for it and the adrenalin to excite anyone present. I left that day feeling optimistic as I felt we had got on well and Ken knew the company I was working for.

I got a second interview and was offered a job with a good salary and a company car and I immediately accepted. What I didn't know then were the plans that Ken had for the company and how I would be involved in a life changing experience. The plans for the Blackborne Road site that meant the old offices were demolished and a brand new office and warehouse development, car park and canteen were built. His plans were to make the company one of the most successful of its time.

I also learned that not only was Ken very much a family man, but also an inclusive man to those he trusted. He had an inner circle of business contacts in retail, wholesale, cash and carry and manufacturing. Later he was to add the most important contacts of his and our lives, those in the City.

He enjoyed the success of the business with his employees, suppliers, customers and friends and family. 'Clarks Night' was the biggest example of this but there were also smaller events: the factory "beanos" at Margate I was often left to supervise, the Circus Tavern with all the staff together, the football at his beloved QPR, the cricket at Chelmsford and some wonderful evenings at Ken and Lynn's home in Hornchurch.

However there was to be only one thing I believe Ken enjoyed more. That was to lead the MBO and become the owner, Chairman and Chief Executive. That became a life changing event for us all.

He describes very well in the book '50 Golden Years' how this was achieved. But behind the scenes there were many moments of joy as well as concern. I wonder if he remembers:

The threatened lock-out of a friend of George Pitt who wanted to buy the company

The Gateway deal and envelopes

The double Woolworth deal that would never work…but it did

Directors midnight feast of McDonald's in the boardroom after another "normal" day

The astonishing loyalty of many of the buyers to help the MBO

The time we were introducing hairnets and beard snoods as hygiene controls for Tesco and Ken took the part to encourage staff by walking around the factory with bee-keepers head gear on.

Sitting around a pool in Palm Springs reading about Black Monday on the stock exchange and how this nearly cancelled the MBO

Personal memories of Ken

I was excited at joining House of Clarks in September 1981 but feared losing my job shortly after as the company suffered in the recession of the early eighties. I know Ken supported me to stay in his team against other Directors' views.

Ken was not seen at the factory very often. He had his New Year tour of the UK with his sales team then he was off to do deals with the largest customers we had and, of course, holidays with his family when they could catch up. But he gave us a yearly performance review which always made me feel nervous.

He would say *'I know you don't see me very much but I know what you do for the company'*. I used to wonder how he knew before I learnt the trust he gave Chris his PA. I always felt undermined by my manager but Ken had a different view.

I was privileged to be asked to join the MBO and become a Director of HOC. I know it was down to Ken to include me and it was to prove the most important invitation I've ever had. It wasn't a financial benefit at the beginning as we all took on debts to own the company but it was definitely a shared ownership. Ken allowed us to purchase as many shares as we could afford before he agreed his share.

The ownership of HOC and the MBO is the most exciting time I've had in my whole career. We had HOC (the 'David') against HS (the supposed 'Goliath') whilst the true giants of industry bent over backwards to help us secure incredible sales and profits for HOC. Sadly but correctly it came to an end in less than one year.

Yes we had together made an incredible success of the MBO but now it was to break up. When I watched Ken and Chris leave the company I felt removed from a family. I never settled in the new company, but kept in contact with Ken and Chris (Howes).

In fact Ken never left me because I joined him again at Lovells and we worked together once more in the Midlands for Cornpoppers.

For me the legacy of Ken is professionalism, dedication, commitment, companionship and fairness. He included me in key decisions that became milestones in my own life. I shared this with my own family who mainly never met Ken, but knew him from afar.

Don Doody (American Friend)
Good old British common sense

My wife and I met the Lewises in 1990 when we were neighbours in Gainey Ranch where they presently reside. We developed a close friendship over the course of the next 20 years and got together often when they were in the States or when we visited them in England. What follows are some memories, anecdotes, etc. If you have any questions or wish more details please feel free to email or write me.

One of the truly funny memories I have of Ken came while we were discussing his having attended his first American baseball game. He wondered why, if a player hits the ball over the fence for a home run, he then has to run around all the bases. Why doesn't he just go back into the dugout?

It seemed silly to him and was something I had never thought of myself, but the more I pondered it, the more sense it made to me too. That's when it hit me and I couldn't stop laughing. Good old British common sense.

It was fun watching their children grow up. One of our first memories is of their sweet daughter Cheralyn, riding her tricycle in front of our home when she was about six. It was actually through her that we finally met Ken and Lynn. As children will do, Cheralyn developed a close relationship with my wife and was always knocking at our door asking to see Jeannie. It's hard to believe she is grown and married now.

We had a community pool in our neighbourhood of 21 homes and you needed a key, which each homeowner was given, to get in. One day, somehow, Ken had locked himself in the pool area and couldn't get out. I don't remember how long he was stuck there before I heard him screaming for someone to come get him out.

Long and short of it, that is how I met good old Ken Lewis and became fast friends.

Brian Dudley (Friend and colleague)
Choose your words carefully...
I first met Ken when I was Finance Director of Hunter Saphir plc after we'd just acquired the House of Clarks Group. I explained to him that, as with all the businesses we bought, to help induct them into the group I would become Chairman and that we would have formal board meetings each month with the group company secretary Barry Homer. Ken got very interested and said *'and these will be formal meetings then, Brian'?*

'Oh yes' I replied, most impressed with this keen new member of the group.

So imagine my surprise when Barry and I entered the Board Room for our first meeting, to find it covered in balloons with all of the male Directors in Dinner Jackets and Ken's secretary Chris in a lovely ball gown!

'Well you did say it was formal' was all Mr. Lewis said. It was then that I learnt that you have to be very careful what you say to Ken and to choose your words carefully or you could live to regret it!

One of Ken's many skills is the ability to throw a great party and I well remember the House of Clarks night, shortly after they joined the group. As always it was superbly organised, with Ken even managing to get everyone to dip in to their pockets to raise enough money to pay for a new Variety Club bus.

Various family parties at Hyde Park hotels still live in the memory too and there is no doubt that for Ken, family has always come first. I am proud to say that nearly 25 years later we are still friends with Ken and Lynn and always have our pre-Christmas lunch with them and Mike and Val Cannon in London every year.

Whether we are talking about politics, the city or the fortunes of West Ham, Ken is always totally up to date, fully researched and right on the button.

Furthermore, I don't know any American who has visited every state in the USA, but he has. A sharp, incisive mind and a great individual to boot – truly he is one in a million!

Peter French (Friend)
Who pinched my pants?

Privileged to be invited to Lynn's 60th birthday bash (I have just got my own back!) in Sardinia I had researched the security and crime trends on that island. As a former senior police detective it is always a good thing to prepare for one's journey. Whilst the area is relatively safe I didn't prepare for the "criminals within".

Weather was due to be fine and therefore several pairs of shorts were packed and for the first few days all was good. Then, one night after a few drinks, Linda my wife and I noticed that our key was missing from the dinner table. We went to the concierge to get another one. Rather unusual as the key weighed a kilo!

We returned to our villa to find that someone had broken in, stacked chairs to obstruct our way to bed and made it obvious that entry had been gained. I couldn't find any motive however until the following morning, when I went to put on my prized shorts!

Having dropped my guard I was now in 'work mode' interviewing and casting aspersions at everyone, apart from the senior Lewis's. Several searches of nearby rooms including the room occupied by the young Ms Lewis (Conservative councillor) revealed zilch. No warrant was used, but my powers under the Ways and Mean Act of 1066 were used several times to no avail. Somebody had nicked Pete's Pants!

Intrigue followed on our return to Blighty where I have to say I felt a lot safer, until photos of my shorts began appearing around the world. A website called "Where's Pete's Pants" appeared on the net and a ransom was demanded.

Disguised criminals, but not that disguised! They included a certain female, the wife of a then soon to be MP – her children wearing the pants were photographed with them. Others took them on cruises.

In accordance with Home Office and Foreign Office procedures no ransom was paid. Eventually, after forensic testing and discovery of 25 different persons DNA on the exhibit, Pete's Pants were returned …not washed but in a good quality frame which was worth 10 times that of the shorts. This proves that crime doesn't pay!

Twelve months after the crime the Lewis's made admissions. If I had been wearing them at the time Lynn (Lewis) would had been nicked for handling!!

Tony Gillet (Friend)
A man who lives life to the full.

That all Southerners are cold, selfish and unfriendly is a notion that we Northerners have long held to be true. I can now report that the said notion is incorrect, for I have known Southerners for over 30 years, and I recently I found a friendly one! But I am not here to write about her; I want to tell you something about Ken. Or is it Kenneth? Or Jack? Or..??

I first met Ken (and Lynn) about 10 years ago. We each have homes on Gainey Ranch in Scottsdale, Arizona and both divide our time between there and our native England.

I had been warned about his exuberant personality, but there was no way that I could be prepared for his all-embracing generosity. His kindness seems to know no bounds.

One cannot help but notice two things about Ken…his personality and his lifestyle. Pictures of him with royalty, government officials etc., seem equally at home with photographs of his much-loved family. Tales of his far-flung travels, his contacts with the rich and famous, all help to build up a picture of a man who lives life to the full.

What is as attractive as his trials and successes is the humility with which he shares his experiences. And my tale is one that reveals that humility to the full. In 2004, I had arranged for 40 visitors from England to spend time in the US south west.

Their visit encompassed various dance festivals and venues, and tours of many of our noteworthy sights. The Grand Canyon; Tombstone and the OK Corral; Las Vegas to name but a few. Ken and Lynn joined us for part of the tour...I particularly remembering him e-mailing Mr. Eric Pickles as we were about to embark on a private tour of the Navajo Nation lands in Monument Valley.

They were not going to stay with us for the whole tour, so I needed to arrange flights to get them back from Las Vegas to Phoenix. It was important that I had Ken's name exactly as it appeared in his passport, and so I asked him if it was Ken or Kenneth or...??

"Actually", he replied, "it's 'Lord'." End of conversation. End of subject. It had never been mentioned before that time, nor has it been mentioned since.

Maybe it is because I encounter many people with lesser skills and larger egos, that I value Ken's modesty. For a man who has achieved so much, both professionally and personally, he has every right to broadcast his success. That he keeps it hidden only serves to increase the respect and affection that he so richly deserves.

If only he came from Lancashire, he would be perfect!

Roy Hall (Friend)
A fun guy

Ken was my best man at the wedding to my wife Reggie back in 1980! It was a little different, Butterkist popcorn was used as confetti! Not only was he my best man back then, but KEN LEWIS will always be MY best man!

When they stayed with us in Cheshire he was a fun guy! e.g. he put Rice Krispies in our bed! He also had a fetish for turning all our ornaments so that they faced the wall or moving them around the house. One can imagine what Reggie said to him – too blue to go into the book.

Chris Howes (nee Standing) (Friend and PA)
He gave us a lifestyle

I joined Clarks in March 1971 as Ken's secretary and several years later he appointed me as his PA. He was away from the office a great deal and

I carried on there, talking to customers and keeping sales force records etc.

A lot of my time was taken up organising Clarks Night each year. The paperwork was horrendous and working out table plans for a large number of guests, time consuming.

I remember one Clarks Night in particular because Ken gave Bob (my husband) a large wad of cash to look after while he went to change into another suit. At this point a raffle was being held for the Variety Club and, without thinking clearly (perhaps having had a couple of brandies) Bob put the whole lot (later found to be £800) into the raffle on Ken's behalf.

Later, when Ken asked for his money back, we realised it had not been intended for the raffle but in fact had been Ken's own money and not for the Variety Club. Very embarrassing all round but funny in hindsight.

On the run up to the buy-out Ken sold me a share in the company and I still have a plaque saying: *'Whatever it takes. Welcome to my Board. I sold you your first share you know. Congratulations from the Boss. 12th September 1986'.*

My husband and I were included in quite a few of the trips and events prior to the buy-out and Ken gave us a lifestyle we could never have enjoyed otherwise. I remember a trip to the USA with quite a few customers when, in the space of about ten days we had almost as many flights, travelling from one cornfield to another. Very tiring to say the least, but Ken was never known for letting you rest for too long.

In the book Ken mentions our celebratory dinner on the Hispaniola, but he didn't mention that on arrival there I sat down and went right off to sleep. It had been an exhausting day and I can't even remember eating the meal or getting home afterwards.

I would like to mention at this point that both Lynn and my husband Bob were absolute gems, supporting us and putting up with the horrendous number of hours we spent away from home.

Ken was not always an easy boss to work for. He seldom understood that one had a life outside of Clarks and home-going time meant nothing to him. Fortunately Bob lived with this understanding that I enjoyed my job but sometimes family and friends didn't understand why it was nearly always the case I turned up late to a dinner or an evening visit.

Nevertheless Ken was extremely fair in all his dealings with staff, me included, and looked after my best interests at all time.

When it came to the selling of the company, Ken's negotiations on this made me, Chris Day and David Jones financially comfortable and enabled us to have a life without financial worry. When we used our money to buy Clarks, having mortgaged and borrowed funds, Ken gave me a David Winter ornament titled 'Alms Houses'. With it came a note saying that's where we would be if things went wrong.

When the sale had taken place and we were financially ok, he gave me another David Winter house, this time titled 'Fairytale Castle' with a note saying *We made it'*. Among so many presents Ken and Lynn have given me over the years these two really meant something special.

Ken and Lynn have always treated Bob and me as part of the family which is so much appreciated. We have seen Brandon, Bradley and Cheralyn grow from lovely babies to mature adults and we have been included in the majority of family occasions. It has been a pleasure being with Ken and Lynn for so many years and Lynn is like a sister to me.

I still work for Ken – 40 years later. That speaks for itself.

A note to Chris from Lynn
"I would like to say a big big thank you to Auntie Chris... for being my best friend, the sister I never had, and so much more to me through my life. She has given me such loyalty and friendship throughout the years. We have shared such memories that only family would share, and that is exactly what she is... family to me."

Jack and Nancy Karczewski (American friend)
He is without guile
We are trying to think back to when we first met the Lewis's and our best guess is the mid to late 1990's. Nancy met Ken when he visited the American Express office in Scottsdale to book a trip on one of his many visits within the United States. I recall that Nancy returned home from work that evening and told me that she'd met a most interesting client that day.

She said that he was a Brit and had visited a great number of US state capitals and it was his goal to visit all fifty US state capitals. This turned out to a long and interesting relationship with the Lewis family; we have met all family members at one time or another and what an interesting bunch they are.

We have felt we have participated in the modern history of this successful and accomplished family. There are two characteristics that stand out with Ken; the first is obviously his success in business and politics, the second is his generosity and I will comment on each.

It becomes obvious that Ken has, because of his business acumen, acquired what we will call the trappings of wealth. What is unique in his case is that these are never demonstrated in a vain way, they just are what they are. I would even characterize Ken's success as incidental in his behaviour; he is without guile in his personal dealings.

We must at this point talk about his generosity too. We learned of this early on when he felt that his ticket for the travel that Nancy obtained for him was so small in revenue and that, she delivered what he considered superior service so he invited us to dinner. This had become a tradition for him and just about every trip here to Scottsdale has resulted in a dinner, home visit or other social gathering. What we find so pleasurable is this is where we meet friends of the family or other family members.

The Lewis' have a plethora of interesting friends and family, mostly from business and they are like Ken successful in their endeavours also. I just love these gatherings because they give me, and hopefully them, an opportunity to share ideas and of course talk politics, economics and business. While there is some disagreement it is minor when compared with the agreements. It is truly astonishing at how much Brits and Yanks agree on major policy positions.

In this day and age, when marriage too often seems to be a transitory state, we have to acknowledge the fact of the success of the marriage of these two fine people. One can observe that this works and it is commendable and unusual.

We would like to summarise by saying that we are really happy to have met the Lewis' and are happy to contribute to his book.

Mike and Pat Large (Friends)
One of the cleverest people I have ever met
It has only been during the last decade or so that the Lewis family became part of our life. Originally it was Pat who met Lynn via a mutual friend, Brenda, when they played Badminton together. My own first encounter

with Ken was at the birthday party of Brenda and Ron Warmington's daughter, Julie, when we shared a table at the Masonic Hall in Hutton.

First impressions are important and Ken immediately struck me as a self-assured, fun loving person with gravitas and humour; a difficult combination. His smile and laugh were like trademarks and defined his character well. What you saw was what you got! I don't think I have ever come across a more generous person in both the financial sense, and the ability to give just the right present or gift by thinking about the recipient and what they would really want.

This generosity always extended to sharing in many of the good things acquired over many years of hard work. Several holidays spent with Ken and Lynn in their home in Scottsdale, Arizona, has shown us the workings behind the man and what makes him the great success he became. Above all else, he is a salesman. It's not hard to see how he successfully sold popcorn to every major retailer in the UK and beyond because this was all great training for the selling of the ultimate product of 'Brand Lewis'.

Having never been successful in the academic world at school, it is hard to understand how Ken became one of the cleverest people I have ever met; until you have a conversation with him about something in which he has a real interest. It is then that you realise that every fact, no matter how small, has been stored carefully for instant recall, emphasising the depth of knowledge and common sense that lurks behind that smiling visage.

The three children of the next generation have inherited some of that, along with their mother's wisdom, but most importantly they have the 100% backing of the whole 'Team Lewis', to ensure they achieve everything they want in life. Each of them has benefited from the patience, wisdom and tenacity of their parents, while achieving much in their own right. A financial helping hand has always been there, but ultimately they have to make the best of their opportunities themselves, and do.

Ken would have made a great politician, albeit lacking in tolerance for those just wanting to play the game of politics rather than making a real difference for the public they serve. However, he took the next best option and did what he could to ensure his first born made the Lewis impact in Parliament.

This entailed walking the streets of Great Yarmouth and delivering hundreds of thousands of leaflets with numerous doorstep conversations as to why the occupants should vote for Brandon Lewis. The sales pitch never centred on economic policy or the intricacies of the defence budget, but rather to state simply that Brandon was his son and that he'd been brought up to be honest and to work hard. This proved to be a real vote winner, if the results were anything to go by; simplistic honesty. Not rocket science, is it?

Our holidays in Scottsdale have always been the high spot of our year. We've thoroughly enjoyed being taken around the area and receiving the usual history lesson about what battles had taken place, and which tribe had been involved, while enjoying some of the best steaks ever eaten anywhere in the world. It is said that everything in America is bigger and better than elsewhere and that is especially true of Arizona, where even the Retail Warehouses are enormous with more stock than you would find in many a city, at prices that would barely cover the packaging.

Dillards for example was a favourite stop and although the visit was usually instigated for our benefit, neither Ken nor Lynn would ever leave empty handed. Thank goodness the store also sold suitcases so we could take our purchases home without it appearing too obvious that we had bought so much. This is also one of the reasons for Ken's sartorial elegance, but learning the secret of the other reason has cost me dearly!

An English company called Brook Taviner make suits, jackets, trousers and shirts. They are all good quality and sold at bargain prices, even before the 2 for 1 offers and discounts that are nearly always obtainable these days. It is these bargain prices that encouraged Ken to buy four jackets at a time, rather than make a decision on which one looks best. Now I too have 'saved' a fortune, and hope that I will have time in my lifetime to wear all that I have collected as bargains as a result.

We also shared in many other trips and outings including rail trips to Padstow, or Rick Stein City as it has become known and Yorkshire via steam train which adds an appropriate dimension (and many extra hours) to the journey. We've even enjoyed a couple of Eurostar trips to Luxembourg and Paris. All these trips entailed eating good food, drinking fine wine and enjoying great company.

Returning from Luxembourg at the end of November 2010 proved challenging because we arrived back in Kent to a total white out, with motorways closed. Driving conditions were unsuitable for anything other than snow ploughs; unless you had a Jeep Grand Cherokee, which we did.

The police, having been convinced that the hardest part of the journey of getting out from Ebbsfleet was now behind us, and if we could tackle that we could tackle anything, allowed us on to the M2.

A couple of hours later, we'd travelled the M2 into London and the A12 out of it so the Lewis party were once again resident in Roundwood Lake. It has to be said that male Lewis's are in the main, more optimistic than the females, but both were equally delighted to be home.

Although Ken is always enthusiastic over every success he or his children have, he is equally enthusiastic for the success of his friends. No one could have been more delighted than he was, when I was awarded the OBE in 2008, or when Clare and Gerry got married in 2011. However the election of Brandon to Parliament, and of Cheralyn to Brentwood Council on the same night in 2010, was just about the ultimate. Ken's pride in his children comes through in almost every conversation. We know of Brandon's every major speech in Parliament, each time Bradley secures a new and bigger client and whenever Cheralyn makes a stand in the Council, for her residents.

Being a friend of the Lewis family is an honour and a privilege but, above all, great fun!

Keith Morton (Friend)
An inspirational character

I have known Ken for about 4 years, after he became a member of our Personal Fitness Club in Hutton. Since then I have got to know him very well.

I have competed myself at a World Level in a Sport, training and helping many people achieve fantastic levels of fitness. That includes helping Frank Bruno become WBC World Boxing Champion, and I have to put Ken Lewis in the same elite category of people who possess the same attributes. They are:

Focus, Disciplined and being Very determined to be the best he can be. A man who always gives 110 % with his fitness training, and a regular winner of our Monthly Fitness Challenges – beating people over half his age, and in many cases easily

I recall a few months ago on one of the challenges whereby I asked him to Bench Press on a certain weight just one repetition, then pause for 3 seconds and repeat on the same weight for two repetitions. Pause again and then perform three repetitions etc. I told him that he would not get any further than 8, maybe 10, repetitions as this was the best that anyone had achieved in the Club and this was including some very fit + strong guys. He looked at me, said nothing and just Focused on the Job.... He actually did 14 in one go – no one got close to this!

Apart from being a pleasure to teach – the conversation and guidance he gives are of the highest value. I can't speak highly enough of Ken as an individual – he is generous through and through and an inspirational character whom I am pleased to refer to as my friend.

Arthur Perkins (Friend)
A person of great character

My name is Arthur Perkins and I have known Ken personally for in excess of 43 years, the first 25 of which were as a business friend involved in the selling and distribution nationally of his company's products through the company I worked for, Palmer & Harvey.

I first met Lynn shortly afterwards when, together with my wife, we were invited to join them on a trip to Tunisia with a number of trade colleagues. From then on we enjoyed many other trips and various events together, and have remained the very best of friends ever since.

I remember when, being appointed as a main holding board director of my company in 1978, receiving a call from Ken expressing his congratulations. He invited me and Thelma to join him and Lynn to dinner to celebrate, which I duly accepted. This was the first time that we had been out together on our own and from that point it became something we have continued to enjoy to this day.

We now meet up for lunch in London on a regular basis, every couple of months or so and have a tradition of paying the bill on an alternative basis. This works fine but, unfortunately, we will quite often have a debate as to whose turn it is to pay. Fortunately, our wives seem to have better memories than us when it really matters, and step in accordingly to resolve the issue. All in good faith, fun and banter.

A couple of years ago we met up for lunch at a fashionable restaurant in the city where we had spent two hours enjoying champagne, fine wine and an excellent meal. We had just finished our dessert when the fire alarm rang out and everybody was asked to leave the premises immediately. We quickly gathered our coats from the cloakroom, much against the wishes of the manager, but made the point that it was very cold outside and we were taking our wives wellbeing into consideration.

Having had to clamber down five flights of stairs we duly assembled outside on the pavement, with all the other guests. We waited anxiously to be allowed back into the building, in order to finish the remainder of our wine which had been left on the table. By this time the fire services had arrived and duly entered the building to investigate the problem.

The time went by and after about fifteen minutes many of the waiting guests decided to give up and left. We waited for about another ten minutes at which point we thought the wait could go on and I said to Ken, *'let's call it a day, I will contact the restaurant later, explain the position and settle the bill accordingly over the phone with my credit card as it was my turn'*. Having agreed, we said our farewells and left.

On contacting the restaurant later that evening I spoke to the manager and explained that we were pushed for time and had had to leave without awaiting the outcome, so could I settle the bill? The manager stated that it had been a false alarm and, due to the circumstances, offered his apologies saying that in this instance there is nothing to pay and we look forward to welcoming you back again very soon. I phoned Ken and told him the result and he immediately said *'What! You have got away without paying all that money?'*

I don't think he has ever forgiven me for my good fortune that day and often brings up the subject just to remind me. I did make the point however, that in order to put his mind at ease I had donated the money to a worthwhile charity.

I could tell so many funny stories relating to our times together but, that would entail writing my own book on the subject. I will however mention an embarrassing moment for Ken which he will always remember, and that was when he bumped into a young lady at a function in London. He said how lovely it was to see her again after such a long time, as the last time he believed they had met was at 'The Sandy Lane' hotel in Barbados some year's previously.

In total disbelief the lady responded, *'That, young man was my mother.'* The lady was the daughter of my Chairman, one of his major clients. I did point out that on the basis the lady in question did bear a resemblance to her mother he could be forgiven for the 'faux pas'.

In conclusion, I can only say of Ken that he is a person of great character and standing, someone who set out his goals and aspirations early in life and succeeded in achieving them through hard work, belief and determination. His success has been truly earned and deserved. He is a devoted family man and is rightly very proud of his children who are a credit to both him and Lynn.

He is also a very caring person and compassion comes naturally to him when he knows of people in need of help or words of comfort.

Over the years we have had many enjoyable times and laughs together, both in business and domestically, sharing our same type of humour and banter. I feel privileged to consider Ken, and indeed Lynn, as very close friends because without them life would be a great deal less fun

Rt. Hon. Eric Pickles MP (Friend)
(following news of Ken's heart operation in America)
Both Irene and I are very pleased to know that our dear friend is well and thriving.

You and Lynn are a very important part of our life, welcoming us into your home and treating us like members of your family

You are full of fun and have always made me laugh and I am glad that you will be around for a good few decades yet

Take care of yourself and I will see you soon.

Geoff and Val Purdy (Friends)
Ken? Well he is different!
One memory that Val and I have of Ken is from the 1980's, when we went out dinner one evening at a restaurant in Hornchurch that he'd recommended. We were driven there in Ken's new car – I think it was a Bentley, that had only been delivered that day.

We pulled up outside the restaurant only to find the central locking on the car had malfunctioned and we were locked in. Both Val and Lynn looked very elegant exiting the very new, very expensive car via the rear windows!

He knows how to show the girls a good time!

Kevin Springham (Friend)
Many happy memories with true friends
Strangely, my first contact with Ken was a letter of complaint. Having just

started to run 'under eighteen nights' at Sam's nightclub in Brentwood late in October '98, a couple of days after the first event, a letter arrived from him, commenting upon the time taken to admit the young people as being *'rather too long'.*

'Mmnn' I thought. *'I'd like to see him admit 700 kids, in 45 minutes'.* A nice reply followed, but little did I know that in less than a year, we would be working together – trying unsuccessfully, to get 700 young people through the doors in anything less than 40 minutes!

There it began, four years of Cheralyn then just 15 and various friends promoting under 18 nights, with Ken, most of the family, friends and indeed anybody else who could be coerced into spending Tuesday nights surrounded by 700 fourteen and fifteen year olds, all overly excited and dancing to 'dreadful, banging, loud music'. (Eric Pickles words, not mine).

By coincidence, I met Sam, now my wife, about the same time and Ken, learning that I had a new girlfriend in tow, suggested that we meet in London for Dinner at the Savoy Grill. *'Most of the important decisions that I have ever made, happened in this room'* explained Ken, who proceeded to share a number of wonderful memories, a thoroughly enjoyable evening.

The following day he popped into the office and, having discussed a little business, declared, *'I really like Sam, totally different to the person I expected. We're having a little party on Sunday and you two should come.....'*

Well from there I think that it would be fair to say we have shared many of the good things that have happened in our lives with Ken, Lynn and the Lewis family, many, many happy memories, with true friends.

Ron Warmington (Friend)
Time with Ken is always well spent

I'm very much looking forward to reading Ken's book because, although we've been pals for over twenty years, my knowledge of his early years is pretty light. That's because Ken is a modest man, who wouldn't dream of boasting of his business and personal successes. So learning more about HOW he climbed so high will be fascinating. Understanding WHY he succeeded is, as the Meerkats say, *'Simples!'.*

Among his many qualities, Ken has more 'Emotional Intelligence' than anyone else I've ever met. He's just as comfortable talking to a Prime

Minister as to a postman... and both would feel equally at ease with him. Both will immediately know that he is genuinely interested in what they have to say, that he is really listening to them and that he really cares.

A man more generous with his time would be very hard to find, and time with Ken is ALWAYS well spent. Most of us will have met a few of those arrogant and self-important men who endlessly trot out advice that we've learned – sometimes the hard way – to ignore because, over time, we've seen that much of it results in disaster.

With Ken, his advice is occasional, subtle and influential. It's never dictatorial... and, as I've found over the years, is unfailingly good.

Another clue to Ken's success is to notice the LOYALTY that surrounds him. Ken has a circle of friends to whom he gives... and from whom he clearly receives... total loyalty. Just look at all those business associates, friends and employees who have stayed with Ken for decades.

It has been a delight and a privilege to be in that circle of friends and I wish him, and Lynn... and their burgeoning family, yet more happiness and success in the years to come. Come to think of it, it's a jolly good thing that Ken and Lynn are grandparents to such a growing band of youngsters: a good deal more Lewis DNA will be a bloody good thing for Britain!

Peter Wayte (Friend, client and colleague)
I am very pleased and proud to call him a good friend.

The Early Days
Ken Lewis was recommended to me by Stephen Clarke of Charterhouse Development Capital for whom I occasionally did some work. Ken was intent on a buy-out of House of Clark's (the owner of the Butterkist name and mark) for whom he had worked for many years.

I first met him at my offices in New Square, Lincoln's Inn in *[I think around 1986]* and I was immediately struck by a number of things. He was not the usual 'City client'. His dress was sharper, his approach more down to earth, he had a very clear idea of what he wanted to achieve and could explain his position in extra-ordinary detail.

I doubted that he was going to be successful in his aim of a management buy-out of House of Clark's largely because the major shareholder and his family had set their face against it. Nevertheless I liked Ken and his style and I was keen not to upset Stephen Clark so I agreed to help on the legal side.

I can't now remember exactly what we said about fees but I suspect that I agreed to act on a no win/no fee basis, or something similar, which may well have been why Ken decided to use me and Wilkinson Kimbers & Staddon on this venture.

Over the next weeks and months Ken deluged me with letters explaining what he had done, memoranda recording meetings particularly with George Pitt (the Chairman of House of Clark's) and requests for advice.

The detail of some of the memoranda was extraordinary. In one particular meeting, which I had not attended, Ken's memo ran to 28 pages. I did however manage to develop a technique to read his epistles sufficiently quickly that it wouldn't bankrupt the Firm if we weren't able to render a fee at the end of the day.

One of the things that did strike me in the early days, and which has been reinforced many times since, is Ken's clarity of objective and tenacity in achieving that objective. He may not have left school with many formal qualifications and he may have worked his way up from a driver at the House of Clark's, but by then he was very much in charge of the business which he knew inside out and was determined to buy. An unwilling vendor was merely a challenge not a prohibition.

It didn't take me that long to realise that Ken was likely to be successful if he could raise the money. He grasped the process and structure of buy-outs very quickly and he led his team with a degree of paternal control which I don't think I have seen matched by anybody else. Those who were key to the objective of acquiring the business and developing it, would be rewarded beyond, it has to be said, their realistic expectations. Ken, however, was realistic enough to want to keep the lion's share for himself. He was Butterkist and he would be the one who would drive it.

I don't recall exactly how Ken ended up with Nat West Ventures as the provider of the equity finance but I think he struck up a strong rapport with Sydney Donald, their lead director, and was prepared to put up with Alistair Gibbons (their 'bull terrier'). We had many meetings with Travers Smith & Braithwaite, the lawyers for Nat West Ventures, and throughout these meetings Ken was patient, clear and unwavering. He wasn't unreasonable but he wasn't going to be shifted once he had made up his mind.

He wanted a larger slice of the equity than was becoming usual for managers participating in a management buy-out and he had agreed to put up a lot of money (£300,000) in order to get this. My main concern throughout was how Ken was going to raise this money. He told me not to worry and that friends of his were going to lend it to him. I was extremely doubtful but consoled myself with the thought that we could renegotiate the equity share against a lower investment, if and when we got to the point of being able to do a deal.

Ultimately George Pitt, his advisers and the other shareholders of House of Clark's bowed to the inevitable and agreed to sell to Ken, his team and their financial backers. The acid test now was upon us and, lo and behold, Ken's friends came up with the money, doing so on the basis of no paperwork whatsoever. To get the acquiring company off the ground I think we might have issued a couple of shares to Ken's friends, but I'm not sure we ever sent them the certificates. They weren't looking for part of the investment, merely to help Ken. I never did know the full extent of the arrangement he had with his friends but the money arrived and was available for Ken's investment alongside County Nat West and Royal Bank of Scotland and thus the House of Clark's was purchased.

Shortly thereafter I was invited to my first Clark's night. My wife, Liz, and I went along to the Royal Lancaster Hotel for what I had discovered was pretty much an annual event run by the House of Clark's to say thank you to customers and suppliers. It was a dinner dance. The menu was always the same, the entertainment largely Ken and his marketing team not so dissimilar year on year and everybody loved it.

On this particular night I remember being much struck by Ken's eldest son, Brandon, who was at the time 14 years old and gave a very polished and mature welcome and an introductory speech that very few 14 year olds could have managed. Ken himself then spoke at some length (which I was beginning to realise was something he did) and amazed me by telling the audience that the House of Clark's was now British, independent, and management owned.

He said that he needed all the customers to buy more goods and all the suppliers to supply at cheaper prices. Everybody lapped it up and, amazingly, did as he asked. During his speech he also introduced all of his advisers and it will always remain with me that when he introduced Sydney Donald of Nat West Ventures, a somewhat mild looking and very respectable English Venture capitalist, he introduced him as '*Sid wot lent me all the millions*'.

The House of Clark's Years

There were not many years between Ken's buy-out of the House of Clark's and its sale to Hunter Saphir, in fact only eleven months. My contact with him during that period was largely dealing with numerous small legal issues some arising from the buy-out and some arising from the House of Clark's business.

We started to have a good deal more social contact and I would frequently meet him at the House of Clark's box at Queens Park Rangers. Indeed I found that so enjoyable that I persuaded my own Firm to take a box at Loftus Road – particularly when I found one on the halfway line where the box holder had gone broke and QPR were selling it off cheap for the season. Socialising with Ken is always down to earth and lunch at QPR was sausage and mash.

The Company was doing exceedingly well and it wasn't long before Ken and Nat West turned their thoughts to a sale. Nat West were certainly initially keener than Ken and as a result Ken was able to do a deal with them whereby they took a slightly larger slice of any upfront purchase consideration, while Ken and his team took all of any deferred consideration, most of which it was realised would be based on post-sale performance.

Hunter Saphir were a young quoted company who were largely in the wholesale fruit and veg business but wanted to diversify on the back of what at the time was a good cash flow. They liked the profitability of House of Clark's where the margins were extraordinary for a food business and were very keen, indeed far too keen.

Their lawyer, a man called Ronnie Fox of Herbert Oppenheim Nathan & Vandyke, saw this and did his best to hold them back, but it was obvious that they were a very willing buyer indeed and ultimately the terms of the deal reflected this. There was a substantial payment up front and the potential for an even larger payment, dependent upon performance. The performance terms were such that, given the House of

Clark's profit margins, you could imagine that the contract was a licence to print money, provided you could increase sales.

Throughout the period of the sale Ken stuck to a few clear principles of what he wanted to achieve in terms of money upfront, deferred terms and the terms of the deal. The purchasers' lawyers would try to chip away at every turn, culminating in one meeting where he asked their lawyer how many outstanding points he had. Ronnie Fox said that there were two and on that basis Ken agreed to continue with the meeting. Without any embarrassment Ronnie Fox then produced a list with eight points on it whereas Ken terminated the meeting and went home.

The next day I had a very humble Ronnie Fox on the phone trying to get the show back on the road. He agreed to drop not only his six additional points, but the two he'd originally raised and at the end of that week, very late on the Friday night (more likely Saturday morning), we signed a deal to sell the House of Clark's to Hunter Saphir. The terms of the deal included about 1m Hunter Saphir shares that Ken and his team had to take and keep, which represented somewhere around 10% of the upfront consideration. The deferred consideration of which Ken and his team had 100% was, however, the prize as this was 4.5 times the profits of the first two years with very little restriction on what could be counted as profit.

We signed that deal early on a Saturday morning and *(the next part is my recollection and like many recollections I may have truncated the timescales)* on the following Monday stock markets around the world collapsed. Hunter Saphir had relied on a rights issue to produce the cash to pay the upfront consideration – a deal they'd signed with Charterhouse Bank at the same time that they signed to buy the House of Clark's.

If we had gone home on that Friday night and come back on the Monday there would have been no deal. Charterhouse Bank was left with almost the entire underwritten rights issue. Ken and his team faced an immediate loss on the Hunter Saphir shares, but they comprised only a very small part of the overall consideration.

Immediately following the signing of the sale of the House of Clark's (indeed that very night) there was another Clark's night. I can't say that I felt on top form that time but nevertheless Liz and I, and all Ken's various advisers, bowled up at the Royal Lancaster Hotel. I asked Ken how he was going to explain that the business was no longer independent and management owned.

True to form he appeared on stage at Clark's night with Nick Saphir, announced the deal, told everyone of his 'earn out' and that it was going to be doubly important that the suppliers reduce their prices and that the customers increased their purchases! What face and what a result. All of them did at least what he asked them for and the friends who put up the money to help him get their money back. Ken and his team got a reasonable amount of money (several millions in Ken's case) and continued to operate the business pretty much without interference during the 'earn out' period.

By way of a thank you for working on the sale, Ken was extremely generous to me and my family and took us with his family on a week long holiday to Disneyworld in Florida, flying first class. Our children had never flown first class and I remember how they sat up all night watching films and eating. They couldn't believe it was possible. We had a wonderful time at Disneyworld and, while we haven't been there as often as Ken and his family, it did cause us to go back twice more in the ensuing years.

In the two years following the sale of the House of Clark's I saw Ken less than I had before but we kept in touch about the earn out and it was clear that the business was going like a train. His customers were doing exactly as he asked them, buying all that they possibly could. Indeed I imagined there must be hundreds of warehouses across the UK stuffed full of Butterkist!

In the second year of the 'earn out' Ken and I had discussions about what he would do at the end of it. By then John Saphir, who had been one of the leading lights, had died in a car accident and, while Ken continued to get on very well with Finance Director Brian Dudley, he did not get on so well with the Chairman, Nick Saphir. Nick in any event felt that the Company was too dependent on Ken and was looking to break that dependency.

As a result it wasn't difficult to agree that at the end of the earn out period Ken would cease to work for the Company full-time and go onto a very part-time consultancy arrangement, for which he was handsomely paid. The terms of the 'earn out' were such that for every £1 of turnover that could be generated, more than £1 of earn out was earned. I don't think he ever did it but it would have paid Ken to pay his customers to buy the popcorn, because the resulting margin multiplied by 4.5 was around two and a half times the cost of buying the popcorn.

The 'earn out' reached amounts never envisaged by anybody (although perhaps by Ken when he realised quite how generous the terms were). I recall that towards the end of the 'earn out' period Ken asked me whether there was anything else that he could do increase the amount to be paid and jokingly I told him he could buy the Roller!

To my surprise he did for its then value of £70,000. As the car had been written down to nothing in the books of the company, according to the terms of the 'earn out' Ken was entitled to 4.5 times the resulting profit of £70,000 so, for an outlay of £70,000 he and his team received £350,000. Ken thought that was pretty good business and no-one at Hunter Saphir complained.

I think Ken was a little disappointed at his treatment following his retirement from full-time working for the Company. He had a great affection for the people and for Dagenham and I think he would have liked to have continued to help, maybe in some more subsidiary role. Perhaps not surprisingly however Hunter Saphir thought it was very unlikely that Ken would take a subsidiary role and they effectively shut him out of the business.

It wasn't long before the business started to suffer, sales dropped, clients were lost and costs increased. Hunter Saphir had done at least one other acquisition on far too generous terms and got into serious financial difficulties. As a result they put House of Clark's up for sale. The business, by this time, was considerably depleted but the factory and the workforce remained at Dagenham and Ken was keen to help people retain their jobs if he could, so he approached the owners of Hunter Saphir with regard to a sale. They wouldn't talk to him and they wouldn't talk to me on his behalf either. In the end we put together an offer with virtually no information but with the intention of buying the business if it could be continued in Dagenham for the benefit of the workforce.

Ken offered £3m which was a fraction of what he had sold the business for. No-one ever responded to Ken's offer and the business was sold for a few hundred thousand pounds less than he'd offered. Within months warranty claims by the buyer had reduced the price below Ken's offer. Ken was livid particularly because the business was not being turned around and people's livelihoods were at stake. As a result he spoke to the Financial Times, who published pretty much a full page story outlining what had gone on.

Post House of Clark's

Ken was now a very rich man but facing a very significant tax bill because of the very large amount he had received by way of deferred consideration. He had not however settled the tax on the initial sale and, after some discussion, I suggested he should look to offer to value the deferred consideration on the initial sale at a high price. The capital gains tax rate at that time was 30% and it was 40% by the time the deferred consideration was received. The Revenue accepted a high value for the deferred consideration, as a result of which Ken's tax bill on the whole sale was closer to 30% than to the 40% it would otherwise have been.

Once again Ken was extremely generous to Liz and me and our then two children, Dan and Jen, by taking us, together with our third child John who was at the time 'en ventre sa mere', on a week-long cruise on the QE2 by way of a thank you. It was totally unnecessary but very much appreciated. We had a wonderful time and during the cruise Dan got to eat sweetbreads and was then told what they were. Being 11 years of age he then rushed out to be sick, but the cruise gave us the opportunity to get to know Ken, Lynn, Brandon, Bradley and Cheralyn somewhat better.

Ken was now largely a man of leisure and he set about looking for investments to make with his money and for a while he and I visited a few businesses with a good story, sometimes a good product, sometimes good management but with not enough capital. Unfortunately on the whole the businesses didn't have the good products and the good management at the same time, so Ken made little or no investments.

He did, however, have Cheralyn at the independently owned Woodlands School near Brentwood and it was clear that the school, while very successful on the educational front, was a great deal less successful on the business front. It was very close to going under, when Ken did a deal with Linda and Alan Tingle to take a stake in the business for a substantial sum.

This was much against my advice as I doubted very much whether the school would ever be a particularly profitable business but we structured the arrangements so that most of the investment was by way of a loan secured on the school premises and paying a reasonably high rate of interest. Over the years since then Ken and his family have acquired most of the remaining shares, and (once again against my advice) opened a sister school in Hutton. The business now operates very much as a Lewis family business providing high quality primary education and latterly nursery education in the Brentwood area.

Ken has thrown himself into the business and it's largely through his efforts, perseverance and energy that the schools have remained in business and profitable. He has had the opportunity to sell the schools for a substantial amount, but to date he has resisted that.

During the period soon after leaving House of Clark's, Ken was asked to get involved in one or two confectionary businesses and I can particularly remember the work he did in saving the company that made Peanut Brittle, almost as iconic as Butterkist. I think he might even have bought the company were it not for the fact that he'd become exhausted by the commute to South Wales.

During the more than 20 years since the sale of the House of Clark's I have dealt with Ken less on the business front and much more socially. Our families have become close friends (Ken is Godfather to our youngest son, John) and we have had many enjoyable occasions together, including nearly all of the Footballer Writer's Association dinner and dance nights in January each year. What has struck me over the time I have known Ken Lewis is his love for, and his commitment to, his family. Yes he had a good business brain because he could identify the main issues and seek to resolve those without losing focus but it's the family side that's often been expressed in business decisions which has impressed me most.

I am very pleased and proud to have been associated with Ken over nearly 30 years and to be able, at this time, to call him a good friend.

John Walker (Friend)
Thanks a million Ken
The first of two memorable moments (as told to me by my late wife, as my own memory of it is vacant due to excessive drinking) was that day in Majorca on a trip I won in a House of Clarks sales competition.

We were in Ken and Lynn's hotel room in some kind of get together when, apparently, I began bouncing on the bed believing it to be a trampoline and onto the balcony floor (we were eight floors up). It seems I was convinced I could fly and was about to launch myself into the wild blue yonder when, thankfully, someone pulled me back and saved my bacon.

I still have nightmares about this story, which was told to me by my late and very irate wife Christine. It was due to this trip that, to my knowledge, Ken and I became new fathers to be, with both Lynn and Christine getting pregnant at the same time. The birth of my own daughter, Joanne, was overshadowed by the birth of Bradley.

On a later occasion we were at the Holiday Inn in Newcastle when Ken and I were having dinner and he spotted an old friend eating alone. Well, not quite alone because he had a dog with him. It was Bernie Winters, the comedian, and the dog was Schnorbitz, a giant and slavering St Bernard who used to be part of his act and they were in pantomime in Newcastle.

Bernie joined us and we consumed a few bottles of wine – well Bernie did mostly – and I made the mistake of offering the dog some meat off my plate. After that it wouldn't leave me alone and by the end of the evening my trousers were wet through with dog slaver.

Then Bernie invited a British Airways crew to join us and some party that turned out to be with other hotel guests joining in too. A great deal of laughter on that fantastic, never to be repeated, night.

I spent eighteen years in a job I absolutely loved and never had a dull moment. I am one of the luckiest guys around and thanks a million, Ken. You are a very special person and you gave me the inspiration to make a success of my life.

Ian Yates (Friend)
He said, 'Sell 'em as fudge'

My relationship with Ken & Lynn, and all their family truly transcends that of Business, and there was a fair amount of that conducted between House of Clarks and Sovereign Cash & Carry. Over many years.

He once sold me 2 tons of wrapped caramels, at an extortionate price, as I am extremely gullible and have often fallen foul of "Southern Slickers". When they arrived it was quickly noted that the caramels were to put it as kindly as possible... antediluvian and very soft. When I gently pointed this out to Ken, his response was "SELL 'EM AS FUDGE". I would never have thought of that! I did sell them and they were highly regarded.

Our relationship has at varying times been that of father & son, or older brother, or even younger brother, but it always has been – and will be in whatever category, for both my wife Patricia and myself – unequalled in our lives.

Memories! Ken once turned up at a Nottingham confectionery ball, dressed as Robin Hood, and proceeded to cavort much like Errol Flynn did in the film. At the time I remembered the remarks in the film that Prince John used 'You are a Cheeky Fellow' Ken was never lacking in CHUTZPAH.

I introduced Ken to the world of Rolls-Royce cars, in the sense that I virtually gave my beautiful Mediterranean Blue Silver Shadow to him. Legend has it that he actually won it from me at cards, whilst we were queuing up to meet a Captain of a cruise ship on one of our family jaunts. The cruise weather was somewhat robust on the way to Madeira, but both Ken's wife Lynn and I were very keen Table Tennis players, and notwithstanding the motion we won the Singles and the Mixed Doubles tournament on the ship.

On another of what I chose to call a JKL C….yourself holiday at a DUDE RANCH in Texas, he inveigled me to accompany a party of colleagues and friends to the small village of Bandera to visit a, 'Best Little Whorehouse in Texas' sort of place or have fried chicken and ride the ELECTRIC BULL in the Plaza. Naturally, we chose the Chicken & Bull. Well, it was not so much that we chose, but that our wives held the casting vote.

We quietly ambled up to this Plaza del Toro, and we noticed that the bull was completely surrounded with massive sheets of sorbo rubber and I wondered what the reason was. It was agreed by others that I would go on first, followed by the other gentlemen. This becoming a painful remembrance…for me! I stayed on, but had difficulty walking for a week. There was no 'No.2' for the bullride.

I won't even mention the fact that on the way to the airport, the ultra-economy bus that Ken had chartered (perhaps chartered is not the right word) got a flat tyre. So the trip had kind of changed from a JKL C…yourself excursion into a JKL DIY holiday, because I had to change the wheel. One has to be fit to be a friend of Kens!

We attended many House of Clark's 'DOs' at the Royal Lancaster hotel. On one particular occasion President Jomo Kenyatta had hired several floors for himself and entourage, complete with many 9' tall security guards. On this particular night, as indeed on several others Ken as host was flogging himself to death ensuring the usual superb evening. He'd taken the odd libation more than his tired body could take, on top of an incredibly boring speech about hybrid corn.

I saw him aimlessly wandering out of doors, and knowing that there were a plethora of large guards with guns prowling around, I felt that sooner or later he would be buying hybrid corn from them or selling them popcorn. So I felt a breath of fresh air was needed, and carted him outside of the hotel. He was staggering along and muttering incomprehensively (the passers by didn't know he was merely preparing another boring speech).

So I put my arms around his shoulders, and we walked around the hotel, people didn't know whether he was being mugged... or we were just good friends. A policeman approached, and I think Ken tried to get me arrested. However, he recovered, we went back inside the ballroom and he continued to bore anyone who was prepared to be bored. (Mainly customers who owed HOC money), As we say in Lancashire, They were all Gradely Do's.

We also went on a trip to the Hawaiian Islands, during which the Lewis's and Yates's called in at a local Pizza Hut in Maui. We asked for some Beer, and these were served in what I call high class buckets. They really were El Massivo. So Ken & I not wanting to waste any, supped the lot. We were not only bloated... but happily inebriated. Ken said we were Pissed, but we Northerners are far more cultured than WOT E is.

The Bill duly arrived, and Ken and I decided that we were each going to pay the tab, amidst the joviality etc. we got into a kind of wrestling match. We were quickly surrounded by 8 or 9 heavily built native waiters, but Ken bribed them with a couple of packets of Pop-corn, and I believe he got them to pay the bill.

Ken had a really nasty, nay vile habit, at speechtimes, of arranging that I followed David Lodge, a supremely nice, caring, compassionate person who everybody in the audience loved. I then went on as somewhat like a cross between Frank Randall and an East End gangster. People used to come for miles around to see and hear me Boo'd off. I was so sensitive in those days!

Perhaps one of the greatest calumnies of all time, is when I felt that from a Northern hayseed, I would really get into the big time, and bought 2 shares in the House of Clark's company. Some readers may be surprised and mortified to learn that I never got paid for my powerful shareholding, or any dividends. I still hurt thinking of it!

In conclusion I would merely say that the Lewis family success story has given me terrific pleasure. As I have seen the movements and progress by Ken, aided admirably by Lynn & Christine. Impeccable choices! The ability to choose the people who will provide 'Lift Off' is a quality that few people have. Ken has it still…in Spades!

At a considerably humbler and somewhat impoverished level, I have endeavoured to emulate his style and achievements, alas at 84 years of age I am still struggling and working hard to keep Patricia in the style she has never been accustomed to. But Life is about continuing to STRIVE!

I owe a lot of people money, therefore I have not too many friends, but I count Ken & Lynn Lewis as our BEST FRIENDS.

Derek Shaw
The Three sides of Ken Lewis

One:

The hard headed, focused business man. He will be as tough as is required to be but also fair and very honest. Above all else he is loyal to all he works with and would stand by all regardless.

Two:

The family man. He loves his family as if they were the be all and end all of his life and is so proud of every one of them. He Loves Lynn with all his heart.

Three:

A great human being, who is loyal to his friends and values their friendship. He is a real softy if truth be told, but he would never admit it. We both worked together as our careers took off. He would be brutally honest with you and we both learnt from one and another – my career was better for it

We got stuck in Chicago it was so cold we ended buying overcoats. Ken being Ken took a fancy to a rather large furry coat which matched his beard too! He looked just like a cuddly bear. We got hooked on Dallas and watched about six episodes one afternoon as it snowed so hard outside

We checked in for our flights, but British Airways were very reluctant to tell us the flights were being delayed so we tried other airlines. This is a lesson I learnt and have used this anecdote many times. We went to the TWA desk where the guy was getting all kinds of abuse. When it came to our turn Ken asked very quietly and very courteously what our chances were. He treated the guy with great respect and I quote his reply: 'Sir you are the first person today to treat me like a human being, and I will get you on a flight. Where do you want to go?'

As it happens BA were able to take off on time but a lesson was learnt and as I say used many times since. Even my son will quote it to you and now my grandsons too. Although it is a long time since my children have seen Ken, they both hold him in great regard and still have giant cuddly toys he gave them some 30 years ago.

"Run when you can
Walk if you have to
Crawl if you must
But never give up"